STATISTICS

Sara Miller McCune founded SAGE Publishing in 1965 to support the dissemination of usable knowledge and educate a global community. SAGE publishes more than 1000 journals and over 800 new books each year, spanning a wide range of subject areas. Our growing selection of library products includes archives, data, case studies and video. SAGE remains majority owned by our founder and after her lifetime will become owned by a charitable trust that secures the company's continued independence.

Los Angeles | London | New Delhi | Singapore | Washington DC | Melbourne

STATISTICS WITH R

A BEGINNER'S GUIDE

ROBERT STINEROCK

Los Angeles | London | New Delhi
Singapore | Washington DC | Melbourne

Los Angeles | London | New Delhi
Singapore | Washington DC | Melbourne

SAGE Publications Ltd
1 Oliver's Yard
55 City Road
London EC1Y 1SP

SAGE Publications Inc.
2455 Teller Road
Thousand Oaks, California 91320

SAGE Publications India Pvt Ltd
B 1/I 1 Mohan Cooperative Industrial Area
Mathura Road
New Delhi 110 044

SAGE Publications Asia-Pacific Pte Ltd
3 Church Street
#10-04 Samsung Hub
Singapore 049483

Editor: Jai Seaman
Assistant editor: Alysha Owen
Production editor: Ian Antcliff
Copyeditor: Richard Leigh
Indexer: Martin Hargreaves
Marketing manager: Susheel Gokarakonda
Cover design: Shaun Mercier
Typeset by: C&M Digitals (P) Ltd, Chennai, India
Printed in the UK

© Robert Stinerock 2018

First published 2018

Apart from any fair dealing for the purposes of research or private study, or criticism or review, as permitted under the Copyright, Designs and Patents Act, 1988, this publication may be reproduced, stored or transmitted in any form, or by any means, only with the prior permission in writing of the publishers, or in the case of reprographic reproduction, in accordance with the terms of licences issued by the Copyright Licensing Agency. Enquiries concerning reproduction outside those terms should be sent to the publishers.

Library of Congress Control Number: 2016951887

British Library Cataloguing in Publication data

A catalogue record for this book is available from the British Library

ISBN 978-1-4739-2489-5
ISBN 978-1-4739-2490-1 (pbk)

At SAGE we take sustainability seriously. Most of our products are printed in the UK using FSC papers and boards. When we print overseas we ensure sustainable papers are used as measured by the PREPS grading system. We undertake an annual audit to monitor our sustainability.

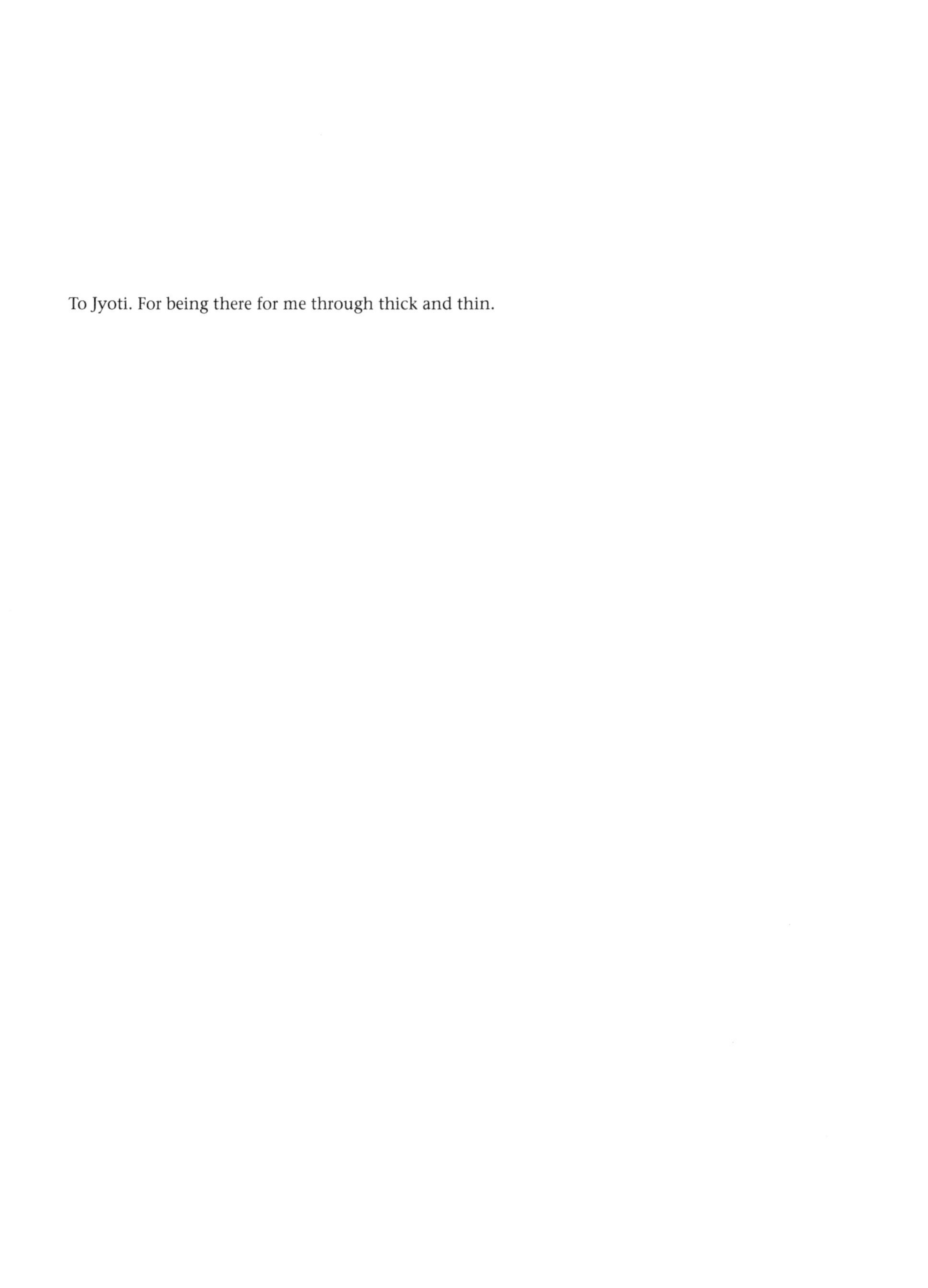

To Jyoti. For being there for me through thick and thin.

CONTENTS

ONLINE RESOURCES

Statistics with R: A Beginner's Guide is supported by a wealth of online resources for both students and lecturers to aid in study and support teaching, which are available at https://study.sagepub.com/stinerock

FOR STUDENTS

Author-made screencasts give you deeper insight into the key statistical ideas and R functions discussed in each chapter and show you first-hand how to work through some of the examples in the book. The **RStudio projects** the author used in the screencasts are also available so you can follow along on your own computer.

Datasets and all R Scripts from the book ready to upload into R and RStudio generate meaningful information to help you master your statistics and data analysis skills.

Exercises and **multiple choice questions** test your knowledge of key concepts and provide a helpful revision tool for assignments and exams while the **answers to in-text exercises** allow you to check your work and make sure you're on track.

FOR INSTRUCTORS

PowerPoint slides featuring figures, tables, and key topics from the book can be downloaded and customized for use in your own presentations.

Exercise testbanks containing questions related to the key concepts in each chapter can be downloaded and used in class or for homework and exams.

ABOUT THE AUTHOR

Robert Stinerock has more than 30 years of experience teaching statistics and probability to students at both the undergraduate as well as graduate level. He currently teaches statistics at three different universities: the Executive MBA program at Baruch College of the City University of New York; the Quantitative Finance program at the Stevens Institute of Technology in Hoboken, New Jersey; and the Faculdade de Economia, Universidade Nova de Lisboa, in Lisbon, Portugal.

He has received several awards for excellence in the classroom: the *Stevens Howe School Outstanding Undergraduate Teacher Award* (2006); the *Stevens Alumni Association Outstanding Teacher Award* (2005); and the *Fairleigh Dickinson Distinguished Faculty Award for Teaching* (1995).

He has published numerous research articles in academic journals, most recently in the *Journal of Macromarketing*, the *Journal of Business Research*, and *Geoforum*. This is his first book.

He earned his Bachelor's, Master's, and Ph.D. degrees, all from Columbia University.

He and his wife, Jyoti (a native of Mumbai, India), live in New York City.

ACKNOWLEDGMENTS

I am profoundly grateful to all of those who have contributed to the conception and completion of this project; without those contributions, I can honestly say that this book would never have been started, much less completed.

I would like to thank the many special people at SAGE. My first editor, Katie Metzler, shepherded the proposal from inception through the review process to acceptance by the editorial board. Jai Seaman has been the editor with whom I have worked during the last two years, and from the beginning she has been encouraging and patient, even when I did not meet every deadline. Alysha Owen has been that hands-on, go-to person who has responded to every question and problem with a cheerful, can-do attitude that kept me on track even when progress was slow. On the editing side, Ian Antcliff has proven to be a creative and helpful problem-solver, and Richard Leigh has shown that he edits with skill and attention-to-detail. I am fortunate indeed to have had the privilege of working with such dedicated people.

I am also grateful to those in the software community who have created and distributed all their amazing software, free of charge. Special thanks go to both the people at the R Core Team as well as at RStudio. It is no exaggeration to say that you are changing the world.

My friend, Eric Novik, deserves special recognition as someone who has contributed to many aspects of this project. Eric first introduced me to R nearly 10 years ago, and since then has been not only a technical advisor but also a problem solver. Eric also encouraged me to introduce scripting within the context of the RStudio Project, something that is now a feature of the book's screencasts. Eric's influence has been indispensable because he has made the project better than I could have on my own.

I am also indebted to Gary Bronson (of Fairleigh Dickinson University) for providing timely, helpful advice when I sought his help early in this project. Gary himself has published 15 books on programming languages. When he speaks, I listen.

A special word of thanks goes to Donald G. Morrison (of Columbia and UCLA) who, back in 1982, first introduced me to the power and beauty of statistics. I know I speak for many of my Ph.D. classmates, as well as for myself, when I say that Don has been a role model *par excellence*, mentor, and friend. For that, Don, I thank you.

My debt of gratitude to my family is more than I can express here. My grandmother and mother-in-law have been the ones who made my life possible. There is never a day when I do not think of you both; your influence remains with me after all these years. Finally, how I tricked my wife, Jyoti, into marrying me is something I will never understand. During our decades together, her strength of character, integrity, loyalty, fierce courage, honesty, and generosity-of-heart have been her examples for me to live by. Jyoti, you have been the best thing that ever happened to me.

PREFACE

The practice of statistics is primarily concerned with the development and application of methods for collecting, presenting, and analyzing data for the purpose of converting it into useful information. The ability to use these methods effectively is especially important today when the role of data shapes such an important part of our world. Acquiring an understanding of both the strengths and limitations of the most widely-used statistical methods, and then using these methods competently, now form an important part of the foundation of such diverse fields as economics, political science, psychology, sociology, finance, marketing, data mining, production management, quality control, and many other commercial, scientific, and engineering areas. Although one need not be a rigorously trained statistician to understand and apply the statistical methods presented in this book, a grasp of the conceptual foundation underpinning *statistics as a way of thinking* is required.

THE NEED FOR AN R-BASED FIRST-YEAR STATISTICS BOOK

The principal feature of this book is that it provides step-by-step instruction in the use of the R statistical language that is both accessible and comprehensive for those individuals wishing to (1) complete an introductory-level course in statistics, (2) prepare for more advanced statistical courses, (3) gain the necessary analytic skills now required for other disciplines such as the management, natural and social sciences, and (4) acquire a basic competence in the use of R.

R is an extremely powerful, highly versatile, widely used statistical programming system that is free and downloadable. Its particular strengths are in statistical modeling, graphical presentations, and its ability to program user-defined functions. In the last decade, R has gained wide acceptance among statisticians and data scientists in industry, academia, research organizations, and public sectors.

To say that R is only a statistical package, however, is to underclaim all that R can do. Because it offers capabilities beyond those featured by other statistical packages, R should not be characterized as a statistical package at all but rather as a *statistical environment*. While it is true that R is a powerful statistical programming and modeling language, it also has the following features and capabilities:

1. R includes a wide-variety of techniques for generating all sorts of publication-quality graphical presentations and data visualization results.
2. R is a versatile and powerful data-manipulation tool.

3. R includes access to thousands of free, downloadable, add-on packages contributed by practitioners and researchers from different fields that greatly expand the scope and types of problems R can work on. Currently, more than 11,000 user-contributed R packages are available at http://www.r-project.org/, and more are being added every day.
4. R provides a connection to a worldwide community of practitioners and researchers-programmers, data scientists, and statisticians, among others-from almost every conceivable field. These naturally occurring communities are connected and sustained not only by way of social media, blogs, and websites but also through specialized R groups and conferences.
5. R provides a mailing list to which one may subscribe free-of-charge that deals with many commonly encountered problems as well as frequently asked questions.
6. R has the ability to read from, and write to, most of the other commercially available software packages including but not limited to Excel, JMP, Minitab, SAS, SPSS, Stata, and Systat. It has the ability to move data and graphics easily between itself and these other environments.
7. R is platform-independent in that it runs on all the major operating systems including Windows, Mac OS X, and Unix.
8. The source code can be downloaded so that anyone can examine the internal workings of its routines and packages and make modifications, if desired.

To elaborate further as to why the use of R features so prominently in this book, there are two main reasons, one pedagogical, the other professional.

First, to answer why I provide such extensive coverage of a statistical language in an introductory-level book, I concede that in former times this aspect might not have been included at all. A few years ago, many faculty felt that since statistics and probability are essentially conceptual in nature, the real value-added to students of being able to think statistically and probabilistically overrode any consideration of students learning to operate software, especially since such instruction would have been viewed as an unnecessary encroachment on time that might be spent more productively on learning the core ideas of statistics. Although some authors and faculty still adhere to this position, I do not take this view. On the contrary, I believe that the ability to think programmatically, developed in part by learning how to translate the requirements of a given statistical problem into the syntax of a statistical programming language, can actually help students and readers learn, absorb, and apply the statistical methods they will encounter throughout the book.

Second, as to why I choose R over the more ubiquitous Excel, I would add that since today's world of work is more challenging than ever, the people entering that world must be armed with the broadest and most current skill-set possible. Today, the ability to use a programming language like R provides students with a clear advantage in the competitive arenas of both university admissions and subsequent employment. At the very least, just as it allows them to add another line to their vita (under computer skills), it also gives them something to talk about in admissions or job interviews. In my experience at the Stevens Institute of Technology and the Universidade Nova de Lisboa, some of our graduating students have reported that their knowing a bit of R gave them a differentiating advantage over other students with whom they were competing for positions in the financial or pharmaceutical industries. As one corporate recruiter recently said to one of our students after making an offer of employment upon graduation, "that you actually have some experience working with R means that we would not have to spend so much time training you in its use, that you would be able to start contributing at a higher level, and do so sooner. Almost everyone coming in here knows Excel. Few know R."

The demand for people qualified in the use of statistical languages such as R is forecast to grow dramatically over the next decade. So strong is the interest in data-qualified people, that several universities are responding by establishing new academic programs to meet this demand. For example, the University of California at Berkeley is now offering a master's degree in information and data science. In this program, the course description for the *Exploring and Analyzing Data* class states that students "will explore a range of statistical techniques and methods using the open-source statistics language, R" to create "statistics and techniques for analyzing and viewing data, with a focus on applying this knowledge to real-world data problems" (http://bit.ly/berkeley-ds). And in a new development, even MBA programs, such as the NYU Stern School (http://bit.ly/stern-ds) and the University of Washington Foster School of Business (http://bit.ly/foster-ds), are now offering concentrations in areas such as business analysis and data sciences that "require statistics software experience with R."

Apart from delivering accessible and comprehensive R instruction, the book's primary objective is to provide students and readers the conceptual foundation to use application-oriented statistical methods. Each statistical method is developed within the context of practical, real-world examples; theory is invoked only where serving the practical end of making clear why certain ways of thinking help with questions of an applied nature. While there is some mathematical notation in each chapter, it is kept to a minimum and used only to express statistical ideas in a clear and concise manner; a familiarity with algebra should suffice. Ultimately, the aim of the book is to provide a solid and complete foundation both for those interested in moving on to more advanced material as well as for those for whom this constitutes the first-and-last encounter with statistics.

1 Introduction and R Instructions

contents

learning objectives

1. Understand the meaning of the following terms: data, elements, variables, observations, data set, population, sample, population parameters, and sample statistics.
2. Obtain an appreciation of what can be done with data that are quantitatively scaled versus those that are qualitatively scaled.
3. Learn about the difference between data that are cross-sectional and data that are longitudinal.
4. Grasp the connection between descriptive statistics, probability, and statistics.
5. Be able to distinguish between a population and a sample.
6. Appreciate the role a sample plays in statistical estimation and statistical inferences about a population parameter.
7. Learn a bit about R, how to download it, how to install it, and how to operate it in some basic ways.

BASIC TERMINOLOGY

Statistics can be seen as a methodological discipline, and, like all areas of methodology, statistics has its own basic set of terms for describing the components and methods that form its conceptual foundation. In this vein, we begin with nine definitions of key components upon which the most widely used statistical methods are based. Throughout the book, we build upon and extend these terms by introducing additional definitions.

Definition 1.1. Data. Data are the facts or measurements that are collected, analyzed, presented, and interpreted. As such, data comprise the raw material of all statistical analyses. Data are further categorized as either quantitative or qualitative—and either longitudinal or cross-sectional—distinctions which are developed in more detail in Sections 1.2 and 1.3. Methods of summarizing and displaying data are provided in Chapters 2 and 3.

As an example of data that might be found in a typical marketing study, consider Table 1.1. In this case, a market researcher contacts all individuals in a statistics class with the purpose of learning something about banking habits, and asks four questions. Do you bank online? What is your age? How many years of formal education do you have? What is your family status (single and never married, married without children, married with children, separated, divorced, or widowed)? The answers to these questions are entered in each of the columns; the column on the far left has the surname of each of the 10 students as well as the title of the instructor. The information about each of the 11 individuals is displayed across each row.

The next eight definitions are described in terms of the different aspects of Table 1.1.

Definition 1.2. Elements. An element is a unit of data which is represented as a set of attributes or measurements. Elements are the entities on which the data are collected.

Examples of elements include households, cities, companies, products, transactions, and persons. In Table 1.1, the elements consist of the 10 students and instructor comprising the statistics class.

Table 1.1 A set of data: 11 observations on four variables for a study of banking habits

Name	Bank online	Age	Years of education	Family status
Adams	yes	28	16	single never married
Butler	yes	31	19	married with children
Danielson	no	22	16	single never married
Fitzgerald	yes	26	17	single never married
Johnson	no	23	16	single never married
Martinez	yes	27	18	married with children
Park	yes	24	16	single never married
Shah	yes	28	17	married with children
Smith	no	21	16	single never married
Taylor	yes	30	19	married without children
Instructor	yes	41	20	married with children

Definition 1.3. Variables. A variable is an attribute of an element that may assume different values. Examples of variables are income, age, weight, occupation, industry classification, presence or absence of a disease, gender, and marital status. Variables are the measurements or the characteristics of interest of the elements, and they are what is usually analyzed using statistical methods. In Table 1.1, there are four variables, one for each question: (1) Do you bank online? (2) What is your age? (3) How many years of formal education do you have? (4) What is your family status?

Definition 1.4. Observations. An observation is the set of values on the variables for a single element. In Table 1.1, the observation corresponding to the instructor consists of the following set of values: yes, 41, 20, married with children. For the student named Adams, the observation is composed of these values: yes, 28, 16, single never married. These four pieces of information completely characterize the person who is the element in question for this data set.

Definition 1.5. Data Set. A "data set" is all the data, across all observations and all variables, collected for any given study. A single data item is referred to as a "datum." Table 1.1 is an example of a data set.

To find the total number of data values in a data set, it is normally necessary only to multiply the number of elements by the number of variables. Exceptions to this rule of thumb occur, however, when there is missing information about any variable measurement for any elements. In this case, it is said that the data set contains missing values.

In Table 1.1 all 11 persons are represented by four variables each, and there are no missing values. Thus, by multiplying 11 times 4, it can be seen that this data set consists of 44 data values.

Definition 1.6. Population. A population consists of all the elements of interest in a study that have some quality (or qualities) in common. In the Table 1.1 data set, the population is the set of all persons enrolled in this particular statistics class: Adams, Butler, Danielson, Fitzgerald, Johnson, Martinez, Park, Shah, Smith, Taylor, and the Instructor. As another example, consider an opinion poll which seeks to predict the outcome of the election of the mayor of London. In this case, the population would consist of all elements having a characteristic in common: they are registered voters in London. Residents of Manchester or Hong Kong are not members of this population since they do not possess the quality of being registered voters in London. Similarly, in a study concerning the effectiveness of a drug intended to help patients control their level of cholesterol, the population would be made up of all persons known to be suffering from high levels of cholesterol.

Definition 1.7. Sample. A sample is a subset of the population that is selected for the purposes of the study. There are many possible unique samples that can be drawn from any given population. For example, for the population specified in Table 1.1, there are 165 samples consisting of 3 elements that can be selected from the population of 11 elements. One such sample would contain Butler, Taylor, and the Instructor; another would consist of Danielson, Johnson, and Smith. In Chapter 7, several methods of selecting samples from a population are discussed.

Often it is not practical or even possible to work with the entire population. Accordingly, most statistical analyses involve working with a sample rather than a population. The choice to use a sample instead of a population is a trade-off decision, however, and it involves sacrificing some richness and accuracy in the findings for the advantage of working with a more manageable, more readily available, less expensive set of data.

Definition 1.8. Population Parameters. Population parameters are the characteristics of interest in a study. But unless the entire population is available, the values of the population parameters are rarely (if ever) known with certainty. Population parameters are typically true but unknown; while they represent the unchanging truth about some characteristic of the population at a given moment in time, they are usually unobservable. Population parameters are often referred to simply as "parameters." Since Table 1.1 displays the entire population of interest in this particular study, the parameters can be derived easily. For example, one parameter, the mean age, can be found by summing the age of all 11 individuals of the population and dividing the result by 11:

$$\mu = \frac{28+31+22+26+23+27+24+28+21+30+41}{11} = \frac{301}{11} \approx 27.4.$$

Thus, the mean age for the population, denoted by the Greek letter μ, is approximately 27.4 years. Chapter 3 includes a more complete discussion of population parameters such as the population mean.

Definition 1.9. Sample Statistics. Sample statistics are the characteristics of interest derived from a sample rather than a population. The values of these sample statistics vary from sample to sample. That is, when a sample is drawn, the sample statistic assumes one value; when another sample is selected, the sample statistic usually takes on a different value. Sample statistics are often referred to simply as "statistics."

Returning to Table 1.1, the sample mean age of the sample consisting of Butler, Taylor, and the Instructor (see Definition 1.7 above) is

$$\bar{x} = \frac{31+30+41}{3} = \frac{102}{3} = 34,$$

while the sample mean age for the other sample (made up of Danielson, Johnson, and Smith) is

$$\bar{x} = \frac{22+23+21}{3} = \frac{66}{3} = 22.$$

Note that the values of the statistics from the two samples differ from one another as well as from the population mean of 27.4 years. This is not surprising since the population and the samples consist of entirely different elements. In later chapters, various methods for measuring and controlling this difference or error are introduced and developed in detail.

DATA: QUALITATIVE OR QUANTITATIVE

Now that we have defined the terms that form the basis of the statistical methods we encounter in subsequent chapters, we are in a position to draw the distinction between qualitative and quantitative data, and between data that are cross-sectional and longitudinal.

Definition 1.10. Qualitative Data. Qualitative data are measurements that can be categorized into one of several classifications. That is, qualitative data are typically labels or names that are used to identify a quality of each element in a data set. They are characteristics but not numerical measurements of anything. In general, qualitative data are either nominal-scaled or ordinal-scaled.

Nominal-Scaled Data. As an example of nominal-scaled data, consider the case of the Stevens Institute of Technology, which has three schools in which undergraduate students may enroll: Sciences, Engineering, and Business Technology. If the elements in a data set consist of the undergraduate students at Stevens, it is clear that each student can be classified in terms of the undergraduate school in which she is enrolled. For this reason, nominal-scaled data are sometimes referred to as "categorical" data: they indicate into which category the element should be placed. Note that this representation can be a non-numeric label such as Sciences, Engineering, and Business Technology. Alternatively, it is possible to employ a numeric representation such as Sciences = 1, Engineering = 2, and Business Technology = 3.

It is important to note, however, that since numerically represented, nominal-scaled data are not inherently quantitative—that is, they are not actually numbers but rather labels—we cannot perform quantitative operations on them in the usual ways. (There are some quantitative methods of a more advanced nature that make use of nominal-scaled data, but they are beyond the coverage of this book.) Just as it would make no sense to calculate the average of a list of telephone numbers, or the average of the numbers on the jerseys of a soccer team's players, it is pointless to find the average of the schools in which students are enrolled. Mathematically, it can be done; the result, nevertheless, would have no meaning. Chapter 2 gives several descriptive methods of presenting and summarizing qualitative data.

Ordinal-Scaled Data. As an example of data that are ordinal-scaled, each element (or student) from the above data set can be further classified in terms of his class standing: freshman, sophomore, junior, or senior. This variable is ordinal-scaled because it has all the properties of a nominal-scaled variable—that is, each undergraduate year constitutes a category—and yet it contains some additional information beyond the simple classification. In this case, the rank of the data is meaningful: seniors normally have rank over juniors, juniors over sophomores, and sophomores over freshmen. As with nominal-scaled data, this information can be represented using the non-numeric label such as senior, junior, sophomore or freshman; it also can be represented using a number, for example senior = 4, junior = 3, and so on. However, we must remember that since numerically represented, ordinal-scaled data are not strictly quantitative or metric, we typically cannot perform quantitative operations on them as if they were. Even so, some statisticians consider ordinal-scaled data to be *somewhat quantitative*. In fact, ordinal-scaled data can be summarized by the use of statistical measures known as "nonparametric methods."

Consider the rank order of the population of the world's five most populous countries. Those countries are:

1 China
2 India
3 US
4 Indonesia
5 Brazil.

The difference between any two elements on an ordinal-scaled variable is not necessarily meaningful, however. If one considers only the ordinal-scaled data (the ranking) above, one might conclude that the US and India have comparable populations when in fact they do not (see Table 1.2).

Table 1.2 Population of the world's five most populous countries

Country	Population
China	1,350,000,000
India	1,200,000,000
US	314,000,000
Indonesia	246,000,000
Brazil	204,000,000

The population of India is almost four times as great as that of the US. The difference between these two data elements, India and the US, is not equal to the difference between the US and Indonesia, the fourth-ranked country. Indonesia's population is clearly much closer to that of the US than is India's. Ordinal-scaled data often mask these differences while the original data do not.

Definition 1.11. Quantitative Data. Quantitative data are those that can be characterized as metric (or quantitative): they report *how many* or *how much*. In general, quantitative data are one of two types: interval-scaled or ratio-scaled.

Interval-Scaled Data. A variable is interval-scaled if the data have all the above-mentioned properties of ordinal data, and if the interval between the values is expressed in terms of fixed units of measurement. An example of interval-scaled data is temperature. The difference between 50 and 51 degrees Celsius is the same as the difference between 75 and 76 degrees. Zero degrees Celsius, however, has no special meaning in that it does not imply the absence of the underlying construct being measured. Zero degrees Celsius is simply one degree warmer than –1°C, and one degree colder than +1°C. Returning to the example concerning the students, it is also possible to measure them in terms of their SAT admission test scores, an interval-scaled variable. Since interval-scaled data are quantitative, many quantitative operations can be performed on them. For example, it is possible to report meaningfully the average SAT score of engineering undergraduates.

Ratio-Scaled Data. A variable is ratio-scaled if the data have all the properties of interval data, and (additionally) if the ratio of two values is meaningful. Examples of ratio-scaled data abound: distance, height, weight, time, money, and so on. Note also that in the case of ratio-scaled data, zero now indicates the absence of the construct being measured: zero distance, zero height, zero weight, zero money, and zero time are universally understood concepts. To understand the difference between ratio-scaled and interval-scaled data, consider the matter of *meaningful ratios*: 50 kilometers is twice as great a distance as 25 kilometers, but 50°C is not twice as warm as 25°C. Finally, data that are ratio-scaled allow the widest range of quantitative operations because ratio-scaled data contain more information than any other kind of data.

The practical reason why it is important to draw the distinction between quantitative and qualitative data is that the statistical analysis that is appropriate depends on whether the data for the variable are quantitative or qualitative. In general, there are more alternatives for statistical analysis when the data are quantitative. Moreover, quantitative data indicate either how many, in which case the data are described as discrete, or how much, in which case the data are characterized as continuous. We return to develop these properties further in Chapters 5 and 6.

 DATA: CROSS-SECTIONAL OR LONGITUDINAL

A final important characteristic to consider is whether the data are cross-sectional or longitudinal.

Definition 1.12. Cross-Sectional Data. Cross-sectional data are collected at the same (or approximately the same) point in time. For example, Table 1.3 is a cross-sectional data set consisting of the population of each of the five counties comprising New York City on July 1, 2012.

Table 1.3 Population of the five counties of New York City: July 1, 2012

County	Population
Bronx	1,408,473
Brooklyn	2,565,635
Manhattan	1,619,090
Queens	2,272,771
Staten Island	470,728

Note that while the population of each of the five counties is reported on July 1, 2012, it is clear that the exercise of counting such a large number of people no doubt took considerable time. Put another way, it is misleading for anyone to think that the population of Brooklyn was exactly 2,565,635 on July 1, 2012. All that number really represents is the best estimate by the Census Bureau of what the actual population figure is likely to be. The real population is bound to be some other number, either larger or smaller.

Table 1.4 Population of Kings County (Brooklyn), New York: 1900-2010

Year	Population
1900	1,166,820
1910	1,634,510
1920	2,018,560
1930	2,560,010
1940	2,698,285
1950	2,738,175
1960	2,627,319
1970	2,602,012
1980	2,231,028
1990	2,300,664
2000	2,465,326
2010	2,504,700

Definition 1.13. Longitudinal Data. Longitudinal data, also known as time-series data, are collected over several time periods. As an example of longitudinal data, consider the population of Brooklyn, New York, for the years 1900–2010 (Table 1.4). In this case, we are measuring the same quantity repeatedly, over time.

Some data sets are both cross-sectional and longitudinal. For example, consumer products companies and market research firms often test-market new-to-the-world, frequently purchased, packaged goods, such as salty snacks or personal care items, before readying the product for a nationwide roll-out. They might do this by monitoring the monthly purchases of 10,000 continuously reporting households in a selected test market city, like Minneapolis–St. Paul, Minnesota, who have agreed to participate in a consumer panel over a 12-month period. The data set then would be structured something like the arrangement depicted in Table 1.5 where each cell would contain the number of purchases made by each household of the product in question over each of the 12 months of the year.

Table 1.5 Cross-sectional and longitudinal (time series) data in table format

	Jan. 15	Feb. 15	Mar. 15	Apr. 15	...	Dec. 15
Household 1	0	2	0	1	...	0
Household 2	1	1	1	0	...	2
Household 3	2	2	2	1	...	1
...	...	...	...	...	...	...
Household 10,000	0	1	0	0	...	0

Clearly, this data set is both cross-sectional and longitudinal in nature. Note that there are 10,000 elements or households, and that each element is represented 12 times over the course of a year. As indicated above, the measurement would be the number of units purchased by the household of the new product over the period of one month. Thus, assuming no missing data items, the total number of data values in this data set is 10,000 times 12, or 120,000.

Having discussed some of the most important characteristics associated with data, data sets, and scales of measurement, we now consider the difference between descriptive statistics (covering the first three chapters of this book), probability (treated in Chapters 4–6), and statistical estimation and inference (our main focus in Chapter 7 and beyond).

1.4 DESCRIPTIVE STATISTICS

Definition 1.14. Descriptive Statistics. Descriptive statistics consists of a wide variety of methods of organizing, summarizing, and reporting data. In general, these methods are classified as either tabular, graphical, or numerical methods, and are developed in detail in Chapters 2 and 3.

While descriptive statistics consists of the three aforementioned data summarization approaches, we first look at tabular methods that can be used to present data in tables (hence the name "tabular"). We then move on to the graphical methods that often can be thought of as pictures (such as pie charts, bar graphs, and histograms) of the information organized in a table. Tabular and graphical methods are covered in Chapter 2. Finally, in Chapter 3, we introduce and discuss a number of the most useful numerical methods that provide additional procedures for summarizing data.

Regardless of the particular method of descriptive statistics we employ, the objective in using them is to provide insights about the data that cannot be easily or quickly obtained by a cursory examination of the original data.

1.5 PROBABILITY

Definition 1.15. Probability. We encounter probability problems whenever we draw a sample from a population, and then attempt to estimate the probability that the sample will have certain characteristics. At least for the type of probability problems encountered in this book, the primary focus is on the sample rather than the population. Here are two examples of this type of probability problem.

1. If a single card is drawn from a deck of 52 playing cards, what is the probability the card will be an ace?
   In this instance, the characteristics of the population are well known: there are four aces in a normal deck of 52 playing cards. The probability that the sample (consisting of only one playing card) has a certain characteristic (it is an ace) is $4/52$.
2. The campaign manager for a certain political candidate knows that 75% of visitors to her website are men and 25% are women. In a sample of the next 100 visitors to the website, what is the probability that at least 80% will be men?
   Here the population is comprised of all visitors to the website, and the relevant population parameter is known at the outset: the percentage of male visitors to the website is 75%. The sample consists of the next 100 visitors to the website, and the issue concerns what the sample will most likely look like. In other words, in light of what is known about the population, what will the sample most probably be like? The emphasis here is on the characteristic of the sample, not the population.

 STATISTICS: ESTIMATION AND INFERENCE

Definition 1.16. Statistics. We encounter problems of statistics whenever we select a sample from a population and want to draw conclusions about the population's properties based on what we learn from the sample. Unlike in the case of the probability problem, the population parameters are unknown. Here is an example of a statistics problem.

The leadership of a political party recently surveyed 1200 registered party members with the purpose of determining how receptive they would be to the party nominating a particular candidate for an open seat in the Senate. Once the survey results had been collected and analyzed, the leadership announced that because 624 of the 1200 survey respondents, or 52%, expressed their approval of the candidate, "The majority of our members favor our running this particular candidate for the Senate seat." How confident can we be that the leadership is correct in this conclusion? Is it possible that they have drawn the wrong conclusion about the population from the sample data? How strong is the evidence supporting their conclusion?

In this example, the members of the political party comprise the population, and the 1200 people whose preferences were sought constitute the sample. We note, however, the crucial difference between probability and statistics: in probability, we draw a sample from a population with known parameters, and make statements about what the sample might look like. By contrast, in statistics, we draw a sample with the purpose of estimating or inferring what the population characteristics might be. In other words, in statistics problems, we do not know the characteristics of the population, but we would like to know them. Accordingly, we draw a sample from that population in order to estimate or infer statistically what those population characteristics might be. The methods of statistics comprise the lion's share of material in this book.

There are several approaches we can take when using statistical methods, but in this book we will make abundant use of statistical estimation and statistical inference. As we will see in Chapters 7 and 8, estimation consists of both point estimation and confidence interval estimation, and the motivation of each is to puzzle out how small or how large something may be.

As an example of a research question for which we might employ a statistical estimation method, consider the following: in the 2012 US Presidential election, what percentage of women and men voted for President Obama?

Note that the research issue in question involves developing an understanding of how large or small something might be. In this example, that *something* is the percentage vote received by a political candidate for public office.

In Chapter 9, we learn that statistical inference involves testing formal hypotheses for the purpose of drawing conclusions or inferences. As an example of a research hypothesis which we might wish to test using the methods of statistical inference, consider the following statement: in the 2012 US Presidential election, a higher percentage of women voted for President Obama than of men.

A research hypothesis is a formal statement that can be tested for the purpose of determining if it is true or false. Because the statement above (concerning the relatively greater support that President Obama enjoyed among women over men) is a claim we could confront with real data, statistical inference would be a research methodology we might use when considering whether the statement is true.

On the other hand, a statement such as "Bill Clinton was a better president than Barack Obama has been" is not a claim that can be tested using empirically grounded data: there are none. We sometimes hear that people try to make these types of comparisons—historians and journalists among them—but in doing this they inevitably resort to subjectively chosen criteria on which the presidents might be measured. Naturally, because there are no universally agreed-upon standards for what criteria are used, and what are not used, different people select different criteria for inclusion. Many people will have different views on the question, but there is no objective evidence pointing either way. Therefore, we would say that this type of hypothesis is not one that can be tested for the purpose of establishing its truth.

Clearly, both statistical approaches—estimation and inference—can be used to get at the same research question. Which we use depends on what specifically we want to know.

SUMMARY

There is a reason why descriptive statistics is covered first, probability second, and statistical estimation and inference last. Broadly speaking, the three areas are sequenced this way because they build on one another. The methods used to solve probability problems could not be effectively applied by someone unfamiliar with some of the concepts from descriptive statistics, such as the mean and the standard deviation (discussed in Chapter 3). Furthermore, problems involving statistical estimation and inference (beginning with Chapter 8) cannot be solved, or perhaps even understood, by someone who is unaware of how to use probability distributions, a topic at the very heart of probability (introduced in Chapters 5 and 6).

These three areas form the content and sequencing of the course material. The first area, descriptive statistics, introduces and develops methodologies for organizing, summarizing, and presenting data that many students and readers use in their work lives. The second area, probability, is approached from several vantage points. While the central ideas of probability are inherently interesting to many students, they are often found to be challenging and abstract. We do our level best to reduce the ambiguity surrounding some of the more difficult ideas and to make almost everything accessible to everyone in a language that is conversational and user-friendly. The third area, statistical inference, is also rather challenging for many students. Like probability, however, it can be seen as *formalized common sense*. Its usefulness and power, however, cannot be overstated. Indeed, it comprises numerous tools and methods that many students and readers find of immediate relevance in both their coursework and workplace.

definitions

Cross-Sectional Data Cross-sectional data are collected at the same (or approximately the same) point in time.

Data Data consist of facts or measurements that we collect, analyze, and interpret; they comprise the raw material of statistical analysis, and may be either quantitative or qualitative.

Data Set A data set refers to all the data, across observations and variables, collected for any given investigative purpose. A single data item is referred to as a "datum."

Descriptive Statistics Descriptive statistics consists of a wide variety of methods of organizing, summarizing, reporting, and interpreting data characteristics, both qualitative and quantitative. In general, these methods are classified as tabular, graphical, or numerical methods.

(a) **Tabular Methods** A collection of data summarization procedures designed to display data in a table format.
(b) **Graphical Methods** A group of pictorial methods for presenting in a pictorial format the information reported in a table.
(c) **Numerical Methods** A collection of numerical measures which summarize various characteristics of a set of data such as the measures of central tendency, location, dispersion, and association.

Elements An element is a unit of data which is represented as a set of attributes or measurements. Elements are the entities (e.g., the households, cities, companies, products, transactions, and persons) on which the data are collected.

Longitudinal Data Longitudinal data, also known as time-series data, are collected over several time periods.

Observations An observation is the set of values of the variables for an element. Observations represent the set of measurements for a single data entity.

Population A population consists of all the entities of interest in an investigative study.

Population Parameters These are the characteristics or qualities of the population in terms of the variables of interest.

Probability We encounter probability problems whenever we draw a sample from a population with known parameters, and then attempt to estimate the probability that the sample will have certain characteristics.

Qualitative Data Qualitative data are those data items that can be classified into categories or classes. That is, qualitative data are typically labels or names that are used to identify a characteristic of each element in a data set. In this book, we will consider qualitative data as one of two types, nominal-scaled or ordinal-scaled.

(a) **Nominal-Scaled Data** Nominal-scaled data are sometimes referred to as "categorical" data: they indicate into which category the data element should be placed. Such data may be represented either numerically or non-numerically.

(b) **Ordinal-Scaled Data** Ordinal-scaled data have all the properties of nominal-scaled data but, in addition, have the quality that order is meaningful. Such data may be represented either numerically or non-numerically.

Quantitative Data Quantitative data are those data items which can be characterized as metric (or quantitative), and which report *how many* or *how much*. In this book, we will consider quantitative data as one of two types, interval-scaled or ratio-scaled.

(a) **Interval-Scaled Data** Interval-scaled data have all the above-mentioned properties of ordinal-scaled data, plus the additional quality that the interval between the values is expressed in terms of fixed units of measurement.

(b) **Ratio-Scaled Data** Ratio-scaled data have all the above-mentioned properties of interval-scaled data, plus the additional quality that the ratio of two values is meaningful.

Sample The portion or subset of the population we select for the purposes of our study.

Sample Statistics These are the characteristics or qualities of the sample in terms of the variables of interest.

Statistics We encounter problems of statistics whenever we select a sample from a population and want to draw conclusions about the population's properties based on what we learn from the sample. Unlike in the case of a probability problem, the population parameters are unknown.

(a) **Statistical Estimation** Statistical estimation consists of both point estimation and confidence interval estimation, and the motivation of each is to puzzle out how small or how large something may be.

(b) **Statistical Inference** Statistical inference involves testing formal hypotheses for the purpose of drawing conclusions or inferences.

Variables A variable is an attribute of an element that may assume different values. Examples of variables are income, age, weight, occupation, industry, disease, gender, and marital status. Variables are the measurements or the characteristics of interest for the elements, and they are what we usually analyze using statistical methods.

R functions

`c()` The concatenate function combines elements within the parentheses, called arguments, into a single entity, called a "vector."

`data.frame()` Combines elements within the parentheses into a single entity, called a "data frame." The data frame is one of the most important structures used in connection with R statistical methods.

`head()` Shows the first six lines (by default) of a data object. To see *n* lines instead of six lines, include *n* in the argument: `head(,n)`.

`mean()` Reports the mean of the data object.

(Continued)

(Continued)

`str()` Displays the internal structure of the data object (e.g., vector, data frame.)

`summary()` Reports the minimum and maximum values plus the median, first and third quartiles, as well as the mean.

`tail()` Shows the last six lines (by default) of a data object. To see *n* lines instead of six lines, include *n* in the argument: `tail(,n)`.

APPENDIX: AN INTRODUCTION TO R

1. Where to Get It and How to Install It

Before we embark on our statistical and probabilistic journey, let us describe R (and RStudio), the statistical programming language we will be using. We describe how to download and install it, how to read data into it, how to write data and analytic results out of it, and how to perform some elementary computations.

Before we can work with R, we have to install it. R is provided free of charge, and can be downloaded from the following website:

`http://www.r-project.org/`

Once you get to this location, note the area in the left-hand margin named "Download." Just below this heading, click on the CRAN link. When you do this, you are presented with the list of hosts called CRAN mirrors (arranged by geographic location) which contain identical R content. Click on the location closest to your own, because the download will typically be faster. For example, since we live in New York City, we used the link to the National Institutes of Health in Bethesda, Maryland: `http://watson.nci.nih.gov/cran mirror/`

Depending on whether you use Windows or Mac OS, the next steps differ slightly.

(a) **Windows.** If you are a Windows user:

  (i) Click on `Download R for Windows`.
  (ii) When the next screen appears, click on `base`.
  (iii) Once you see the next page, click on the link `Download R 3.2.3 for Windows`. (The number 3.2.3 is associated only with the current version of R; this number changes as updated versions of R are made available.)
  (iv) Save the file `R-3.2.3-win.exe`, double-click, and follow the onscreen instructions. Assuming the installation has been successful, there will be an entry in the All Programs area of the Start Menu. By right-clicking on `R 3.2.3`, you may place a shortcut R icon on the desktop. To start up R, simply click on the icon in the usual way.

(b) **Mac OS X.** If you are a Mac user:

  (i) Click on the `Download R for (Mac) OS X` link.
  (ii) Click on the latest `pkg` file. As of this writing, the latest file is `R-3.2.3.pkg`. (The number will change, however, as updated versions of R are made available.) Once downloaded, the file will appear in the Downloads area.

(iii) Move `R-3.2.3.pkg` from the Downloads area to the Applications area and double-click on its entry (icon). Follow the instructions for full installation.

(iv) The installation process should create an R entry in the Application area. Drag the R entry to the desktop for an R shortcut. To start up R, simply click on the icon in the usual way.

You will also want to install RStudio, an integrated development environment, once you have downloaded the R statistical programming package itself. RStudio can be thought of as a shell in which R operates. It simplifies many basic functions and facilitates the running of R itself, thus making R easier to interact with and more user-friendly. RStudio is provided free of charge and can be downloaded from:

`http://rstudio.com`

(a) When you get to this location, click `Download RStudio`.

(b) When the next screen appears, select `Desktop`.

(c) At the next screen, select `Download RStudio Desktop`.

(d) Depending on whether you use Windows or a Mac, follow the above steps (for installing R). The installation steps are the same for RStudio as they are for R.

Make sure that you have installed R before installing RStudio. RStudio by itself does not include the R program. Once both R and RStudio have been successfully downloaded and installed, a double-click on the RStudio icon launches the program (Figure 1.1) and you are ready to start using R.

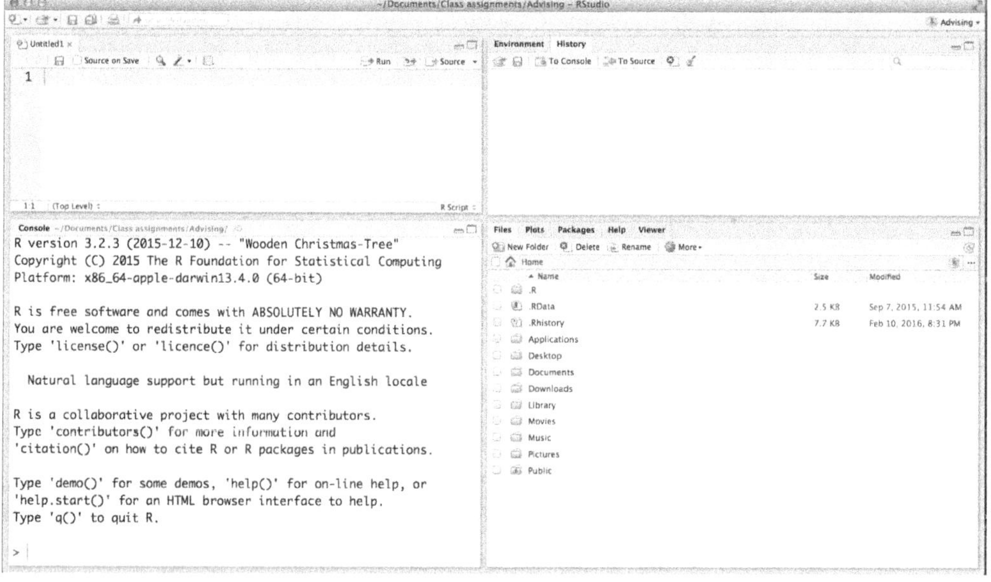

Figure 1.1 Screen view of the RStudio interface

There are four panes or windows in the RStudio interface.

(a) The **Source** window, located in the upper left-hand quadrant, is where we write code for our programs. It includes an intuitive, feature-rich text editor that makes it easy to run, save, and access programs.
(b) The **Console** is in the lower left-hand window and is the location where interactive work is done. The RStudio Console is the same as the Console in R.
(c) As the name implies, the tabbed **Environment/History** pane in the upper right-hand area is where the data sets and variables are listed and described (in Environment), and where the history of R commands is displayed (in History).
(d) The tabbed **Files/Plots/Packages/Help/Viewer** pane in the lower right-hand area is a repository of helpful tools which we discuss in subsequent chapters.

We point out that it is not absolutely necessary to run R through RStudio. While RStudio is a relatively new addition to R, the R package itself has been around for a couple of decades, and people ran (and still run) R very well without RStudio. However, since RStudio makes interacting with R more straightforwardly intuitive, we will use it throughout this book.

To exit RStudio, enter `q()` at the R prompt and hit the enter key. The R prompt can be seen on the command line of the Console, the lower left-hand pane. It is the *greater-than* symbol >, and it is the location where we write our R commands when working in an interactive mode.

2. Basic File Management and Working with Data

(a) Installing the `introstats` package that accompanies this book

This book comes with an R package called `introstats` which includes the data sets used with the examples and exercises for the chapters. Packages are extensions to R that implement various methods and provide package-specific data sets, and we will encounter more of them in later chapters. In order to access the data sets used in this book, you will want to install the package by entering the following two commands at the R prompt in the Console.

```
install.packages("devtools")
devtools::install_github("ericnovik/introstats")
```

Once these two steps have been executed, it is necessary to enter one final command at the R prompt in the Console each time we begin an R session requiring one of the data sets:

```
library(introstats)
```

This option for importing data into the R environment (referred to as the R Workspace) is used for examples and exercises throughout the book. But because this approach cannot be taken when we are using R in any other context, two additional methods are introduced below (see (b) and (c)): entering the data directly in the R Console, and importing the data from a spreadsheet.

(b) How to get data into R: entering the data directly in the R Console

Even though it is an abstract characterization, R is often referred to as an *object-based* programming language. In R, two of the most common data objects are *vectors* and *data frames*. One can think of vectors as a single column in a spreadsheet that contains elements of the same type. One example of a vector might consist of the following elements: 1, 3, 5, 7. Another vector could be made up of these items: "a," "d," "t." However, 1, 5, "d," "t" do not make up a valid vector since the elements are not of the same type.

(i) How to use R to analyze a data set if it is organized in a vector

Analyzing data that are organized in vectors is convenient when we have a small set of data and want to analyze it quickly. Consider the data in Table 1.6, which consist of the US unemployment rates (percent) for the 12 months from January to December 2012.

Table 1.6 Official monthly US unemployment rate (%) for 2012.

Rate	8.3	8.3	8.2	8.1	8.2	8.2	8.2	8.1	7.8	7.9	7.8	7.8

Source: US Bureau of Labor Statistics

In this book, we write out the R code in a shaded block similar to the one below. We refer to these as R blocks. When explanation is helpful, each line of code in the R block is accompanied by a comment. When there is more than one comment in an R block, the comments are numbered. Finally, whenever the code requires more detailed explanation, it is written just after the R block itself in numbered comments. This is done with an eye to keeping a more clutter-free R block environment.

As a naming convention, we identify an object by three elements: a letter indicating whether the object is associated with a chapter (C) or its exercises (E), and two numbers, the first indicating the chapter number, the second the object number. For example, the first object of Chapter 1 is `C1_1`; the first object in Chapter 2 is `C2_1`; and the second object in Chapter 3 is `C3_2`. Similarly, `E1_1` names the first object of the Chapter 1 exercises, while `E3_4` names the fourth object in the Chapter 3 exercises. When the data objects are named unambiguously, there is less chance of confusion.

Consider the following R block in which we create an object `C1_1` in the R Workspace, check its accuracy, and find the mean of `C1_1`.

```
#Comment1. Read data into a vector named C1_1.
C1_1 <- c(8.3, 8.3, 8.2, 8.1, 8.2, 8.2, 8.2, 8.1, 7.8,
          7.9, 7.8, 7.8)

#Comment2. To confirm that C1_1 contains what we want.
C1_1
```

```
##  [1] 8.3 8.3 8.2 8.1 8.2 8.2 8.2 8.1 7.8 7.9 7.8 7.8
```

```
#Comment3. Find the mean of C1_1.
mean(C1_1)
```

```
## [1] 8.075
```

Some explanation of these R commands is helpful.

A To enter the Table 1.6 data into the R Workspace, place the cursor at the command line in the Console next to the R prompt >, write out the following line of code, and enter.

```
C1_1 <- c(8.3, 8.3, 8.2, 8.1, 8.2, 8.2, 8.2, 8.1, 7.8, 7.9, 7.8, 7.8)
```

The `c()` expression is referred to as the "concatenate" function and it combines all the elements in the parentheses into a vector. The symbol <- is known as the assignment operator, and it assigns whatever is on its right-hand side to whatever is on its left-hand side, in this case `C1_1`. Even though it is constructed from two symbols, the *less-than* sign and a *hyphen*, we should think of <- as a single symbol. Finally, the direction of the assignment operator -> can be reversed so that whatever is on its left-hand side is stored in whatever is on its right-hand side.

B To make certain that the vector `C1_1` contains the data items we want, enter the vector name `C1_1` at the R prompt >, hit enter, and visually inspect the result. In this case, we need only confirm that all the data values from Table 1.6 are indeed stored in the vector named `C1_1`.

C Once we are satisfied that `C1_1` includes the desired data values, we calculate their mean with the function `mean()`.

The R function `c()` is the first of many we will use; `mean()` is another. The values that are entered within the parentheses of the function are referred to as "arguments," and each R function has rules governing how its arguments are to be specified. If a function has two or more arguments, they are separated by commas. A third function is `data.frame()`, and it can be used to assign a heading (or variable name) to a vector; it can also be used to bring together more than one vector to form a matrix-like object.

(ii) How to use R to analyze a data set if it is organized in a data frame

Working with data frames (rather than vectors) is more common when performing statistical analysis, particularly when one desires to incorporate variable names in the objects. (`C1_1` did not include a variable name.) Once the set of data extends to more than one variable, it usually becomes necessary to include variable names. Below, the function `data.frame()` is used to include a variable name `rate` (for % unemployment rate).

```
#Comment1. Use function data.frame() to read C1_1 into C1_2.
C1_2 <- data.frame(rate = C1_1)
```

```
#Comment2. Examine contents of first 3 rows of data in C1_2.
head(C1_2,3)
```

```
##   rate
## 1 8.3
## 2 8.3
## 3 8.2
```

```
#Comment3. Find the mean of the variable named rate.
mean(C1_2$rate)
```

```
## [1] 8.075
```

The three R commands above require additional explanation.

- A To add the variable name `rate` to vector `C1_1`, use the function `data.frame(rate = C1_1)` and assign the result to a data frame `C1_2`.
- B Use the function `head(C1_2,3)` to check that `C1_2` includes the variable name `rate`. Note that the second argument of `head(C1_2,3)` (which is 3) specifies that only the first three rows `C1_2` should be reported. Remember: if a function has two or more arguments, they are separated by commas.
- C Using the function `mean(C1_2$rate)`, find the mean value of `rate`. Note that `C1_2` and the variable name `rate` are separated by the dollar sign `$`.

  The function `data.frame` can also be used to create a single object with two or more variables. For example, suppose that six students are measured on three variables: grade point average (`gpa`); math Scholastic Aptitude Test (SAT) score (`satm`); and verbal SAT score (`satv`).

```
#Comment1. Read data into 3 vectors: gpa, satm, and satv.
gpa <- c(2.7, 3.5, 3.7, 3.3, 3.6, 3.0)
satm <- c(450, 560, 700, 620, 640, 570)
satv <- c(540, 650, 700, 720, 540, 750)
```

```
#Comment2. Use function data.frame() to read 3 vectors into
#C1_3. Name each vector GPA, SATM, and SATV, respectively.
C1_3 <- data.frame(GPA = gpa, SATM = satm, SATV = satv)
```

```
#Comment3. Examine the contents of C1_3.
C1_3
```

```
##   GPA SATM SATV
## 1 2.7  450  540
## 2 3.5  560  650
## 3 3.7  700  700
## 4 3.3  620  720
## 5 3.6  640  540
## 6 3.0  570  750
```

```
#Comment4. Find the mean of the variable named GPA.
mean(C1_3$GPA)
```

```
## [1] 3.3
```

The data frame `C1_3` now contains all three variables—`GPA`, `SATM`, and `SATV`. The mean of `GPA` is 3.3; the mean of the other variables is found in the same manner, taking care to separate `C1_3` from the variable names (`SATM` or `SATV`) with a dollar sign `$`.

(c) How to get data into R: importing the data from a spreadsheet

While the method described above works well with small data sets, we do not recommend using it for larger data sets. There are many ways to import data into the R Workspace; one of the more widely used methods involves carrying out the following two steps: (1) convert a spreadsheet data file to a comma-separated values (csv) file; (2) import the csv file into the R Workspace. Spreadsheets are widely used, and most have the ability to convert data to csv files. Here is how this can be done if your spreadsheet software is Excel or Numbers.

1 Convert a spreadsheet data file to a csv file: first Excel, then Numbers.

   A Once the Excel file is loaded, select the `File` drop-down menu and click on the `Save As...` option.

   B Once the `Save As` dialog box appears, enter the desired filename in the `Save As` window; change from `Excel Workbook` to `Comma Separated Value (.csv)` in the `Format` window. Click on `Save`.

   If you use a Mac and your preferred speadsheet software is Numbers:

   A Once the Numbers file is loaded, select the `File` drop-down menu and click on `Export` option.

   B Once the `Export` dialog box appears, select `CSV` and click on `Next`. When the `Save As` dialog box appears, enter the desired filename in the `Save As` window. Click on `Export`.

2 Import the csv file into the R Workspace.

Now that your spreadsheet data file has been converted to the csv format, the second (and final) step is to import it into the R Workspace. There are several ways of doing this but we believe that the best method exploits a feature of RStudio known as Project. RStudio Project helps us organize and automate the migration of our data files between the various folders that might reside in the Documents area of our hard drive and the R Workspace where the actual data analysis must be done.

To demonstrate how to use Project, we first recreate the data sets above, `C1_2` and `C1_3`, but this time using a spreadsheet such as Excel or Numbers, making sure to save both in the csv format (see step 1 above). In this demonstration, we save `C1_2.csv` and `C1_3.csv` in folders named `Economics` and `Advising`, respectively, for course material for two university classes, Economics and Educational Psychology. The `Economics` and `Advising` folders are organized within a folder named `Class Assignments`. When successfully executed, the tabbed window of the lower right-hand area of the RStudio interface—`Files/Plots/Packages/Help/Viewer`—provides confirmation (see Figures 1.2 and 1.3). Figure 1.2 shows that `C1_2.csv` is located in the `Economics` folder which itself is organized inside another folder, `Class Assignments`. Similarly, Figure 1.3 reports the path address for the other data set, `C1_3.csv`.

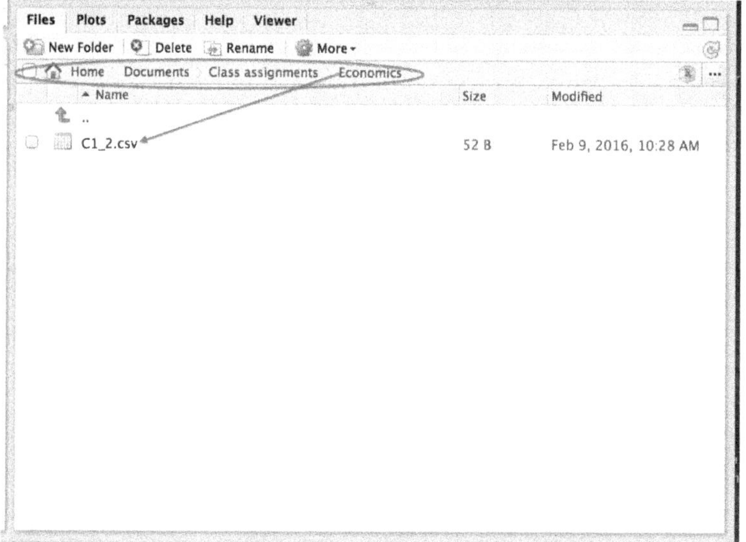

Figure 1.2 Path `Documents > Class assignments > Economics > C1_2.csv`

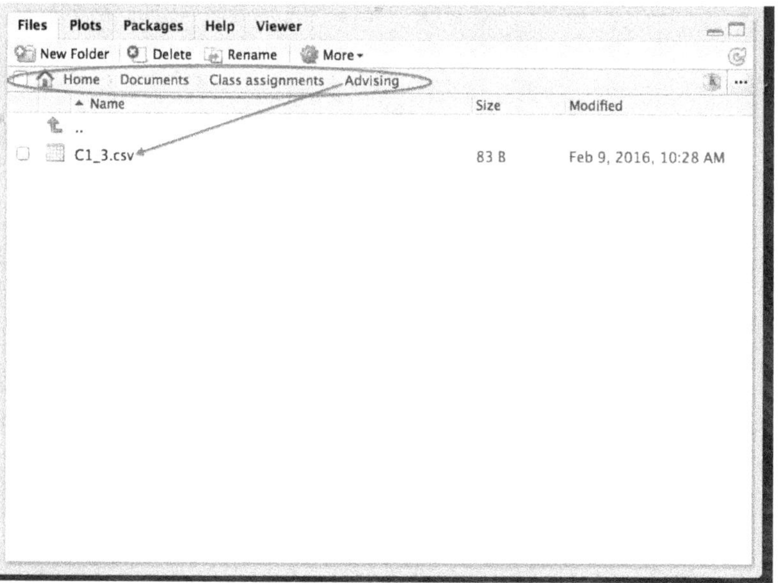

Figure 1.3 Path `Documents > Class assignments > Advising > C1_3.csv`

Suppose we wish to create two projects, one each for our two courses, because we want to organize all of our work—data files, R programs, and graphical illustrations such as plots, histograms, and so on—in its own designated space. Here is how RStudio Project helps us do that. After opening RStudio, click on `File` and select `New Project...` from the drop-down menu. When the New Project window opens, click on `Existing Directory`. (Note that "directory" and "folder" are two terms that refer to the same thing.) When the next window appears, identify the target directory in the `Project working directory` field by clicking on the `Browse` button and navigating to the desired directory. In this case, the desired directory is the `Advising` folder. Click on the `Create Project` button (see Figure 1.4).

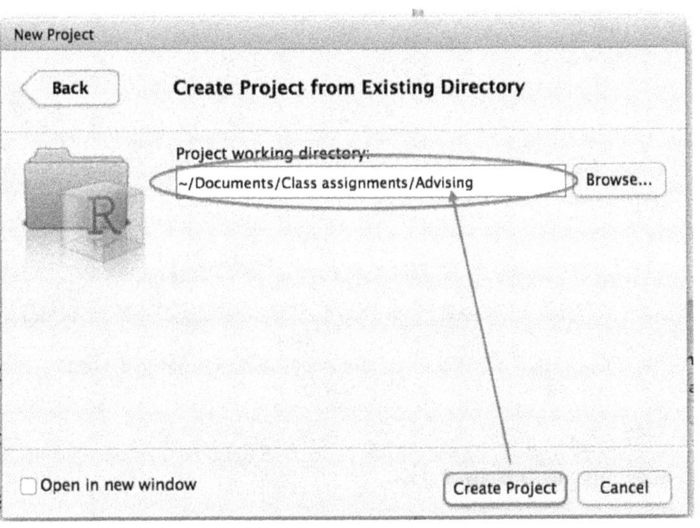

Figure 1.4 Final step of creating the `Advising` project

That the `Advising` project has been successfully created is confirmed in two ways: `Advising` is now indicated in the upper right-hand corner, next to the RStudio icon; and `Advising`, as reported in the lower right-hand panel, now includes two new files, `.Rhistory` and `Advising.Rproj`, along with the data set we want to import into the R Workspace, `C1_3.csv` (see Figure 1.5).

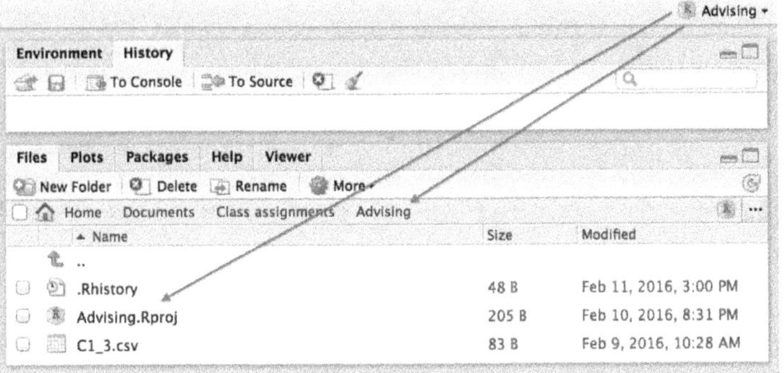

Figure 1.5 The `Advising` project is now created

In this demonstration, the next step requires a simple repetition of the above procedure to create the Economics Project. Everything is executed in the same way except that at Figure 1.4, we specify Economics rather than Advising. Assuming the execution is successful, the upper right-hand corner of the RStudio interface will now show the two project names, Advising and Economics. When the contents of Economics is examined, we will once again find two new files, .Rhistory and Economics.Rproj, along with the data set we want to import into the R Workspace, C1_2.csv. Both Economics and Advising projects can be thought of as ordinary folders residing in the Class Assignments folder.

Remember that our purpose here is to demonstrate how to import, export, and organize our files. To this end, we now (1) import the data set C1_3.csv to the R Workspace, (2) perform a simple statistical summarization procedure, and (3) export the output back to the Advising folder.

We open the Advising project by clicking on the down arrow next to the RStudio icon in the upper right-hand corner of the RStudio interface and then navigating to Advising (see Figure 1.5). Once in the Advising project, we enter C1_3 <- read.csv("C1_3.csv") at the prompt in the Console to import C1_3.csv to the Workspace. Note that the argument of the function read.csv() does not specify the full path address (an advantage of using RStudio) but does require that the filename itself be expressed within quotes, either single or double: "C1_3.csv" (see Figure 1.6).

As with the first time we used C1_3 above, we only need to enter C1_3 at the prompt to examine the contents of the new object (see Figure 1.6). Now that C1_3 resides in the Workspace, we are in a position to perform our statistical analysis.

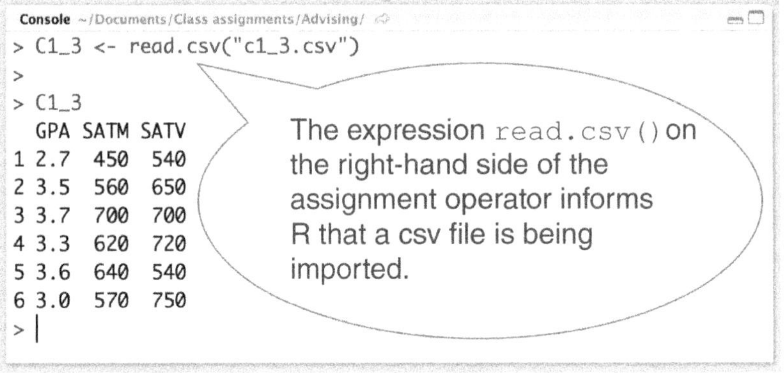

Figure 1.6 Importing C1_3.csv into the R Workspace

We use the function summary(C1_3) to provide the minimum, maximum, mean, median, and first and third quartiles for all three variables in C1_3. Once the results are assigned to an object named Descriptives, we review the contents by entering the object name at the prompt (see Figure 1.7).

```
Console ~/Documents/Class assignments/Advising/
> Descriptives <- summary(C1_3)
>
> Descriptives
      GPA              SATM            SATV
 Min.   :2.700   Min.   :450.0   Min.   :540.0
 1st Qu.:3.075   1st Qu.:562.5   1st Qu.:567.5
 Median :3.400   Median :595.0   Median :675.0
 Mean   :3.300   Mean   :590.0   Mean   :650.0
 3rd Qu.:3.575   3rd Qu.:635.0   3rd Qu.:715.0
 Max.   :3.700   Max.   :700.0   Max.   :750.0
>
```

Figure 1.7 Summary statistics for `C1_3.csv` assigned to `Descriptives`

The `summary()` function is only one among many that we might use in this instance. The important point to bear in mind is that our purpose here is to demonstrate how to organize, import, and analyze our files.

(d) How to export data and analysis results out of R

Finally, we show how to export an object from the R Workspace to an external folder that might reside in the `Documents` area on the hard drive, a capability that is useful when one wishes to share data or analysis files with colleagues. In this instance, we use the function `write.csv()` to send the object we created above, `Descriptives`, back to the `Advising` project folder (see Figure 1.8).

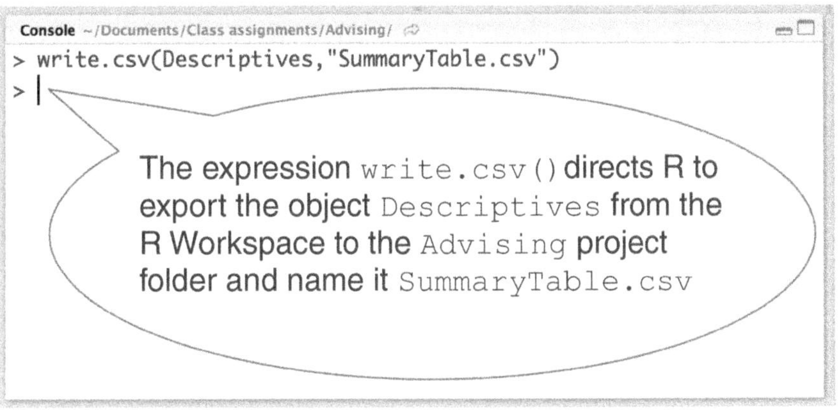

Figure 1.8 Exporting the object `Descriptives` to the `Advising` project folder

Note that the `write.csv()` function does not specify the full path address to the external folder (this was done when we created the Project) but does require two arguments: the name of the object in the R Workspace, `Descriptives`, and the name of the data file once it has been exported to the folder, `SummaryTable.csv`. Note that quotes must enclose the file name.

A final inspection of the `Advising` project folder now lists the four files that reside there, including `SummaryTable.csv` (see Figure 1.9).

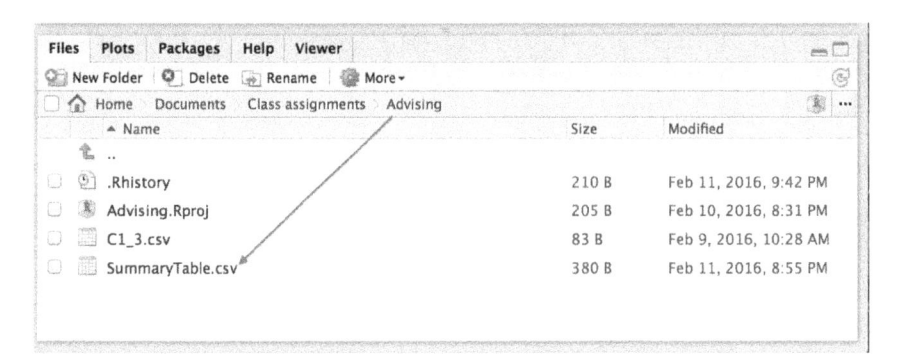

Figure 1.9 The `Advising` project folder with four files

We have just summarized three methods that can be used to import data into the Workspace: (a) installing the `introstats` package that accompanies this book; (b) entering data directly into the R Console; and (c) most useful of all, importing the data from a spreadsheet. Despite the fact that we have just taken nearly six pages to cover method (c), it is not the approach we use in the examples and exercises for this book. Instead, we use method (a) and to a lesser extent method (b). The reason why we take so much care and so many pages to demonstrate method (c) is that it is the approach you will use most often when working with R in any context unconnected with the book, particularly in your other classes or in your work life.

3. Five Hints for Using R

1. Since R is case sensitive, remember that *x* and *X* are not the same thing.
2. If a line of code is incomplete, a + sign will appear, prompting us to finish the line.
3. Remember that comments (preceded with a #) describe what lines of R code are intended to accomplish, and can be very helpful when we cannot otherwise make out the purpose of the code.
4. We can avoid re-entering R commands by using the up-arrow key, an action that recovers the lines above for recycling. In fact, it is possible to go back through as many lines of code as necessary by repeatedly hitting this key.
5. We can confirm that R is connected to a certain external directory by entering `getwd()` at the prompt in the Console. Similarly, we can connect R to a desired directory by entering `setwd()`, where the argument is the path address enclosed in quotes. Even so, one of the advantages of working with RStudio Projects is that these steps are usually unnecessary.

OUR APPROACH TO WRITING THIS BOOK

There is much additional material we could have included but have not. Textbooks are normally defined as much by what they leave out as by what they include, and this one is no exception. This book is primarily about statistics and probability, and only secondarily about the R statistical programming language. Moreover, R provides many different ways to solve the problems we encounter in this book. We have chosen to include those concepts and methods that have worked best for the thousands of graduate and undergraduate students we have had when teaching statistics at four different universities in the US and Europe.

exercises

1.1 Using R, create a vector consisting of the following elements: 81, 17, 7, 55, 2, 98, 71, 47, 19, 8, 3, 10, 28, 65, 80. Name it `E1_1`.

   (a) How many data values are in `E1_1`? Use the function `length()`.
   (b) What is the mean of `E1_1`?
   (c) What is the median of `E1_1`? Use the function `median()`.
   (d) Use the functions `min()` and `max()` to find the minimum and maximum values.
   (e) What is the sum of the values in `E1_1`? Use the function `sum()`.

1.2 Use the functions `sum()` and `length()` to find the mean of `E1_1`.

1.3 Using the built-in data set `LakeHuron`, please answer the following questions.

   (a) What are the first five values in `LakeHuron`?
   (b) How many data values are in `LakeHuron`?
   (c) What is the lowest level (in feet) of Lake Huron during the 1875-1972 period?
   (d) What is the highest level of Lake Huron?
   (e) What is the mean level?
   (f) What is the median level?
   (g) What are the last four values in `LakeHuron`? Use the function `tail(,4)`.

1.4 Suppose we interview five individuals who are registering to vote in the 2016 US Presidential election, and learn the following about them in terms of their age (years) and annual income (US$): voter 1 is 25 years of age with an income of $24,000; voter 2 is 37 years with an income of $42,000; voter 3 is 45 years with an income of $39,000; voter 4 is 57 years with an income of $77,000; and voter 5 is 65 years with an income of $84,000. Use R to create a data frame consisting of these five individuals and two variables, named `Age` and `Income`. Name the data frame `E1_2`.

1.5 Use the function `summary()` to find the minimum, maximum, mean, median, and first and third quartiles of `E1_2`.

https://study.sagepub.com/stinerock

Descriptive Statistics: Tabular and Graphical Methods

contents

learning objectives

1 Learn how to report qualitative data using summarization procedures such as frequency distributions, bar graphs, and dot charts.
2 Learn how to report quantitative data using summarization procedures such as frequency and relative frequency distributions.
3 Learn how to construct a histogram as a graphical summary of quantitative data. Learn how the shape of a data distribution is revealed by a histogram.
4 Learn how to create cross-tabulations and scatter diagrams of bivariate data.

Throughout this chapter, we use R extensively to achieve each of these four objectives.

Although Chapter 1 introduces probability and statistics from a big-picture perspective, this chapter introduces and develops material of a more applied nature: tabular and graphical methods of summarizing data. The objective of using these methods is to provide insights about the data that cannot be grasped by examining the original raw data.

2.1 METHODS OF PRESENTING QUALITATIVE DATA

Over the course of a recent semester, data were collected on the region of origin for the 40 graduate students enrolled in a statistics course. When the students' origins are represented as regions such as Latin America and Europe—as well as the nations of China, India, and the US—the results might be tabulated and reported as in Table 2.1.

Table 2.1 Graduate students' country-of-origin data

US	US	Latin America	India	China	China	China	US
China	China	China	India	India	US	China	India
China	China	India	China	Latin America	US	US	India
China	Europe	Latin America	China	US	China	Europe	Europe
India	India	US	China	India	China	Europe	India

These data are not quantitative but qualitative; the places of origin represent a quality of each student. Even if we were to code the countries with a number—China = 1, Europe = 2, and so on—the data still are not inherently numerical, and thus we cannot perform numerical analysis on them. The best we can do is report the counts of the students representing their countries/region, and organize those counts in tables or pictures. Also, the importance of being able to summarize qualitative data in this way is greater when we are no longer dealing with 40 students but rather with (say) 10,000. Fortunately, these methods work just as well on larger data sets as they do on smaller ones.

Definition 2.1. Frequency Distribution. A frequency distribution is a tabular summary of the number of observations falling into each of two or more mutually exclusive, collectively exhaustive categories.

Example 2.1. Construct a frequency distribution of the data in Table 2.1.

Table 2.2 Frequency, relative frequency, and percent frequency distributions

1	2	3	4
Country	**Frequency**	**Relative frequency**	**Percent frequency**
China	15	15/40 = 0.38	38%
Europe	4	4/40 = 0.10	10%
India	10	10/40 = 0.25	25%
Latin America	3	3/40 = 0.07	7%
US	8	8/40 = 0.20	20%
	40	1.00	100%

Taken together, columns 1 and 2 of Table 2.2 make up the frequency distribution. We can use R to create both Table 2.1 and the frequency distributions.

```
#Comment1. Use rep() to generate the data values; assign result to C2_1.
C2_1 <- c(rep('Latin', 3), rep('Europe', 4), rep('US', 8),
          rep('India', 10), rep('China', 15))

#Comment2. Use head(,8) to review the first 8 items of C2_1.
head(C2_1, 8)

## [1] "Latin" "Latin" "Latin" "Europe" "Europe" "Europe" "Europe" "US"

#Comment3. Use table() for frequency distribution; assign result to C2_2.
C2_2 <- table(C2_1)

#Comment4. Review contents of C2_2, the frequencies.
C2_2

## C2_1
##   China Europe  India  Latin  US
##      15      4     10      3   8
```

Some explanation of these commands should be helpful.

1 Our first step involves using an R function to generate the data set. The function `rep()` replicates (or repeats) the elements reported in Table 2.1. In this case, `rep('Latin',3)` replicates "Latin" 3 times; `rep('Europe',4)` repeats "Europe" 4 times; `rep('US',8)` repeats

"US" 8 times; `rep('India',10)` repeats "India" 10 times; and `rep('China',15)` repeats "China" 15 times. The result, referred to as a "character vector," is bound together by the `c()` function and assigned to the object named `C2_1`. Note that 'Latin' is used as an abbreviation for 'Latin America.'

2 The function `head(C2_1,8)` reports the first eight elements of `C2_1`. This is a useful feature that makes it possible to check on exactly what an object contains.

3 The function `table()` classifies the elements of an object into categories and provides the frequency (or counts) for each category. The frequencies are then assigned to a new object, `C2_2`, making possible still other graphical and tabular representations such as relative frequency distributions, bar graphs, and dot charts (see below).

Definition 2.2. Relative Frequency Distribution. A relative frequency distribution reports the proportion, rather than number, of observations falling into each category.

Example 2.2. Construct a relative frequency distribution of the data in Table 2.1.

From columns 1 and 2 of Table 2.2, we can develop two other related frequency distributions, the relative frequency and the percent frequency distributions. Columns 1 and 3 provide the relative frequency distribution, while columns 1 and 4 report the percent frequency distribution. Two R commands can be used to find relative frequencies.

```
#Comment1. Use the function sum() to find the number of elements in the
#object C2_2; assign that number to the object n.
n <- sum(C2_2)

#Comment2. Divide object C2_2 by n; assign result to object C2_3.
C2_3 <- C2_2 / n

#Comment3. Review the contents of C2_3, the relative frequencies.
C2_3

## C2_1
##  China  Europe  India  Latin     US
##  0.375   0.100  0.250  0.075  0.200
```

Relative frequencies are created by dividing each category count of `C2_2` by n. Note that R operates on `C2_2` to provide the relative frequency for each category with a single command (that is, by dividing `C2_2` by n). This is an example of *vectorization*, and it is an important feature of R because it simplifies many operations, basic (like this one) as well as more complicated (like some of the operations we encounter later in the book).

Two graphical methods of presenting qualitative data are the bar graph and dot chart. Remember that graphical methods are basically pictures of information reported in tables.

Definition 2.3. Bar Graph. A bar graph is a picture depicting qualitative data. Bars representing the different categories are typically placed along a horizontal axis; the heights of the bars drawn above the axis indicate the frequency, relative frequency, or percent frequency for each category.

Example 2.3. Create a bar graph of the data in Table 2.1 (see Figure 2.1).

```
barplot(C2_2, col = c('purple', 'red', 'blue', 'yellow', 'green'),
        xlab = 'Country/Region', ylab = 'Count', ylim = c(0, 20),
        main = 'Bar Graph of Student Origin Data')
```

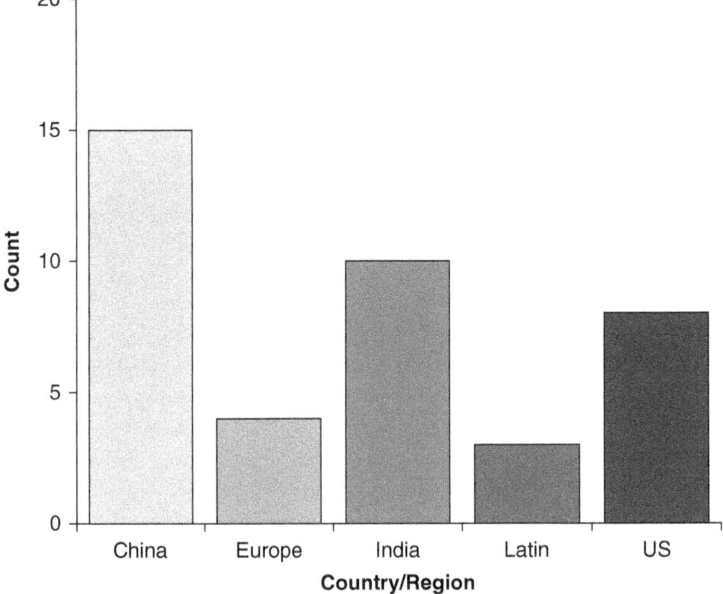

Figure 2.1 Distribution of 40 students from five countries/regions

The six arguments of the function `barplot()` require some explanation.

1 The object name is `C2_2`.
2 The colors for each bar are specified, from left to right, with `col = c()`.
3 The label for the horizontal axis is defined by `xlab =`.
4 The label for the vertical axis is defined by `ylab =`.
5 The range of values to be assumed by the vertical axis is specified by `ylim = c()`.
6 The main title (above the bars) is added by the use of `main =`.

It bears repeating that the objective of using tabular and graphical methods is to provide insights about the data that cannot be grasped by a cursory inspection of it in its original form: of the sample of 40 students enrolled in the statistics class, the largest number come from China, then India, then the US, then Europe, and lastly Latin America.

Note that when `barplot()` is executed, the bar graph is displayed in the lower right-hand quadrant of the RStudio interface where a `Plots` tab is highlighted. When the `Plots` tab is selected, Export displays the options `Save Plot as Image...`, `Save as PDF...`, and `Copy to Clipboard...`. These choices make it possible to export the bar graph (as well as other R-based graphical representations) in various image formats: PDF, PNG, JPEG, TIFF, BMP, SVG, and EPS.

Definition 2.4. Dot Chart. A dot chart is a simple graphical representation of qualitative data expressed in terms of frequencies of category occurrence.

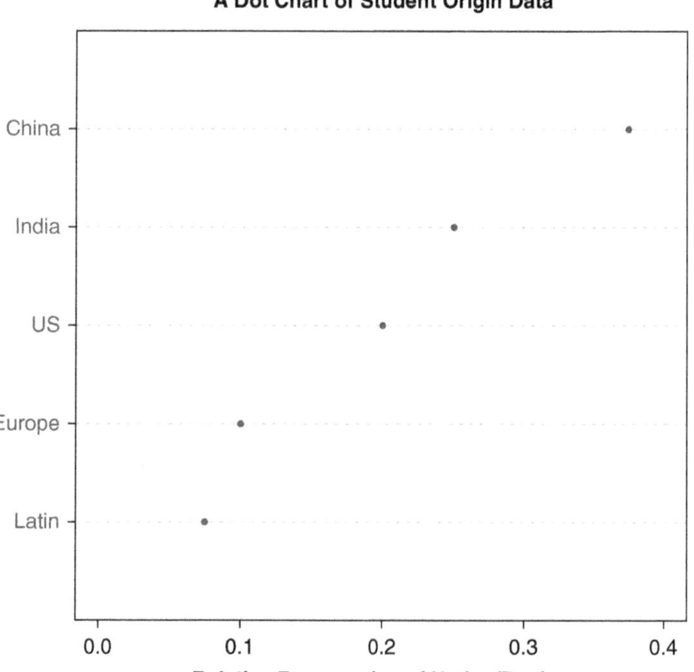

Figure 2.2 Distribution of 40 students from 5 countries/regions

Example 2.4. Create a dot chart of the data in Table 2.1 (see Figure 2.2).

```
dotchart(sort(C2_3), xlab = 'Relative Frequencies of Nation/Region',
         main = 'A Dot Chart of Student Origin Data',
         xlim = c(0, 0.40), pch = 20, col = 'blue')
```

The six arguments of the function `dotchart()` are explained here.

1 To sort the elements of `C2_3` in order of frequency, use `sort()`. Otherwise, the elements on the vertical axis are displayed alphabetically by default with the result that the image is a bit more difficult to interpret.
2 The label for the horizontal axis is defined by `xlab =`.
3 The main title (just above the chart) is added by the use of `main =`.

4 The range of values to be assumed by the horizontal axis is specified by `xlim = c()`.

5 The plotting character is defined by `pch =`; `pch = 20` results in a small solid circle. For the full menu of `pch =` options, enter `?pch` at the prompt in the Console.

6 The color of the plotted points is specified by `col =`.

Note: R sometimes responds with warning messages that we can safely ignore because the desired result is produced even as the warning is issued.

2.2 METHODS OF PRESENTING QUANTITATIVE DATA

Although the tabular and graphical methods of presenting quantitative data are similar to those discussed above, there are some differences. As before, the objective of applying these methods to quantitative data is to provide insights about the data that cannot be quickly obtained by looking only at the original set of data.

As an example, suppose marketing research data have been collected across 100 households in connection with an advertising effectiveness study on the hours of television viewing occurring during the two-day holiday period from New Year's Eve through New Year's Day. The hours of viewing time are arranged in ascending order and reported in Table 2.3.

Table 2.3 Hours of TV viewing across 100 households during a two-day holiday period

2.37	2.41	3.29	3.92	4.57	4.67	4.98	5.58	5.86	5.97
6.31	6.38	6.94	7.05	7.13	7.30	7.50	7.90	8.22	8.49
8.51	8.53	8.56	9.22	9.23	9.33	9.35	9.50	9.56	9.61
9.70	9.85	9.94	9.96	10.25	10.27	10.48	10.55	10.62	10.72
10.72	11.00	11.03	11.08	11.19	11.35	11.54	11.64	11.67	11.71
11.73	11.79	11.83	12.22	12.35	12.59	12.61	12.63	12.85	12.96
12.97	12.98	13.18	13.21	13.23	13.42	13.49	13.53	13.68	13.74
13.77	14.00	14.09	14.14	14.19	14.20	14.40	14.61	14.94	14.95
15.10	15.20	15.27	15.52	15.75	15.79	15.87	15.88	16.09	16.30
16.78	17.25	17.29	17.37	17.75	17.93	18.58	19.42	20.22	20.82

Note that despite being presented in ascending order, one cannot gain much insight into television-viewing patterns by inspecting the data in their present form. However, by organizing the data in a frequency distribution, we can improve on its interpretability. But unlike the previous frequency distribution (see Table 2.2), we must decide on the number and width of classes.

In general, between 5 and 20 collectively exhaustive, mutually exclusive, equal-width classes capture the distribution of the data pretty well. Since this is an inexact science, it is sometimes useful to try different numbers of classes.

Example 2.5. Organize the Table 2.3 data into a frequency distribution (see Table 2.4).

Table 2.4 Frequencies: relative, percent, and cumulative

	2	3	4	5	6	7	8
Class	**No. hrs**	**Freq.**	**Rel. freq.**	**% freq.**		**Cum. freq.**	**Cum. rel. freq.**
1	0-5.00	7	.07	7%	≤ 5.00	7	.07
2	5.01-10	27	.27	27%	≤ 10.00	34	.34
3	10.01-15	46	.46	46%	≤ 15.00	80	.80
4	15.01-20	18	.18	18%	≤ 20.00	98	.98
5	20.01-25	2	.02	2%	≤ 25.00	100	1.00
Totals		100	1.00	100%			

In this example, five classes of an equal width of 5 seem to distribute and reveal the data in a way that allows insight into its grouping, central tendency, and dispersion. What can now be seen immediately—and what was obscured when reviewing the Table 2.3 data—is that (a) only 7% of households in this sample view television 5 hours or less during this period, while 2% watch more than 20 hours; (b) 34% of the households view 10 hours or less; and (c) the greatest percentage of households, 46%, view between 10 and 15 hours.

Note that the Table 2.4 frequencies, relative frequencies, and percent frequencies in columns 3, 4, and 5, respectively, are obtained in the same manner as they were in Table 2.2. Note also that columns 6, 7, and 8 report the cumulative frequencies. A review of Table 2.4 should suffice to make clear how the numbers in these columns are obtained.

Here is how we use R to obtain the frequency distribution for this data set. To demonstrate how this might be done, we use the data set `tv_hours` from the book's companion website. See Section 2(a) in the Chapter 1 Appendix for direction, if necessary.

```
#Comment1. Examine contents of first 2 rows of data in tv_hours.
head(tv_hours, 2)

##    hours
## 1  2.37
## 2  2.41

#Comment2. Use cut() to break the variable hours (the name of the
# variable in tv_hours) into classes.
C2_4 <- cut(tv_hours$hours, c(0, 5, 10, 15, 20, 25))
```

#Comment3. Use table() for frequency distribution; assign result to C2_5.

```
C2_5 <- table(C2_4)
```

#Comment4. Review contents of C2_5, the frequencies.

```
C2_5
```

```
## C2_4
##    (0,5]  (5,10]  (10,15]  (15,20]  (20,25]
##        7      27       46       18        2
```

Further explanation of these steps should make clear how frequencies are found.

1 As a first step, we (a) make sure that the data set is what we expect (the first two values should be the same as those in Table 2.3) and (b) learn what the variable name is.
2 We use `cut()` to stipulate that the five classes are (0,5], (5,10], (10,15], (15,20], and (20,25], where the first class includes those households falling in the range greater than 0 hours (of TV viewing) up to and including 5 hours; the second class includes households reporting greater than 5 hours but less than or equal to 10 hours; and so on. The result of this operation is assigned to the object `C2_4`.
3 The function `table()` classifies the elements of `C2_4` into classes and produces the frequencies for each. When the result is assigned to another object, `C2_5`, we can use it for other descriptive representations such as relative frequencies and histograms.
4 The final step reports the frequency values that are stored in `C2_4`.

Example 2.6. Organize the Table 2.3 data into a relative frequency distribution.

#Comment1. Divide C2_5 by the sum of its elements; assign result to C2_6.

```
C2_6 <- C2_5 / sum(C2_5)
```

#Comment2. Review the contents of C2_6, the relative frequencies.

```
C2_6
```

```
## C2_4
##    (0,5]  (5,10]  (10,15]  (15,20]  (20,25]
##     0.07    0.27     0.46     0.18     0.02
```

Thus, in this sample of 100 households, a proportion 0.07 of households viewed television less than 5 hours; 0.27 of households viewed between 5 and 10 hours; and so on.

A graphical method of presenting quantitative data is the histogram.

Definition 2.5. Histogram. A histogram partitions data into classes on the horizontal axis; the heights of the bars above the axis indicate the frequency for each class.

Example 2.7. Create a histogram of the data in Table 2.3. Use the object `tv_hours`.

For a histogram, the variable of interest is usually placed on the horizontal axis, the frequencies on the vertical axis. A rectangle is drawn above each class interval, its height corresponding to the interval frequency. If we combine the Table 2.4 information from columns 2 and 3 into a histogram, we obtain the picture in Figure 2.3.

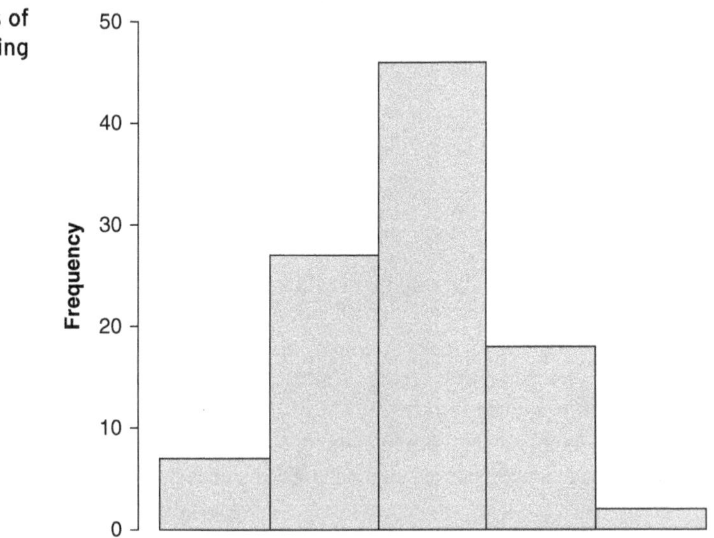

Figure 2.3 One hundred households by hours of TV viewing

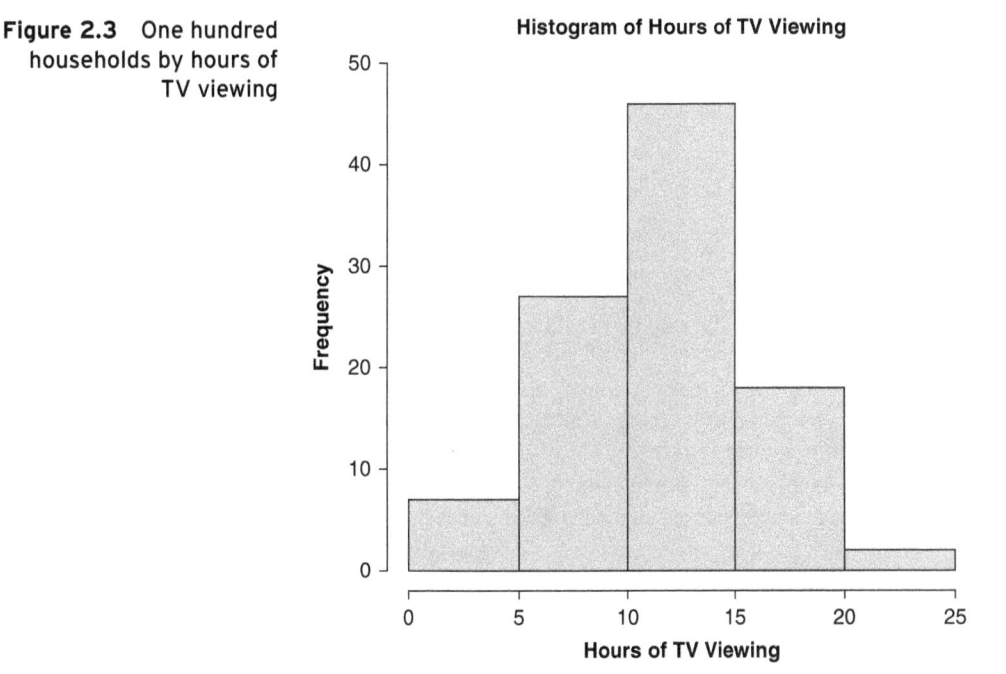

The six arguments of the function `hist(tv_hours$hours, breaks = 5, xlab = "Hours of TV Viewing", ylim = c(0, 50), main = "Histogram of Hours of TV Viewing", col = "blue")` in the above R block are:

1 The object name is `tv_hours`; the variable name is `hours`.
2 The number of breaks (or categories) is specified by `breaks =`.
3 The label for the horizontal axis is defined by `xlab =`.
4 The range of values to be assumed by the vertical axis is set by `ylim = c()`.
5 The main title (above the bars) is added by use of `main =`.
6 The color is specified by `col =`.

The point of summarizing data with either tabular or graphical methods is to provide insights that cannot be obtained by inspecting it in its original, unprocessed form.

2.3 CROSS-TABULATIONS AND SCATTER PLOTS

Thus far, we have focused on methods that are used to summarize one variable at a time, such as the hours of television viewing. Very often, however, we would like to be able to capture something about the relationship between two variables taken together. We now consider two methods—one tabular, one graphical—to help us explore and summarize the relationships between two variables: the cross-tabulation and the scatter diagram.

Definition 2.6. Cross-tabulation. A cross-tabulation (or contingency) table is a tabular method for summarizing the relationship between two variables simultaneously. It is a flexible approach in that it can be used when both variables are qualitative, both are quantitative, or when one variable is qualitative and the other quantitative.

Let us consider an example of the last type. Many undergraduate degree programs report uneven student satisfaction with the college experience. On a closer look, however, student satisfaction is not uniformly distributed across the student cohorts: students who are in their sophomore and junior years (i.e., their second and third years) often express lower satisfaction with their academic programs than do either their freshman or senior counterparts (i.e., students who are in their first or fourth years). Suppose we ask 100 undergraduates, 25 from each class cohort, to express their level of satisfaction on an eight-point Likert scale where a score of 1 indicates a level of satisfaction which is poor and 8 represents a satisfaction level which is excellent.

Most of us have used the Likert scale, even if we are unfamiliar with the designation. It is a flexible and easy-to-administer rating measurement methodology that is widely used in survey research by those conducting investigative social science studies, public opinion polls, and customer satisfaction questionnaires. The Likert is an itemized rating scale on which respondents register their opinions or attitudes on everything from television programs and political candidates to their favorite laundry detergent. In general, the scale consists of response categories which run from "strongly disagree" to "strongly agree," or in this example from "poor" to "excellent," and the respondent registers her answer by selecting the response category that most closely aligns with her own attitude or opinion.

Table 2.5 Cross-tabulation table of student satisfaction ratings by class cohort

	Poor	Below average	Above average	Excellent	Totals
Freshmen	0	1	17	7	25
Sophomores	1	13	11	0	25
Juniors	4	17	4	0	25
Seniors	0	0	4	21	25
Totals	5	31	36	28	100

Organizing the 100 observations into a cross-tabulation table, we find that the patterns emerge between the two variables of interest (see Table 2.5). The column headings have been re-expressed in terms of labels where poor indicates a satisfaction rating of either 1 or 2; below average means a satisfaction score of either 3 or 4; above average signifies a rating of either 5 or 6; and excellent indicates a rating of either 7 or 8.

We see from Table 2.5 that freshmen and seniors seem more satisfied with their undergraduate experience than do sophomores and juniors. In particular, 24 of 25 freshmen rate their experience as above average or excellent whereas only 1 freshman rates the experience as below average. Among the 25 seniors polled, all rate their satisfaction as either above average or excellent. Only 11 sophomores (of the 25) rate their satisfaction as above average, while none rates her satisfaction as excellent. Among juniors we see a similar pattern of dissatisfaction, with 21 of 25 students rating their satisfaction as either below average or poor; not a single junior rates her satisfaction as excellent. As with the other methods of descriptive statistics, the real power of a cross-tabulation table lies in its ability to provide insights into the nature of the data.

Example 2.8. Use R and the `students` data set (from the book website) to create Table 2.5. Although we applied the function `head()` in Example 2.5 to identify the variable name (it was `hours`), we can also use the function `names()`—see Comment 1 in the R block below. Once we have determined the variable names, R produces a rough-looking cross-tabulation table in only two steps (see Comments 2 and 3). At Comment 4, we display the table itself.

```
#Comment1. Use function names() to identify the variable names.
names(students)

## [1] "year" "rating"

#Comment2. Use cut() to break the variable "rating" into 4 classes.
C2_7 <- cut(students$rating, c(0, 2, 4, 6, 8))

#Comment3. Use table() to create crosstabulation; name the object C2_8.
C2_8 <- table(students$year, C2_7)

#Comment4. Review contents of C2_8, the cross-tabulation table.
C2_8

##              C2_7
##               (0,2] (2,4] (4,6] (6,8]
## freshmen         0     1    17     7
## juniors          4    17     4     0
## seniors          0     0     4    21
## sophomores       1    13    11     0
```

Here is an explanation of steps 2 and 3; the rationale for step 1 is provided above, and, by now, the purpose of step 4 should be self-explanatory.

1 We use the function `cut()` to define the four classes as (0, 2], (2, 4], (4, 6], and (6, 8], where the first class includes those students whose ratings are either 1 or 2; the second class includes student ratings that are either 3 or 4; the third class includes those whose ratings are either 5 or 6; and the final class includes all whose ratings are either 7 or 8. The result of this operation is assigned to object `C2_7` (Comment 2).

2 The function `table()` classifies the elements of `C2_7`, or `rating`, by the four values of the other variable, `year`: `freshmen`, `sophomores`, `juniors`, or `seniors`. The result of this cross-classification is assigned to the object `C2_8` (see Comment 3).

Three improvements that might be made to the cross-tabulation table are: (1) include the column and row totals; (2) reorder the rows to resemble the arrangement in Table 2.5 (by default, R has reordered the row names alphabetically); and (3) rename the columns and rows. We begin by finding the column and row totals and then adding them to `C2_8`.

```
Total <- rowSums(C2_8)
C2_8 <- cbind(C2_8, Total)
Total <- colSums(C2_8)
C2_9 <- rbind(C2_8, Total)
C2_9
```

```
##             (0,2] (2,4] (4,6] (6,8] Total
## freshmen        0     1    17     7    25
## juniors         4    17     4     0    25
## seniors         0     0     4    21    25
## sophomores      1    13    11     0    25
## Total           5    31    36    28   100
```

An explanation of the five lines of R code from the above R block should be helpful.

1 The function `rowSums()` finds the sum of values for each row across all columns of `C2_8`. These row sums are then stored in the object named `Total`.
2 The function `cbind()` binds together (column-wise) `C2_8` and `Total`. Note that in these steps, we recycle the names `C2_8` and `Total`.
3 The function `colSums()` finds the sum of values for each column across all rows of `C2_8`. These column sums are then stored in the object named `Total`.
4 The function `rbind()` binds together (row-wise) `C2_8` and `Total`. Note that in these steps, we again recycle the names `C2_8` and `Total` but assign the result to `C2_9`.
5 `C2_9` displays the updated table along with column and row totals.

We now (a) reorder the rows and (b) rename the columns and rows.

```
C2_10 <- rbind(C2_9[1, ], C2_9[4, ], C2_9[2, ], C2_9[3, ], C2_9[5, ])
rownames(C2_10) <- c('Freshmen', 'Sophomores', 'Juniors', 'Seniors',
                     'Column Total')
colnames(C2_10) <- c('Poor', 'Below.Avg', 'Above.Avg', 'Excellent',
                     'Row Total')
C2_10
```

```
##               Poor Below.Avg Above.Avg Excellent Row Total
## Freshmen         0         1        17         7        25
## Sophomores       1        13        11         0        25
## Juniors          4        17         4         0        25
## Seniors          0         0         4        21        25
## Column Total     5        31        36        28       100
```

Additional explanation of these three steps should make clear what has been done.

1. In the first step, we rearrange the rows of `C2_9` and assign the result to a new object, `C2_10`, in which the row order is restored to that of Table 2.5. We do this by specifying the order of the five arguments of the `rbind()` function. That is, in the resulting object, `C2_10`, the first row is `C2_9[1, ]`, which is also the first row of `C2_9`; the second row of `C2_10` is `C2_9[4, ]`, which is the fourth row of `C2_9`; the third row of `C2_10` is `C2_9[2, ]`, which is the second row of `C2_9`; the fourth row of `C2_10` is `C2_9[3, ]`, which is the third row of `C2_9`; and the fifth row of `C2_10` is `C2_9[5, ]`, which is also the fifth row of `C2_9`. The notation `[]` is sometimes referred to as the indexing operator, and is a powerful tool that will be exploited in future chapters. For now, you are encouraged to read this chapter's Appendix for a brief introduction to how it works and what it can accomplish.
2. The function `rownames()` is used to rename the rows of `C2_10`; note the use of the `c()` function to create a character vector consisting of all five row names.
3. The function `colnames()` is used to rename the columns of `C2_10`; note the use of the `c()` function to create another character vector, this time of the ratings.

Finally, row and column percentages form a simple extension of the cross-tabulation table. Row percentages are found by dividing each frequency by its corresponding row total. For example, the row percentage entry for freshmen who rate their satisfaction as above average is found by dividing 17 by 25, giving 0.68 or 68%; similarly, the row percentage entry for seniors who rate their satisfaction as excellent is found by dividing 21 by 25, giving 0.84 or 84%. The entire row percentage table is displayed in Table 2.6.

Table 2.6 Row percentages for each student class year

	Poor	Below average	Above average	Excellent	Totals
Freshmen	0.00	0.04	0.68	0.28	1.00
Sophomores	0.04	0.52	0.44	0.00	1.00
Juniors	0.16	0.68	0.16	0.00	1.00
Seniors	0.00	0.00	0.16	0.84	1.00
Totals	0.05	0.31	0.36	0.28	1.00

Among the four groups of students, seniors appear most satisfied, followed closely by freshmen. In fact, of the 50 students who are either freshmen or seniors, only 1 expressed a satisfaction rating as below average. While sophomores and juniors are decidedly less satisfied with their undergraduate experience, juniors are least satisfied of all. No sophomores or juniors rated their satisfaction as excellent.

Column percentages are found by dividing each frequency in the cross-tabulation table by its corresponding column total. The column percentage table is displayed in Table 2.7.

Table 2.7 Column percentages for different levels of satisfaction

	Poor	Below average	Above average	Excellent	Totals
Freshmen	0.00	0.03	0.47	0.25	0.25
Sophomores	0.20	0.42	0.31	0.00	0.25
Juniors	0.80	0.55	0.11	0.00	0.25
Seniors	0.00	0.00	0.11	0.75	0.25
Totals	1.00	1.00	1.00	1.00	1.00

Of those students rating their level of satisfaction as excellent, 75% are seniors while 25% are freshmen. Of those students rating their level of satisfaction as below average, 55% are juniors, 42% are sophomores, and 3% freshmen. Of all students rating their satisfaction as poor, 80% are juniors and 20% are sophomores.

Definition 2.7. Scatter Plot. A scatter plot, or scatter diagram, is a graphical presentation of the association between two quantitative variables. One variable is shown on the horizontal axis, the other on the vertical axis. The general pattern of the plotted points suggests the nature of the relationship between the two variables.

Table 2.8 Twelve US states from various regions represented in terms of four variables

State	Education	Poverty	Obesity	Wind
Alabama	22.0%	13.4%	32.0%	11.4 mph
California	29.9%	10.6%	23.8%	12.6 mph
Connecticut	35.6%	6.7%	24.5%	13.5 mph
Illinois	30.6%	9.9%	27.1%	16.6 mph
Kentucky	21.0%	14.4%	30.4%	13.4 mph
Maryland	35.7%	6.1%	28.3%	14.0 mph
Massachusetts	38.2%	7.0%	22.7%	19.8 mph
Minnesota	31.5%	7.0%	25.7%	16.9 mph
Mississippi	19.6%	17.3%	34.9%	13.2 mph
New York	32.4%	10.8%	24.5%	14.6 mph
Texas	25.5%	13.4%	30.4%	12.2 mph
Washington	31.0%	8.1%	26.5%	14.2 mph

Consider the data collected on four variables for 12 states in the US shown in Table 2.8. The data are from the US Census Bureau, the Centers for Disease Control and Prevention, and the National Weather Service, all agencies of the US government. The four variables are described as follows:

1. `Education` denotes for each state the percentage of residents, 25 years of age and older, who have attained (at least) a bachelor's degree at a college or university.
2. `Poverty` reports for each state the percentage of households below the US poverty line.
3. `Obesity` indicates for each state the percentage of residents classified as obese.
4. `Wind` denotes for the capital city of each state the average wind velocity (mph).

Example 2.9. Use the function `plot()` and the `poverty` data set (from the book's website at https://study.sagepub.com/stinerock) to create a scatter plot with `Poverty` on the horizontal axis and `Obesity` on the vertical axis.

First, use function `names()` to identify the variable names of the data set `poverty`.

```
names(poverty)
```

```
## [1] "State" "Education" "Poverty" "Obesity" "Wind"
```

Second, use the function `plot()` to create the scatter plot diagram of the two variables (see Figure 2.4).

```
plot(poverty$Poverty, poverty$Obesity, xlab = 'Percent in Poverty',
    ylab = 'Percent Designated Obese', pch = 19, col = 'red')
```

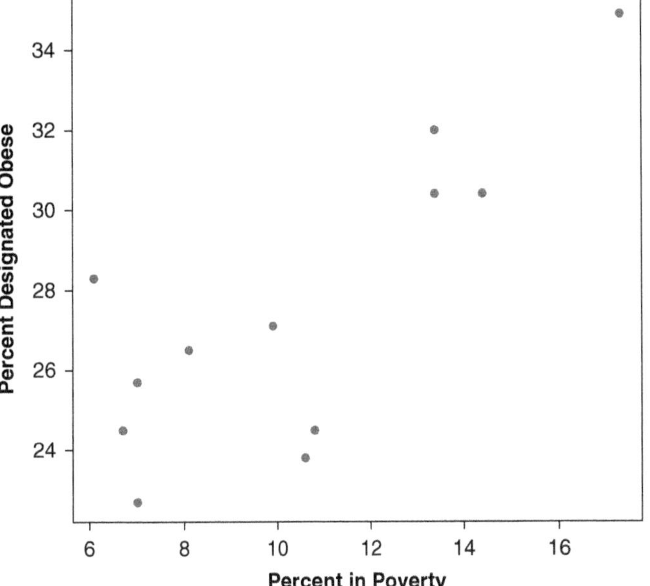

Figure 2.4 A scatter plot of the relationship between obesity and poverty

The six arguments of the function `plot()` in the above R block are as follows:

1. The object name is `poverty`; the variable name for the horizontal axis is `Poverty`.
2. The object name is `poverty`; the variable name for the vertical axis is `Obesity`.
3. The label for the horizontal axis is defined by `xlab =`.
4. The label for the vertical axis is specified by `ylab =`.
5. The plotting character is defined by `pch =`.
6. The color of the plotted points is set by `col =`.

The scatter plot reveals a positive relationship between the two variables, suggesting that higher (lower) rates of obesity are associated with higher (lower) levels of poverty. This does not mean that either variable has caused the other, however. By themselves, statistical methods typically deal only with relationships or associations between variables, not with establishing causality. Although we might try to make the case that poverty causes obesity, or even that obesity causes poverty, we cannot use statistical methods to prove such a causal connection, even if one actually exists.

Example 2.10. Create a scatter plot with `Education` on the horizontal axis and `Obesity` on the vertical axis.

```
plot(poverty$Education, poverty$Obesity, xlab = 'Percent with College
     Degree', ylab = 'Percent Designated Obese', pch = 19, col = 'red')
```

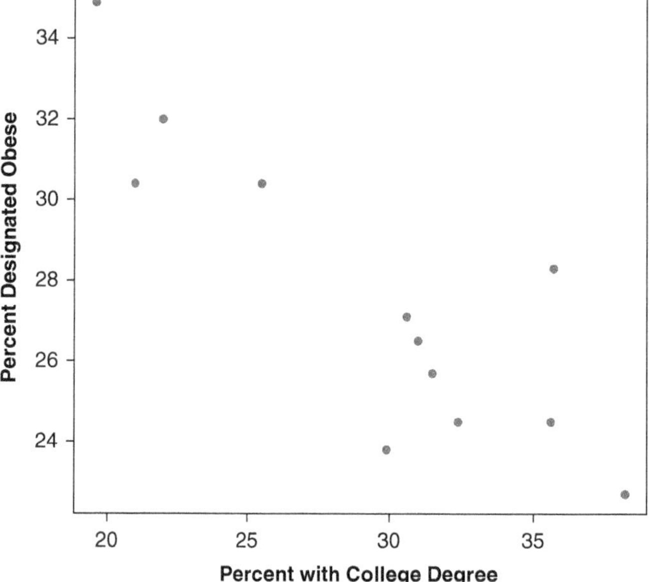

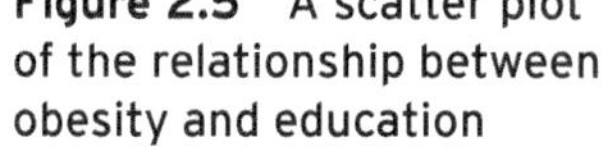

Figure 2.5 A scatter plot of the relationship between obesity and education

Figure 2.5 shows the negative relationship between `Education` and `Obesity`. In this case, the points run in a band from the upper left-hand to the lower right-hand corners of the scatter plot, suggesting that higher (lower) levels of education are associated with lower (higher) rates of obesity. Once again, we remind the reader that no causality is demonstrated here. What is the most we can claim from representing the data and relationships in this manner? The two variables appear to be negatively related.

SUMMARY

Chapter 2 introduces and develops two of the three general approaches to descriptive statistics: tabular and graphical methods. (The final approach, numerical methods, is the focus of Chapter 3.) Among the variations of tabular methods are (a) frequency distributions, (b) relative frequency distributions, (c) cumulative frequency distributions, and (d) cumulative relative frequency distributions. Also included among descriptive methods are those of a graphical nature. In the case of qualitative data, graphical methods include the bar graph and dot chart; for data that are quantitative, we have extended the graphical methods to the histogram. Finally, in the instance where we are interested in expressing and understanding the relationship between two variables, we use R to create both a cross-tabulation table and a scatter plot.

We point out that it is possible to misuse many of the methods of descriptive statistics. When done so intentionally, it is often for the purpose of supporting someone's predetermined argument or point of view. If it is done unintentionally, the weakness in the approach often lies in the skill of the person using the methods. For example, some will note that we did not introduce one highly popular and widely used graphical method, the pie chart. The pie chart is not so easily read and interpreted as the bar graph or the dot chart. Research has shown that the human eye has more difficulty discerning differences in areas (as depicted in pie charts) than it does differences in lengths. For this reason, we have decided not to include the pie chart among the best graphical methods, and encourage students and readers to employ those methods that work best. However, in the best case, effective application of descriptive statistical methods usually results in insights that are not possible by a cursory examination of the original data.

Throughout Chapter 2, we make extensive use of the basic R installation in support of the tabular and graphical methods being applied. We hasten to point out that R extends to graphical capabilites not covered in this textbook which involve using other packages such as `ggplot2` and `lattice`. Students who are interested in learning more about these features of R are encouraged to explore the numerous online sources available.

Finally, an important point to make early in this book is that even though tabular and graphical methods can be used to identify the relationship (if any) between variables, we cannot assume that one variable *causes* another just because they are related. By themselves, statistical methods cannot establish causality, although there are some methods of a more advanced nature that attempt to do just that. Typically, statistical methods are about relationships and associations between and among variables, not causality.

definitions

Bar Graph A graphical method representing qualitative data. Bars representing the categories are placed along a horizontal axis; the heights of the bars indicate the frequency, relative frequency, or percent frequency for each category.

Cross-tabulation A tabular method for summarizing the relationship between two variables simultaneously. It can be used when both variables are qualitative, both are quantitative, or when one variable is qualitative and the other quantitative.

Cumulative Frequency Distribution A tabular method of summarizing quantitative data which displays the running total of the number of data items that are less than or equal to the upper limit of each given class.

Cumulative Relative Frequency Distribution A tabular method of summarizing quantitative data which displays the running total of the proportion of data items that are less than or equal to the upper limit of each given class.

Dot Chart A simple graphical representation of qualitative data expressed in terms of the frequencies, or relative frequencies, of category items.

Frequency Distribution A tabular summary of the number of observations falling into each of two or more mutually exclusive, collectively exhaustive categories.

Histogram A graphical method that partitions quantitative data values into sub-range categories of equal width on the horizontal axis; the heights of bars indicate the frequency, relative frequency, or percent frequency for each category.

Percent Frequency Distribution A tabular method which reports the percentage, rather than the number, of observations falling into each category.

Relative Frequency Distribution A tabular method which reports the proportion, rather than the number, of observations falling into each category.

Scatter Plot A graphical presentation of two quantitative variables. One variable is shown on the horizontal axis, one on the vertical axis. The general pattern of the plotted points suggests the nature of the relationship between the two variables.

R functions

Note that some of the R functions listed below are used in the exercises found on the companion website, but not in this chapter. The practice of introducing R functions either in the website exercises or in the chapters is followed elsewhere in this book.

`abline()` Provides a reference line to a scatter plot.

`barplot()` Produces a bar graph of the count or frequency of observations falling into two or more mutually exclusive, collectively exhaustive categories.

`cbind()` Binds together a column of data values with a separate object.

`colnames()` Changes the names of the columns in a table.

`colSums()` Provides sums of values down all columns of a table for each row category.

(Continued)

(Continued)

`cut()` Divides the range of quantitative values into interval categories and then assigns those values to the interval in which they fall.

`dotchart()` Provides a simple graphical representation of the frequency, or relative frequency, of qualitative data.

`head()` Displays the first six lines of a data object.

`hist()` Provides a histogram of the count or frequency of quantitative data values; the bar can be either vertically or horizontally arranged.

`length()` Can be used to count the number of data values in a data object.

`lm()` Runs linear model methods (e.g., linear regression, analysis of variance).

`mosaicplot()` Provides a mosaic plot of the relationship between two (or more) categorical variables.

`ncol()` Can be used to count the number of columns in a data object.

`nrow()` Can be used to count the number of rows in a data object.

`plot()` Creates a scatter diagram of points based on the position of each observation on two quantitative variables.

`prod()` Provides the product of a sequence of numbers. That is, `prod(n:N)` reports the product of all numbers running from the smallest value *n* to the largest value *N*.

`rbind()` Binds together a row of data values with a separate object.

`rep()` Replicates or repeats values defined in `()`.

`rnorm()` Generates a set of data values that are normally

`rownames()` Changes the names of the rows of a table.

`rowSums()` Provides sum of values across all rows of a table for each column category.

`sort()` Sorts data into ascending order (or descending, if preferred).

`sum()` Provides the sum of data values defined in `()`.

`summary()` Reports the five-number summary (the minimum and maximum values plus the first quartile, the median, and third quartile) as well as the mean.

`table()` Creates tabular representations of categorical data.

data sets

Note that some of the data sets listed below are used in the exercises found at https://study.sagepub.com/stinerock, but not in this chapter. The practice of using data sets either in the website exercises or in the chapters is followed elsewhere in this book.

1 `a`
2 `caferts`
3 `Cars93`
4 `hotel`
5 `longley`
6 `mktsurvey`
7 `plot1`
8 `plot2`
9 `plot3`
10 `poverty`
11 `students`
12 `tv_hrs`

APPENDIX: BASIC DATA MANIPULATION

1. Can We Get Help?

When you do not know how to do something, there are ways to get help that are part of the installation. Here are some commands you can enter at the R prompt:

`help()` brings up a page that describes how to use functions and operators. For example, `help(table)` provides an explanation of `table()`; it also describes how we might specify the results we want. If we need help with a symbol, however, we must enclose it in single or double quotes. For example, if we would like to understand the assignment operator better, we might enter `help("<-")` at the prompt.

`example()` provides examples of uses of functions. For instance, `example(table)` displays the execution of `table()` using various data sets, along with the results and commentary.

`help.search("table")` provides a list of help topics matching the term `table`. Note that we must always include in quotes the term being searched.

`apropos("table")` provides a list of functions or commands that include the term "table." Once again, we must include the term in quotes.

`args(table)` lists the arguments associated with `table()`.

Another helpful source is the internet. When searching for an answer to a question about R, we typically encounter countless blogs and sources—from students, faculty, and researchers who are happy to help out. Since the community of R users is growing every day, the internet has emerged as one of the most promising sources of answers to questions about R. Other R users have the same questions you have. The answer to your question can often be found after a bit of online searching.

2. Can We Create Our Own Data?

Yes, we can, and there are several ways to do it. For now, we describe briefly a handful of the most commonly used methods for creating our own data.

(a) Creating numeric and non-numeric objects

The function `c()` can be used to create objects that contain numeric and non-numeric elements.

```
#Comment1. Use function c() to create 3 objects, a, b, and c.
#Examine contents of a to ensure that it contains 1, 2, and 3.
a <- c(1, 2, 3)
b <- c(4, 5, 6)
c <- c(7, 8, 9)
a

## [1] 1 2 3
```

```
#Comment2. Use c() to create object d from objects a, b, and c.
#Examine contents of d.
d <- c(a, b, c)
d

## [1] 1 2 3 4 5 6 7 8 9

#Comment3. Use operator + to create object e from a+b+c. Examine
#contents of e; note e consists of sums of elements of a, b, and c.
e <- a + b + c
e

## [1] 12 15 18

#Comment4. Use operator - to create f from a-b. Examine f; note
#elements of f are the differences of elements of a and b.
f <- a - b
f

## [1] -3 -3 -3

# Comment5. Use operators * and / to multiply and divide a and b, creating
#objects g and h, respectively. Note that elements of g and h are the
#product and ratio of the elements of a and b.
g <- a * b
h <- a / b
g

## [1] 4 10 18

h

## [1] 0.25 0.40 0.50
21

#Comment6. Use function c() to create object i consisting of
#non-numeric elements. Examine contents of i.
i <- c("Red", "White", "Blue")
i

## [1] "Red" "White" "Blue"

#Comment7. Use functions rep() and c() for repeated values.
#Name result j and examine. (Sequence (1, 2, 3) is repeated 3 times.)
#Note that c() is the first argument of the rep() function.
j <- rep(c(1, 2, 3), 3)
j

## [1] 1 2 3 1 2 3 1 2 3
```

```
#Comment8. Use function c(n:N) to create a sequence from a lower-
#value n to a higher-value N. Name result k and examine.
k <- c(5 : 15)
k

## [1] 5 6 7 8 9 10 11 12 13 14 15

#Comment9. Use function seq (from=n, to=N, by=x) to create sequence
#from n to N in increments of x. Name result l and examine.
l <- seq(from = 5, to = 6, by = 0.1)
l

## [1] 5.0 5.1 5.2 5.3 5.4 5.5 5.6 5.7 5.8 5.9 6.0
```

(b) Generating random values from probability distributions

We can also use R to generate data values that are distributed according to probability distributions. Here we use two distributions, the normal and the uniform.

```
#Comment1. Use function rnorm() to draw 10,000 data values from
#normal distribution with mean 100, standard deviation of 15.
#Name the data set m; create a picture (histogram) of data set
#m for purpose of visualization.
m <- rnorm(10000, 100, 15)

#Comment2. Show histogram of m with 50 bars; set color as red.
hist(m, breaks = 50, ylim = c(0, 600), col = 'red')
```

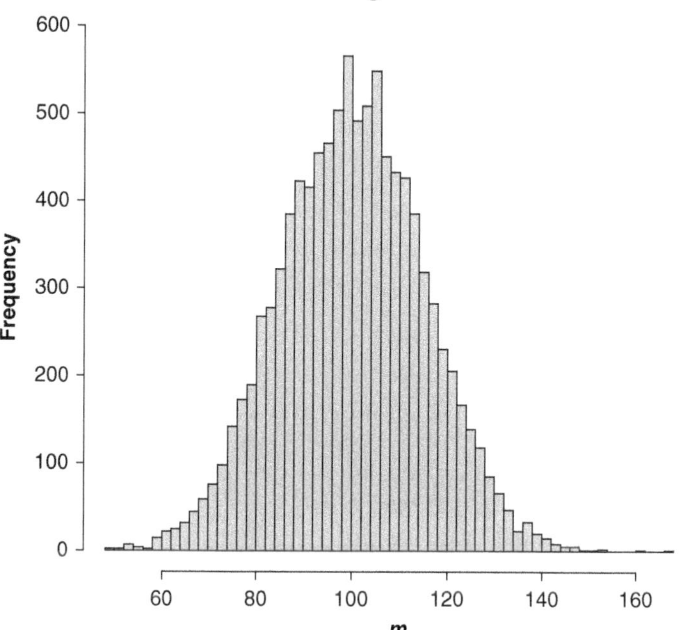

From the histogram, the data run from (roughly) 40 to 160 with a mean of 100.

```
#Comment1. Use function runif() to draw 20,000 data values from
#uniform distribution running from 75 to 125. Name data set n.
n <- runif(20000, 75, 125)

#Comment2. Show histogram of n with 50 bars; set color as blue.
hist(n, breaks = 50, xlim = c(70, 130), ylim = c(0,500),col = 'blue')
```

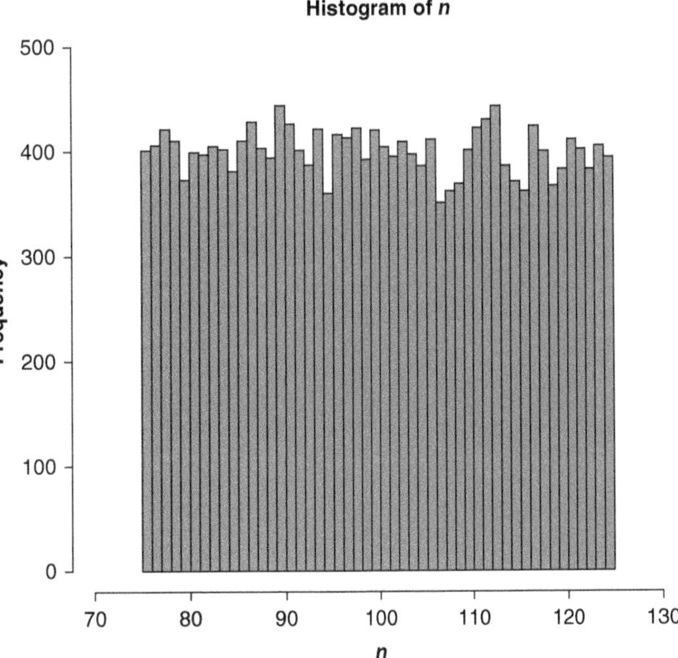

From the histogram, we see that the data are distributed uniformly from 75 to 125. R has other data-generating capabilities that will be introduced in later chapters. For now, it is enough that we have introduced the topic early in the book for the purpose of demonstrating some of the features of R to readers.

3. Can we extract a data subset from a larger data set?

Recall that for Exercise 1.3 at the end of Chapter 1, we used one of the built-in R data sets, `LakeHuron`. For this demonstration, we use another of the built-in data sets, `longley`. (To see the entire list of built-in R data sets, enter `data()` at the R prompt in the Console.) To inspect `longley`, we need simply to enter the file name at the R prompt; to get more information about the data set, enter `?longley` at the prompt. For our purpose, it is enough to know that the data set consists of 16 years of data (1947–1962) on seven variables of a macroeconomic nature:

```
names(longley)
```

```
## [1] "GNP.deflator" "GNP"          "Unemployed" "Armed.Forces"
## [5] "Population"   "Year"         "Employed"
```

To extract a data subset from a larger data frame, we use the same square-bracket operator, `[,]`, employed above to reorder the rows of the cross-tabulation table, `C2_9`. In that instance, we used `[,]` to carve out, or extract, rows of `C2_9` where the particular row was identified by the two-element notation within the squared bracket: the first element indicated the number of the row, the second element the number of the column. Thus, `C2_9[1,]` indicates the first row of `C2_9`, and `C2_9[4,]` the fourth; but `C2_9[,2]` identifies the second column `C2_9` and `C2_9[,3]` the third. If the second element is omitted, the result is returned as the entire row across all columns; if the first element is missing, the operation returns the entire column down all rows. We may even specify a single data value within an object: `C2_9[2,3]` would return the item in the second row of the third column of `C2_9`. Consider the following examples in which we use square bracketing and the `longley` data frame.

```
longley[, 3:7]
```

```
##      Unemployed Armed.Forces Population Year Employed
## 1947      235.6        159.0    107.608 1947   60.323
## 1948      232.5        145.6    108.632 1948   61.122
## 1949      368.2        161.6    109.773 1949   60.171
## 1950      335.1        165.0    110.929 1950   61.187
## 1951      209.9        309.9    112.075 1951   63.221
## 1952      193.2        359.4    113.270 1952   63.639
## 1953      187.0        354.7    115.094 1953   64.989
## 1954      357.8        335.0    116.219 1954   63.761
## 1955      290.4        304.8    117.388 1955   66.019
## 1956      282.2        285.7    118.734 1956   67.857
## 1957      293.6        279.8    120.445 1957   68.169
## 1958      468.1        263.7    121.950 1958   66.513
## 1959      381.3        255.2    123.366 1959   68.655
## 1960      393.1        251.4    125.368 1960   69.564
## 1961      480.6        257.2    127.852 1961   69.331
## 1962      400.7        282.7    130.081 1962   70.551
```

Because the first element in the brackets has been omitted, the subset is returned with all rows; and because the second element includes all columns from 3 to 7 (`3:7` is 3, 4, 5, 6, 7), the subset returns with all columns except the first two.

```
longley[longley$Year > 1959, 7]
```

```
## [1] 69.564 69.331 70.551
```

```
mean(longley[longley$Year > 1959, 7])
```

```
## [1] 69.81533
```

In this case, the returned subset includes only those rows for which the variable `Year` exceeds 1959 (1960, 1961, and 1962) and also column 7, `Employed`. If we want the mean of `Employed` for those three years, we apply the function `mean()` to see that it is 69.81533; that is, an average of roughly 69.8 million people were employed in the US during this 3-year period. If we wish to compare that with the average of `Employed` from the first 3 years (i.e., 1947, 1948, and 1949) we simply specify the first argument within `[,]` to reflect this change. The mean of `Employed` for this 3-year post-war period is lower at about 60.5 million.

```
longley[longley$Year < 1950, 7]

## [1] 60.323 61.122 60.171

mean(longley[longley$Year < 1950, 7])

## [1] 60.53867
```

For yet another way of slicing and extracting information from `longley`, consider the following example.

```
C2_11 <- longley[longley$Armed.Forces > 300, c('Year', 'GNP')]
C2_11

##      Year     GNP
## 1951 1951  328.975
## 1952 1952  346.999
## 1953 1953  365.385
## 1954 1954  363.112
## 1955 1955  397.469
```

Here is what we have done:

(a) The first element, `longley$Armed.Forces > 300`, specifies that only those rows for which the variable `Armed.Forces` exceeds 300 should be extracted.
(b) The second element, `c('Year', 'GNP')`, stipulates that only the `Year` and `GNP` columns be selected; all other columns should be excluded.
(c) The data subset is assigned to `C2_11`. This operation returns the `Year` and `GNP` columns on (only) those rows for which `Armed.Forces > 300`.

This method of subsetting data sets is sometimes referred to as "indexing." It is an important capability of R and we return to it later in the book. In the meantime, a good way to learn how to exploit its power is to work through several examples on a data set such as `longley`.

exercises

2.1 A survey of 1095 households investigating attitudes toward six brands, A, B, C, D, E, and F, in a certain product category reveals the following preference structure: of the 1095 households, 272 express a preference for brand A; 212 prefer B; 297 prefer C; 38 prefer D; 181 prefer E; and 95 prefer F.

(a) Use R to create a character vector containing all 1095 items; name it `E2_1`.

(b) Confirm that `E2_1` includes the desired information. Hint: there are many ways this could be done but in this case use the `table()` function to report the frequency distribution. Since we use it again below, assign the result to the object `fd` (for frequency distribution) and report the contents of `fd`.

2.2 Use `E2_1` for all parts of this exercise.

(a) Produce the frequency distribution of `E2_1`. Store result in object `rf` (for relative frequency distribution).

(b) Produce the relative frequency distribution of `E2_1`. Color the six bars, from left to right: red, blue, green, violet, orange, and cyan. Use argument `ylim = c(0, 300)` to set scale of vertical axis; use `main='` to specify a main title; use `xlab='and ylab='` to define the labels for the horizontal (`x`), and vertical (`y`) axes, respectively.

2.3 Produce a bar graph of relative frequencies for `E2_1`. Color the bars brown and purple, alternately; set vertical axis from 0 to 0.35; include a main title and define labels for the horizontal and vertical axes, respectively. Hint: use `rf`.

2.4 Use the `Cars93` data set (included in the `MASS` package) to answer the next questions.

(a) Use `names(Cars93)` function to print out the variable names of `Cars93`.

(b) Provide the frequency and relative frequency distributions for the variable `Type`. What percentage are large cars?

(c) Provide a cross-tabulation table in which the variables `Origin` and `Type` are organized along the two margins. Are most of the vehicles of US origin?

2.5 Using the data set `poverty` (from https://study.sagepub.com/stinerock), produce a scatter plot with `Wind` on the horizontal axis and `Poverty` on the vertical. Label the horizontal and vertical axes "Wind" and "Percent Below Poverty Line," respectively. Also, set the color of the points as blue, and express the points as empty circles. (Hint: you can enter `?pch` at the prompt in the Console to inspect the various plotting characteristics.)

https://study.sagepub.com/stinerock

Descriptive Statistics: Numerical Methods

contents

learning objectives

1. Learn how to compute the mean, median, mode, quartiles, and various percentiles.
2. Learn how to use and interpret the box plot display.
3. Learn how to compute the range, interquartile range, variance, standard deviation, and coefficient of variation.
4. Understand how to derive *z*-scores and how they may be used.
5. Know how the empirical rule finds the percentage of data items within a specified number of standard deviations from the mean.
6. Understand the problem posed by statistical outliers: what they are, why they matter, how one identifies them, and what one can do about them.
7. Learn how to compute and interpret covariance and correlation as measures of linear association between two variables.
8. Learn how to compute and interpret the geometric mean.

In Chapter 2, we learned how to use tabular and graphical methods to organize, summarize, and present data. In this chapter, we learn how to use numerical methods.

3.1 MEASURES OF CENTRAL TENDENCY

We begin by considering three measures of central tendency: the mean, median, and mode.

Definition 3.1. Mean. The mean of a data set is the average of all the data values.

Whether the data are drawn from a sample or an entire population, the mean is calculated in exactly the same way, although the mathematical expressions differ slightly. If the data consist of a sample drawn from a population, the mean is denoted

$$\bar{x} = \frac{\Sigma x_i}{n}.$$

However, if the data consist of the entire population, the mean is denoted

$$\mu = \frac{\Sigma x_i}{N}.$$

In statistics, Greek letters (such as μ) are often associated with a population while Latin letters (such as $\bar{x}$) indicate a sample. The other difference between the two expressions is found in the denominator: n indicates the sample size, N the population size.

Example 3.1. Table 3.1 lists monthly rental prices (in US dollars) of 70 one-bathroom, one-bedroom apartments in New York. The data are reported in ascending order, from the lowest to the highest. Using this data set, let us consider how we might derive several useful measures of central tendency, dispersion, and relative location. What is the mean?

Since the data in Table 3.1 form a sample, the expression for the mean is

$$\bar{x} = \frac{\Sigma x_i}{n} = \frac{\$274{,}020}{70} = \$3915.$$

Table 3.1 Monthly rent ($) for 70 apartments in New York City

2950	3020	3030	3060	3070	3110	3145	3320	3420	3490
3520	3530	3540	3560	3570	3590	3600	3610	3620	3640
3660	3660	3720	3740	3740	3740	3755	3760	3770	3790
3830	3860	3870	3890	3900	3970	3975	3975	3975	3990
3990	4020	4070	4100	4120	4160	4170	4180	4180	4190
4220	4240	4260	4290	4300	4315	4400	4400	4420	4430
4440	4450	4450	4470	4480	4510	4610	4660	4680	4850

To find the mean of a data set using R, we use the function `mean()`. In this instance, the data set name is `housing` and the variable name is `rent`. Remember to separate the data set name from the variable name with a dollar sign, `$`. Recall also that whenever we need to access data files from this book's website (at https://study.sagepub.com/stinerock), we must begin the analysis by entering the command `library(introstats)` at the R prompt > in the R Console.

```
mean(housing$rent)

## [1] 3914.571
```

Definition 3.2. Median. The median of a data set is the middle value when the data items are arranged in ascending (or descending) order.

For an odd number of observations, the median is the middle value; for an even number of observations, it is found by taking the mean of the two middle values. The median is often preferred to the mean whenever the data set contains outliers, or values that are extremely large or small for that particular data set. For example, the median is the measure of central tendency most often used for income and property value data, instances in which outliers are often present. The reason the median is preferred is that it only takes a few outsized incomes or property values to over-inflate the mean.

Example 3.2. What is the median of the rental data? Since there are 70 values (an even number), the median is found by taking the mean of the middle two data values. The mean of the values in the 35th and 36th places (in bold type in Table 3.2) is the median = ($3900 + $3970)/2 = $3935.

Table 3.2 The two middle values of the apartment rental data are in bold type

2950	3020	3030	3060	3070	3110	3145	3320	3420	3490
3520	3530	3540	3560	3570	3590	3600	3610	3620	3640
3660	3660	3720	3740	3740	3740	3755	3760	3770	3790
3830	3860	3870	3890	**3900**	**3970**	3975	3975	3975	3990
3990	4020	4070	4100	4120	4160	4170	4180	4180	4190
4220	4240	4260	4290	4300	4315	4400	4400	4420	4430
4440	4450	4450	4470	4480	4510	4610	4660	4680	4850

We can use the R function `median()` to find the median.

```
median(housing$rent)
```

```
## [1] 3935
```

Note that the median and the mean are different values, even though both are derived from the same data set. This is because each measure is a different interpretation of what is meant by the term *central tendency*. Ordinarily, the mean and median are equal only when the data are distributed symmetrically about the mean. When the data are skewed to the right, the mean typically exceeds the median, whereas when the data are skewed to the left, the median is normally greater than the mean.

Example 3.3. As an example of when we would prefer the median to the mean, consider a hypothetical problem. The 31 recent graduates of a computer science degree program have landed jobs and reported their starting salaries accordingly: 15 students are starting at $90,000/year; 1 student at $100,000/year; 14 students at $110,000/year; and the final student at $10,000,000/year. (The final student has been signed by the New York Yankees baseball team because he can throw five different pitches, including an unhittable 102 mph split-finger fastball.) What is the mean salary? What is the median salary? The mean is

$$\mu = \frac{\sum x_i}{N} = \frac{\$12,990,000}{31} = \$419,032,$$

while the median salary is $100,000. Remember that for a data set containing an odd number of values, the median is the middle value. Since our data set includes 31 values, the median is located at the 16th position, and is thus found to be $100,000. The median represents the typical salary more accurately than the mean because the mean includes an outlier, the Yankees pitcher, whose income distorts the computation. That is, the mean is sensitive to the presence of outlier values in a way that the median is not.

Example 3.4. Consider a different example concerning property values. For the fourth quarter of 2014, the median price of an apartment in Manhattan is reported to be $980,000. Is the mean price higher? Lower? Or about the same? It is higher: the mean price is reported to be $1,720,000. The reason the mean exceeds the median by so much lies in the skewed nature of the distribution of property values: the lowest price of any apartment of this type in Manhattan is about $500,000; the highest price is very high, sometimes over $100,000,000. Put another way, the data representing apartment prices are not distributed symmetrically; in fact, they are highly skewed to the right.

Definition 3.3. Mode. The mode is the value that occurs most frequently. The greatest frequency can occur at more than one value. If the data have two modes, then they are bimodal; if they have more than two modes, then they are multi-modal.

Example 3.5. What is the mode of the 70 rental values? The data are bimodal since $3740 and $3975 both occur 3 times.

3.2 MEASURES OF LOCATION

The are several related ways to identify the location of data items within a rank-ordered data set. Among them are percentiles and quartiles.

Definition 3.4. Percentiles. The *p*th percentile of a data set (arranged in ascending order) is the value such that at least p% of the observations fall at or below this value, and at least $(100 - p)$% fall at or above it.

Percentiles provide insight into how data are distributed over their entire range, from the smallest to the largest value; a particular percentile value cuts the data into two pieces. There are several methods of deriving percentiles and they all provide values that differ very little from one another. Here is one commonly used approach.

To find the *p*th percentile, calculate the following index m on the ranked-ordered data set, where p is the percentile of interest and n is the number of data items:

$$m = \frac{p}{100}n.$$

If m is not an integer, round up. The *p*th percentile is the data value located at the position of the next integer greater than m. But if m is an integer, the *p*th percentile can be found by calculating the mean of the data values in positions m and $m + 1$.

Example 3.6. In the case of the apartment rental values, what is the 90th percentile? Using the formula above, we find the index m:

$$m = \frac{p}{100}n = \frac{90}{100}70 = 63.$$

Since $m = 63$ is an integer, the 90th percentile is found by taking the average of the data values in the 63rd and 64th positions, which gives ($4450 + $4470)/2 = $4460. Note that 90% (63/70) of the data values are less than $4460 while 10% (7/70) are greater.

Definition 3.5. Quartiles. The three quartiles are specific percentages: the first quartile is the 25th percentile; the second quartile is the 50th percentile or the median; the third quartile is the 75th percentile.

Example 3.7. For the rental values, what are the first, second, and third quartiles?

1. For the first quartile or 25th percentile, $m = (25/100)(70) = 17.5$. Therefore, the first quartile falls in the 18th position, and is $3610.
2. For the second quartile or 50th percentile, $m = (50/100)(70) = 35$. Therefore, the second quartile is the average of the items in the 35th and 36th positions, or $3935.
3. For the third quartile or 75th percentile, $m = (75/100)(70) = 52.5$. Therefore, the third quartile is in the 53rd position, and is $4260.

The function `quantile()` reports any desired percentile if we specify the values in the `probs = c()` argument. We obtain the three quartiles and 90th percentile as follows:

```
quantile(housing$rent, type = 2, probs = c(0.25, 0.50, 0.75, 0.90))
```

```
## 25% 50% 75% 90%
## 3610 3935 4260 4460
```

Thus, we confirm that the value of the 25th percentile is \$3610, the 75th percentile is \$4260, and the 90th percentile is \$4460; the 50th percentile, or median, is \$3935. Of the various ways that might be used to calculate percentiles, the argument `type = 2` provides the same answers as those we worked out manually above.

3.3 EXPLORATORY DATA ANALYSIS: THE BOX PLOT DISPLAY

Exploratory data analysis consists of a broad set of methods for visually presenting data in an easy-to-understand manner for the purpose of revealing characteristics such as the central tendency, the dispersion, and the shape of the data. One commonly used technique of exploratory data analysis is the box plot.

Definition 3.6. Box Plot. The box plot is a graphical display which is based on five values: the minimum, maximum, median, and first and third quartiles (the five-number summary mentioned in Chapter 2). It has the advantage of simultaneously providing comparisons of the distribution of data across several categories.

Example 3.8. Using data set `jobs`, provide a box plot display of the Table 3.3 data which report the starting salaries (in Australian dollars) for graduates of one of Australia's highly regarded MBA programs in the areas of accounting, finance, management, and marketing.

Table 3.3 Starting salaries for four areas of study

	Minimum	First quartile	Median	Third quartile	Maximum
Accounting	79,000	81,500	84,500	89,250	93,000
Finance	72,000	74,000	77,500	80,000	82,000
Management	49,000	66,750	69,000	71,250	74,000
Marketing	67,000	68,000	69,000	70,250	96,000

The R function `boxplot()` produces the boxplot in Figure 3.1. The data set is `jobs` and can be found on the website. It contains variables `Salary` and `Position`.

```
boxplot(Salary ~ Position, data = jobs,
        xlab = 'Starting Salaries for Four Areas of Study',
        ylab = 'Starting Annual Salaries ($000)', col = 'grey', pch = 19)
```

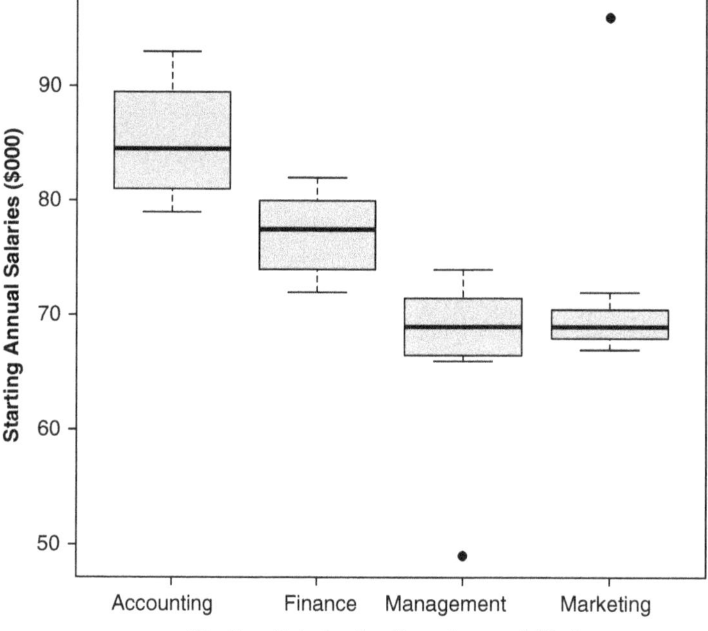

Figure 3.1 Box plot display of starting salaries for four areas of study

The six arguments of the function `boxplot` require some explanation.

1. `Salary~Position` is the model formula that specifies the basic elements of the graphical figure. `Salary` is a quantitative variable that includes the dollar amount of salary; `Position` is a categorical variable that, in this case, includes `Accounting`, `Finance`, `Management`, and `Marketing`. Note that, in this model, the first variable, `Salary`, must be quantitative since a box plot includes measures such as the minimum, maximum, median, and first and third quartiles.
2. `data` = `jobs` directs R to look in `jobs` for the variables `Salary` and `Position`.
3. `xlab` = specifies the horizontal axis label.
4. `ylab` = specifies the vertical axis label.
5. `col` = defines the color (in this case, grey).
6. `pch` = indicates the plotting character (in this case, a solid dot).

In Figure 3.1, the median is the dark horizontal line in each box: the median salary is highest for those in accounting, then in finance, followed by management and marketing. The bottom and top of each box denote the first and third quartiles. There are two outliers, indicated by the black points: $49,000 for management and $96,000 for marketing.

3.4 MEASURES OF VARIABILITY

We now consider five measures of variability, the simplest of which is the range.

Definition 3.7. Range. The range is the difference between the largest and smallest values in a data set.

Because the range is based only on the largest and smallest values, it is sensitive to the presence of statistical outliers. For instance, in the hypothetical example concerning average salaries, the range is \$10,000,000 – \$90,000 = \$9,910,000 because a professional baseball player (an outlier whose salary is \$10,000,000) is included.

Example 3.9. What is the range for the rental data? It is \$4850 – \$2950 = \$1900. Using R, we subtract `min()` from `max()` to find the range of the data:

```
max(housing$rent) - min(housing$rent)
```

```
## [1] 1900
```

Definition 3.8. Interquartile Range. The interquartile range (IQR) is the difference between the third and first quartiles, and is the range of the middle 50% of the data. Its advantage is that it overcomes the problem of outliers in the data.

Example 3.10. What is the IQR of the rental data? We have already obtained the first and third quartiles, so we subtract the former from the latter: $\text{IQR} = Q_3 - Q_1 = \$4260 - \$3610 = \$650$. The R function `IQR()` provides the interquartile range.

```
IQR(housing$rent, type = 2)
```

```
## [1] 650
```

When we include `type = 2` as an argument (as we did with `quantile()` in Example 3.7), `IQR()` finds the interquartile range by subtracting $Q_1 = 3610$ from $Q_3 = 4260$.

Unlike the range and interquartile range, the variance uses all the available information.

Definition 3.9. Variance. The variance is a measure of variability that uses all the data and is derived from the average of squared deviations from the mean of the data.

More specifically, the variance is based on the difference between the value of each observation and its mean, either $x_i - \bar{x}$ for a sample, or $x_i - \mu$ for a population. This value is often referred to as the *deviation about the mean* or simply the *deviation*. To calculate the variance, the deviation of each data value from its own mean is first squared, and then summed over all elements in the data set, and divided either by N in the case of a population or by $n - 1$ for a sample. The expression for the population variance is

$$\sigma^2 = \frac{\sum(x_i - \mu)^2}{N},$$

while the expression for the sample variance is

$$s^2 = \frac{\sum(x_i - \bar{x})^2}{n-1}.$$

Note the differences in notation and computation between the two expressions. First, the sum of squared deviations (i.e., the numerator) is divided by the sample size minus one, or $n - 1$, in the case of the sample variance; it is divided by the population size, or N, in the case of the population variance. Second, note the use of the Greek letters in the case of the population, μ and σ, and the Latin letters in the case of the sample, $\bar{x}$ and s. This is a continuation of the convention, mentioned earlier, of ordinarily using Greek letters when a population is concerned but Latin letters when a sample is being used.

Since what we are trying to estimate is the average of squared deviations about the mean, one might ask why (in the case of a sample) we divide by $n - 1$ rather than N? The short answer is that if the sum of squared deviations about the sample mean is divided by $n - 1$ rather than N, then the resulting sample variance provides an unbiased or (on average) more accurate estimate of the population variance than if we divided by N. Remember that one reason we use samples is to obtain accurate estimates of the population's characteristics without having to work with the entire population.

Example 3.11. The Smithson Bus Line provides a regular service between London's Victoria Coach Station and cities in the British West Midlands. Suppose that on a recent weekday, five Birmingham-bound buses depart London Victoria with the following numbers of passengers: 40, 45, 38, 50, and 47. What is the sample variance? Use both formulae above (see Table 3.4 for computations) and the R function `var()`.

Table 3.4 Number of passengers on five buses between London and Birmingham

No. of passengers per bus x_i	Deviation about the mean $x_i - \bar{x}$	Squared deviation $(x_i - \bar{x})^2$
40	40 – 44 = –4	16
45	45 – 44 = 1	1
38	38 – 44 = –6	36
50	50 – 44 = 6	36
47	47 – 44 = 3	9
$\bar{x} = 44$	$\sum(x_i - \bar{x}) = 0$	$\sum(x_i - \bar{x})^2 = 98$

The sample variance is

$$s^2 = \frac{\sum(x_i - \bar{x})^2}{n-1} = \frac{98}{5-1} = \frac{98}{4} = 24.5\,(\text{passengers})^2.$$

Define an object containing the data values using `c()` and name it `C3_1`.

```
C3_1 <- c(40, 45, 38, 50, 47)
var(C3_1)

## [1] 24.5
```

In deriving the variance, it is important to square each deviation before summing. Otherwise, the sum of simple deviations about the mean (i.e., the sum of unsquared terms in the middle column of Table 3.4) is always zero. Another question concerns the relative uninterpretability of the units, (passengers)^2. That the meaning of the units is not intuitive leads to the next widely used measure of dispersion, the standard deviation.

Definition 3.10. Standard Deviation. The standard deviation of a data set is the positive square root of the variance.

Example 3.12. Find the sample standard deviation of the bus passenger data. We simply take the positive square root of the answer to Example 3.11:

$$s = \sqrt{s^2} = \sqrt{24.5\,(\text{passengers})^2} = 4.95 \text{ passengers.}$$

The R function `sd()` provides the standard deviation:

```
sd(C3_1)

## [1] 4.949747
```

In the instance of the population standard deviation, the expression is

$$\sigma = \sqrt{\sigma^2} = \sqrt{\frac{\Sigma(x_i - \mu)^2}{N}}.$$

An advantage of using the standard deviation rather than the variance is that it is easier to interpret. Since it is expressed in the same units as the mean, it is more easily compared to statistics that are expressed in the same units as the original data.

Definition 3.11. Coefficient of Variation. The coefficient of variation (CV) is a measure of relative variability; it is found by dividing the standard deviation by the mean.

The CV is a measure without units, and it indicates how large the standard deviation is, relative to the mean. Depending on whether we are dealing with a sample or a population, the notation (but not the computational form) is slightly different: the sample CV is $s / \bar{x}$, while the population CV is σ/μ.

Example 3.13. Find the CV for the passenger data using both the formula and the ratio of the R functions `sd()` and `mean()`: $s / \bar{x} = 4.95 / 44 = 0.1125$.

```
sd(C3_1) / mean(C3_1)

## [1] 0.1124943
```

In other words, the sample standard deviation is 11.25% of the sample mean.

Example 3.14. What is the CV for the apartment rental data? Since $s = \sqrt{s^2} = \$451.29$ and $\bar{x} = \$3914.57$, the CV is \$451.29 / \$3914.57 = 0.1153.

```
sd(housing$rent) / mean(housing$rent)

## [1] 0.1152837
```

That is, the sample standard deviation is 11.53% of the mean. Clearly, the two data sets have almost the same degree of variability with one another, an insight that would not be possible had we considered only the standard deviations. The rental data (with a standard deviation of \$451.29) would seem to be far more variable than the passenger data (with a standard deviation of only 4.95 passengers). By using the CV, however, it is possible to gain a deeper insight into this issue of comparability across data sets.

Example 3.15. One method of gauging the risk associated with a company's stock involves consideration of the variability of its share price. One approach compares the standard deviation of one company's share price with that of another. Suppose that an analysis of the closing share prices of two companies over the last 6 months provides these standard deviations and means: for company A, $s_A = \$5$ and $\bar{x}_A = \$1000$; for company B, $s_B = \$5$ and $\bar{x}_B = \$10$.

While the standard deviations imply that the two companies' share prices are equally volatile, the CVs make clear that this is not the case: the CV for company A is 0.005; for company B it is 0.50. If one's investment goal is to preserve capital—for example, to save for a down payment on a home purchase—it would be important to know that A's share price volatility is only 0.50% of its mean, while B's is 50% of its mean. Clearly, the CV captures the degree of share price volatility better than the standard deviation alone.

Although we have described several measures of location and variability, the mean and the standard deviation are the most widely used measures of central tendency and variability, respectively. In fact, using only the mean and the standard deviation of a data set, we can also learn much about the relative location of items in a data set.

THE *z*-SCORE: A MEASURE OF RELATIVE LOCATION

Definition 3.12. *z*-Scores. The *z*-score is a measure that indicates the relative position of a data value with respect to the data set of which it is a member.

Deriving *z*-scores calls for a standardization process that involves subtracting the mean from each data value, and dividing the difference by the standard deviation. The result indicates the relative position of a data value in terms of the number of standard deviations it is from the mean. For a population, the *z*-score is given by

$$z_i = \frac{x_i - \mu}{\sigma};$$

and for a sample, it is produced by applying

$$z_i = \frac{x_i - \bar{x}}{s}.$$

Associated with each data value x_i is another value z_i, called its *z*-score or its standardized value; z_i indicates the number of standard deviations x_i is from its own mean. In general, a data value less than the mean has a negative *z*-score; a data value greater than the mean has a positive *z*-score; a data value equal to the mean has a *z*-score of zero.

Example 3.16. Standardize the London–Birmingham passenger data. Recall that $\bar{x} = 44$ and $s =$ 4.95 (see Table 3.5).

Table 3.5 Bus passenger data converted into z-scores: standardized data

No. of passengers per bus x_i	Deviation about the mean $(x_i - \bar{x})$	z-score $z_i = (x_i - \bar{x}) / s$
40	40 – 44 = –4	–4 / 4.95 = –0.8081
45	45 – 44 = 1	1 / 4.95 = 0.2020
38	38 – 44 = –6	–6 / 4.95 = 1.2121
50	50 – 44 = 6	6 / 4.95 = 1.2121
47	47 – 44 = 3	3 / 4.95 = 0.6061
$\bar{x} = 44$	$\Sigma(x_i - \bar{x}) = 0$	$\Sigma z_i = 0$

Note that the new variable z has a distribution with mean $\bar{z}$ of 0 and standard deviation s_z of 1. Note also that in converting x to z, the relevant units change from *passengers* to *standard deviations*. This is true of all standardized data sets: the mean is 0, the standard deviation is 1, and the unit of a standardized variable is the standard deviation. Standardizing data with R is straightforward:

```
(C3_1 - mean(C3_1)) / sd(C3_1)

## [1] -0.8081220 0.2020305 -1.2121831 1.2121831 0.6060915
```

Example 3.17. For the apartment rents, we can standardize all 70 data values in exactly the same way. In that case, recall that $\bar{x} = \$3914.57$ and $s = \$451.29$. To standardize the first value, the least expensive apartment priced at $x_1 = \$2950$,

$$z_1 = \frac{\$2950 - \$3914.57}{\$451.29} = -2.14;$$

and to standardize the 70th value, the most expensive priced at $x_{70} = \$4850$,

$$z_{70} = \frac{\$4850 - \$3914.57}{\$451.29} = 2.07.$$

Thus, a rent of \$2950 is 2.14 standard deviations below the mean of this particular data set, while a rent of \$4850 is 2.07 standard deviations above the mean.

Definition 3.13. Empirical Rule. Whenever it is known that the data are *normally* distributed, the empirical rule can be used to make statements about the proportion of data values that fall within a given number of standard deviations from the mean.

Many phenomena are characterized by a normal, bell-shaped distribution, and we make extensive use of it in later chapters. Figures 3.2 and 3.3 show the *standard normal* distribution of the variable z, a special case of the normal distribution when z has a mean of 0 and a standard deviation of 1. For both the normal as well as the standard normal distribution, the empirical rule states:

- approximately 68% of data values fall within 1 standard deviation of the mean;
- approximately 95% of data values fall within 2 standard deviations of the mean;
- approximately 99.7% of data values fall within 3 standard deviations of the mean.

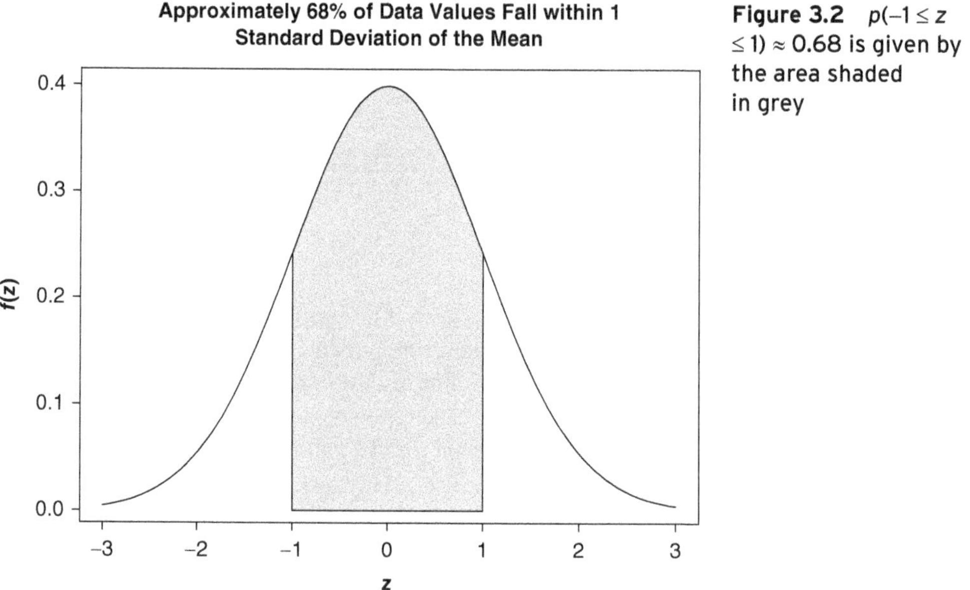

Figure 3.2 $p(-1 \leq z \leq 1) \approx 0.68$ is given by the area shaded in grey

In those cases where the data are (roughly) normally distributed, it is possible to identify outliers in a data set—that is, those observations with unusually large or small values—by what the empirical rule tells us. The ability to identify outliers in a data set is an important first step before deciding what, if anything, to do about them.

There are several reasons why a data set might include outliers. First, an outlier could be a data value that *was mistakenly recorded*. For example, although a household providing demographic information for a survey may have reported that it has 3 children, the person entering the data may have mistakenly entered 30 children. In this case, a correction can be made by consulting the original survey. Second, an outlier could be an observation that *was included in the data set by mistake*. For instance, if the purpose of the above study is to investigate voting attitudes among young families with newborn children, it would be a mistake to include surveys completed by

Figure 3.3 $p(-2 \leq z \leq 2) \approx 0.95$ is given by the area shaded in grey

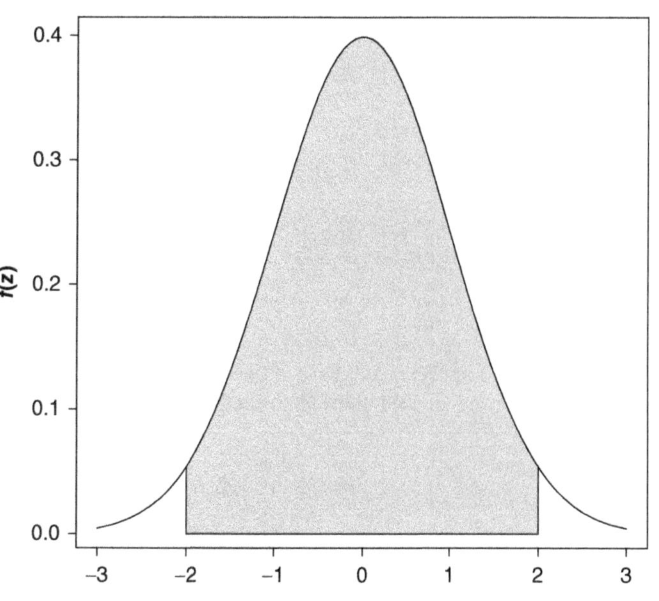

elderly people whose age is much higher. This error can be rectified by simply removing this household from the data set. Third, an outlier might simply be an unusually large or small data value that *has been included and entered correctly*. In this instance, the outlier is normally retained in the data set but the descriptive methods would take into account the presence of outliers. In the case of the recent graduate who signed a contract for $10 million to play baseball, we would use the median rather than the mean to report average salaries.

Here is a simple, two-step procedure for identifying outliers:

1 Standardize the data. That is, convert all original data values into their z-scores.
2 Identify and flag any z-score less than –3 or greater than +3. If there are any z-scores for which $|z_i| > 3$, then the associated data value x_i is an outlier and should be reviewed for accuracy and appropriateness for inclusion in the data set.

Example 3.18. Applying this procedure to the rental data, are there any outliers? No. For all $i = 70$ values, $-3 < z_i < +3$. The lowest rent of $2950 has a standardized value of –2.14, while the most expensive rent of $4850 has a standardized value of 2.07. R makes it an easy matter to efficiently identify outliers using the function `scale()` nested within `min()` and `max()`, where `scale()` returns the z-scores of the data set, and `min()` and `max()` provide the minimum and maximum z-scores, respectively.

```
min(scale(housing$rent))

## [1] -2.137383
```

```
max(scale(housing$rent))

## [1] 2.072806
```

MEASURES OF ASSOCIATION: THE BIVARIATE CASE

Thus far, the numerical measures introduced in this chapter have concerned only one variable. The last topic of the chapter introduces two different but related numerical measures of linear association between two variables, the *covariance* and the *correlation coefficient.*

Definition 3.14. Covariance. The covariance is a numerical measure of linear association between two variables. A positive value indicates a positive linear relationship between the variables, while a negative value indicates a negative linear relationship. A covariance of 0 is indicative of no linear relationship between the variables, either positive or negative. The population covariance between variables x and y is found with the expression

$$\sigma_{xy} = \frac{\sum(x_i - \mu_x)(y_i - \mu_y)}{N},$$

while the sample covariance between x and y is

$$s_{xy} = \frac{\sum(x_i - \bar{x})(y_i - \bar{y})}{n-1}.$$

Example 3.19. Table 3.6 reports the high and low daily temperatures (in degrees Celsius) for March 3, 2015 for seven cities scattered across the world. What is the covariance?

Table 3.6 High and low temperatures (degrees Celsius) for seven cities

City	High temperature, x_i	Low temperature, y_i
Mumbai	33	22
Nairobi	31	14
Paris	9	2
São Paulo	28	20
Sydney	27	20
Tokyo	9	3
Toronto	–3	–12

Intuitively, one might suspect that these two measures would be positively related: within a given day, cities with the higher of the high temperatures would be expected to have the higher of the low temperatures as well. The derivation of the covariance of the two temperature readings is shown in Table 3.7.

Table 3.7 Calculations for the sample covariance: high and low temperatures

x_i	y_i	$x_i - \bar{x}$	$y_i - \bar{y}$	$(x_i - \bar{x})(y_i - \bar{y})$
33	22	13.86	12.14	168.27
31	14	11.86	4.14	49.12
9	2	−10.14	−7.86	79.69
28	20	8.86	10.14	89.84
27	20	7.86	10.14	79.69
9	3	−10.14	−6.86	69.55
−3	−12	−22.14	−21.86	483.98
$\bar{x} = 19.14$	$\bar{y} = 9.86$	$\Sigma(x_i - \bar{x}) = 0$	$\Sigma(y_i - \bar{y}) = 0$	$\Sigma(x_i - \bar{x})(y_i - \bar{y}) = 1020.14$

Thus the sample covariance is

$$s_{xy} = \frac{\Sigma(x_i - \bar{x})(y_i - \bar{y})}{n-1} = \frac{1020.14}{6} = 170.02.$$

To find the sample covariance with R, we use the function `cov()`. The data set name is `city` and the two variable names are `high_cent` and `low_cent`.

```
cov(city$high_cent, city$low_cent)

## [1] 170.0238
```

That the units on which the variables are measured affect the magnitude of the covariance means that the covariance itself reveals little about the *strength of the association* between those variables. To understand this limitation better, consider the next example.

Example 3.20. Table 3.8 reports information on 16 voters: their age, annual income, view of same-sex marriage, and average amount of weekly television viewing (in both hours and minutes). Find the covariance of x_1 = `Age` with x_4 = `Hrs TV` and x_5 = `Min TV`.

(Note: x_3 is measured on a 1–7 rating scale as a reaction to the statement, "I approve of the right of same-sex couples to marry," with a person indicating strong approval with a 7, strong disapproval with a 1, and relative indifference with a number in between.)

The covariance of x_1 and x_4, as well as of x_1 and x_5, can be found using the function `cov()` and the data set `polling`.

```
cov(polling$x1, polling$x4)

## [1] 2.816667

cov(polling$x1, polling$x5)

## [1] 169
```

Table 3.8 Some personal information about 16 voters

x_1 = Age	x_2 = Annual income	x_3 = Same-sex	x_4 = Hrs TV	x_5 = Min TV
25	$24,000	7	21 hrs	1260 mins
27	$24,000	7	8 hrs	480 mins
31	$38,000	7	18 hrs	1080 mins
32	$40,000	7	0 hrs	0 mins
37	$42,000	5	22 hrs	1320 mins
39	$48,000	4	20 hrs	1200 mins
40	$44,000	7	12 hrs	720 mins
44	$46,000	4	18 hrs	1080 mins
45	$39,000	7	6 hrs	360 mins
46	$51,000	3	18 hrs	1080 mins
52	$54,000	2	21 hrs	1260 mins
53	$60,000	1	0 hrs	0 mins
57	$77,000	1	20 hrs	1200 mins
59	$71,000	3	18 hrs	1080 mins
63	$78,000	2	8 hrs	480 mins
65	$84,000	1	18 hrs	1080 mins

In this example, the covariance of `age` (x_1) and hours of TV viewing (x_4) is 2.817, but the covariance of `age` (x_1) and `minutes` of TV viewing (x_5) is 169. While the covariance confirms that the relationship is positive, how strong that positive relationship might be remains a question. To gain more insight into the strength of the relationship, we introduce a new but related statistic, the correlation coefficient.

Definition 3.15. Correlation Coefficient. The correlation coefficient is a numerical measure of linear association between two variables. Its advantage over the covariance is that it indicates not only whether the association is positive or negative, but also how strong that association might be. When two variables are strongly negatively related, the correlation approaches –1; when they are strongly positively related, it approaches +1; when they are unrelated, it is near 0. The population correlation cofficient between x and y is

$$\rho_{xy} = \frac{\sigma_{xy}}{\sigma_x \sigma_y}, \quad \text{where } -1 \le \rho_{xy} \le +1,$$

in which σ_{xy} is the population covariance, and σ_x and σ_y are the population standard deviations of x and y, respectively. The sample correlation coefficient between x and y is

$$r_{xy} = \frac{s_{xy}}{s_x s_y}, \quad \text{where } -1 \le r_{xy} \le +1,$$

in which s_{xy} is the sample covariance, and s_x and s_y are the sample standard deviations of x and y, respectively.

Example 3.21. Use the R function `cor()` to find the correlation of x_1 = `Age` with x_4 = `Hrs TV` and x_5 = `Min TV`. Figure 3.4 also confirms the lack of assocation between the two variables.

```
cor(polling$x1, polling$x4)

## [1] 0.02972137

cor(polling$x1, polling$x5)

## [1] 0.02972137
```

The correlations of x_1 = `Age` with x_4 = `Hrs TV` and x_1 = `Age` with x_5 = `Min TV` are now the same, $r = 0.0297$, whether the second variable is expressed in terms of hours or minutes.

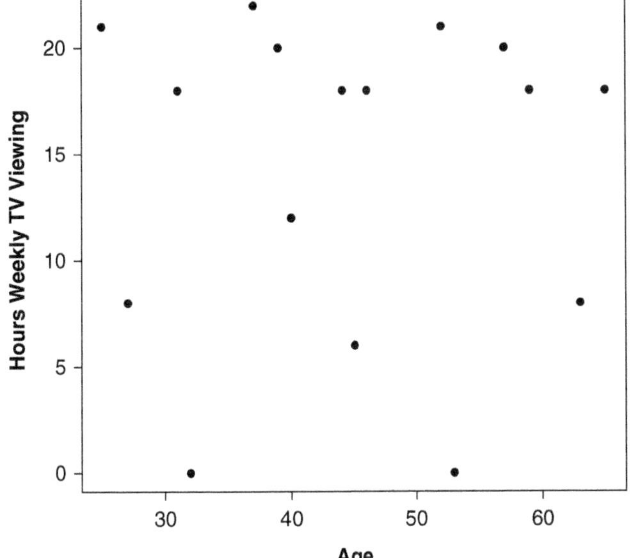

Figure 3.4 Plot of TV viewing and age: no linear relationship with $r = -0.0297$

```
plot(polling$x1, polling$x4, xlab = 'Age',
     ylab = 'Hours Weekly TV Viewing', pch = 19)
```

Consider two other relationships—one positive (between age and income) and one negative (between age and view of the right of same-sex couples to marry).

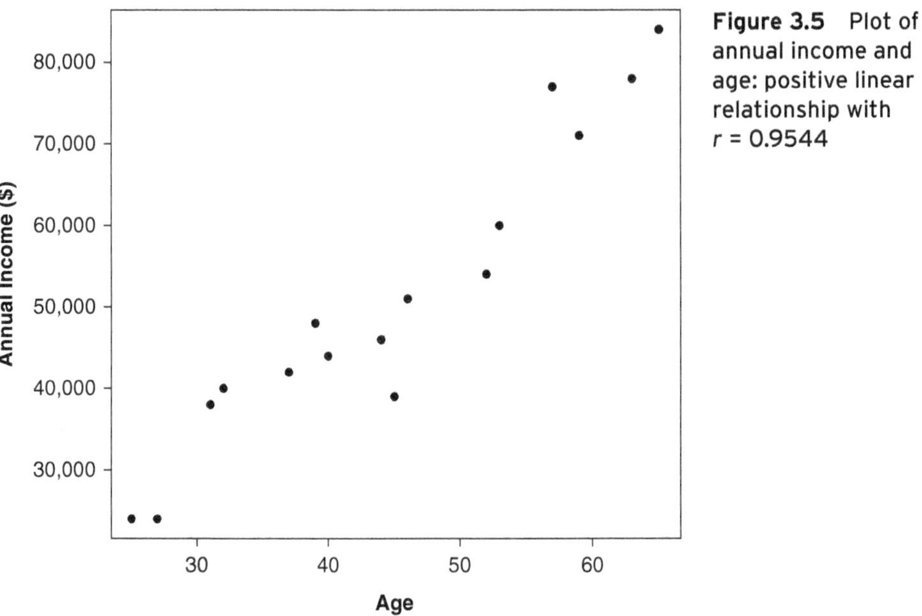

Figure 3.5 Plot of annual income and age: positive linear relationship with $r = 0.9544$

```
plot(polling$x1, polling$x2, xlab = 'Age',
     ylab = 'Annual Income ($)', pch = 19)
```

Both the scatter plot in Figure 3.5 and the correlation coefficient $r_{xy} = 0.9544$ reveal the positive linear relationship between age and annual income. This is not a surprising finding, of course, given that younger people are typically just beginning their work lives.

Finally, consider the association between age and view of the right of same-sex couples to marry. In general, younger people tend to be more receptive than their elders to the idea of same-sex marriage, a relationship revealed in both the plot in Figure 3.6 as well as a correlation coefficient of –0.8612.

```
plot(polling$x1, polling$x3, xlab = 'Age',
     ylab = 'Views of Same-Sex Marriage', pch = 19)
```

The correlation coefficient captures both the *direction* and *strength* of the linear association between two variables. It is a widely used measure with many applications, and we will return to it later in this book.

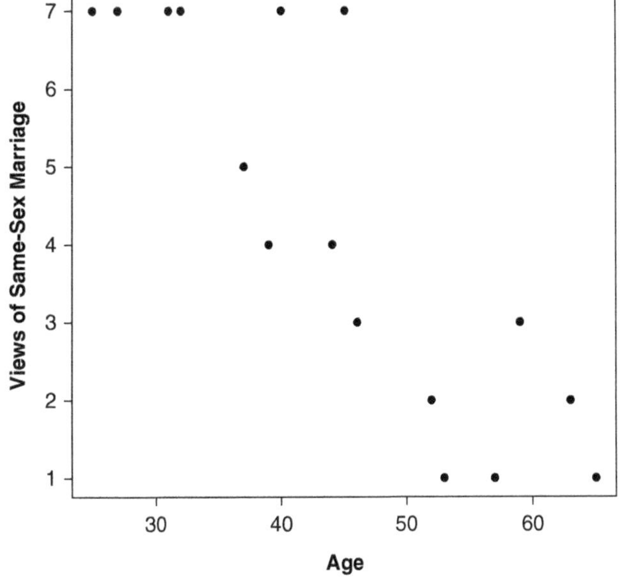

Figure 3.6 View of same-sex marriage and age: negative relationship with $r = -0.8612$

3.7 THE GEOMETRIC MEAN

In this section, we introduce a different measure of central tendency known as the *geometric mean*. The geometric mean differs from the ordinary mean (also known as the *arithmetic mean* or simply the mean; see Definition 3.1) in that it is the preferred measure of central tendency when the phenomenon under consideration is multiplicative rather than additive. Since these two terms may be unfamiliar, we begin by drawing the distinction between what is meant by an additive process and a multiplicative process.

The mean provides a measure of central tendency when the data values on which it is applied are independent of one another. For example, suppose that over a 2-week period, a department store manager randomly interviews six customers with the purpose of learning something about their purchase patterns, and finds that they have spent these amounts: \$37.14, \$56.74, \$11.81, \$90.07, \$117.56, and \$9.16. Since the purchases of each customer are made independently, the arithmetic mean is a reasonable measure of central tendency (since the process is additive) and, in this case, is \$53.75.

Now consider a situation where we also desire a measure of central tendency, but one where there is dependence of one data measurement on the previous one. Table 3.9 reports the percentage annual return for the S&P500 over 8 years, 2008–2015. For each year, the annual return plus dividends (center column) has been converted to the growth rate from the previous year (right-hand column). Thus, if we had invested \$1000 at the beginning of 2008, the value of that investment would have fallen to $\$1000 \times 0.63 = \$630$ by the year's end. But if we had invested the \$1000 at the beginning of 2009, the investment would have increased to $\$1000 \times 1.2646 = \$1264.60$ by the year's end.

Table 3.9 Annual return and growth rate (%) for S&P500 index: 2008-2015

Year	Annual return plus dividends (%)	Growth rate from previous year
2008	−37.00%	0.6300
2009	26.46%	1.2646
2010	15.06%	1.1506
2011	2.11%	1.0211
2012	16.00%	1.1600
2013	32.39%	1.3239
2014	13.69%	1.1369
2015	1.38%	1.0138

Suppose $1000 was invested in an S&P500 index fund on January 2, 2008 and held until December 31, 2015. To what amount would $1000 grow if invested for the full 8 years? To answer this question, we need to apply the average growth rate, compounding regularly, over all periods the $1000 is held. But what growth rate should be used?

One approach is to apply the mean growth rate to the initial investment of $1000. That is, (0.630 + 1.2646 + 1.1506 + 1.0211 + 1.1600 + 1.3239 + 1.1369 + 1.0138) / 8 = 1.0876 or about 8.76%.

```
(0.630 + 1.2646 + 1.1506 + 1.0211 + 1.1600 + 1.3239 + 1.1369 + 1.0138) / 8

## [1] 1.087613
```

Thus, for 8 years, the initial investment of $1000 would be expected to grow to about $1.0876^8 \times \$1000 = 1.9579 \times \$1000 = \$1958$. This calculation is reported (and confirmed) in the bottom row of the column headed "End-of-year balance at 8.76%" in Table 3.10.

Table 3.10 Growth of $1000 over 8 years at 8.76% and 6.51%

Year	End-of-year balance at 8.76%	End-of-year balance at 6.51%
2008	1.0876 × $1000 = $1088	1.0651 × $1000 = $1065
2009	1.0876 × $1088 = $1183	1.0651 × $1065 = $1135
2010	1.0876 × $1183 = $1286	1.0651 × $1134 = $1208
2011	1.0876 × $1286 = $1399	1.0651 × $1208 = $1287
2012	1.0876 × $1399 = $1522	1.0651 × $1287 = $1371
2013	1.0876 × $1522 = $1655	1.0651 × $1371 = $1460
2014	1.0876 × $1655 = $1800	1.0651 × $1460 = $1555
2015	1.0876 × $1800 = $1958	1.0651 × $1555 = $1657

Although this approach seems reasonable, it is incorrect. To see why, consider this question by applying the growth rate from the previous year (right-hand column of Table 3.9) to the initial investment of $1000 and compounding annually for the 8-year period. The calculations and actual end-of-year balances are reported in Table 3.11.

Table 3.11 Actual growth of $1000 over 8 years applying year-to-year growth rate

Year	Actual end-of-year balance
2008	0.630 × $1000 = $630
2009	1.2646 × $630 = $797
2010	1.1506 × $797 = $917
2011	1.0211 × $917 = $936
2012	1.1600 × $936 = $1086
2013	1.3239 × $1086 = $1437
2014	1.1369 × $1437 = $1634
2015	1.0138 × $1634 = $1657

As we see, over the 8-year period from 2008 through 2015, the initial investment of $1000 would be expected to grow to only $1657, not $1958. This calculation is reported in the bottom row of the column headed 'Actual end-of-year balance' in Table 3.11.

While the computations reported in Table 3.11 result in the correct amount of $1657, we prefer to use a more straightforward method to derive this amount. And since applying the average growth rate of 8.76% does not work, we want to use one that is appropriate to the multiplicative nature of the phenomenon in question. What we use instead is the *geometric mean*, which is defined as the *nth root of the product of n growth rates*, or

$$(x_1 \times x_2 \times x_3 \times \ldots \times x_n)^{1/n}.$$

Applying this expression to the growth rates (from Table 3.9), the geometric mean is $(0.630 \times 1.2646 \times 1.1506 \times 1.0211 \times 1.1600 \times 1.3239 \times 1.1369 \times 1.0138)^{1/8} = 1.0651$, or about 6.51%. Thus, for 8 years, the initial investment of $1000 would be expected to grow to about $1.0651^8 \times \$1000 =$ $1657. See the right-hand column of Table 3.10 for confirmation.

```
(0.630 * 1.2646 * 1.1506 * 1.0211 * 1.1600 * 1.3239
 * 1.1369 * 1.0138) ^ (1/8)

## [1] 1.065146
```

The geometric mean can be applied in those situations where we want to calculate the average rate of change over a number of time intervals. Areas of application include but are not limited to the rates of change in populations, epidemics, the sea level, various economic phenomena, and even microbial growth. Although in this example we developed it over 8 periods (years), it can be derived for any number of time intervals. Finally, the length of interval does not need to be years; it can be anything, including quarters, months, weeks, days, or even shorter durations.

SUMMARY

Chapters 2 and 3 identify and describe three general approaches to descriptive statistics. In Chapter 2, we learned how to use various *tabular* and *graphical* methods whereas in this chapter, we acquired the ability to apply a number of *numerical* methods. Among the outcomes of numerical methods are: (1) measures of central tendency such as the mean, the median, the mode, and (when the phenomenon under consideration involves rates of change over a number of time intervals) the geometric mean; (2) measures of location, including percentiles and quartiles; (3) measures of dispersion, such as the range, the interquartile range, the variance, the standard deviation, the coefficient of variation, and standardized data values; and (4) measures of linear relationship between two variables, including the covariance and correlation coefficients. We also saw an example of exploratory data analysis, the box plot.

Regardless of the particular method of descriptive statistics being applied, the purpose is always the same: to provide insights about the data that cannot be gleaned by a perfunctory or superficial examination of the original data. In the best case, however, the effective application of descriptive statistical methods can result in insights that are not possible by a simple exploration of the data in its original form.

Descriptive statistics forms the first part of this book because a firm grasp of its concepts and organizing principles is essential if we are to understand the next topic, probability. For example, many of the ideas that form the foundation of probability are developed on measures of location and variation such as the mean and the standard deviation. Moreover, the use of cross-tabulation tables and frequency distributions proves invaluable when introducing and using such probability concepts as the random variable and probability distribution.

Finally, we have seen how R makes many of the computational aspects of descriptive statistics quick to do as well as more accurate. In future chapters, we propose to build on our understanding and use of R whenever possible and practical to do so.

definitions

Box Plot The box plot is a graphical display which is based on five values: the minimum, maximum, median, and first and third quartiles. It has the advantage of simultaneously providing comparisons of the data across several categories.

Coefficient of Variation The coefficient of variation is a measure of relative variability of a data set, and is found by dividing the standard deviation by the mean.

(Continued)

(Continued)

Correlation Coefficient The correlation coefficient is a numerical measure of linear association between two variables. It indicates not only whether the association is positive or negative, but also how strong that association might be.

Covariance The covariance is a measure of linear association between two variables. It is typically expressed as σ_{xy} if the data set is a population, s_{xy} if a sample.

Empirical Rule Whenever it is known that the data are normally distributed, the empirical rule can be used to make statements about the proportion of data values that fall within a given number of standard deviations from the mean.

Exploratory Data Analysis A set of methods for visually representing data in an easy-to-understand manner for the purpose of revealing the important characteristics such as the central tendency, the dispersion, and the shape of the data.

Geometric Mean A measure of central tendency that provides the average rate of growth over several periods. It is the preferred measure when the phenomenon under consideration is multiplicative rather than additive.

Interquartile Range The interquartile range is the difference between the third and first quartiles of a data set. It is the range of the middle 50% of data values.

Mean The mean of a data set is the average of all the data values in that data set.

Median The median of a data set is a middle value when the data items are arranged in ascending (or descending) order.

Mode The mode of a data set is the value that occurs most frequently.

Outlier A data value that is extraordinarily small or large.

Percentiles The *p*th percentile of a data set (arranged in ascending order) is the value such that at least *p*% of the observations fall at or below this value, and at least (100 - *p*)% fall at or above it.

Quartiles The quartiles are the 25th, 50th, and 75th percentiles.

Range The range is the difference between the largest and smallest values of a data set.

Standard Deviation The standard deviation is the square root of the variance.

Variance The variance is a measure of variability that uses all the data values, and is based on the average of squared deviations from the mean of the data set.

z-Score The *z*-score is a measure that indicates the relative position of a data value with respect to the data set of which it is a member.

formulae

Coefficient of Variation: Population:

$$= \frac{\sigma}{\mu}$$

Coefficient of Variation: Sample:

$$= \frac{s}{\bar{x}}$$

Correlation: Population:

$$\rho_{xy} = \frac{\sigma_{xy}}{\sigma_x \sigma_y}$$

Correlation: Sample:

$$r_{xy} = \frac{s_{xy}}{s_x s_y}$$

Covariance: Population

$$\sigma_{xy} = \frac{\sum(x_i - \mu_x)(y_i - \mu_y)}{N}$$

Covariance: Sample

$$s_{xy} = \frac{\sum(x_i - \bar{x})(y_i - \bar{y})}{n-1}$$

Geometric Mean

$$(x_1 \times x_2 \times x_3 \times \ldots \times x_n)^{1/n}$$

Interquartile Range

$$IQR = Q_3 - Q_1$$

Mean: Population

$$\mu = \frac{\sum x_i}{N}$$

Mean: Sample

$$\bar{x} = \frac{\sum x_i}{n}$$

Standard Deviation: Population

$$\sigma = \sqrt{\sigma^2} = \sqrt{\frac{\sum(x_i - \mu)^2}{N}}$$

Standard Deviation: Sample

$$s = \sqrt{s^2} = \sqrt{\frac{\sum(x_i - \bar{x})^2}{n-1}}$$

Variance: Population

$$\sigma^2 = \frac{\sum(x_i - \mu)^2}{N}$$

Variance: Sample

$$s^2 = \frac{\sum(x_i - \bar{x})^2}{n-1}$$

***z*-Score: Population**

$$z_i = \frac{x_i - \mu}{\sigma}$$

***z*-Score: Sample**

$$z_i = \frac{x_i - \bar{x}}{s}$$

R functions

Note that some of the R functions listed below are used in the exercises, found on the companion website, but not in this chapter. The practice of introducing R functions either in the website exercises or in the chapters is followed elsewhere in this book.

`boxplot()` A method of exploratory data analysis, `boxplot()` creates a box plot display of quantitative data. It is mostly based on the five-number summary (see `summary()` below).

`cor()` Provides the correlation coefficient between two quantitative variables.

`cov()` Provides the covariance between two quantitative variables.

`IQR()` Reports the interquartile range: the difference between the third and first quartiles of a set of quantitative data.

`length()` Reports the number of data items in an object.

(Continued)

(Continued)

`max(scale())` Note that `scale()` is nested within `max()`, and provides the maximum standardized value in a set of quantitative data.

`mean()` Reports the arithmetic mean of a set of quantitative data.

`median()` Reports the median of a set of quantitative data.

`min(scale())` Here `scale()` is nested within `min()`, and provides the minimum standardized value in a set of quantitative data.

`quantile()` Reports the values of any desired percentiles.

`rexp()` Generates a series of data values that are exponentially distributed.

`rnorm()` Generates a series of data values that are normally distributed. The default normal distribution is the standard normal, but it is possible to override this by specifying the preferred values for the mean and standard deviation.

`scale()` Provides the standardized values, or *z*-scores, of all data items.

`sd()` Provides the standard deviation of a quantitative variable.

`seq()` Can be used to generate a sequence of numbers whose minimum, maximum, and inter-value distance is defined by the arguments in ().

`var()` Provides the variance of a quantitative variable.

data sets

Note that some of the data sets listed below are used in the exercises and found on the book's website, but not in this chapter. The practice of using data sets either in the website exercises or in the chapters is followed elsewhere in this book.

1 `city`
2 `daily_idx_chg`
3 `housing`
4 `jobs`
5 `LakeHuron`
6 `polling`
7 `temps`
8 `top20`

APPENDIX: VECTORIZATION

A vector is simply an ordered collection of elements (see the Chapter 1 Appendix, Section 3(a)). A useful feature of R is its ability to perform operations on entire vectors. To appreciate this capability, consider these examples of vectorization.

#Comment1. Create an object and name it vector1. Examine contents.

```
vector1 <- c(1, 2, 3, 4, 5)
vector1

## [1] 1 2 3 4 5
```

```
#Comment2. Subtract 3 from vector1 and assign the result to vector2.
#Examine contents of vector2 and note the result of this operation.
vector2 <- vector1 - 3
vector2

## [1] -2 -1 0 1 2

#Comment3. Add 5 to vector1 and assign the result to vector3.
#Examine contents of vector3 and note the result of this operation.
vector3 <- vector1 + 5
vector3

## [1] 6 7 8 9 10

#Comment4. Multiply vector1 by 2 and assign the result to vector4.
#Examine contents of vector4 and note the result of this operation.
vector4 <- vector1 * 2
vector4

## [1] 2 4 6 8 10

#Comment5. Divide vector1 by 2 and assign the result to vector5.
#Examine vector5 and note the result of this operation.
vector5 <- vector1 / 2
vector5

## [1] 0.5 1.0 1.5 2.0 2.5

#Comment6. Square vector1 and assign the result to vector6.
#Examine vector6 and note the result of this operation.
vector6 <- (vector1) ^ 2
vector6

## [1] 1 4 9 16 25

#Comment7. In separate operations, add and multiply the values in vector1.
sum(vector1)

## [1] 15

prod(vector1)

## [1] 120

#Comment8. Square and then sum the values in vector1.
sum((vector1) ^ 2)

## [1] 55

#Comment9. Using vectorization, find the mean of the elements in vector1.
sum(vector1) / length(vector1)

## [1] 3
```

The vectorization capability of R is one to which we return later in the book.

exercises

See the website for full solutions to these exercises.

3.1 Use R to find the 90th percentile, the first, second, and third quartiles, as well as the minimum and maximum values of the `LakeHuron` data set. (Recall that R has a number of data sets included; `LakeHuron` is the name of the data set that contains the "Annual measurements of the level, in feet, of Lake Huron, 1875-1972." To see all the available data sets, simply enter `data()` at the R prompt.) What are the mean and the median?

3.2 Use R to find the range, interquartile range, variance, standard deviation, and coefficient of variation of the `LakeHuron` data set.

3.3 Use R to create a vector with the following elements: –37.7, –0.3, 0.00, 0.91, e, π, 5.1, $2e$, and 113,754, where e is the base of the natural logarithm (roughly 2.718282) and π the ratio of a circle's diameter to its radius (about 3.141593).
Name it `E3_2` and find the mean, median, 78th percentile, variance, and standard deviation.
Note: R understands `exp(1)` as e, `pi` as π.

3.4 Use R to define two vectors, `x` and `y`, where `x` contains 24, 22, 22, 21, and 19, and `y` contains 27, 24, 23, 21, and 19. Which is the most likely correlation coefficient describing the relationship between `x` and `y`: –0.90, –0.50, –0.10, 0.00, +0.10, +0.50, or +0.90? Use R to find the correlation and covariance of `x` and `y`.

3.5 Use R to define a vector with the following elements: 10, 20, 30, 40, 50, 60, 70, 80, 90, and 100. Making use of the vectorization capability of R, find the sample variance and standard deviation of this set of data. Check answers against those using the functions `var()` and `sd()`. The expression for the variance is.

$$s^2 = \frac{\sum_{i=1}^{n}(x_i - \bar{x})^2}{n-1}.$$

https://study.sagepub.com/stinerock

Introduction to Probability

contents

learning objectives

1. Gain an appreciation for the role that probability plays in our understanding of the world we live in.
2. Be able to apply the three methods commonly used for assigning probabilities to experimental outcomes, and understand when each should be used.
3. Be able to apply the laws that are available for computing probabilities of events.
4. Understand how new information can be used to revise initial (prior) probability estimates using Bayes' theorem.

Originally, the formal study of probability emerged as a response to the need of gamblers to understand better the games of chance they played: flipping a coin, casting a pair of dice, spinning a roulette wheel, and drawing cards from a deck. As probabilistic thinking evolved, however, people realized that it could also serve as a model of other phenomena, particularly in the physical and social sciences.

 SOME IMPORTANT DEFINITIONS

Definition 4.1. Probability. Probability is a numerical measure of the likelihood that an outcome will occur; it can assume values between 0 and 1 (inclusive). A probability close to 0 indicates that an outcome is highly unlikely to occur, while a probability near 1 indicates that the outcome is very likely to occur. A probability in the neighborhood of 0.5 indicates that the occurrence of an outcome is about as likely as it is unlikely.

Definition 4.2. Experiment. An experiment is any process that can result in one of several well-defined outcomes that cannot be predicted with certainty beforehand. Whenever an experiment is performed, one and only one of the experimental results occurs. Table 4.1 lists some experiments and their associated experimental outcomes.

Table 4.1 Examples of experiments and their experimental outcomes

Experiment	Experimental outcomes
Roll a die	1, 2, 3, 4, 5, or 6
Make an investment	Financial loss, gain, or break-even
Draw a single playing card	Any one of the 52 possible playing cards
Inspect a part coming off an assembly line	Defective or non-defective

Definition 4.3. Sample Space. Each experiment has an associated sample space that is the set of all possible experimental outcomes. We denote the sample space by S.

Definition 4.4. Sample Point. A sample point is a member of the sample space. It is any one particular experimental outcome.

If an experiment consists of drawing a card from a deck of 52, there are 52 possible experimental outcomes. This set of all possible outcomes of the experiment is the sample space. A six of hearts is one of the 52 possible sample points. Similarly, if an experiment consists of observing the closing price of a common stock on the last day of trading for the year, the sample space is made up of all possible closing prices.

4.2 COUNTING RULES

Counting rules make it possible to identify and count the sample points of an experiment. Such rules are useful because they help us understand what may happen when certain kinds of experiments occur. We consider three widely used counting rules: the counting rule for the multiple-step experiment, the counting rule for combinations, and the counting rule for permutations.

The Counting Rule for the Multiple-Step Experiment

Also known as the *multiplication principle*, here is a formal definition of this rule: If an experiment can be characterized as a sequence of N steps with n_1 possible results on the first step, n_2 possible results on the second step, and so on, then the total number of experimental outcomes for the overall experiment is equal to $n_1 n_2 \ldots n_N$. That is, the number of experimental outcomes for the overall experiment is the product of the number of results on each step.

Example 4.1. An experiment consists of tossing three coins. How many experimental outcomes are associated with this experiment?

This multiple-step experiment has $N = 3$ steps with $n_1 = 2$ results on the first step, $n_2 = 2$ results on the second, and $n_3 = 2$ on the third. Therefore, there are $n_1 n_2 n_3 = 2 \times 2 \times 2 = 8$ possible experimental outcomes or sample points.

To write out all the sample points of the sample space S, let H be heads and T be tails. We obtain

$$S = \{(HHH), (HHT), (HTH), (THH), (HTT), (THT), (TTH), (TTT)\}.$$

Note that there are eight sample points, just as the counting rule indicates. See the tree diagram in Figure 4.1 to visualize the sequence of three steps.

Example 4.2. The Department of Motor Vehicles (DMV) for the state of California wants to issue new license plates to the roughly 35 million vehicles in the state next year. They are proposing to use all numbers, arranged in seven positions or places on the new plates. Will they have a sufficient number of unique license plates for every vehicle in the state?

This question can be framed as a multiple-step experiment of $N = 7$ steps with $n_1 = 10$ outcomes on the first step, $n_2 = 10$ outcomes on the second, and so on, for all 7 steps. That is, all positions can be filled in any of 10 ways: 0, 1, 2, 3, 4, 5, 6, 7, 8, or 9.

Figure 4.1 A tree diagram of three coin tosses

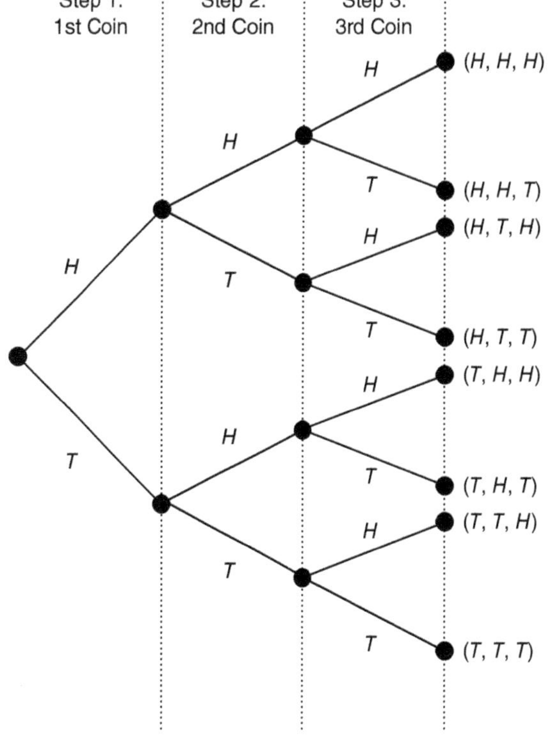

As currently planned, there will not be a sufficient number of unique plates. In fact, there would be only 10 million,

$$n_1 n_2 n_3 n_4 n_5 n_6 n_7 = 10 \times 10 \times 10 \times 10 \times 10 \times 10 \times 10 = 10^7 = 10{,}000{,}000$$

—far shy of the required 35 million.

To get around this problem, the DMV might use letters instead of numbers in a few of the positions. In this way, they would increase the number of results on each of those steps, or positions, from 10 to 26. In particular, suppose instead they decide to use 3 letters followed by 4 numbers arranged in the 7 places. How many unique plates are now possible? Now the experiment has $N = 7$ steps with $n_1 = n_2 = n_3 = 26$ and $n_4 = n_5 = n_6 = n_7 = 10$. Applying the counting rule, the number of possible experimental outcomes (the number of unique license plates) is now 175,760,000:

$$n_1 n_2 n_3 n_4 n_5 n_6 n_7 = 26 \times 26 \times 26 \times 10 \times 10 \times 10 \times 10 = 26^3 \times 10^4 = 175{,}760{,}000.$$

```
#Comment. Use operators ^ and * to perform basic computations using R.
(26 ^ 3) * (10 ^ 4)

## [1] 175760000
```

States having larger populations use more (not fewer) letters on their license plates.

The Counting Rule for Combinations

This rule provides the number of combinations of N distinct objects taken n at a time: that is, the number of unique subsets of size n. In the present case, it makes it possible for us to count the number of experimental outcomes when n objects are to be selected from a larger set of N objects. This number is typically expressed as C_n^N or $\binom{N}{n}$, given by

$$C_n^N = \binom{N}{n} = \frac{N!}{n!(N-n)!},$$

where

$$N! = N(N-1)(N-2)...(2)(1),$$

$$(N-n)! = (N-n)(N-n-1)(N-n-2)...(2)(1),$$

$$0! = 1.$$

Example 4.3. Place three balls (numbered 1, 2, and 3) in an urn. In drawing two balls at random, how many different pairs are possible? That is, how many combinations of $N = 3$ objects can be taken $n = 2$ at a time? Applying this counting rule, we find

$$C_n^N = \binom{N}{n} = \frac{N!}{n!(N-n)!} = \frac{3!}{2!1!} = \frac{3\times 2\times 1}{2\times 1\times 1} = 3.$$

The sample space is $S = \{(1,2),(1,3),(2,3)\}$ and contains 3 sample points.

```
#Comment. Use the function choose(N, n) to find the number of combinations
#of N items taken n at a time.
choose(3, 2)

## [1] 3
```

This counting rule makes it unnecessary to identify and count all of an experiment's sample points, something which is helpful when it is impractical or impossible to do so.

Example 4.4. How many unique five-card hands are possible with a deck of 52 cards?

$$C_n^N = \binom{N}{n} = \frac{N!}{n!(N-n)!} = \frac{52!}{(5!)(47!)} = \frac{311,875,200}{120} = 2,598,960.$$

```
#Comment. Use function choose(52, 5) to find the number of combinations
#of N = 52 items taken n = 5 at a time.
choose(52, 5)

## [1] 2598960
```

As we see, 2,598,960 unique five-card hands can be drawn from a deck of 52.

The Counting Rule for Permutations

This rule makes it possible to count the number of experimental outcomes when n objects are selected from a larger set of N objects when the order of selection matters. The crucial distinction between combinations and permutations lies with the order of the items selected. Note that with combinations, the sample point $(1, 2)$ is counted only once because $(1, 2)$ and $(2, 1)$ are viewed as the same sample point. In the case of permutations, however, $(1, 2)$ and $(2, 1)$ are seen as two different sample points. Since the number of permutations exceeds the number of combinations, the computation must be adjusted to reflect this. The number of permutations should be expressed as P_n^N, where

$$P_n^N = n!C_n^N = n!\binom{N}{n} = n!\frac{N!}{n!(N-n)!} = \frac{N!}{(N-n)!}.$$

Thus the number of permutations of N objects taken n at a time equals the number of combinations (of N objects taken n at a time) multiplied by $n!$. As can be seen, this expression collapses to a simpler form than the expression for combinations. To draw the distinction between combinations and permutations, consider Examples 4.5 and 4.6.

Example 4.5. Suppose five balls (numbered 1, 2, 3, 4, and 5) are placed in an urn. In selecting two balls, how many different pairs are possible? That is, how many combinations of $N = 5$ balls can be taken $n = 2$ at a time? First, list the entire sample space S.

$$S = \{(1,2),(1,3),(1,4),(1,5),(2,3),(2,4),(2,5),(3,4),(3,5),(4,5)\}.$$

Applying the expression for combinations confirms that there are 10 combinations:

$$C_n^N = \binom{N}{n} = \frac{N!}{n!(N-n)!} = \frac{5!}{2!3!} = 10.$$

Example 4.6. How many permutations of 2 out of 5 are possible? Using the formula

$$P_n^N = \frac{N!}{(N-n)!} = \frac{5!}{(5-2)!} = \frac{5!}{3!} = 20.$$

That there are 20 permutations (of 2 of 5 objects) makes sense given that there are 2 possible arrangements for each of the 10 combinations. That is, $(1, 2)$ can be rearranged as $(2, 1)$; $(1, 3)$ can be rearranged as $(3, 1)$; and so on. Each of the 10 combinations can be arranged in 2 different ways, providing for $10 \times 2 = 20$ permutations in all. See below how R is used to derive permutations. Note that `factorial(N)` calculates $N!$.

```
#Comment. Use the ratio of factorial expressions for permutations.
factorial(5) / factorial(5 - 2)

## [1] 20
```

4.3 ASSIGNING PROBABILITIES

Counting rules are useful because they count the number of sample points of an experiment, something which is often an important preliminary step to assigning probabilities and understanding what may happen when certain kinds of experiments occur.

There are two requirements that must be met when assigning probabilities: (1) the probability of any sample point must be between 0 and 1, inclusive; and (2) the sum of the probabilities for all sample points must be 1. Expressing these conditions formally:

1. $0 \le p(E_i) \le 1$, for each experimental outcome *i*.
2. $\Sigma_{i=1}^{n} p(E_i) = 1$, where there are *n* experimental outcomes.

As long as the method of assigning probabilities satisfies these two requirements, the method is acceptable, at least from a mathematical point of view. The three general methods of assigning probability values to experimental outcomes are the *classical method*, the *relative frequency method*, and the *subjective method*. We briefly consider each.

The Classical Method

The classical method of assigning probabilities rests on the assumption of equally likely outcomes. When this assumption is met, the expression to derive probabilities is

$$\text{probability of an outcome} = \frac{\text{number of favorable cases}}{\text{total number of cases}}.$$

Note that if the assumption of equally likely outcomes is justified, we know that when the sample space contains n sample points, then the probability of any one of them is $1/n$. Consider Examples 4.7 and 4.8.

Example 4.7. What is the sample space S for the experiment of tossing two coins?

$$S = \{(HH), (HT), (TH), (TT)\}$$

Assuming equally likely outcomes, one can assign probabilities to each sample point:

$$p(HH) = p(HT) = p(TH) = p(TT) = 0.25.$$

Since there are $n = 4$ outcomes in the sample space, the probability of any one of these outcomes is $1/4$. Note that both requirements specified for assigning probabilities are satisfied.

Example 4.8. An experiment consists of drawing one card from a deck of 52 cards. How many experimental outcomes are there? What is the probability of drawing a five of hearts?

There are 52 possible outcomes consisting of all the cards in the deck. Since the assumption of equally likely outcomes seems valid, the probability of drawing a five of hearts is $1/52$.

As elegant as the method may seem, however, the assumption of equally likely outcomes restricts its applicability because many experiments have sample spaces composed of non-equally likely sample points. There are two other methods of assigning probabilities.

The Relative Frequency Method

This method of assigning probabilities is based more on real-world empirical observation than on theoretical assumptions about the likelihood of any experimental outcome, a fact that makes its use appropriate both when the assumption of equally likely outcomes is valid as well as when it is not. Consider the application of this method in Example 4.9.

Example 4.9. A sales manager wants to estimate the probability that customers will buy her company's new product. When her sales force calls on potential customers, we can view this as an experiment with two outcomes, S ={sale, no sale}. Applying the classical method of assigning probabilities to these two outcomes, we have p(sale) = p(no sale) = 0.50. The problem is that since there is no reason to assume that these two outcomes are equally likely, the classical method of assigning probabilities is clearly an inappropriate approach.

Instead of using the classical method to assign probabilities, suppose that another approach is taken. In a test market evaluation, 1000 potential customers were contacted, with the result that 250 purchased the product but 750 did not. In effect, the experiment of *contacting a customer* has been repeated 1000 times, and the outcome of *sale* occurred with a frequency of 0.25 while the outcome of *no sale* occurred with a frequency of 0.75. Incorporating this empirically based information, the probabilities are assigned as p(sale) = 0.25 and p(no sale) = 0.75.

The relative frequency method of assigning probabilities works just as well in those situations where the assumption of equally likely outcomes is justified.

The Subjective Method

A final approach to assigning probabilities is the subjective method. The classical and relative frequency methods cannot always be applied to all situations requiring probability assessments because either the experimental outcomes are not equally likely, or the relative frequency data are either unavailable or uncollectable. Consider a simple example.

Example 4.10. Suppose one wanted to predict the outcome of the Euro 2016 soccer championship final. France and Portugal faced one another for the purpose of determining who would carry the day and be crowned champion. In this example, the experiment could be defined as the final match between these two teams, and the sample space could be specified as S = {France wins, France loses}. What method might one use to assign probability estimates to these two outcomes? While the classical method would assign probabilities in the usual way—p(France wins) = p(France loses) = 0.50—there was no reason to assume that these two experimental outcomes were equally likely. Nor was the relative frequency method useful because the two teams had not played a sufficient number of times (in this case, not at all in 2016), and therefore relative frequency data were simply not available. The best approach in this case was to assign probability estimates that were subjectively based on experience, intuition, injury reports, momentum, and so on. By the way, Portugal defeated France 1–0.

4.4 EVENTS AND PROBABILITIES

Before moving on to the basic relationships of probability, we call attention to two additional definitions that will be important to us as we move ahead. We have been using the term *event* rather casually thus far, but we will now provide a more formal definition.

Definition 4.5. Event. An event is a well-defined collection of sample points. By "well-defined" we mean that either the sample points can be identified and listed or, when there are too many to list, we can describe them. An event is a subset of the sample space.

Definition 4.6. Probability of an Event. The probability of an event equals the sum of the probabilities of the sample points comprising that event. If we can identify all the sample points of an experiment, and assign a probability to each, we can compute the probability of any particular event.

Example 4.11. Consider the scheduling problem faced by a large, full-service travel agency, Bon Voyage, in January of this year as it attempts to design holiday packages for people traveling from Toronto, Canada to Mumbai, India for a two-week trip over the December–January period, nearly 11 months in the future. This type of problem is fraught with uncertainy—in terms of the cost and availability of passenger seats on commercial airlines as well as of rooms at Western-style, up-market hotels in the expensive city of Mumbai—and the stakes are high for at least two reasons. First, reservations and payment for flights and hotel accommodations must be made by Bon Voyage to the airlines and hotels far in advance as the December–January travel period is the most congested of the year. Indecision and delay inevitably mean higher costs and poorer choices. Second, since Bon Voyage finds itself in a difficult competitive environment in which it must compete with other types of international travel businesses as well as online travel booking websites, it strives to position itself as offering a highly personalized service in which reliability and good value for money are aspects at which it excels. Accordingly, it is essential that Bon Voyage gets things like scheduling right.

In this case, Bon Voyage wishes to price its India holiday packages at a guaranteed level of $15,000 (Canadian). The risk to which the agency is exposed is that the costs it faces (for air tickets and hotel accommodations) will fluctuate over the course of the year, making it difficult if not impossible to know with certainty what those costs may turn out to be. If the costs float above $15,000, the agency will be forced to sell the packages at an advertised price that will not cover those costs, and it will lose money on each sale.

As a result, Bon Voyage wants to make a realistic assessment of the choices its clients will face in terms of the amount to be paid for (1) two round-trip air tickets between Toronto and Mumbai and (2) a double-room in a luxury hotel. In this connection, the agent in charge examined the costs they incurred on behalf of clients who made the same trip during the most recent Indian holiday travel season.

The agent felt that because of the persistent worldwide economic slump, the prices from the previous travel season would probably remain the same for the approaching travel season. Accordingly, the agent selected a sample of 100 of last season's clients making the India trip with the purpose of identifying the array of airline and hotel prices. Based on the particular carrier and exact travel dates, the expected round-trip airfare for two passengers from Toronto to Mumbai is anticipated to be one of three prices: $5000, $6000, or $7000. For hotel accommodations, the expected cost is also forecasted to be one of three levels: $8000, $9000, or $10,000. From the data, the agent also noted that for 10 of the 100 clients, the airfare was $5000 and the hotel accommodation was $8000; for 17 of the 100 clients, the airfare was $5000, the hotel accommodation was $9000; for 17 clients, the airfare was $5000, the hotel $10,000; and so on. See Table 4.2.

Table 4.2 Nine outcomes and probability assignments for proposed India holiday

1	2	3	4	5	6
Step 1: Airfare	**Step 2: Hotel**	**Experimental outcome**	**Total price of package**	**Number of packages**	**Probability of each outcome**
$5000	$8000	($5000, $8000)	$13,000	10	p($5000, $8000) = 0.10
$5000	$9000	($5000, $9000)	$14,000	17	p($5000, $9000) = 0.17
$5000	$10,000	($5000, $10,000)	$15,000	17	p($5000, $10,000) = 0.17
$6000	$8000	($6000, $8000)	$14,000	15	p($6000, $8000) = 0.15
$6000	$9000	($6000, $9000)	$15,000	12	p($6000, $9000) = 0.12
$6000	$10,000	($6000, $10,000)	$16,000	8	p($6000, $10,000) = 0.08
$7000	$8000	($7000, $8000)	$15,000	11	p($7000, $8000) = 0.11
$7000	$9000	($7000, $9000)	$16,000	6	p($7000, $9000) = 0.06
$7000	$10,000	($7000, $10,000)	$17,000	4	p($7000, $10,000) = 0.04

Since there are three possible values for both airfares (column 1) and accommodations (column 2), there are a total of nine possible outcomes (column 3). From column 4, which sums the two costs, this season's holiday package should cost no less than $13,000 but no more than $17,000. The frequencies of costs, for all 100 clients, are reported in column 5.

Because Bon Voyage intends to price the India holiday package at $15,000, the total cost must come in below that amount. But in view of the information in Table 4.2, how realistic is a $15,000 price? To answer that question, we first define the sample space S.

$$S = \{(\$5K, \$8K), (\$5K, \$9K), (\$5K, \$10K), (\$6K, \$8K), (\$6K, \$9K), (\$6K, \$10K), (\$7K, \$8K), (\$7K, \$9K), (\$7K, \$10K)\}.$$

Let E be the event that the cost comes in at exactly $15,000. Since an event is simply a collection of sample points, E can be defined as

$$E = \{(\$5K, \$10K), (\$6K, \$9K), (\$7K, \$8K)\}.$$

Because the probability of an event equals the sum of the probabilities comprising that event, the probability of event E can be calculated (see column 6 of Table 4.2):

$$p(E) = p(\$5K, \$10K) + p(\$6K, \$9K) + p(\$7K, \$8K) = 0.17 + 0.12 + 0.11 = 0.40.$$

Thus, if the costs for next winter's packages are the same as they were during the previous holiday period, there is a 0.40 probability that they will come to \$15,000.

Similarly, if G is the event that the cost will be greater than \$15,000, then

$$G = \{(\$6K, \$10K), (\$7K, \$9K), (\$7K, \$10K)\}$$

and

$$p(G) = p(\$6K, \$10K) + p(\$7K, \$9K) + p(\$7K, \$10K) = 0.08 + 0.06 + 0.04 = 0.18.$$

Thus, assuming the future looks like the past in terms of costs, there is a 0.18 probability that the packages will come in above \$15,000.

Finally, the probability that the costs will be at or below $\$15,000$ equals 1 minus the probability that they will not be. That is, $1 - p(G) = 1 - 0.18 = 0.82$.

This result can be confirmed by simply summing the probabilities of all sample points for which the costs are less than or equal to \$15,000.

Example 4.12. An experiment consists of casting two dice, one red and one blue. Suppose we are interested in the sum of the two values coming up.

Applying the counting rule for the multiple-step experiment, we can see that the number of experimental outcomes for the overall experiment is the product of the number of results on each step. Since there are six possible results for the throw of both the red and blue dice, there are $6 \times 6 = 36$ sample points comprising the sample space:

$$S = \{(1,1), (1,2), (1,3), (1,4), (1,5), (1,6), \ldots, (6,1), (6,2), (6,3), (6,4), (6,5), (6,6)\}.$$

Table 4.3 shows the experimental outcomes in terms of the sums of the two values coming up. The margins at the top and left-hand side of the table indicate the values that the blue and red dice can take. The sums of those two values are entered in the cells.

What is the probability of obtaining a value of 5? To answer this question, let E_5 be the event that the values of the two dice coming up sum to 5:

$$E_5 = \{(4,1), (3,2), (2,3), (1,4)\}$$

so

$$p(E_5) = p(4,1) + p(3,2) + p(2,3) + p(1,4) = 1/36 + 1/36 + 1/36 + 1/36 = 1/9.$$

Table 4.3 Summary table of the sums of all possible values coming up on two dice

	Blue: 1	Blue: 2	Blue: 3	Blue: 4	Blue: 5	Blue: 6
Red: 1	2	3	4	5	6	7
Red: 2	3	4	5	6	7	8
Red: 3	4	5	6	7	8	9
Red: 4	5	6	7	8	9	10
Red: 5	6	7	8	9	10	11
Red: 6	7	8	9	10	11	12

What is the probability of obtaining a value of 4 or less? Let $E_{2,3,4}$ be the event that the values of the two dice coming up sum to 4 or less:

$$E_{2,3,4} = \{(1,1),(2,1),(1,2),(3,1),(2,2),(1,3)\}$$

so

$$p(E_{2,3,4}) = p(1,1) + p(2,1) + p(1,2) + p(3,1) + p(2,2) + p(1,3) = 6/36 = 1/6.$$

4.5 PROBABILITIES OF UNIONS AND INTERSECTIONS OF EVENTS

It is now possible to extend this foundation in a more powerful way. There are many experiments where the number of sample points is impossibly large, or the identification of the sample points (as well as the determination of their associated probabilities) is difficult. In these situations, another approach must be used which builds on several ideas fundamental to the relationships of probability: the complement of an event, the union of two events, the intersection of two events, mutually exclusive events, and independent events. By extending these ideas, it is possible to provide several new approaches to deriving probabilities: the addition law, the multiplication law, and conditional probability.

Definition 4.7. Complement of an Event. Given an event A, the complement of event A, denoted A^c, is the event consisting of all sample points that are not in event A.

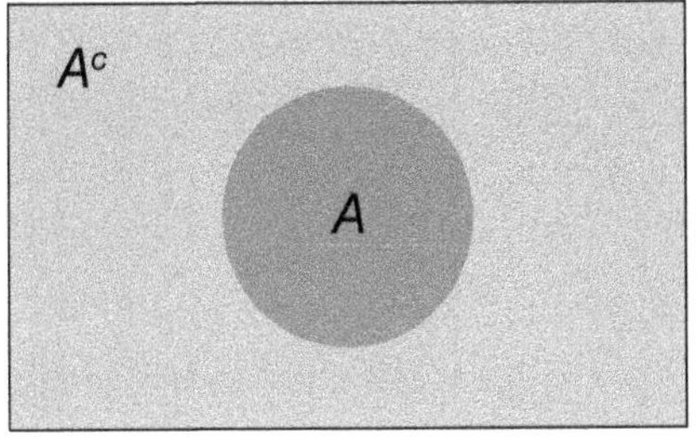

Figure 4.2 Events A and A^c

Figure 4.2 illustrates how the sample space can be partitioned between events A and A^c. In any probability application, either event A or its complement A^c must occur. Therefore, $p(A) + p(A^c) = 1$, and so $p(A) = 1 - p(A^c)$.

Example 4.13. If an experiment consists of tossing three coins, the sample space is

$$S = \{(HHH), (HHT), (HTH), (HTT), (THH), (THT), (TTH), (TTT)\}.$$

If event A consists of all sample points that have at least two heads, then A and A^c are

$$A = \{(HHH), (HHT), (HTH), (THH)\}, \quad A^c = \{(HTT), (THT), (TTH), (TTT)\}.$$

Definition 4.8. Union of Events. The union of two events, A and B, is another, new event containing all the sample points belonging to event A *or* event B *or* both events A and B. This new event is denoted $A \cup B$ (see Figure 4.3).

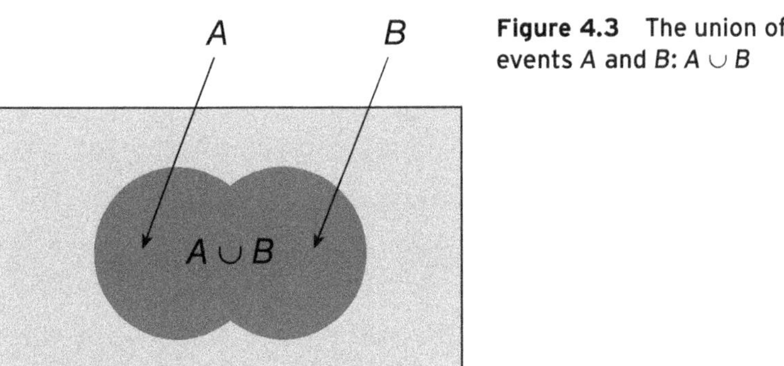

Figure 4.3 The union of events *A* and *B*: $A \cup B$

Definition 4.9. Intersection of Events. The intersection of two events, A and B, is another, new event containing all sample points belonging to *both* events A and B. This new event is denoted $A \cap B$ (see Figure 4.4).

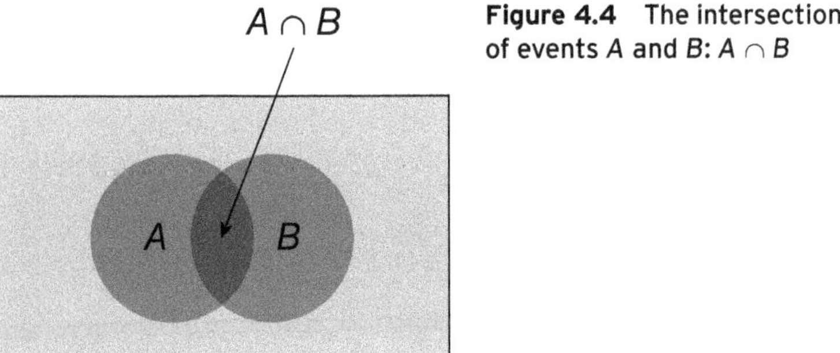

Figure 4.4 The intersection of events *A* and *B*: $A \cap B$

Example 4.14. An experiment consists of rolling a single die. The sample space for this experiment is $S = \{1, 2, 3, 4, 5, 6\}$. Define two events, $A = \{1, 2, 3, 4\}$ and $B = \{3, 4, 5, 6\}$.

What is the event $A \cap B$?

$$A \cap B = \{3, 4\}$$

What is the event $A \cup B$?

$$A \cup B = \{1, 2, 3, 4, 5, 6\}$$

What is the event A^c?

$$A^c = \{5, 6\}$$

What is the event B^c?

$$B^c = \{1, 2\}$$

What is the event $A^c \cup B^c$?

$$A^c \cup B^c = \{1, 2, 5, 6\}$$

What is the event $A^c \cap B^c$?

$$A^c \cap B^c = \{\} = \varnothing$$

where $\varnothing$ denotes the empty set.

Definition 4.10. Addition Law. The addition law provides a way to calculate the probability of event A, event B, or both events A and B. In other words, it provides a way to calculate the probability of the union of two events. It is given by

$$p(A \cup B) = p(A) + p(B) - p(A \cap B).$$

Definition 4.11. Mutually Exclusive Events. Two events are said to be *mutually exclusive* if the events have no sample points in common: $A \cap B = \varnothing$ (see Figure 4.5).

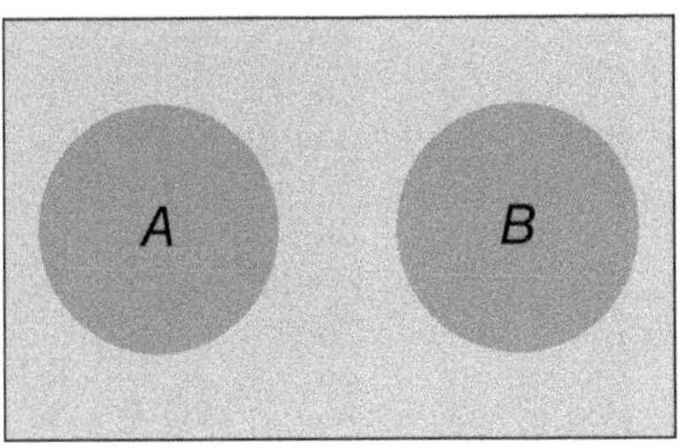

Figure 4.5 The mutually exclusive events *A* and *B*

When $A \cap B = \varnothing$, $p(A \cap B) = 0$. In other words, the probability of finding an element in the event $A \cap B$ is zero. Thus, in the special case when two events have no sample points in common, the addition law collapses to a simpler form:

$$p(A \cup B) = p(A) + p(B) - p(A \cap B)$$

$$= p(A) + p(B) - 0$$

$$= p(A) + p(B).$$

Example 4.15. In Chapter 2, 40 graduate students were identified by their countries of birth; 15 were born in China, 10 in India, 8 in the US, and so on. Define A as the event that a student was born in China, and B as the event a student was born in India. In this case, $A \cap B$ is the event that a student was born in *both* China *and* India. Clearly, this is the empty set and the probability of finding such a person (born both in China and India) is 0. There never could be such a person.

Example 4.16. According to the US Centers for Disease Control and Prevention (CDC), over the 8-year period from 1999 to 2006, an average of 16,375 teenagers died each year in the US. Among the leading causes of death are accidents (7860), homicide (2129), and suicide (1801). Let A, H, and S represent the events that a person dies from accident, homicide, or suicide, respectively. What are $p(A)$, $p(H)$, and $p(S)$? They are

$$p(A) = 7860 / 16{,}375 = 0.48,$$

$$p(H) = 2129 / 16{,}375 = 0.13,$$

$$p(S) = 1801 / 16{,}375 = 0.11.$$

Are the events A and H mutually exclusive? Yes, if one assumes that a person can die of only one primary cause, then the event $A \cap H$ is an empty set, and $p(A \cap H) = 0$.
What is the probability a person dies from an accident or homicide?

$$p(A \cup H) = p(A) + p(H) - p(A \cap H) = 0.48 + 0.13 - 0.00 = 0.61$$

What is the probability a person dies from homicide or suicide?

$$p(H \cup S) = p(H) + p(S) - p(H \cap S) = 0.13 + 0.11 - 0.00 = 0.24$$

What is the probability that someone dies from a cause other than from A, H, or S?

$$1 - [p(A) + p(H) + p(S)] = 1 - [0.48 + 0.13 + 0.11] = 1 - 0.72 = 0.28$$

4.6 CONDITIONAL PROBABILITY

We are now in a position to discuss two important and powerful probability ideas: conditional probability and Bayes' theorem. In many probability situations, it is useful to be able to determine the probability of an event given that another event is known to have occurred. Let event A have probability $p(A)$. If another (possibly related) event B has occurred, it is possible to incorporate this new information in calculating the probability of event A. This idea is written $p(A \mid B)$, and is read "the probability of A given B."

Definition 4.12. Conditional Probability. The conditional probability of A given B is the probability of event A given that the condition designated as event B is known to exist.

The formal definition of conditional probability is

$$p(A \mid B) = \frac{p(A \cap B)}{p(B)}.$$

Example 4.17. Although the records of the 2218 people traveling on the ill-fated *Titanic* ocean liner on April 15, 1912 are incomplete, many researchers agree on the composition of survivors among the passengers and crew: 488 of the 1300 passengers survived the disaster, while 215 of the 918 crew members did (see Table 4.4).

Table 4.4 Cross-tabulation table of survivors among *Titanic* crew and passengers

	Passenger (*P*)	Crew member (*C*)	Totals
Survived (*S*)	488	215	703
Did not survive (S^c)	812	703	1515
Totals	1300	918	2218

A journalist wrote in a newspaper column that the *Titanic* crew members were more likely to survive the shipwreck than were the *Titanic* passengers, pointing out that of the 1515 people to perish that night, 812 were passengers while only 703 were crew members. A reader claiming to be a descendant of one of the surviving crew members wrote a letter to the editor disputing the journalist's conclusion, claiming that the reverse was actually true, and that crew members were more likely to die than the passengers on the *Titanic*.

Conditional probability can shed light on this question. Define the following four events:

P is the event that a person was a passenger on the *Titanic*.

C is the event that a person was a crew member on the *Titanic*.

S is the event that a person survived.

S^c is the event that a person did not survive.

Sometimes it is helpful to think about certain probability problems in terms of a ball-and-urn framework. Suppose that an urn contains 2218 balls, and that each ball has painted on it a pair of letters, either P or C (denoting *passenger* or *crew member*) and S or S^c (indicating *survivor* or *not survivor*). Suppose further that the 2218 balls are apportioned in exactly the same combination as the passenger/crew data in Table 4.4: 488 balls have the letters P and S; 215 balls have C and S; 812 balls have P and S^c; and 703 balls have C and S^c. After stirring the contents of the urn, draw a single ball at random; or, what is exactly the same process, randomly select a single person from the list of 2218 passengers and crew members. Here are a few questions:

1 What is the probability that a randomly selected person is both a passenger and a survivor? That is, what is $p(P \cap S)$?

$$p(P \cap S) = 488 / 2218 = 0.2200$$

2 What is the probability that a randomly selected person is both a passenger and someone who did not survive? That is, what is $p(P \cap S^c)$?

$$p(P \cap S^c) = 812 / 2218 = 0.3661$$

3 What is the probability that a randomly selected person is both a crew member and a survivor?

$$p(C \cap S) = 215 / 2218 = 0.0969$$

4 What is the probability that a randomly selected person is both a crew member and someone who did not survive?

$$p(C \cap S^c) = 703 / 2218 = 0.3170$$

Now to derive the marginal probabilities, we find $p(P), p(C), p(S)$, and $p(S^c)$.

5 What is the probability that a randomly drawn person will be a passenger? To answer this question, add the probabilities of the two ways a passenger could be selected: (a) passenger and survivor and (b) passenger and non-survivor. That is,

$$p(P) = p(P \cap S) + p(P \cap S^c) = 0.2200 + 0.3661 = 0.5861$$

6 What is the probability that a randomly selected person will be a crew member?

$$p(C) = p(C \cap S) + p(C \cap S^c) = 0.0969 + 0.3170 = 0.4139$$

7 What is the probability that a randomly selected person will be a survivor?

$$p(S) = p(S \cap P) + p(S \cap C) = 0.2200 + 0.0969 = 0.3169$$

8 What is the probability that a randomly selected person will be a non-survivor?

$$p(S^c) = p(S^c \cap P) + p(S^c \cap C) = 0.3661 + 0.3170 = 0.6831$$

Now we organize the answers to questions 1–8 (above) in Table 4.5.

Table 4.5 Table of joint probabilities and marginal probabilities

	P	C	Totals
S	$p(P \cap S) = 0.2200$	$p(C \cap S) = 0.0969$	$p(S) = 0.3169$
S^c	$p(P \cap S^c) = 0.3661$	$p(C \cap S^c) = 0.3170$	$p(S^c) = 0.6831$
Totals	$p(P) = 0.5861$	$p(C) = 0.4139$	1.0000

Table 4.5 is referred to as a *joint probability table*. The joint probabilities are the probabilities of the intersection of two events; they are entered in the cells of the table. The marginal probabilities are the probabilities of one event taken separately; they are entered in the margins of the table. Each probability value is derived from the data in Table 4.4.

Conditional probability makes it possible to resolve the issue of whether the passengers on the *Titanic* were less likely to survive than the crew members. The answer lies not in the relative number of passengers and crew members who survived or died, but in comparing the probability that a crew member survived with the probability that a passenger survived. More formally, does $p(S|C)$ exceed $p(S|P)$?

Recall that $p(S|P)$ denotes the probability of event S (survival) given that the condition designated as event P (the person is a passenger) is known to exist. Thus, $p(S|P)$ is concerned only with the survival status of the 1300 passengers. What proportion of the 1300 passengers survived? Using the data from either Table 4.4,

$$p(S|P) = 488 / 1300 = 0.3754,$$

or the probabilities from Table 4.5,

$$p(S|P) = \frac{p(S \cap P)}{p(P)} = \frac{0.2200}{0.5861} = 0.3754,$$

it is clear that there was a 37.54% chance of survival if the person was a passenger.

What proportion of the 918 crew members survived? Using the original raw data from Table 4.4,

$$p(S|C) = 215 / 918 = 0.2342,$$

or the probabilities from Table 4.5,

$$p(S|C) = \frac{p(S \cap C)}{p(C)} = \frac{0.0969}{0.4139} = 0.2342,$$

we see that there was a 23.42% chance of survival if a person was a crew member.

Comparing the conditional probabilities, $p(S|P)$ and $p(S|C)$, it seems the newspaper columnist misinterpreted the meaning of the data, perhaps because he knew nothing about the explanatory power of conditional probability. Since $p(S \mid P) > p(S \mid C)$, it is clear that crew members were more likely than passengers to have perished on the *Titanic*.

Before moving on to Bayes' theorem, we consider two additional topics that are relevant to conditional probability: independent events and the multiplication law.

Definition 4.13. Independent Events. Two events A and B are said to be independent if $p(A \mid B) = p(A)$, or, what is the same thing, $p(B \mid A) = p(B)$. Otherwise, events A and B are not independent.

In the example concerning those aboard the *Titanic*, it has been found that survival and crew member/passenger role are not independent since $p(S|P) \neq p(S)$. The fact that someone was a passenger, and not a crew member, improves their chances of survival.

We now consider the multiplication law for two events, A and B. Recall that the addition law provides the probability of the union of two events. What the multiplication law does is make it possible to find the probability of the intersection of two events.

Definition 4.14. Multiplication Law. The multiplication law provides a way to calculate the probability of *both* event A *and* event B. In other words, it provides a way to calculate the probability of the intersection of two events. It can be derived from the expression for conditional probability:

$$p(A \mid B) = \frac{p(A \cap B)}{p(B)}$$

or

$$p(A \cap B) = p(A \mid B)p(B).$$

If events A and B are independent, however, this expression collapses to a simpler form. That is, since $p(A \mid B) = p(A)$ when events A and B are independent, we have

$$p(A \cap B) = p(A \mid B)p(B) = p(A)p(B).$$

Thus the form of the multiplication law depends on whether the events A and B are independent:

1. $p(A \cap B) = p(A \mid B)p(B)$, if the events A and B are not independent.
2. $p(A \cap B) = p(A)p(B)$, if the events are independent.

Example 4.18. A movie theater conducts weeknight promotions in which coupons can be redeemed for free admission by any couple if one member pays the full price. If a couple appears bearing one coupon, both are admitted for the price of one adult. Historically, 30% of couples redeem the coupons. What is the probability that the next two couples redeem coupons? Let A and B be the events that the first and second couples redeem a coupon, respectively, so that $A \cap B$ is the event that both couples redeem a coupon. Assuming that the events A and B are independent,

$$p(A \cap B) = p(A)p(B) = 0.30 \times 0.30 = 0.09.$$

4.7 BAYES' THEOREM

By now, it is clear that revising probabilities by incorporating new information can be an important phase of probability analysis. In the previous example concerning persons on the *Titanic*, the probability of survival was 0.3169 (see Table 4.5). But when information about whether the person was a passenger or crew member is incorporated into the probability assessment, the probability changed: $p(S \mid P) = 0.3754$ but $p(S \mid C) = 0.2342$ (see Section 4.6). In a similar way, Bayesian analysis begins with initial or *prior probability* estimates for the specific events of interest. If additional relevant information about these events becomes available, the prior probability values can be updated by calculating revised probabilities, referred to as *posterior probabilities*. Bayes' theorem provides a method for making these new probability calculations.

Example 4.19. As an example of how Bayes' theorem can be applied, consider the following story appearing in the *Wall Street Journal*, "On Orbitz, Mac Users Steered to Pricier Hotels" (June 26, 2012). The article describes how internet-based companies employ data-mining methods with the purpose of defining and targeting different market segments. As an example, if Orbitz, the online travel-booking retailer, knows that a website visitor is using a Mac, it assumes that the visitor is a less price-sensitive consumer since Mac users have a higher mean income than non-Mac users.

Let S denote the event that a website visitor is price-sensitive, I the event that the visitor is price-insensitive. Suppose that market research has shown that 60% of visitors to the Orbitz website are considered price-sensitive while 40% are thought to be price-insensitive. Thus, in randomly selecting a shopper from among those visiting the website each day, the prior probabilities are $p(S) = 0.60$ and $p(I) = 0.40$. Note that these prior probabilities are derived from the prior knowledge of how the two types of shoppers are distributed across the population of website visitors.

Suppose also that price-insensitive consumers are thought to be four times as likely to use a Mac than are price-sensitive consumers. If M is the event that a website visitor is using a Mac, then the relationship between Mac users and price-sensitivity can be expressed as follows: $p(M \mid I) = 0.80$ and $p(M \mid S) = 0.20$. Although these values of $p(M \mid I)$ and $p(M \mid S)$ have been selected arbitrarily, any two values for the conditional probabilities can be used in this analysis as long as their ratio to one another is 4 to 1.

Bayesian analysis can be used to update the prior probabilities, $p(S)$ and $p(I)$, by incorporating the information expressed in the conditional probabilities, $p(M \mid S)$ and $p(M \mid I)$. That is, in applying Bayesian analysis, we move from the left-hand to the right-hand sides of the arrows below:

$$p(S) \Rightarrow p(S \mid M),$$

$$p(I) \Rightarrow p(I \mid M).$$

One method of updating the prior probabilities to the posterior probabilities is the tabular approach. As the name implies, this method involves organizing all the information in a table (see Table 4.6).

Table 4.6 Bayesian tabular method of organizing probabilities for price-sensitivity problem

1	2	3	4	5
Events	**Prior probabilities**	**Conditional probabilities**	**Joint probabilities**	**Posterior probabilities**
S	$p(S) = 0.60$	$p(M \mid S) = 0.20$	$p(M \cap S) = 0.120$	$p(M \mid S) = 0.273$
I	$p(I) = 0.40$	$p(M \mid I) = 0.80$	$p(M \cap I) = 0.320$	$p(I \mid M) = 0.727$
	1.00	1.00	$p(M) = 0.440$	1.00

Table 4.6 organizes the above information in columns 1, 2, and 3. For column 4, the multiplication law is applied to the information in columns 2 and 3 to provide joint probabilities. That is, the entries in column 4 are the result of the product of the entries in columns 2 and 3. Note that when the column 4 entries are summed, they provide the marginal probability that a website visitor is using a Mac: $p(M) = p(M \cap S) + p(M \cap I)$. Put another way, to find the probability that any randomly selected website visitor is a Mac user, we simply add the probabilities of the two ways a visitor could be a Mac user: the probability that a visitor is price-sensitive *and* a Mac user, plus the probability that a visitor is price-insensitive *and* a Mac user. Column 5 reports the posterior probabilities, and its entries are found by a simple application of the expression for conditional probabilities:

$$p(S \mid M) = \frac{p(M \cap S)}{p(M)} = \frac{0.120}{0.440} = 0.273,$$

$$p(I \mid M) = \frac{p(M \cap I)}{p(M)} = \frac{0.320}{0.440} = 0.727.$$

Thus, the Bayesian tabular method makes it possible to incorporate the new information (i.e., the relation between price-insensitivity and Mac use) into the prior probabilities. In this case, it is not surprising that the posterior probabilities differ considerably from the prior probabilities. After all, since Mac use is a characteristic more strongly associated with price-insensitivity, the probability that a Mac-using website visitor is price-insensitive should be higher:

$$p(S) = 0.60 \Rightarrow p(S \mid M) = 0.273,$$

$$p(I) = 0.40 \Rightarrow p(I \mid M) = 0.727.$$

Accordingly, Orbitz is no doubt wise to direct the Mac-using website visitor to higher-priced accommodations and transportation alternatives.

Although most students prefer using the tabular method of working out posterior probabilities, here is a more general formulation of Bayes' theorem:

Given an event A and K mutually exclusive, collectively exhaustive events, $B_1, B_2, \ldots, B_k$,

$$p(B_i \mid A) = \frac{p(B_i \cap A)}{p(A)}$$

$$= \frac{p(A \mid B_i)p(B_i)}{p(A)}$$

$$= \frac{p(A \mid B_i)p(B_i)}{p(A \mid B_1)p(B_1) + p(A \mid B_2)p(B_2) + \ldots + p(A \mid B_k)p(B_k)}.$$

Finally, note that the posterior probabilities sum to 1 just as did the prior probabilities. Bayes' theorem has provided a formal method for incorporating this new and relevant information in a logically clear manner.

SUMMARY

As we bridge what may seem like a gap between descriptive statistics, probability, and statistics (the three areas covered in this book), a clearer picture of the rationale for both the inclusion and sequencing of these topics begins to emerge. The three areas are introduced in this order because they build on one another. The methods used to solve probability problems could not be effectively applied by someone unfamiliar with some of the concepts from descriptive statistics, such as the mean, standard deviation, cross-tabulation tables, and frequency distributions. Moreover, problems involving statistical estimation and inference cannot be solved, or perhaps even understood, by someone who is unaware of how to use probability distributions—topics we consider in Chapters 5 and 6.

In this chapter, too, we have introduced a number of concepts which build on one another: probability, experiment, sample space, methods of assigning probabilities to events, mutually exclusive events, independence, conditional probability, and Bayes' theorem. These ideas provide the very foundation for most of what comes later in the book.

We can think of probability as the mathematical language of uncertainty. Every day, each of us must make decisions—and draw conclusions—based on incomplete information. This is true whether we are scientists, engineers, financial investors, social scientists, or ordinary people attempting to navigate day-to-day life, and we must make those decisions in the face of uncertainty about how well they will turn out to be. While probability alone does not tell us how to make decisions or draw conclusions, it does give us ways of evaluating the level of risk to which we are exposed when making a decision or drawing a conclusion. Ultimately, probability reflects a thoughtful attempt to come to grips with the uncertainty characterizing much of life.

definitions

Addition Law A probability relation which makes it possible to compute the probability of the union of two events: $p(A \cup B) = p(A) + p(B) - p(A \cap B)$.

Bayes' Theorem A method for obtaining updated posterior probabilities which incorporates additional, relevant information into prior probabilities.

Classical Method of Assigning Probabilities The classical method of assigning probabilities rests on the assumption of equally likely outcomes.

Complement of an Event Given an event A, the complement of A, denoted A^c, is defined to be the event consisting of all sample points that *are not in event A*.

Conditional Probability The conditional probability of A given B is the probability of event A given that the condition designated as event B is known to exist.

Event An event is a well-defined collection of sample points.

Experiment An experiment is a process that results in well-defined outcomes. If an experiment is performed, one and only one of the possible outcomes can occur.

Independent Events Two events A and B are independent if $p(A \mid B) = p(A)$ or $p(B \mid A) = p(B)$. Otherwise, events A and B are not independent.

Intersection of Events The intersection of events A and B, denoted $A \cap B$, is the event containing all sample points belonging to both A and B.

Joint Probability Found in the cells of the joint probability table, joint probabilities are probabilities of the intersection of two events.

Marginal Probability Found in the margins of the joint probability table, marginal probabilities are the probabilities of the events taken separately.

Multiplication Law The multiplication law provides a way to calculate the probability of *both* event A *and* event B. In other words, it provides a way to calculate the probability of the intersection of two events.

Mutually Exclusive Events Mutually exclusive events have no sample points in common. Since $A \cap B = \varnothing$, it follows that $p(A \cap B) = 0$.

Posterior Probability In Bayesian analysis, the posterior probability is the conditional probability of an event once the new information has been incorporated.

Prior Probability In Bayesian analysis, the prior probability of an event is the probability of that event before any new information has been introduced.

Probability Probability is a numerical measure of the likelihood that an outcome will occur; it can assume values between 0 and 1 (inclusive).

Probability of an Event Adding up the probabilities of the sample points in an event provides the probability of that event.

Relative Frequency Method of Assigning Probabilities An empirically based method of assigning probability to events based on the ratio of favorable cases to the total number of cases.

Sample Point A sample point is an element of the sample space. It is any one particular experimental outcome.

Sample Space Each experiment has associated with it a sample space that is the set of all possible experimental outcomes.

Subjective Method of Assigning Probabilities A personalized method of assigning probability to events based on individual hunches, intuition, or instinct. This method is appropriate when the other methods of assigning probabilities–the classical or relative frequency methods–cannot be used.

Union of Events The union of events A and B, denoted $A \cup B$, is the event containing all the sample points belonging to A or B or both A and B.

formulae

Addition Law for Two Mutually Exclusive Events

$p(A \cup B) = p(A) + p(B)$

Addition Law for Two Non-mutually Exclusive Events

$p(A \cup B) = p(A) + p(B) - p(A \cap B)$

Bayes' Theorem Given an event A and K mutually exclusive, collectively B_1, B_2 exhaustive events, $B_1, B_2, \ldots, B_k$,

$$p(B_i \mid A) = \frac{p(B_i \cap A)}{p(A)}$$

$$= \frac{p(A \mid B_i)p(B_i)}{p(A)}$$

$$= \frac{p(A \mid B_i)p(B_i)}{p(A \mid B_1)p(B_1) + p(A \mid B_2)p(B_2) + \ldots + p(A \mid B_k)p(B_k)}$$

Conditional Probability

$$p(A \mid B) = \frac{p(A \cap B)}{p(B)}$$

$$p(B \mid A) = \frac{p(A \cap B)}{p(A)}$$

Counting Rule for Combinations

$$C_n^N = \binom{N}{n} = \frac{N!}{n!(N-n)!}$$

Counting Rule for Permutations

$$P_n^N = n!C_n^N = n!\binom{N}{n} = n!\frac{N!}{n!(N-n)!} = \frac{N!}{(N-n)!}$$

Multiplication Law for Independent Events

$p(A \cap B) = p(A)\,p(B)$

Multiplication Law for Non-independent Events

$p(A \cap B) = p(A \mid B)p(B)$

Probability of an Event in Terms of its Complement

$p(A) = 1 - p(A^c)$

R functions

`choose(N, n)` Number of combinations of n objects drawn from a larger set of N.

`factorial(N)` Provides $N!$ (factorial) and equals $N(N-1)(N-2)\ldots(2)(1)$.

`factorial(N)/factorial(N - n)` Number of permutations of n objects drawn from a larger set of N.

exercises

4.1 If we have a two-step experiment in which we flip a coin and cast a die, how many outcomes are there for the entire experiment? Using H for heads and T for tails, write out the entire sample space.

4.2 In one of the best-known versions of the card game of Solitaire, cards are dealt from a deck of 52 cards. How many different hands of 7 cards can be drawn from 52? Use R to find the answer.

4.3 Consider a class of first-year statistics students in which 20 undergraduate students are enrolled. What is the probability that two or more students will be found to share the same birthday? As a simplifying assumption, ignore leap years. Use R to find the answer. Hint: recall that the probability of an event A equals 1 minus the probability of the complement of that event, A^c: i.e., $p(A) = 1 - p(A^c)$.

4.4 The following data from a sample of 100 families show the record of college attendance by fathers and their oldest sons: in 22 families, both father and the son attended college; in 31 families, neither father nor son attended college; in 12 families, the father attended college while the son did not; and in 35 families, the son attended college but the father did not.

(a) What is the probability a son attended college given that his father attended college?

Organizing this information in a simple table

	Son Attended	Son Did Not	Totals
Father Attended	22	12	34
Father Did Not	35	31	66
Totals	57	43	100

Define the following events

S_c is event that the son attended college
S_n is event that the son did not attend college
F_c is event that the father attended college
F_n is event that the father did not attend college

(b) What is the probability a son attended college given that his father did not attend college?
(c) Is attending college by the son independent of whether his father attended college?

4.5 Consider the following facts: (a) in random testing, you test positive for a disease; (b) all people who have the disease test positive for it; (c) in 5% of the cases, this test shows positive even when a person does not have the disease (that is, there is a 5% chance of a *false positive*); and (d) in the population-at-large, one person in a thousand has the disease. What is the probability that you have the disease? Hint: define the following events: D is event person has the disease; D^c is event person does not have the disease; P is event person tests positive for the disease.

https://study.sagepub.com/stinerock

Discrete Probability Distributions

contents

learning objectives

1. Understand the concepts of a random variable and a probability distribution.
2. Be able to distinguish between discrete and continuous random variables.
3. Be able to compute and interpret the expected value, variance, and standard deviation of a discrete random variable.
4. Be able to compute and work with probabilities involving the binomial, Poisson, and hypergeometric probability distributions.
5. Learn to use R in connection with the binomial, Poisson, and hypergeometric probability distributions.

In Chapter 4 we introduced and developed some important ideas which form the fundamental building blocks of probability and statistics. We saw how to apply some of these ideas in practical ways, particularly in connection with conditional probability and Bayes' theorem. In the next two chapters, we expand on this discussion by considering discrete and continuous probability distributions. In doing so, we once again appreciate just how practical and powerful these tools, methods, and ways of thinking can be.

5.1 SOME IMPORTANT DEFINITIONS

Before introducing any new definitions, we begin by reminding the reader of three important definitions from Chapter 4: an experiment, a sample space, and a sample point.

Definition 5.1. Experiment. An experiment is any process that can result in one of several well-defined outcomes that cannot be predicted with certainty beforehand. Whenever an experiment is performed, one and only one of the possible experimental results can occur.

Definition 5.2. Sample Space. Each experiment has associated with it a sample space that is the set of all possible experimental outcomes.

Definition 5.3. Sample Point. A sample point is an element of the sample space. It is any one particular experimental outcome.

We now turn to some new definitions and ideas.

Definition 5.4. Random Variable. A random variable is a function that assigns numerical values to the result of an experiment.

Definition 5.5. Discrete Random Variable. A discrete random variable assumes a countable number of distinct values, either finite or infinite in number.

Definition 5.6. Continuous Random Variable. A continuous random variable may take on any value in an interval or series of intervals.

A random variable can be either discrete or continuous, depending on the numerical values it assumes. A discrete random variable assumes either a finite number of values, in the case of the binomial probability distribution, or an infinite sequence of values, as with the Poisson probability distribution. (Both distributions are covered in this chapter.) What is meant by an "infinite sequence of values" can be misunderstood, but an example should clarify the meaning. The number of vehicles driving over San Francisco's Golden Gate Bridge each day is a discrete random variable which assumes an infinite sequence of values. While the number of vehicles can be very large, it is not infinite. The term "infinite sequence" simply means that the uppermost limit on the number is unknown.

A continuous random variable, on the other hand, may assume any numerical value in an interval. Since this is a topic covered in Chapter 6, it will not be discussed further here.

For any given experiment, it is possible to define many different random variables. For example, if the experiment is to observe the vehicles crossing the Golden Gate Bridge over a 24-hour period, one random variable x might be the number of automobiles bearing California license plates; another random variable y could be the number of trucks with out-of-state license plates; and still another random variable z might be the number of vehicles that are pulled over for safety inspection. Any random variable (x, y, or z) is a function that assigns numerical values to the outcome of the experiment. In this case, we have one experiment—observing vehicles crossing the bridge—but three random variables, each of which provides a numerical characterization of the experimental outcome.

Here are two additional new definitions.

Definition 5.7. Probability Distribution. A probability distribution for a random variable reports the way the probabilities are distributed across the various values the random variable can take on.

Definition 5.8. Probability Function. A probability function provides for each value the probability the random variable can assume.

Example 5.1. As an illustration of a discrete random variable and its probability distribution, consider the sales data from a retail business, Phoenix Appliances. Over the past 100 days of business, sales records show that Phoenix sells anywhere from 0 to 6 air conditioners each day. If the random variable x is the number of units sold in a single day, the random variable can take on seven values: 0, 1, 2, 3, 4, 5, or 6.

No. of units sold, x	No. of days	$f(x)$
0	10	10 / 100 = 0.10
1	14	14 / 100 = 0.14
2	21	21 / 100 = 0.21
3	28	28 / 100 = 0.28
4	17	17 / 100 = 0.17
5	8	8 / 100 = 0.08
6	2	2 / 100 = 0.02
	100	1.00

Table 5.1 A tabular representation of the discrete probability distribution

Table 5.1 reports the distribution of unit sales over all 100 days. We note that on 10 days, no air conditioners were sold; on 14 days, 1 unit was sold; on 21 days, 2 were sold; and so on. The left-hand and right-hand columns of Table 5.1 form the probability distribution: the probability function $f(x)$ provides the probability for each value that the random variable x can assume. Figure 5.1 is a picture of the same information: a graphical depiction of the probability distribution of x in terms of $f(x)$.

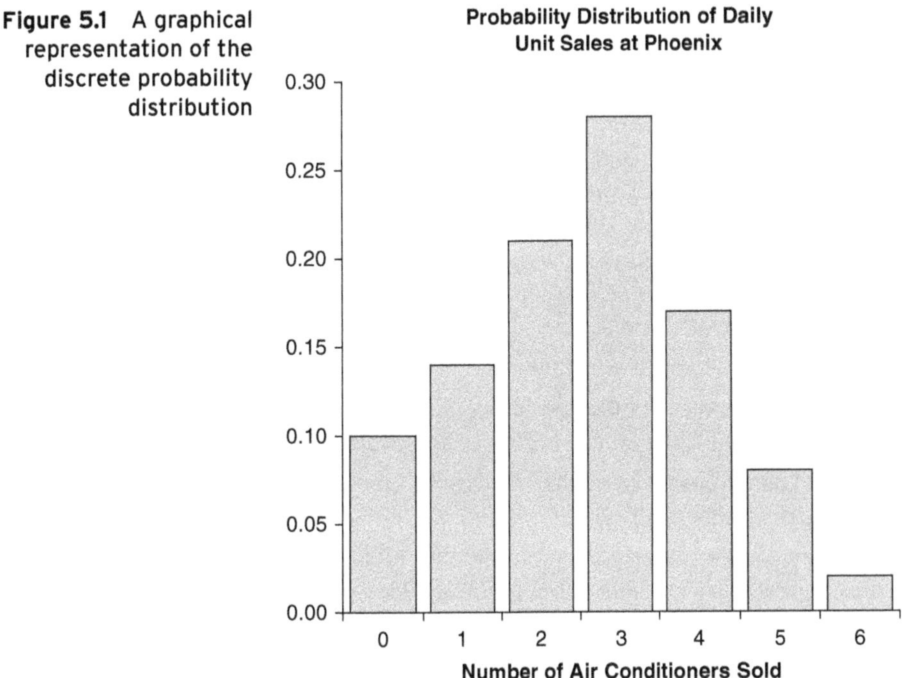

Figure 5.1 A graphical representation of the discrete probability distribution

The discrete probability function $f(x)$ must always satisfy the following two requirements:

1 $0 \leq f(x) \leq 1$, or the probability function is bounded by 0 and 1.
2 $\Sigma f(x) = 1$, or the sum of all probabilities must equal 1.

In addition to tabular and graphical methods of reporting a discrete probability distribution (Table 5.1 and Figure 5.1), it is possible to use a formula that gives $f(x)$ for each value of x. In this chapter, we consider four such discrete probability distributions: the discrete uniform, the binomial, the Poisson, and the hypergeometric probability distributions.

 THE DISCRETE UNIFORM PROBABILITY DISTRIBUTION

Since the formula for the probability function for the discrete uniform probability distribution is very simple, it makes sense to begin here.

Definition 5.9. Discrete Uniform Probability Distribution. This is the probability distribution of a random variable for which all values of x are equally likely. The probability function $f(x)$ of the discrete uniform probability distribution is

$$f(x) = \frac{1}{n},$$

where n is equal to the number of values the random variable x might take on. In this instance, the values the random variable x might assume are all equally likely.

Example 5.2. An experiment consists of the roll of a single die. What is the probability function and probability distribution? Figure 5.2 shows the distribution of outcomes.

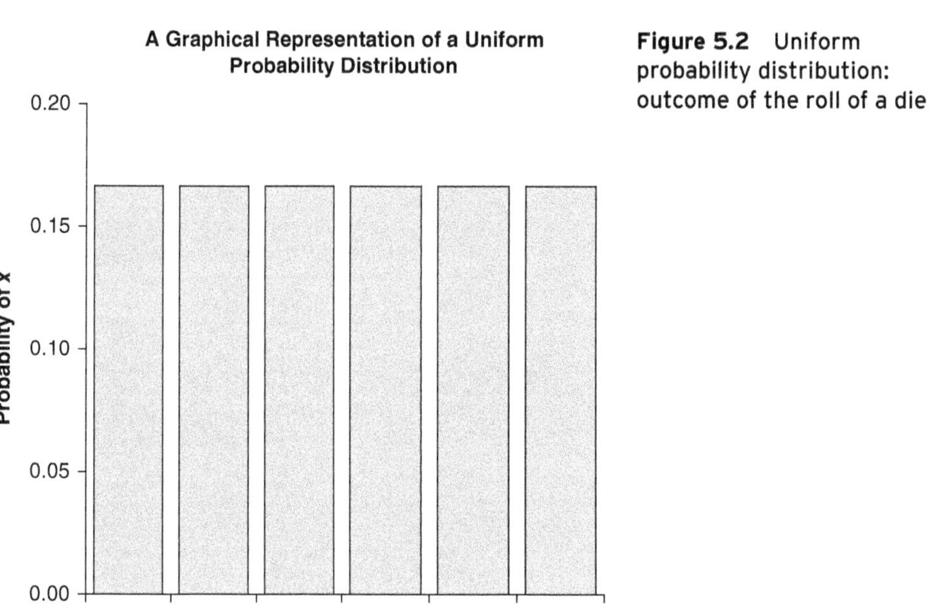

Figure 5.2 Uniform probability distribution: outcome of the roll of a die

For this experiment, the sample space is $S = \{1, 2, 3, 4, 5, 6\}$. Let the random variable x be the number coming up when the die is rolled. Since n is the number of values x might take on, the probability function is

$$f(x) = \frac{1}{n} = \frac{1}{6} = 0.1667.$$

Thus the probability distribution is as follows:

x	1	2	3	4	5	6
$f(x)$	1/6	1/6	1/6	1/6	1/6	1/6

5.3 THE EXPECTED VALUE AND STANDARD DEVIATION OF A DISCRETE RANDOM VARIABLE

The expected value and standard deviation are properties of each random variable.

Definition 5.10. Expected Value. The expected value of a discrete random variable x, $E(x)$, is the weighted value or mean of all values of the random variable:

$$E(x) = \mu = \sum x f(x).$$

Definition 5.11. Variance. The variance of a discrete random variable x, $\text{Var}(x)$, captures the degree of dispersion of all values of the random variable:

$$\text{Var}(x) = \sigma^2 = \sum (x - \mu)^2 f(x).$$

As with the measures of the characteristics of a set of data (see Chapter 3), the standard deviation of a discrete random variable is often the preferred measure of dispersion because it is expressed in the same units as the expected value and the original data.

Definition 5.12. Standard Deviation. The standard deviation of a discrete random variable x is the positive square root of the variance:

$$\sigma = \sqrt{\sigma^2} = \sqrt{\sum (x - \mu)^2 f(x)}.$$

Table 5.2 Calculations for air conditioner daily units sales data

1	2	3	4	5	6
x	$f(x)$	$xf(x)$	$(x - \mu)$	$(x - \mu)^2$	$(x - \mu)^2 f(x)$
0	0.10	0.00	−2.60	6.76	0.6760
1	0.14	0.14	−1.60	2.56	0.3584
2	0.21	0.42	−0.60	0.36	0.0756
3	0.28	0.84	0.40	0.16	0.0448
4	0.17	0.68	1.40	1.96	0.3332
5	0.08	0.40	2.40	5.76	0.4608
6	0.02	0.12	3.40	11.56	0.2312
		$E(x) = 2.60$			$\sigma^2 = 2.1801$

Table 5.2 shows the calculations for the mean and standard deviation of the air-conditioning sales data from Phoenix Appliances. Thus, from column 3, the mean is

$$E(x) = \mu = 2.60 \text{ units}.$$

That is, on an average day, Phoenix Appliances can expect to sell between two and three units.

The entries in column 6 of Table 5.2 are the product of the entries in columns 2 and 5. Note that, unlike the variance, the standard deviation is expressed in the same units of measurement as the original data and the mean. Thus,

$$\sigma = \sqrt{\sigma^2} = \sqrt{2.1801} = 1.4765 \text{ units.}$$

For this reason, many of the statistical methods we encounter in this book make use of the mean as the measure of central tendency (not the median or the mode) and the standard deviation (not the interquartile range or the variance) as the preferred measure of dispersion.

THE BINOMIAL PROBABILITY DISTRIBUTION

Our second discrete probability distribution is the well-known binomial.

Definition 5.13. Binomial Probability Distribution. The binomial probability distribution describes how probabilities are distributed across the values the random variable may assume under conditions characterized by what is called the *binomial experiment*. There are five properties of the binomial experiment, and before the binomial can be applied to any problem, we must be sure that all five properties are satisfied. Otherwise, there is no binomial experiment, and the use of the binomial would be inappropriate. The properties are as follows:

1 The overall experiment is composed of a series of n identical trials.
2 On each trial, there are two possible results, designated S (success) and F (failure).
3 From trial to trial, the probability of success, $p(S) = p$, is unchanging.
4 The trials are independent.
5 The question of interest is: what is the probability of x successes in n trials?

A few small-scale examples illustrate what is meant by each of the conditions.

Example 5.3. What is the probability of two heads in three coin tosses?

First, let us make sure that the problem satisfies all five properties of the binomial experiment:

1 The overall experiment is composed of a series of n identical trials.

In this case, each toss of the coin can be thought of as a single trial; the three tosses of the coin make up the three trials. Thus, the overall experiment has $n = 3$ identical trials.

2 On each trial, there are two possible results, designated S (success) and F (failure).

In the case of tossing a coin, one might designate the outcome "heads" as S, the outcome "tails" as F. Note that when tossing a coin, no third outcome is possible.

3. From trial to trial, the probability of success, $p(S) = p$, is unchanging.

Assuming an unbiased coin, $p(S) = 0.50$ and $p(F) = 0.50$ on any single trial. From one trial to the next, these probabilities do not change.

4. The trials are independent.

When tossing a coin three times, the outcome on any trial does not affect the probability of an outcome on the next trial.

5. The question of interest is: what is the probability of x successes in n trials?

What is the probability of $x = 2$ heads (successes) in $n = 3$ tosses (trials)? Given that the coin-tossing example meets all five properties of the binomial experiment, we can use the binomial to find the probability of two heads in three tosses. However, if even one of the above properties is not satisfied, this is not a binomial experiment, and we would not be justified in using the binomial to answer the question.

To clarify what is meant by the third requirement—that the probability of either outcome remains constant from trial to trial—consider the following. In tossing a coin once, the probability of heads is $p = 0.50$; in tossing the coin a second time, P is still 0.50; and in tossing it a third time, P remains at 0.50. Thus, the trials have a constant probability of S from one trial to the next.

By contrast, consider the experiment of drawing a single playing card from a deck of 52. If S is the event "drawing a heart," what is $p(S)$? Since there are 13 hearts in a deck, $p = p(S) = 13 / 52 = 0.25$. Now suppose the first card selected is a heart but it is not replaced in the deck. What is the probability the second card drawn from this (now smaller) deck is a heart? Is it still 0.25? No, it is now $p = 12 / 51 = 0.2353$. Clearly, the probability of success $p(S)$ is changing from trial to trial. In such a situation, this is not a binomial experiment and the binomial is not strictly appropriate to use on a problem such as this.

Returning to the example: what is the probability of two heads in three coin tosses?

A simple three-step template can be used for this type of problem.

1. Does the problem fall into the binomial framework? That is, does it meet all five properties of the binomial experiment? If the answer is no, finding another approach to the problem is usually called for. If yes, then proceed to the second step.
2. Define the three parameters for the specific problem: n, the number of trials; x, the number of successes; and p, the probability of success on a single trial.
3. Once the parameters n, x, and p have been defined, the probability can be found in any of three ways: it can be calculated using the binomial probability function $f(x)$; it can be found using software, like R; or it can be looked up in a table of probabilities.

The binomial probability function $f(x)$ is

$$f(x) = p(x \mid n, p) = \binom{n}{x} p^x (1-p)^{n-x}, \quad \text{for } x = 0, 1, 2, \ldots, n,$$

where $f(x) = p(x \mid n, p)$ is the probability of x successes in n trials, in which p is the probability of success and $1-p$ the probability of failure.

Applying the three-step template, the first step involves making sure that the problem meets all five properties of a binomial experiment (this was done above). The second step calls for defining the parameters of the problem: $n = 3$, $x = 2$, and $p = 0.50$. The third step requires finding the probability. Using the probability function

$$f(x) = p(x \mid n, p) = \binom{n}{x} p^x (1-p)^{n-x},$$

we have

$$\begin{aligned} f(2) = p(x = 2 \mid n = 3, p = 0.50) &= \binom{3}{2} 0.50^2 (1-0.50)^{3-2} \\ &= 3 \times 0.50^2 \times 0.50 \\ &= 0.3750. \end{aligned}$$

The probability of two heads in three tosses is 0.3750. Using the R function `dbinom(x, n, p)`, however, is a quicker and less error-prone approach to finding binomial probabilities.

```
dbinom(2, 3, 0.50)

## [1] 0.375
```

Example 5.4. What is the probability that there will be fewer than two heads in three tosses? That is, what is $p(x = 0) + p(x = 1)$? Use two R functions: `dbinom()` and `pbinom()`. Note that `pbinom()` provides the cumulative binomial probability. See Comment2 below.

```
#Comment1. Use function dbinom(x,n=3,p=0.50) for x=0 and x=1. Sum.
dbinom(0, 3, 0.50) + dbinom(1, 3, 0.50)

## [1] 0.5

#Comment2. Use pbinom(1, 3,0.50) for p(x=0,n=3,p=0.50) + p(x=1,n=3,p=0.50).
pbinom(1, 3, 0.50)

## [1] 0.5
```

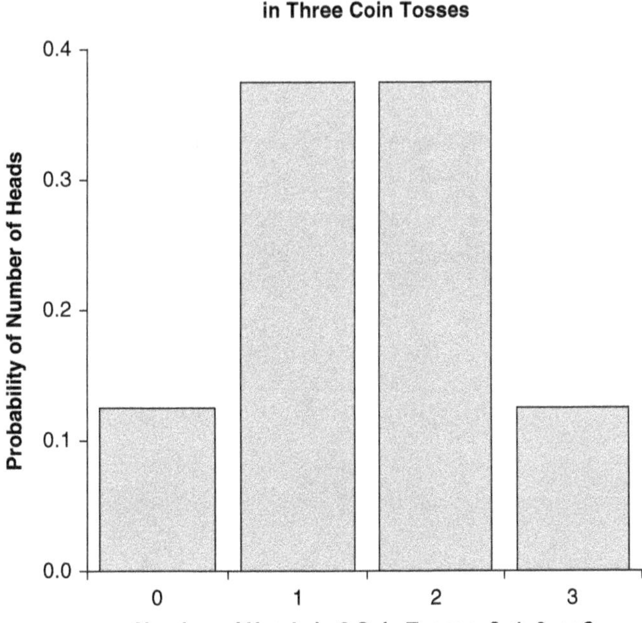

Figure 5.3 Binomial probability distribution of number of heads in three coin tosses

Example 5.5. We can use the function `dbinom(0:n, n, p)` to produce the entire binomial probability distribution. For example, to confirm that the probabilities of 0, 1, 2, and 3 heads in three coin tosses are correct (see Figure 5.3), use function `dbinom(0:3, 3, 0.50)`.

```
#Comment1. Use function dbinom(0:3,3,0.50) to find the 4 probabilities.
dbinom(0:3, 3, 0.50)

## [1] 0.125 0.375 0.375 0.125

#Comment2. Use sum(dbinom(0:3,3,0.50)) to show all probabilities sum to 1.
sum(dbinom(0:3, 3, 0.50))

## [1] 1
```

This confirms that the probabilities (see Figure 5.3) appear to be exactly correct: $p(x = 0) = 0.1250$, $p(x = 1) = 0.3750$, $p(x = 2) = 0.3750$, $p(x = 3) = 0.1250$.

Example 5.6. If a single die is cast three times, what is the probability that 4 will come up exactly once? Recall that the first part of the three-step template is to make sure that the problem conforms with the five properties of the binomial experiment. Clearly, the problem consists of a series of $n = 3$ identical trials. There are two outcomes possible on each trial—4 can be designated as S while 1, 2, 3, 5, and 6 can be named as F. The probability of success is $p(S) = p = 1/6$; the probability of failure is $p(F) = (1 - p) = 5/6$. Significantly, since $p(S)$ and $p(F)$ do not change from trial to trial, the trials are independent.

Second, define the parameters in the usual way: $x = 1$, $n = 3$, and $p = 1/6$.

Third, find the probability using the binomial probability function $f(x)$.

$$f(x) = p(x \mid n, p) = \binom{n}{x} p^x (1-p)^{n-x}$$

$$\begin{aligned} f(1) = p(x = 1 \mid n = 3, p = 1/6) &= \binom{3}{1} (1/6)^1 (5/6)^2 \\ &= 3(1/6)^1 (5/6)^2 \\ &= 0.3472 \end{aligned}$$

Thus, the probability that 4 comes up exactly once in three rolls of the die is 0.3472.

Although it may be unclear why the binomial probability function works at all, consider the issue in light of several Chapter 4 definitions. As an aid to this discussion, see Figure 5.4. Since the die-rolling experiment can be viewed as a sequence of $N = 3$ steps with two possible outcomes on each step (S and F), the counting rule for the multiple-step experiment (see Section 4.2) states that the sample space must have $2 \times 2 \times 2 = 8$ possible experimental outcomes: (SSS), (SSF), (SFS), (FSS), (FFS), (FSF), (SFF), and (FFF), where S is {4} and F is {1,2,3,5,6}. Thus the sample space is

$$\{(SSS), (SSF), (SFS), (FSS), (FFS), (FSF), (SFF), (FFF)\}.$$

If E_1 is the event that 4 (an S) comes up once and only once in three tosses, those elements of the sample space that belong to E_1 are

$$E_1 = \{(FFS), (FSF), (SFF)\}.$$

Event E_1 is a subset of the sample space (see Definition 4.5); see the right-hand side of Figure 5.4.

Because the probability of an event equals the sum of the probabilities of the sample points in that event (see Definition 4.6.),

$$p(E_1) = p(FFS) + p(FSF) + p(SFF) = p(F \cap F \cap S) + p(F \cap S \cap F) + p(S \cap F \cap F),$$

and since the results of each trial are independent (see Definition 4.14),

$$p(E_1) = p(F)\, p(F)\, p(S) + p(F)\, p(S)\, p(F) + p(S)\, p(F)\, p(F).$$

Because in this case, $p(S) = 1/6$ and $p(F) = 5/6$, it is possible to substitute and solve this equation:

$$\begin{aligned} p(E_1) &= (5/6)\,(5/6)\,(1/6) + (5/6)\,(1/6)\,(5/6) + (1/6)\,(5/6)\,(5/6) \\ &= 3\{(1/6)\,(5/6)\,(5/6)\} = 3\{(1/6)\,(5/6)^2\} = 0.3472. \end{aligned}$$

Figure 5.4 A tree diagram of three rolls of a die: *S* is {4} and *F* is {1, 2, 3, 5, 6}

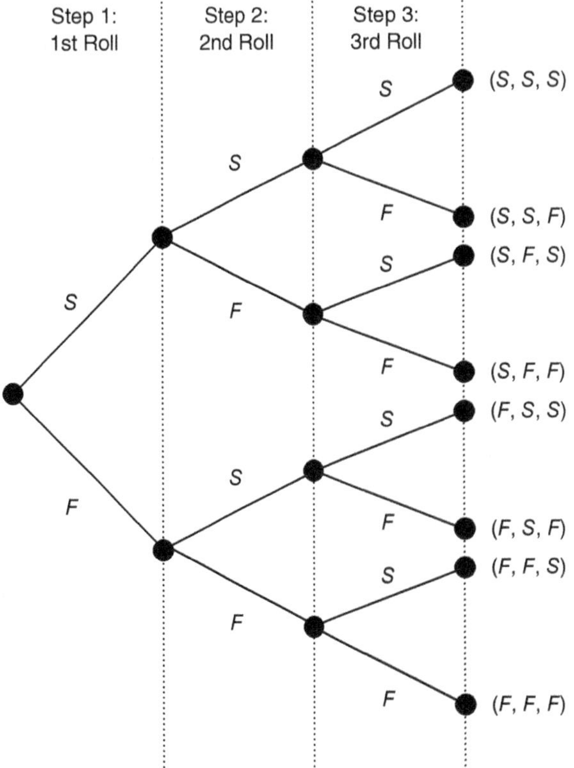

This answer is exactly the same as the value arrived at using the binomial probability function $f(x)$. Two entirely different approaches (applying $f(x)$ but also using a few definitions and probability laws) provide the same answer. The expression $3(1/6)(5/6)^2$ is now more intuitive than at first glance: there are three ways to get one *S* and two *F*s—(*FFS*), (*FSF*), and (*SFF*)—and each occurs with a probability of $(1/6)(5/6)^2$. Multiplying $(1/6)(5/6)^2$ by 3 provides the probability of one success in three trials, or 0.3472.

We can use the function `dbinom(x, n, p)` to confirm this result.

```
dbinom(1, 3, 1/6)

## [1] 0.3472222
```

Example 5.7. Use `pbinom()` to find the probability that 4 comes up at least twice in the three rolls, that is, $p(x = 2) + p(x = 3)$.

```
#Comment1. Use 1-pbinom(1,3,1/6) for binomial probability.
1 - pbinom(1, 3, 1/6)

## [1] 0.07407407
```

#Comment2. Use sum(dbinom(2:3,3,1/6)) for binomial probability.

```
sum(dbinom(2:3, 3, 1/6))
```

```
## [1] 0.07407407
```

Like the other discrete probability distribution encountered above (the Phoenix Appliances data), the binomial also has an expected value, variance, and standard deviation:

$$E(x) = \mu = np,$$

$$\sigma^2 = np(1 - p),$$

$$\sigma = \sqrt{np(1-p)}.$$

Suppose an experiment consists of $n = 100$ coin tosses. Using the first expression, we expect there will be 50 heads, or successes:

$$E(x) = \mu = np = 100 \times 0.50 = 50.$$

Applying the other two expressions, we can easily find both the variance and standard deviation:

$$\text{Var}(x) = \sigma^2 = np(1 - p) = 100 \times 0.50 \times 0.50 = 25,$$

$$\sigma = \sqrt{np(1-p)} = \sqrt{100 \times 0.50 \times 0.50} = \sqrt{25} = 5.$$

5.5 THE POISSON PROBABILITY DISTRIBUTION

The Poisson is the third discrete probability distribution in this chapter, and its focus is on the number of occurrences of an event over some interval of time, area, volume, or some other medium of a continuous nature. The sampling medium is not the discrete trial, as it is for the binomial, but rather some type of continuous medium like time or space.

Definition 5.14. Poisson Probability Distribution. The Poisson probability distribution describes how probabilities are distributed across the values the random variable may assume under conditions characterized by what is called the *Poisson experiment*. There are three properties of the Poisson experiment, and before the Poisson can be applied to any problem, we must be sure that all three properties are satisfied:

1. The probability of an occurrence in a given unit of time, distance, area, or volume is the same for all units of equal magnitude.
2. The occurrence or non-occurrence in any unit of time, distance, area, or volume is independent of the occurrence or non-occurrence in any other unit.
3. The question of interest is: what is the probability of x *occurrences* in a given unit of time, distance, area, or volume?

An example should help clarify both what these properties mean in practice as well as the kind of problem to which the Poisson can be applied.

Example 5.8. A restaurant manager would like to adjust the staffing level during the mid-morning period. The relevant variable in this case is the average number of customers arriving in a 15-minute interval during the 10:00–12:00 noon period. Records show that the average number of customer arrivals during a 15-minute interval is 20 (see Table 5.3).

Table 5.3 Number of customer arrivals in eight 15-minute intervals

Interval no. (time)	No. of arrivals
1 (10:00-10:15)	21
2 (10:15-10:30)	22
3 (10:30-10:45)	18
4 (10:45-11:00)	20
5 (11:00-11:15)	16
6 (11:15-11:30)	24
7 (11:30-11:45)	20
8 (11:45-12:00)	19
	160

Since there are 160 customer arrivals over all eight 15-minute intervals, the mean number of arrivals per 15-minute interval is 20. This value is denoted as $\mu = 20$ in the expression below, and it serves as the main parameter for the Poisson probability distribution.

Here is the type of problem to which the Poisson can be applied: given that $\mu = 20$ arrivals, what is the probability of exactly 15 arrivals in any 15-minute period?

Before using the Poisson probability distribution to answer this question, make sure that the experiment satisfies all three properties of the Poisson experiment.

1. The probability of an occurrence in a given unit of time, distance, area, or volume is the same for all units of equal magnitude.
   During the 10:00-12:00 period, the probability of an arrival during, say, a 1-minute sub-interval should equal the probability in any other 1-minute sub-interval. This may not be true, however, if one were to include different periods of the day, such as the busy breakfast or lunch hours, with the 10:00-12:00 period.
2. The occurrence or non-occurrence in any unit of time, distance, area, or volume is independent of the occurrence or non-occurrence in any other unit.
   Apart from when customers arrive in groups, they usually arrive at a restaurant independent of one another.
3. The question of interest is: what is the probability of *x occurrences* in a given unit of time, distance, area, or volume?
   What is the probability of 15 arrivals given that the mean arrival rate is $\mu = 20$?

Applying the three-step template (as with the binomial), the first step involves making sure that the problem meets all three properties of a Poisson experiment (this was done above). The second step calls for defining the parameters of the problem: $\mu = 20$ and $x = 15$. The third step requires finding the probability. The Poisson probability function is

$$f(x) = p(x \mid \mu) = \frac{\mu^x e^{-\mu}}{x!}, \quad \text{for } x = 0, 1, 2, \ldots,$$

where $f(x) = p(x \mid \mu)$ is the probability of x occurrences in a unit of time, distance, area, or volume; μ is the mean number of occurrences in that unit of time, distance, area, or volume; and $e \approx 2.71828\ldots$ is the base of the natural logarithm. In theory, a Poisson-distributed random variable x could assume a value of 0, 1, 2, or anything above that—a quality very different from a binomially distributed random variable where x could take on values up to but not beyond the number of trials n.

What is the probability of 15 arrivals if the mean arrival rate is $\mu = 20$? Using $f(x)$, we obtain

$$f(15) = p(x = 15 \mid \mu = 20) = \frac{20^{15} e^{-20}}{15!} = 0.0516.$$

To find this answer using R, the function `dpois(x, μ)` provides Poisson probabilities.

```
#Comment. Use function dpois(15,20) for probability of 15 occurrences.
dpois(15, 20)

## [1] 0.05164885
```

Example 5.9. What is the probability of exactly five arrivals in 3 minutes?

Here it is necessary to convert the parameter $\mu = 20$ to the expected number of arrivals during a 3-minute period: 20 arrivals per 15-minute interval is equivalent to 4 arrivals per 3-minute interval. This new arrival rate can be found in the following way:

$$\frac{20 \text{ arrivals}}{15 \text{ minutes}} = \frac{x \text{ arrivals}}{3 \text{ minutes}}$$

so

$$x \text{ arrivals} = (3 \text{ minutes}) \frac{20 \text{ arrivals}}{15 \text{ minutes}} = 4 \text{ arrivals}.$$

Thus, the new expected number of arrivals is now $\mu = 4$ for a time interval of 3 minutes' duration. We are now in a position to find the probability of exactly five arrivals in 3 minutes:

$$f(x) = p(x \mid \mu) = \frac{\mu^x e^{-\mu}}{x!}$$

$$f(5) = p(x = 5 \mid \mu = 4) = \frac{4^5 e^{-4}}{5!} = 0.1563.$$

We can use the R function `dpois()` to confirm this answer.

```
#Comment. Use function dpois(5,4) for probability of 5 occurrences.
dpois(5, 4)

## [1] 0.1562935
```

Example 5.10. The occurrence of potholes in a highway after a particularly severe winter is a Poisson-distributed random variable with a mean of $\mu = 3$ defects per mile. What is the probability there are exactly 12 defects in a 3-mile stretch of highway?

It is often useful to express the parameter μ in a more flexible form for the purpose of solving Poisson problems involving different interval lengths. That is, reexpress μ as

$$\mu = \lambda t,$$

where λ equals the expected rate of occurrence per interval (it can be viewed as the *intensity* of the Poisson process under consideration) and t is the number of intervals. Thus, the product λt is simply the expected rate of occurrence per t intervals. If this seems a little abstract, consider how the idea is applied to this problem.

Converting from 1 mile to 3 miles, it is clear that 9 defects per 3-mile interval is equivalent to 3 defects per 1-mile interval: $\mu = \lambda t = $ (3 defects/mile)(3 miles) = 9 defects. So the probability of 12 defects when 9 are expected is

$$f(x) = p(x \mid \lambda t) = \frac{(\lambda t)^x e^{-\lambda t}}{x!}$$

$$f(12) = p(x = 12 \mid \lambda t = 9) = \frac{9^{12} e^{-9}}{12!} = 0.07277.$$

We can use R function `dpois(12, 9)` to confirm this answer:

```
dpois(12, 9)

## [1] 0.07276505
```

Example 5.11. Use `dpois(a:b, 9)` to display all eight probabilities from $a = 5$ to $b = 12$ defects when 9 are expected.

```
dpois(5:12, 9)

## [1] 0.06072688 0.09109032 0.11711612 0.13175564 0.13175564 0.11858008
## [7] 0.09702006 0.07276505
```

Example 5.12. Use `sum(dpois(a:b, 9))` to find probability of between $a = 5$ to $b = 12$ defects when 9 are expected.

```
sum(dpois(5:12, 9))

## [1] 0.8208098
```

Find this probability using the difference between two cumulative probabilities.

```
ppois(12, 9) - ppois(4, 9)

## [1] 0.8208098
```

Figure 5.5 displays the Poisson probability distribution of the number of occurrences (defects in a 3-mile stretch of a highway) when the expected number is $\mu = 9$. Unsurprisingly, the bars (and probability) indicate that 9 defects are most likely; lesser, or greater, numbers of defects are less likely. The probability of 12 defects is 0.07277.

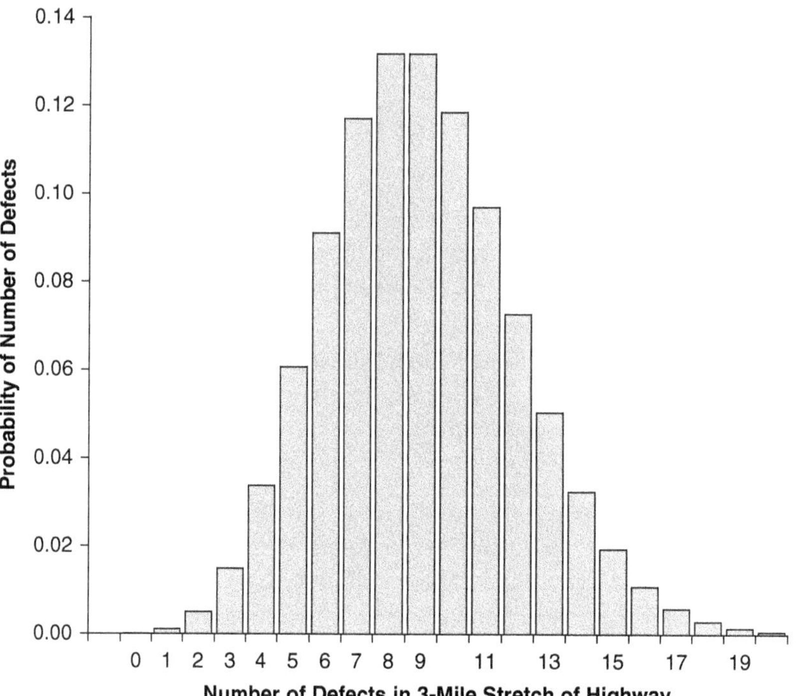

Figure 5.5 Poisson probability distribution of number of defects when $\mu = 9$

Finally, like the binomial probability distribution, the Poisson probability distribution also has an expected value, variance, and standard deviation:

$$E(x) = \mu = \lambda t,$$

$$\sigma^2 = \mu = \lambda t,$$

$$\sigma = \sqrt{\sigma^2} = \sqrt{\mu} = \sqrt{\lambda t}.$$

While $E(x) = \mu$, it is notable that $\sigma^2 = \mu$; that is, for the Poisson probability distribution, the mean and variance are equal. Thus, in the case of the restaurant staff-scheduling problem (Example 5.8), one would expect an average of 20 arrivals in 15 minutes. The variance and standard deviation are 20 and 4.4721, respectively.

$$E(x) = \mu = \sigma^2 = 20,$$

$$\sigma = \sqrt{\mu} = \sqrt{20} \approx 4.4721.$$

The Poisson is associated with one of the continuous probability distributions, the exponential, and it will be encountered again in Chapter 6.

THE HYPERGEOMETRIC PROBABILITY DISTRIBUTION

The hypergeometric is the fourth (and final) discrete probability distribution covered in this chapter. It is quite similar to the binomial, except that two of the five properties of the binomial experiment are not applicable in the case of the hypergeometric: the probability of success is not constant from trial to trial; and the trials are not independent. The practical result is that a different computational approach is called for.

Definition 5.15. Hypergeometric Probability Distribution. The probability distribution of a hypergeometrically distributed random variable provides the probability that elements are selected from a finite population without replacement.

An example will clarify the idea behind the hypergeometric probability distribution.

Example 5.13. An urn has 5 balls, 3 black and 2 white. If 3 balls are drawn randomly, what is the probability of 1 white and 2 black balls? Although this problem may appear to be a binomial experiment, it is not. The reason is that the probabilities from trial to trial are not stationary. That is, after drawing the first ball, the probability of selecting either a black or white ball on the second draw has changed; and after the second ball has been selected, the probabilities have changed yet again. We take three different approaches below.

Approach 1. Each ball is identified with one of the following designations: B_1, B_2, B_3, W_1, and W_2, where B_1 is black ball 1, W_1 is white ball 1, and so on. The sample space S associated with drawing three balls from the urn consists of 10 sample points:

$$S = \{(B_1B_2B_3), (B_1B_2W_1), (B_1B_2W_2), (B_1B_3W_1), (B_1B_3W_2), (B_2B_3W_1), (B_2B_3W_2),$$
$$(W_1W_2B_1), (W_1W_2B_2), (W_1W_2B_3)\}.$$

Applying the classical method of assigning probabilities (see Section 4.3):

$$p(B_1B_2B_3) = p(B_1B_2W_1) = p(B_1B_2W_2) = p(B_1B_3W_1) = \ldots = p(W_1W_2B_3) = 0.10.$$

That is, the probability of any one of the 10 sample points is 0.10. Furthermore, if we define E as the event of one white and two black balls, then

$$E = \{(B_1B_2W_1), (B_1B_2W_2), (B_1B_3W_1), (B_1B_3W_2), (B_2B_3W_1), (B_2B_3W_2)\}.$$

Since the event E occurs if one white and two black balls are selected when drawing three balls from the urn (Definition 4.5), and since the probability of an event equals the sum of the probabilities of the sample points comprising that event (Definion 4.6), we know that

$$\begin{aligned} p(E) &= p(B_1B_2W_1) + p(B_1B_2W_2) + p(B_1B_3W_1) + p(B_1B_3W_2) + p(B_2B_3W_1) + p(B_2B_3W_2) \\ &= 0.10 + 0.10 + 0.10 + 0.10 + 0.10 + 0.10 = 0.60. \end{aligned}$$

Thus, using Approach 1, we find there is a 0.60 probability of one white and two black balls.

Approach 2. Use the hypergeometric probability function $f(x)$ to find the probability:

$$f(x) = \frac{\binom{r}{x}\binom{N-r}{n-x}}{\binom{N}{n}}, \quad \text{for } 0 \le x \le r,$$

where $N = 5$ is the number of balls in the urn (the population size) and $n = 3$ is the number of balls being selected for the sample. Furthermore, the population itself consists of $r = 3$ balls designated success (black) and $N - r = 3$ balls designated failure (white). Finally, the problem concerns the probability of drawing a sample of size $n = 3$ containing $x = 2$ successes and $n - x = 1$ failure. If $f(x)$ is the probability of $x = 2$ successes (black) in $n = 3$ trials, then

$$f(2) = \frac{\binom{3}{2}\binom{2}{1}}{\binom{5}{3}} = \frac{3 \times 2}{10} = 0.60.$$

The expression for the hypergeometric probability function $f(x)$ it is actually quite intuitive. Note that $x = 2$ successes can be selected from a total of $r = 3$ successes in three ways: B_1B_2, B_1B_3, and B_2B_3. That is,

$$\binom{r}{x} = \binom{3}{2} = 3.$$

Moreover, $n - x = 1$ failure can be selected from a total of $N - r = 2$ failures in two ways: W_1 and W_2. That is,

$$\binom{N-r}{n-x} = \binom{2}{1} = 2.$$

By applying the counting rule for the multiple-step experiment (see Section 4.2), the number of outcomes is the product of the number of results on each step, so there are

$$\binom{r}{x}\binom{N-r}{n-x} = \binom{3}{2}\binom{2}{1} = 3 \times 2 = 6$$

ways to draw two black balls and one white ball (see event E above). Finally, there are 10 ways that three balls can be selected from five (see S above):

$$\binom{N}{n} = \binom{5}{3} = 10.$$

Since 6 of the 10 equally probable outcomes satisfy the requirement of the problem, there is a $6/10 = 0.60$ probability of 2 blacks and 1 white ball in a random selection of 3.

Approach 3. Use the R function `dhyper(x, r, N-r, n)`. Note that, in the population, r is the number of elements designated success and $N - r$ is the number of elements labeled failure; n is the size of the sample and x is the number of successes in that sample.

```
dhyper(2, 3, 2, 3)

## [1] 0.6
```

Finally, like the other discrete probability distributions, the hypergeometric probability distribution also has an expected value, variance, and standard deviation:

$$E(x) = n\frac{r}{N},$$

$$\sigma^2 = n\frac{r}{N}\left(1 - \frac{r}{N}\right)\frac{N-n}{N-1},$$

$$\sigma = \sqrt{\sigma^2} = \sqrt{n\frac{r}{N}\left(1 - \frac{r}{N}\right)\frac{N-n}{N-1}}.$$

In the case of drawing a sample of 3 balls from 3 black and 2 white, the expected value is 1.8; the variance and standard deviation are 0.36 and 0.60, respectively:

$$E(x) = n\frac{r}{N} = 3 \times \frac{3}{5} = 1.80,$$

$$\sigma^2 = n\frac{r}{N}\left(1-\frac{r}{N}\right)\frac{N-n}{N-1} = 3\times\frac{3}{5}\left(1-\frac{3}{5}\right)\frac{5-3}{5-1} = 3\times\frac{3}{5}\times\frac{2}{5}\times\frac{1}{2} = 0.36,$$

$$\sigma = \sqrt{\sigma^2} = \sqrt{0.36} = 0.60.$$

Although the expressions for the expected value and variance of the hypergeometric look complicated, they are more intuitive if one recalls that the hypergeometric and binomial experiments are similar. The main distinction between the two is that P changes from trial to trial in the former case but not in the latter. In fact, the two probability functions provide similar, if not exactly the same, results when N is large.

When N is large, P changes very little from trial to trial. Returning to the example where 3 balls are selected from a population of 5—consisting of 3 black balls (success) and 2 whites (failure)—P is 0.60 on the first ball drawn. If a black ball is selected on the first draw, P on the second draw falls from 0.60 to 0.50, but if a white ball is selected on the first draw, P on the second draw rises from 0.60 to 0.75. It should be clear that because P changes so dramatically from trial to trial, this is not a binomial experiment, and the binomial probability distribution cannot be used.

Instead of drawing 3 balls from a population of 3 blacks and 2 whites, suppose 3 balls are selected from a larger population consisting of 3000 blacks and 2000 whites. Because the ratio of black-to-white balls is maintained, P at the first draw is 0.60. Notably, however, P on the second and third rounds remains essentially unchanged regardless of which ball is selected on the first draw. In fact, P falls from 0.60 to only 0.5998 for the second round, if a black ball is selected on the first; it rises from 0.60 to 0.6001 on the second round if a white ball is drawn on the first.

The point is that when the population is large, the hypergeometric probability distribution is very similar to the binomial probability distribution, and the binomial can often be used as an approximation to the hypergeometric. In this situation, the expected value of the hypergeometric is practically the same as the expected value of the binomial:

$$E(x) = n\frac{r}{N} \Rightarrow np.$$

In addition, when the population is large, the term

$$\frac{N-n}{N-1}$$

approaches 1, and the variance of the hypergeometric approaches the variance of the binomial:

$$\lim_{N\to\infty} n\frac{r}{N}\left(1-\frac{r}{N}\right)\frac{N-n}{N-1} = np(1-p), \quad \text{since } \frac{N-n}{N-1} \to 1.$$

5.7 THE HYPERGEOMETRIC PROBABILITY DISTRIBUTION: THE GENERAL CASE

The approach of using `dhyper()` or the hypergeometric probability function $f(x)$ works well when the problem is framed in terms of only two mutually exclusive categories. Consider a way to expand this approach to accommodate more than two categories.

A population contains a finite number W of elements that are grouped into K mutually exclusive classes with w_1 elements in group 1, w_2 elements in group 2, ..., and w_k elements in group K. A random sample of n is selected and is found to contain n_1 elements of group 1, n_2 elements of group 2, ..., and n_k elements of group K. The probability of this is

$$\frac{\binom{w_1}{n_1}\binom{w_2}{n_2}\cdots\binom{w_k}{n_k}}{\binom{W}{n}},$$

where

$$n_1 + n_2 + \ldots + n_k = n \quad \text{and} \quad w_1 + w_2 + \ldots + w_k = W.$$

This is a more general expression for the hypergeometric probability function because it can be used for problems involving any number of mutually exclusive categories. Using the R function `choose()`, the previous two-category problem can be solved differently:

```
#Comment. Divide the product of two combinations by a third combination.
choose(3, 2) * choose(2, 1) / choose(5, 3)

## [1] 0.6
```

Let us apply this expanded approach to a more complicated problem.

Example 5.14. Suppose there is a group of 107 citizens at a public debate, and that, of this group, 35 are registered Democrats, 38 are Independents, and 34 are registered Republicans. What is the probability, in drawing a random sample of 30 (from the 107), that there will be 10 Democrats, 10 Independents, and 10 Republicans?

Substituting into the formula above gives

$$\frac{\binom{w_1}{n_1}\binom{w_2}{n_2}\cdots\binom{w_k}{n_k}}{\binom{W}{n}} = \frac{\binom{35}{10}\binom{38}{10}\binom{34}{10}}{\binom{107}{30}} = 0.03573.$$

To confirm that the expression is structured correctly:

$$W = w_1 + w_2 + w_3 = 35 + 38 + 34 = 107 \quad \text{and} \quad n = n_1 + n_2 + n_3 = 10 + 10 + 10 = 30.$$

By dividing the product of the three combinations in the numerator by the single combination in the denominator, R is able to provide the probability.

```
#Comment. Divide the product of two combinations by a third combination.
choose(35, 10) * choose(38, 10) * choose(34, 10) / choose(107, 30)

## [1] 0.0357304
```

We confirm that there is a 0.03573 probability that a randomly drawn sample contains exactly 10 Democrats, 10 Independents, and 10 Republicans.

The advantage of dividing the product of combinations by a single combination to derive hypergeometric probabilities becomes clear when the complexity of the problem expands to more than two categories. In this instance, the R function `dhyper()` is not useful since it cannot accommodate three or more categories.

SUMMARY

This chapter enlarges upon and develops several probability topics that feature prominently in the treatment of statistical estimation and inference. Of those topics, the most important are the random variable and the probability distribution. This chapter focuses entirely on discrete probability distributions, and, as we will see, Chapter 6 extends the discussion to continuous probability distributions.

A random variable is a function that assigns numerical values to the result of an experiment. The probability distribution of a random variable describes how probabilities are distributed across the various values the random variable can take on. In the case of discrete probability distributions, a probability function reports for each value the probability the random variable can assume; the analog of the probability function in the case of the continuous probability distribution is called a probability density function (a notion to which we return in Chapter 6).

A discrete probability distribution can be described by (a) a tabular method (or table), (b) a graphical method (a picture of the information that is reported in the table, such as a bar graph), or (c) a formula. In addition, just as a set of data can be characterized by the mean and standard deviation, so can a probability distribution.

The binomial probability distribution describes how probabilities are distributed across the values the random variable may assume under conditions characterized by what is called the binomial experiment. There are five properties of the binomial experiment: (a) the overall experiment must consist of a series of n identical trials; (b) on each trial, there are two possible outcomes, denoted S and F; (c) from trial to trial, $p(S)$ is unchanging; (d) the trials are independent; and (e) the question of interest is the probability of x successes in n trials. There are three properties of the Poisson experiment: (a) the probability of an occurrence in a given unit of time, area, or volume is the same for all units of equal magnitude; (b) the occurrence or non-occurrence in any unit of time, area, or volume is independent of what happens in any other unit; and (c) the question of interest is the probability of x occurrences in a unit of time, area, or volume. The hypergeometric is similar to the binomial except that two of the five properties of the binomial are not applicable: the probability of success is not constant from trial to trial and the trials are not independent.

definitions

Binomial Probability Distribution The probability distribution of a binomially distributed random variable shows how the probabilities are distributed across the values the random variable can take on.

Binomial Probability Function A function that reports the probability of each value of a binomially distributed random variable.

Continuous Random Variable A continuous random variable may assume any value in an interval or series of intervals on the real number line.

Discrete Random Variable A discrete random variable assumes either a finite number of values or an infinite sequence of values.

Discrete Uniform Probability Distribution The probability distribution of a random variable for which all values are equally likely.

Expected Value The expected value of a probability distribution is a measure of central tendency, and it is derived by weighing each of the possible values of the random variable by its probability.

Experiment An experiment is any process that can result in any of more than one well-defined outcomes that cannot be predicted with certainty beforehand. Whenever an experiment is performed, one and only one of the possible experimental results can occur.

Hypergeometric Probability Distribution The probability distribution of a hypergeometrically distributed random variable shows how the probabilities are distributed across the values the random variable can take on.

Hypergeometric Probability Function A function that reports the probability of each value of a hypergeometrically distributed random variable.

Poisson Probability Distribution The probability distribution of a Poisson-distributed random variable shows how the probabilities are distributed across the values the random variable can take on.

Poisson Probability Function A function that reports the probability of each value of a Poisson-distributed random variable.

Probability Distribution A probability distribution for a random variable reports the way the probabilities are distributed across the various values the random variable can take on.

Probability Function A function that reports the probability for each value the random variable can assume.

Random Variable A function that assigns numerical values to the outcome of an experiment.

Sample Point A sample point is an element of the sample space. It is any one particular experimental outcome.

Sample Space Each experiment has associated with it a sample space that is the set of all possible experimental outcomes.

Standard Deviation The standard deviation is the positive square root of the variance. It is expressed in the same units as the expected value and the original data, something usually seen as an advantage over the variance.

Variance The variance of a discrete random variable is a measure of dispersion, and it is derived by weighing each of the squared deviations of all possible values of the random variable by its probability.

formulae

Binomial Probability Function

$$f(x) = p(x \mid n, p) = \binom{n}{x} p^x (1-p)^{n-x}$$

Binomial Distribution: Expected Value

$$E(x) = \mu = np$$

Binomial Distribution: Variance

$$\text{Var}(x) = \sigma^2 = np(1-p)$$

Binomial Distribution: Standard Deviation

$$\sigma = \sqrt{np(1-p)}$$

Discrete Random Variable: Expected Value

$$E(x) = \mu = \sum x_i f(x_i)$$

Discrete Random Variable: Variance

$$\text{Var}(x) = \sigma^2 = \sum (x_i - \mu)^2 f(x_i)$$

Discrete Random Variable: Standard Deviation

$$\sigma = \sqrt{\sum (x_i - \mu)^2 f(x_i)}$$

Discrete Uniform Probability Function

$$f(x) = \frac{1}{n}$$

Hypergeometric Probability Function

$$f(x) = \frac{\binom{r}{x}\binom{N-r}{n-x}}{\binom{N}{n}}$$

Hypergeometric Distribution: Expected Value

$$E(x) = n\frac{r}{N}$$

Hypergeometric Distribution: Variance

$$\text{Var}(x) = \sigma^2 = n\frac{r}{N}\left(1 - \frac{r}{N}\right)\frac{N-n}{N-1}$$

Hypergeometric Distribution: Standard Deviation

$$\sigma = \sqrt{n\frac{r}{N}\left(1 - \frac{r}{N}\right)\frac{N-n}{N-1}}$$

Poisson Probability Function

$$f(x) = p(x \mid \mu) = \frac{\mu^x e^{-\mu}}{x!}$$

Poisson Distribution: Expected Value

$$E(x) = \mu$$

Poisson Distribution: Variance

$$\text{Var}(x) = \sigma^2 = \mu$$

Poisson Distribution: Standard Deviation

$$\sigma = \sqrt{\mu}$$

R functions

`dbinom(x, n, p)` Provides the binomial probability of x successes in n trials when the probability of success P is constant from trial to trial.

`dhyper(x, r, N-r, n)` Provides the hypergeometric probability of x successes in n trials.

(Continued)

(Continued)

`dpois(x, μ)` Provides the Poisson probability of x occurrences in an interval when the mean number of occurrences is μ.

`pbinom(x, n, p)` Provides the cumulative binomial probability of x or fewer successes in n trials when the probability of success p is constant from trial to trial.

`phyper(x, r, N-r, n)` Provides the cumulative hypergeometric probability of x or fewer successes in n trials.

`ppois(x, μ)` Provides the cumulative Poisson probability of x or fewer occurrences in an interval when the mean number of occurrences is μ.

`choose (W1, n1)* choose (W2, n2)*... *choose (Wk, nk)/ choose (W, n)` Provides the hypergeometric probability of n_1 successes in class 1, n_2 successes in class 2, ..., and n_k successes in class k, where $W = w_1 + w_2 + ... + w_k$ and $n = n_1 + n_2 + ... + n_k$ in n trials.

APPENDIX: USING R TO FIND PROBABILITIES–BINOMIAL, POISSON, AND HYPERGEOMETRIC

R commands for binomial, Poisson, and hypergeometric probabilities are listed in Tables 5.4, 5.5, and 5.6, respectively.

Table 5.4 R commands for the binomial probabilities

To find this binomial probability	Use this R command
$p(x = a)$	dbinom(a, n, p)
$p(x \le a)$	pbinom(a, n, p)
$p(x < a)$	pbinom(a–1, n, p)
$p(x \ge a) = 1 - p(x < a) = 1 - p(x \le a - 1)$	1–pbinom(a–1, n, p)
$p(x > a) = 1 - p(x \le a)$	1–pbinom(a, n, p)

Table 5.5 R commands for the Poisson probabilities

To find this Poisson probability	Use this R command
$p(x = a)$	dpois(a, μ)
$p(x \le a)$	ppois(a, μ)
$p(x < a)$	ppois(a–1, μ)
$p(x \ge a) = 1 - p(x < a) = 1 - p(x \le a - 1)$	1–ppois(a–1, μ)
$p(x > a) = 1 - p(x \le a)$	1–ppois(a, μ)

Table 5.6 R commands for the hypergeometric probabilities

To find this hypergeometric probability	Use this R command
$p(x = a)$	dhyper(*a*, *r*, *N*–*r*, *n*)
$p(x \leq a)$	phyper(*a*, *r*, *N*–*r*, *n*)
$p(x < a)$	phyper(*a*–1, *r*, *N*–*r*, *n*)
$p(x \geq a) = 1 - p(x < a) = 1 - p(x \leq a - 1)$	1–phyper(*a*–1, *r*, *N*–*r*, *n*)
$p(x > a) = 1 - p(x \leq a)$	1–phyper(*a*, *r*, *N*–*r*, *n*)

exercises

5.1 If 85% of vehicles arriving at the Lincoln Tunnel (connecting New Jersey and New York City) have either New York or New Jersey license plates, what is the probability that, of the next 20 vehicles, two or fewer (i.e., 0, 1, or 2) will bear license plates from states other than New Jersey or New York? Use R to find the solution.

5.2 At a certain university, half the students enrolled in a statistics class take the course on a pass-fail basis; the other half take it for a normal grade of A, ..., F.

(a) If 20 students are selected at random, what is the probability that 12 (of the 20) are taking the course pass-fail?
(b) What is the probability that no more than 5 students are taking the course for a normal grade of A, ..., F?
(c) What is the expected number who are taking the course on a pass-fail basis?

5.3 Calls arrive at a customer-service toll-free number at the rate of 20 per hour. Use R to find the solutions to the following questions.

(a) What is the probability of five or more calls in a 15-minute period?
(b) What is the probability that between 7 and 12 calls, inclusive, will arrive in the next 30 minutes?
(c) If one particular caller has a difficult problem to resolve and requires 15 minutes of the customer-service representative's time, how many callers would we expect to be waiting on hold once the call has been completed?
(d) If the customer-service representative wishes to take a 5-minute coffee break, what is the probability that no calls will be awaiting him once he returns?

5.4 A manufacturer is concerned with the quality of AA batteries being delivered by a certain supplier. Recently, the average battery life has fallen below the manufacturer's standard, and so the manufacturer has begun to test the life of the batteries from this particular supplier more closely. To do this, the quality control inspectors randomly select small samples of batteries from each shipping carton of 100. Even if one of the batteries fails the test, the entire box of 100 is rejected and returned to the supplier. Suppose that unbeknownst to inspectors, a carton of 100 batteries contains 15 defective batteries. Use R to answer all questions.

(Continued)

(Continued)

(a) What is the probability the carton will be returned if a sample of five batteries is selected and tested?

(b) What is the probability the carton will be returned if the sample size is 10?

(c) If the quality control department has decided that it wants (roughly) a 0.85 probability of correctly identifying at least one of the 15 defective batteries in the shipping carton, what sample size should they use?

5.5 Suppose we select a random sample of 5 balls from an urn containing 4 red, 3 white, and 2 blue balls. What is the probability that we draw 2 blue and at least 1 red ball? Use R to find the solution.

https://study.sagepub.com/stinerock

Continuous Probability Distributions

contents

learning objectives

1. Understand the difference between how probabilities are computed for discrete and continuous random variables.
2. Be able to compute probability values for a continuous uniform probability distribution, and be able to derive the expected value and variance for such a distribution.
3. Be able to calculate probabilities using a normal probability distribution, and understand the role of the standard normal distribution in this process.
4. Be able to compute probabilities for the exponential probability distribution.
5. Understand the relationship between the Poisson and exponential probability distribution.
6. Learn to use R in connection with the three major continuous probability distributions.

In Chapter 5 we introduced the concept of the discrete random variable. In this chapter we extend the discussion to continuous random variables and their probability distributions. In making this transition, we begin by developing the distinction between how probabilities are derived for the continuous random variable versus the discrete random variable. To this end, we first consider the continuous uniform probability distribution before moving on to the normal, standard normal, and exponential distributions.

 6.1 CONTINUOUS UNIFORM PROBABILITY DISTRIBUTION

We begin with the example of the simplest continuous probability distribution, the uniform. The simplicity of this particular distribution is both a weakness and a strength: a weakness because the types of problems to which the uniform can be applied are limited; a strength because it provides a helpful and instructive introduction to continuous probability distributions, primarily because the probability computations are so simple.

Definition 6.1. Continuous Uniform Probability Distribution. A continuous uniform probability distribution is one for which all intervals of equal length have the same probability. When graphed, the distribution assumes the shape of a rectangle.

A university makes available a conference room for student activities and meetings. Since there are many requests to use the room, the administration requires students to reserve it in advance for 90-minute blocks of time. A review of the times the room is actually occupied has found that the meeting times are distributed uniformly throughout the 90-minute interval, with some meetings lasting very briefly but others consuming the entire 90-minute time period.

Let x be the random variable indicating the duration of a meeting, where x may take on any value from 0 to 90 minutes. Note that when x is said to assume any value in the interval, that value might be 72 minutes, 64.175 minutes, π minutes, and so on. Since x can assume any value in the interval, x is a continuous (and not a discrete) random variable. This is an important departure from how we define the discrete random variable, and it is this characteristic that differentiates the two types of random variables.

Moreover, if we make the assumption that the probability of meeting-time duration is the same for any 1-minute interval from 0 to 90 minutes, that is,

$$p(0 \le x \le 1) = p(1 \le x \le 2) = \dots = p(89 \le x \le 90),$$

then the probability distribution is not only continuous, it is continuous uniform.

What was referred to as the probability function $f(x)$ of a discrete random variable is called a probability density function in the case of the continuous random variable. Perhaps surprisingly, the probability density function $f(x)$ does not provide probabilities; it simply provides the height of the curve at some specific value of the random variable x.

Definition 6.2. Probability Density Function. A probability density function provides the likelihood that a continuous random variable will assume a particular range of values. When the area under the curve of the function and over the range of values is computed, it provides the probability the random variable will fall in that interval.

In general, if a continuous uniform random variable x is defined to exist between two points a and b, then the probability density function is

$$f(x) = \frac{1}{b-a}, \quad \text{where } a \le x \le b.$$

When $x < a$ or $x > b$, $f(x) = 0$. In general, probability density functions for continuous random variables must satisfy two important conditions. The first condition is that the probability density function can assume only non-negative values. That is,

$$f(x) \ge 0, \qquad \text{for all } x.$$

The second condition is that the area under the graph of the probability density function is always equal to 1. That is,

$$\int_{-\infty}^{\infty} f(x)\,dx = 1.$$

(If the above mathematical notation is unfamiliar, it simply represents the area under the curve of the density function or, what is the same thing, probability. Accordingly, the second condition states that $f(x)$ must provide an area of 1 over the interval on which it is defined.)

In the current example where $a = 0$ and $b = 90$, the probability density function is

$$f(x) = \frac{1}{90-0} = \frac{1}{90} = 0.0111, \quad \text{where } 0 \le x \le 90.$$

Note that the probability that a continuous random variable takes on any legally defined value x is 0. In terms of the hypothetical values of x cited above, this simply means that $p(x = 72) = p(x = 64.175) = p(x = 24\pi) = 0$, and so on. Although this may be counterintuitive—after all, x must assume some value each time an experiment is conducted—consider the following argument.

Returning to the example of the duration of a student meeting, what is the probability that a meeting lasts *exactly* 60 minutes? In fact, there is no chance a meeting lasts exactly 60 minutes. By exactly 60 minutes, we really mean 60.000... minutes, not (say) 60.001 minutes, a different value of x. Since there are infinitely many possible values of x, it is impossible to list all those values. Thus, the probability distribution of a continuous random variable is provided by a continuous curve.

So how are probabilities derived for a continuous random variable? The area under the graph of the probability density function $f(x)$ between a and b is the probability x falls in that interval. Unlike in the case of the discrete random variable, $f(x)$ has no directly useful meaning in the context of the continuous case because it does not represent probability. For a continuous random variable, probability is defined as the likelihood that a random variable falls in a given range, and is equal to the area under the curve with respect to that range. To make this clear, return to the class meeting-time example.

Example 6.1. What is the probability that a meeting will last between 30 and 60 minutes? See Figure 6.1 for a graphical representation. Below are three different approaches.

Approach 1. Find the area under the curve between 30 and 60 by finding the area of the subrectangle. Note that area = length × width, where length is 30 and width is 1/90. So the probability is

$$p(30 \le x \le 60) = (60 - 30)\frac{1}{90} = \frac{30}{90} = 0.3333.$$

Approach 1 only works when the area under the curve is easily computed by simple geometric methods. Approach 2 uses a more general method for finding probabilities.

Approach 2. The area under the curve between 30 and 60 can be found with calculus:

$$p(30 \le x \le 60) = \int_{30}^{60} \frac{1}{90} dx = \left[\frac{x}{90}\right]_{30}^{60} = \frac{1}{90}(60 - 30) = 0.3333.$$

While Approach 2 is a more generally applicable way of finding areas and probabilities, it suffers from being both tedious and error-prone to apply. Approach 3 uses R.

Approach 3. Use the R function `punif(`x_0`, min =` a`, max =` b`)` to find $p(x \le x_0)$, where $f(x) = 1 / (b - a)$. In this case, we find $p(30 \le x \le 60)$ by subtracting the cumulative probability that $x \le 30$ from the cumulative probability that $x \le 60$.

```
punif(60, min = 0, max = 90) - punif(30, min = 0, max = 90)

## [1] 0.3333333
```

Example 6.2. What is the probability that a meeting lasts between 55 and 75 minutes?

Approach 1. Find the area of the subrectangle, where area = length × width:

$$p(55 \le x \le 75) = (75 - 55)\frac{1}{90} = \frac{20}{90} = 0.2222.$$

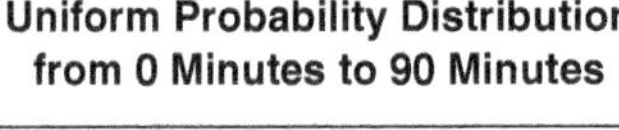

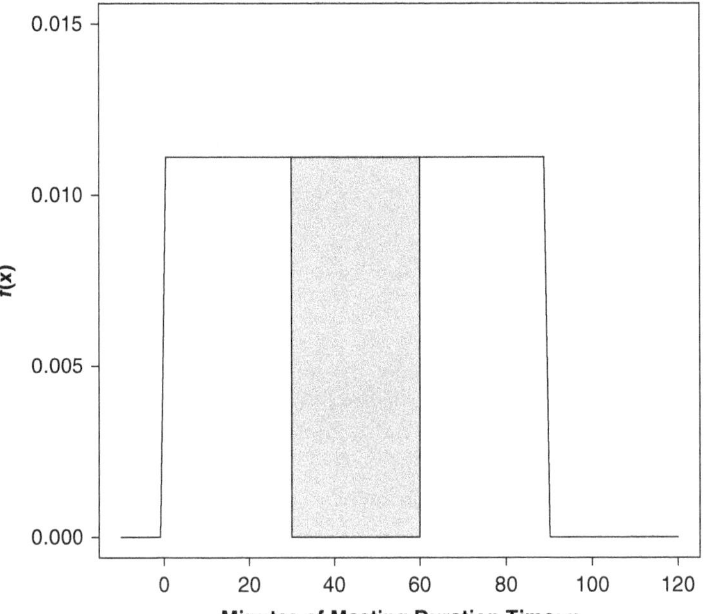

Figure 6.1 The probability $p(30 \le x \le 60) = 0.3333$ is given by the area shaded in grey

Approach 2. Use the method of integral calculus:

$$p(55 \le x \le 75) = \int_{55}^{75} \frac{1}{90} dx = \frac{1}{90}(75 - 55) = 0.2222.$$

Approach 3. Use R. Note that it is not necessary to include '`min=`' and '`max=`' as long as the lower bound is specified first and the upper bound second.

```
punif(75, 0, 90)- punif(55, 0, 90)

## [1] 0.2222222
```

Like discrete random variables, continuous random variables have an expected value, a variance, and a standard deviation:

$$E(x) = \frac{a+b}{2},$$

$$\sigma^2 = \frac{(b-a)^2}{12},$$

$$\sigma = \sqrt{\frac{(b-a)^2}{12}}.$$

Applying these expressions to the current example:

$$E(x) = \frac{a+b}{2} = \frac{0+90}{2} = \frac{90}{2} = 45,$$

$$\sigma^2 = \frac{(b-a)^2}{12} = \frac{90^2}{12} = \frac{8100}{12} = 675,$$

$$\sigma = \sqrt{\frac{(b-a)^2}{12}} = \sqrt{\frac{8100}{12}} = \sqrt{675} = 25.98.$$

Consider one final point concerning the nature of continuous probability distributions: because $p(x=55) = p(x=75) = 0$, it follows that $p(55 \le x \le 75) = p(55 < x < 75) = p(55 \le x < 75) = p(55 < x \le 75)$. In other words, including either or both end points of the interval, in this case either 55 or 75, does not change the value of the calculated probability.

What is true for the uniform probability distribution is also the case for the next three continuous probability distributions: the normal, the standard normal, and the exponential. For any continuous random variable x, the probability that x takes on a value between some lower bound a and another higher bound b can be found by calculating the area under the graph of the probability density function $f(x)$ over the range from a to b.

6.2 NORMAL PROBABILITY DISTRIBUTION

The normal probability distribution is the most important of all. Many continuous random variables across diverse areas of application have distributions for which the normal serves as a good or excellent model. In fact, the normal probability distribution is extensively used in the statistical estimation and inference parts of this book.

Definition 6.3. Normal Probability Distribution. A normal probability distribution is a continuous symmetric distribution for which the values of the variable are distributed in the shape of the bell curve. Although we do not propose to make use of it, the probability density function $f(x)$ for the normally distributed random variable is given by

$$f(x) = \frac{1}{\sigma\sqrt{2\pi}} e^{-(x-\mu)^2/2\sigma^2}, \quad \text{where } -\infty < x < +\infty.$$

Here μ is the mean and σ^2 is the variance. With regard to how data values are distributed in the case of the general normal probability distribution, recall the empirical rule from Section 3.5, which states that, regardless of the value of the mean μ and the standard deviation σ, if the data are known to be normally distributed, then:

1 Approximately 68% of data values will be within 1 standard deviation of the mean (see Figure 6.2).

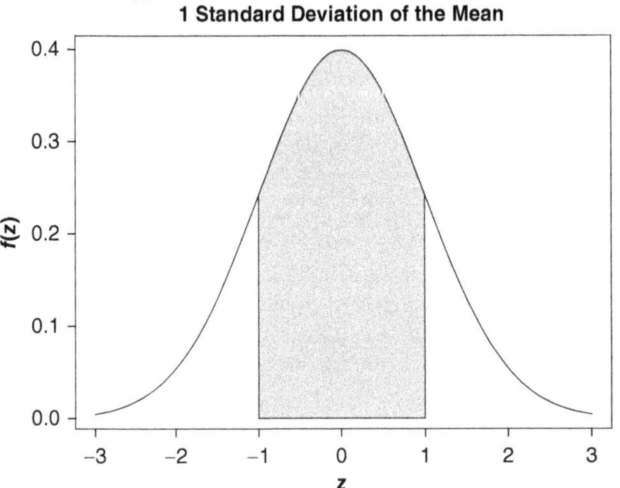

Figure 6.2 $p(-1 \leq z \leq 1) \approx$ 0.68 is given by the area shaded in grey

2 Approximately 95% of the data values will be within 2 standard deviations of the mean (see Figure 6.3).

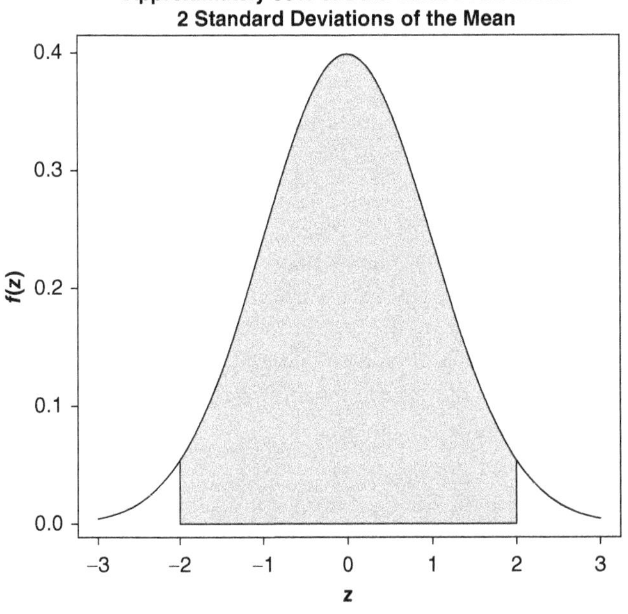

Figure 6.3 $p(-2 \leq z \leq 2) \approx$ 0.95 is given by the area shaded in grey

3 Approximately 99.7% of the data values will be within 3 standard deviations of the mean.

The normal probability distribution is sometimes referred to as the bell curve because of its symmetric, bell-shaped nature (see Figures 6.2 and 6.3). As it is a symmetric distribution, the mean, the median, and the mode are equal, and, like all continuous probability distributions, the area under the curve equals 1. However, there are literally an infinite number of different normal distributions; while each is shaped symmetrically around its mean, each differs as to its mean μ and standard deviation σ. In fact, the mean μ of a normal distribution can assume any real number value, while the standard deviation σ may be any positive number. How does one derive normal probabilities in the face of such complexity? There are two general approaches to getting any probabilities one may desire.

1 Find the probabilities for the normal distribution with $\mu = 0$ and $\sigma = 1$ and organize them in a single table. Then to solve problems requiring the general normal distribution (that is, a normal distribution with $\mu \neq 0$ and/or $\sigma \neq 1$), use these probabilities along with a simple conversion method.
2 Find probabilities using statistical software, such as R.

Definition 6.4. Standard Normal Probability Distribution. The normal probability distribution with mean $\mu = 0$ and standard deviation $\sigma = 1$.

The standard normal probability density function is derived simply by substituting $\mu = 0$ and $\sigma = 1$ into the normal probability density function

$$f(x) = \frac{1}{\sigma\sqrt{2\pi}} e^{-(x-\mu)^2/2\sigma^2},$$

to give

$$f(x) = \frac{1}{\sqrt{2\pi}} e^{-x^2/2}.$$

By convention, the standard normal random variable is expressed as z, not x:

$$f(z) = \frac{1}{\sqrt{2\pi}} e^{-z^2/2}, \quad \text{where } -\infty < z < +\infty.$$

Note that $f(z)$ is actually a bit simpler than $f(x)$, since both the denominator of the first term and the exponent on the second have collapsed to less complicated forms. Even so, $f(z)$ is not what we propose to use to find probabilities. As in the case of the continuous uniform probability distribution, we find probabilities by computing areas under the curve of $f(z)$ over an interval of values that z might assume. The best approach to computing probabilities related to the standard normal random variable is to use R.

Example 6.3. What is $p(z \leq 0)$?

Answer: 0.5000. Since the mean $\mu = 0$, and since the standard normal probability distribution is symmetrical, $p(z \leq 0)$ is 0.5000. Use `pnorm()` to find the cumulative probability.

```
pnorm(0)

## [1] 0.5
```

Example 6.4. What is $p(z \le -0.75)$?

Answer: 0.2266. Since $z = -0.75$ lies to the left of the mean $\mu = 0$, in the lower tail of the distribution, $p(z \le -0.75)$ should be less than 0.5000 (see Figure 6.4).

```
pnorm(-0.75)
```

```
## [1] 0.2266274
```

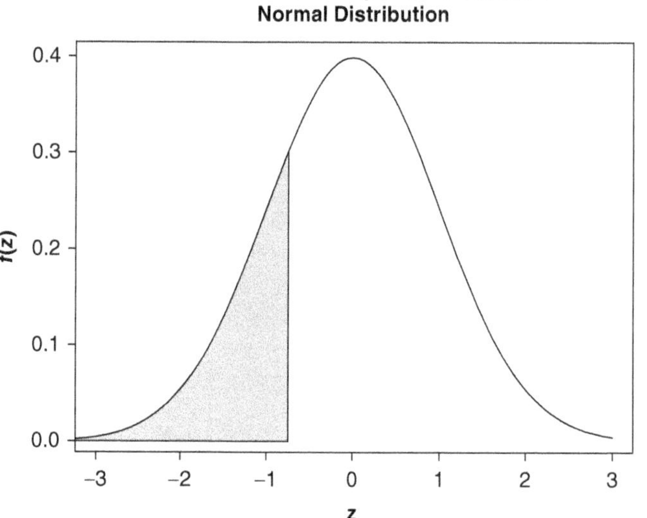

Figure 6.4 $p(z \le -0.75) = 0.2266$ is given by the area shaded in grey

Example 6.5. What is $p(z \le 1.25)$?

Answer: 0.8944. Since $z = 1.25$ lies to the right of the mean $\mu = 0$, in the upper tail of the distribution, $p(z \le 1.25)$ should be more than 0.5000.

```
pnorm(1.25)
```

```
## [1] 0.8943502
```

Example 6.6. What is $p(z \le 1.96)$?

Answer: 0.9750. Since $z = 1.96$ lies to the right of $z = 1.25$, $p(z \le 1.96)$ should be more than 0.8944.

```
pnorm(1.96)
```

```
## [1] 0.9750021
```

Example 6.7. What is $p(z \ge 1.05)$?

Answer: 0.1469. Since $z = 1.05$ lies to the right of the mean $\mu = 0$, in the upper tail of the distribution, $p(z \ge 1.05)$ is less than 0.5000 (see Figure 6.5). R offers two approaches.

```
#Comment1. 1 minus the cumulative probability that z is less than 1.05.
1 - pnorm(1.05)

## [1] 0.1468591

#Comment2. Or pnorm(1.05,lower.tail=FALSE) for area to right of z=1.05.
pnorm(1.05, lower.tail = FALSE)

## [1] 0.1468591
```

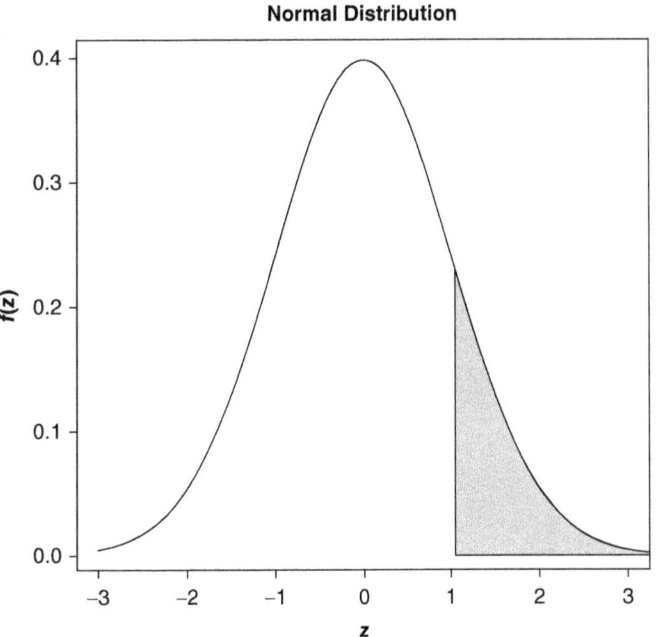

Figure 6.5 $p(z \geq 1.05) = 0.1469$ is given by the area shaded in grey

Example 6.8. What is $p(z \geq -0.25)$?

Answer: 0.5987. Since $z = -0.25$ lies to the left of the mean $\mu = 0$, in the lower tail of the distribution, $p(z \geq -0.25)$ should be more than 0.5000.

```
#Comment1. Use 1 minus pnorm(-0.25).
1 - pnorm(-0.25)

## [1] 0.5987063

#Comment2. Or use pnorm(–0.25,lower.tail=FALSE)
pnorm(-0.25, lower.tail = FALSE)

## [1] 0.5987063
```

Example 6.9. What is $p(z \geq -1.96)$?

Answer: 0.9750. Since $z = -1.96$ lies to the left of the mean $\mu = 0$, in the lower tail of the distribution, $p(z \geq -1.96)$ should be more than 0.5000.

```
1 - pnorm(-1.96)

## [1] 0.9750021

pnorm(-1.96, lower.tail = FALSE)

## [1] 0.9750021
```

Example 6.10. What is $p(1 \leq z \leq 1.96)$?

Answer: 0.1337. From $p(z \leq 1.96)$ subtract $p(z \leq 1)$.

```
pnorm(1.96) - pnorm(1)

## [1] 0.1336574
```

Example 6.11. What is $p(-1.15 \leq z \leq 2.05)$? See Figure 6.6.

Answer: 0.8547. From $p(z \leq 2.05)$ subtract $p(z \leq -1.15)$.

```
pnorm(2.05) - pnorm(-1.15)

## [1] 0.8547458
```

Example 6.12. What is $p(-1.20 \leq z \leq -0.65)$?

Answer: 0.1428.

```
pnorm(-0.65) - pnorm(-1.20)

## [1] 0.1427764
```

Example 6.13. Find the value for z such that the probability of a larger value is 0.05.

Answer: $z = 1.645$. Here we are reversing our direction. In Examples 6.3–6.12 we begin with values of z and end with probabilities; in Examples 6.13–6.16 we start with probabilities and then back out the associated z values. R handles this easily as long as we remember that qnorm(1 – 0.05) = qnorm(0.95), where the argument is simply the area to the left of the z value in question. R provides the single value of z which partitions the area under the curve into two pieces with 0.95 to the left of z, 0.05 to the right. That is the value of z which answers this question.

```
qnorm(0.95)

## [1] 1.644854
```

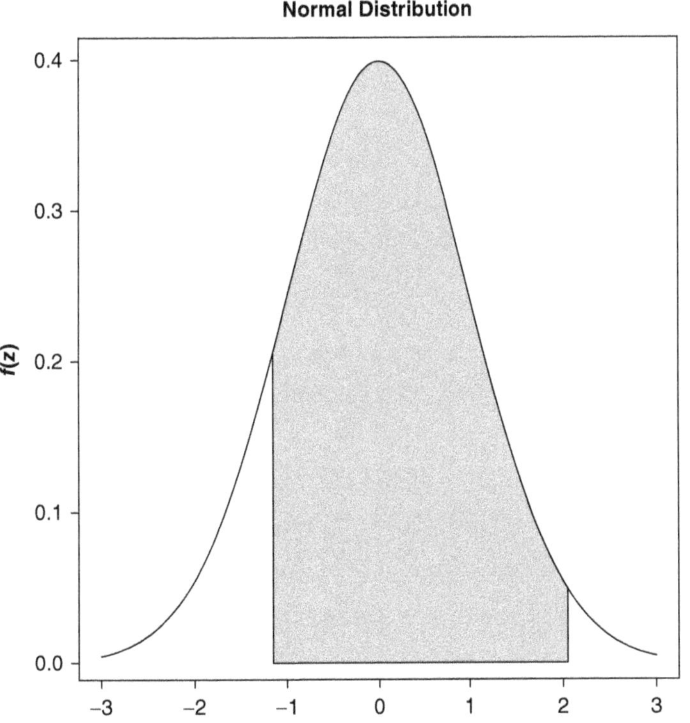

Figure 6.6 $p(-1.15 \leq z \leq 2.05) = 0.8547$ is given by the area shaded in grey

Example 6.14. Find the value for z such that the probability of a larger value is 0.10.

Answer: $z = 1.282$. Use `qnorm(1 - 0.10) = qnorm(0.90)` to find the value of z which divides area under the curve into two pieces with 0.90 to the left and 0.10 to the right.

```
qnorm(0.90)
```

```
## [1] 1.281552
```

Example 6.15. Find the value for z such that the probability of a larger value is 0.7881.

Answer: $z = -0.7998$.

```
qnorm(0.2119)
```

```
## [1] -0.799846
```

Example 6.16. Find the value for z such that the probability of a larger value is 0.9900.

Answer: $z = -2.326$.

```
qnorm(0.0100)
```

```
## [1] -2.326348
```

As important as it is to know how to find probabilities for the standard normal variable z, a question remains: since this approach is only useful for finding probabilities for one particular normal distribution—the one with $\mu = 0$ and $\sigma = 1$—how does one find normal probabilities when the mean is not 0 or the standard deviation is not 1? The key to using the standard normal areas to find probabilities for a general normal variable x is to convert x to the standard normal variable z. The simple two-step transformation of x into z involves (1) subtracting μ from x and (2) dividing the difference by σ. That is,

$$z = \frac{x - \mu}{\sigma}.$$

Most problems of a practical nature take a form similar to this: what is the probability that x is between a and b, where x has a normal distribution with $\mu \neq 0$ and $\sigma \neq 1$; that is, what is $p(a \leq x \leq b)$? While x is normally distributed, it is not *standard* normally distributed. But by performing this transformation, it is possible to use the standard normal probabilities to find $p(a \leq x \leq b)$ as follows:

1 Starting with the initial expression $p(a \leq x \leq b)$, subtract μ from a, x, and b:

$$p(a - \mu \leq x - \mu \leq b - \mu).$$

2 Divide each of the three terms (resulting from step 1) by σ:

$$p\left(\frac{a - \mu}{\sigma} \leq \frac{x - \mu}{\sigma} \leq \frac{b - \mu}{\sigma}\right).$$

Replace the middle term with z:

$$p\left(\frac{a - \mu}{\sigma} \leq z \leq \frac{b - \mu}{\sigma}\right).$$

In other words, the probability that x is between a and b is exactly equal to the probability that z is between $(a - \mu) / \sigma$ and $(b - \mu) / \sigma$. That is,

$$p(a \leq x \leq b) = p\left(\frac{a - \mu}{\sigma} \leq z \leq \frac{b - \mu}{\sigma}\right).$$

To apply the relationship between the general normal variable x and the standard normal variable z, consider the following examples.

Example 6.17. IQ scores are normally distributed with mean $\mu = 100$ and standard deviation $\sigma = 15$. What is the probability someone has an IQ score of 95 or less? That is, what is $p(x \leq 95)$?

Answer: 0.3694. We use two R-based approaches to this question.

Approach 1. Use the above method to transform x to z:

$$p(x \leq a) = p\left(\frac{x - \mu}{\sigma} \leq \frac{a - \mu}{\sigma}\right)$$

$$p(x \leq 95) = p\left(z \leq \frac{95 - 100}{15}\right) = p\left(z \leq -\frac{1}{3}\right) = 0.3694.$$

```
pnorm(-1/3)
```

```
## [1] 0.3694413
```

Approach 2. A better approach uses function `pnorm(95, 100, 15)` to find $p(x \leq 95)$ directly without having first to convert x to z. The standard deviation $\sigma = 100$ and mean $\mu = 15$ are specified as the second and third argument of the function, respectively.

```
pnorm(95, 100, 15)
```

```
## [1] 0.3694413
```

Example 6.18. Referring to Example 6.17, what is the probability someone has an IQ score of 110 or more? That is, what is $p(x \geq 110)$?

Answer: 0.2525.

Approach 1. Use the above method to transform x to z:

$$p(x \geq 110) = p\left(\frac{x-\mu}{\sigma} \geq \frac{110-100}{15}\right)$$

$$p(x \geq 110) = p\left(z \geq \frac{2}{3}\right) = 0.2525.$$

```
1 - pnorm(2/3)
```

```
## [1] 0.2524925
```

Approach 2. Use function `1 - pnorm(110, 100, 15)` to find $p(x \geq 110)$ directly:

```
1 - pnorm(110, 100, 15)
```

```
## [1] 0.2524925
```

Example 6.19. What is the probability someone has an IQ score between 90 and 110?

Answer: 0.495.

Approach 1. Use the above method to transform x to z:

$$p(90 \leq x \leq 110) = p\left(-\frac{2}{3} \leq z \leq \frac{2}{3}\right) = 0.495.$$

```
pnorm(2/3) - pnorm(-2/3)
```

```
## [1] 0.4950149
```

Approach 2. The expression `pnorm(110, 100, 15) - pnorm(90, 100, 15)` gives the answer directly:

```
pnorm(110, 100, 15) - pnorm(90, 100, 15)
```

```
## [1] 0.4950149
```

Example 6.20. A high-IQ society at a large public university requires that anyone seeking to join demonstrate that they have an IQ score placing them in the highest 1% of the population. What IQ score should an aspiring member have in order to be successful?

Answer: 134.9 or 135, rounding up.

Approach 1. Since $z = 2.326$ and $z = (x - \mu) / \sigma$, set these two expressions of z equal to one another and solve for x, the minimum required IQ score. Use the R function `qnorm(0.99)` to find that when $z = 2.326$, the probability of a larger value is equal to 0.01:

```
qnorm(0.99)
```

```
## [1] 2.326348
```

Substituting and solving for x:

$$\frac{x - \mu}{\sigma} = 2.326$$
$$x = \mu + 2.326\sigma.$$

Plugging in the values for the mean $\mu = 100$ and standard deviation $\sigma = 15$:

$$x = \mu + 2.326\sigma = 100 + 2.326 \times 15 = 100 + 34.89 = 134.9 \approx 135.$$

Approach 2. The function `qnorm(0.99, 100, 15)` finds the value of x that divides the area under the curve into two pieces, with 0.99 to the left and 0.01 to the right:

```
qnorm(0.99, 100, 15)
```

```
## [1] 134.8952
```

Example 6.21. The military service sets the minimum acceptable IQ score for enlistees. For example, if the Navy decides that each enlisted man or woman should have an IQ score above the lowest 10% of the population, what IQ score must all volunteers equal or exceed?

Answer: 80.78 or 81, rounding up.

Approach 1. Since $z = -1.282$ and $z = (x - \mu) / \sigma$, set these two expressions of z equal to one another and solve for x, the minimum IQ score. Use the R function `qnorm(0.10)` to find that when $z = -1.282$, the probability of a smaller value is equal to 0.10:

```
qnorm(0.10)
```

```
## [1] -1.281552
```

Substituting and solving for x:

$$\frac{x-\mu}{\sigma} = -1.282$$
$$x = \mu - 1.282\sigma.$$

Plugging in the values for the mean $\mu = 100$ and standard deviation $\sigma = 15$:

$$x = \mu - 1.282\sigma = 100 - 1.282 \times 15 = 100 - 19.23 = 80.77 \approx 81.$$

Approach 2. Find the cut-off point x directly using `qnorm(0.10, 100, 15)`.

```
qnorm(0.10, 100, 15)
```

```
## [1] 80.77673
```

Being able to use the first method to answer this type of question is desirable for the purpose of understanding the reasoning behind the approach. But because the second method is more convenient and precise, we prefer using it to the first method.

EXPONENTIAL PROBABILITY DISTRIBUTION

The exponential is the final continuous probability distribution considered in this chapter. It can be used to model phenomena of a continuous nature such as the *time* between arrivals (e.g., time between customers arriving at a restaurant) and the *distance* between occurrences (e.g., distance between defects in a plate glass window). As we will see, the exponential and Poisson (from Chapter 5) probability distributions are related.

Definition 6.5. Exponential Probability Distribution. A continuous probability distribution that can be used to find probabilities about the time or distance between occurrences which themselves are Poisson-distributed.

Although we will not be using the exponential probability density function to find probabilities, we provide it here to demonstrate how it differs from the other density functions we have encountered in this chapter:

$$f(x) = \frac{1}{\mu} e^{-x/\mu}, \quad \text{where } x \geq 0 \text{ and } \mu > 0.$$

Note that μ represents both the mean and the standard deviation. Instead, probabilities are derived using the cumulative probability function

$$p(x \leq x_0) = 1 - e^{-x_0/\mu}.$$

This expression makes intuitive sense: as x_0 becomes large—that is, the further x_0 is from 0—the smaller is the term subtracted from 1. This is consistent with the nature of cumulative probability functions: as x_0 becomes large, $p(x \leq x_0)$ approaches 1.

Example 6.22. Calls arrive at a customer-service number at a Poisson rate of 20 per hour (or 60 minutes). What is the exponential probability density function $f(x)$? What is the cumulative probability function $p(x \le x_0)$?

If calls arrive at a rate of 20 per hour, then the *time between calls* is exponentially distributed with a mean of $\mu = 3$ minutes (20 calls arriving at rate of 1 call every 3 minutes consume 60 minutes). In view of this, the exponential probability density function $f(x)$is

$$f(x) = \frac{1}{\mu}e^{-x/\mu} = \frac{1}{3}e^{-x/3}$$

and the cumulative probability function is

$$p(x \le x_0) = 1 - e^{-x_0/\mu} = 1 - e^{-x_0/3}.$$

Using the cumulative probability function, what are the following probabilities?

1 What is the probability that the time between calls is less than 2 minutes? That is, what is $p(x \le 2)$?

Answer: 0.4866 (see Figure 6.7).

Approach 1. Use the cumulative probability function to find the probability:

$$p(x \le 2) = 1 - e^{-2/3} = 1 - 0.5134 = 0.4866.$$

Approach 2. Use function `pexp(2, 1/3)` to find the probability that the time between calls is less than 2 minutes when the average time between calls is 3 minutes:

```
pexp(2, 1/3)

## [1] 0.4865829
```

2 What is the probability that the time between calls is less than 5 minutes? That is, what is $p(x \le 5)$?

Answer: 0.8111.

Approach 1. Use the cumulative probability function to find the probability:

$$p(x \le 5) = 1 - e^{-5/3} = 1 - 0.1889 = 0.8111.$$

Approach 2. Use the function `pexp(5, 1/3)` to find the probability that the time between calls is less than 5 minutes when the average time between calls is 3 minutes:

```
pexp(5, 1/3)

## [1] 0.8111244
```

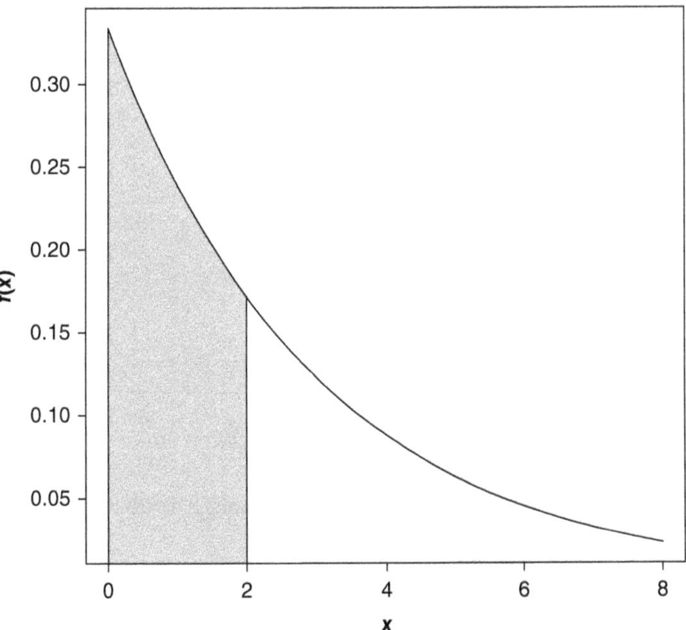

Figure 6.7 $p(x \leq 2) =$ 0.4866 is given by the area shaded in grey

3 What is the probability that the time is greater than 3 minutes? That is, what is $p(x \geq 3)$?

Answer: 0.3679 (see Figure 6.8).

Approach 1. Use the cumulative probability function to find the probability:

$$p(x \geq 3) = 1 - p(x \leq 3) = 1 - (1 - e^{-3/3}) = 1 - (1 - e^{-1}) = e^{-1} = 0.3679.$$

Approach 2. Use 1 minus the function `pexp(3, 1/3)` to find the probability that the time between calls is greater than 3 minutes when the average time between calls is 3 minutes:

```
1 - pexp(3, 1/3)

## [1] 0.3678794
```

4 What is the probability that the time is greater than 6 minutes? That is, what is $p(x \geq 6)$?

Answer: 0.1353.

Approach 1. Use the cumulative probability function to find the probability:

$$p(x \geq 6) = 1 - p(x \leq 6) = 1 - (1 - e^{-6/3}) = 1 - (1 - e^{-2}) = e^{-2} = 0.1353.$$

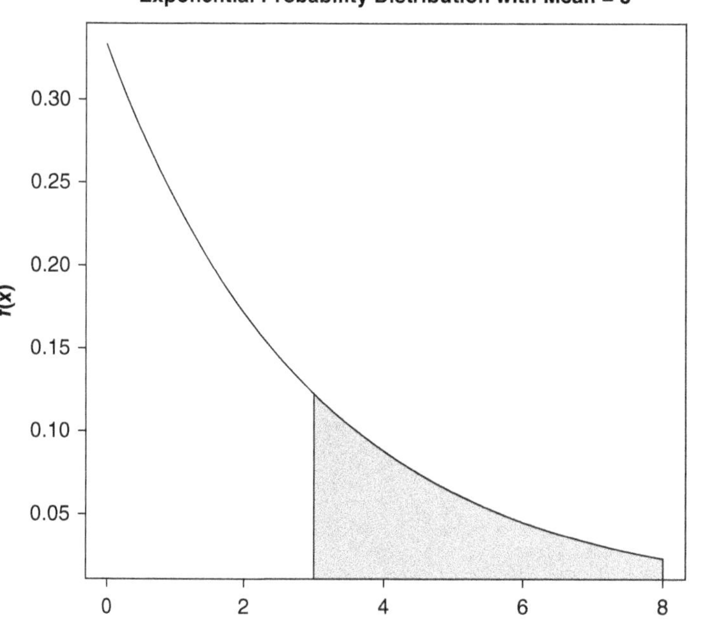

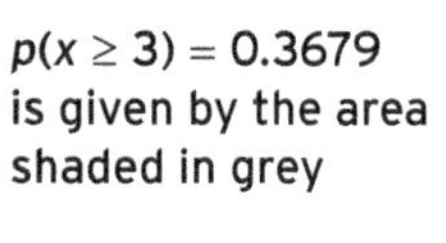

Figure 6.8
$p(x \geq 3) = 0.3679$ is given by the area shaded in grey

Approach 2. Use 1 minus the function `pexp(6, 1/3)` to find the probability that the time between calls is greater than 6 minutes when the average time between calls is 3 minutes:

```
1 - pexp(6, 1/3)
```

```
## [1] 0.1353353
```

5 What is the probability that the time between calls is between 2 and 5 minutes? That is, what is $p(2 \leq x \leq 5)$?

Answer: 0.3245 (see Figure 6.9).

Approach 1. Use the difference between the two cumulative probability functions to find the probability:

$$p(2 \leq x \leq 5) = p(x \leq 5) - p(x \leq 2) = (1 - e^{-5/3}) - (1 - e^{-2/3})$$
$$= 0.8111 - 0.4866 = 0.3245.$$

Approach 2. From `pexp(5,1/3)` subtract `pexp(2,1/3)` to find the probability that the time between calls is between 2 and 5 minutes when the average is 3 minutes:

```
pexp(5, 1/3) - pexp(2, 1/3)
```

```
## [1] 0.3245415
```

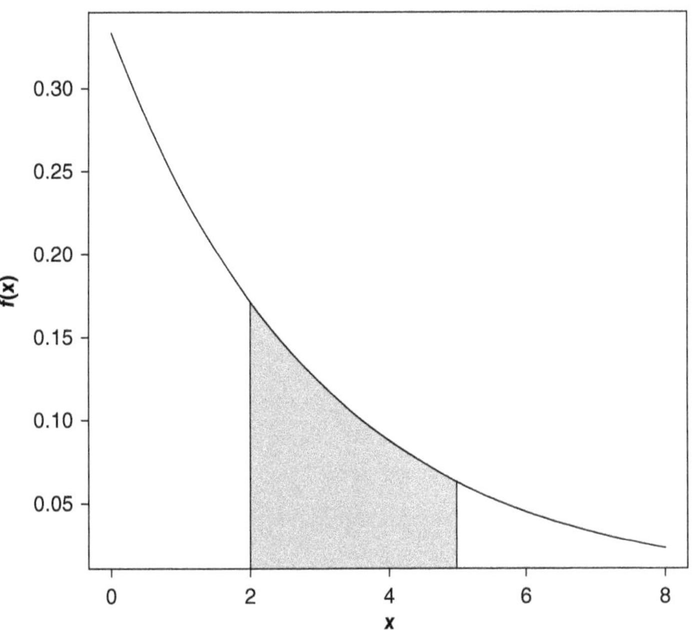

Figure 6.9 $p(2 \leq x \leq 5) = 0.3245$ is given by the area shaded in grey

Example 6.23. If a customer-service representative takes a 5-minute coffee break, what is the probability that no calls await him when he returns?

Answer: 0.1889. This is calculated as follows:

$$p(x \geq 5) = 1 - p(x \leq 5) = 1 - (1 - e^{-5/3}) = e^{-5/3} = 0.1889.$$

```
1 - pexp(5, 1/3)
```

```
## [1] 0.1888756
```

Note that this result can also be found by translating the exponential problem into the Poisson probability framework. In this case, if 20 calls arrive every 60 minutes, then 5/3 calls arrive every 5 minutes, on average. Accordingly, the Poisson calculation would be

$$p(x \mid \mu) = \frac{\mu^x e^{-\mu}}{x!}.$$

Since $\mu = 5/3$ and $x = 0$,

$$p\left(x = 0 \mid \mu = \frac{5}{3}\right) = \frac{(5/3)^0 e^{-5/3}}{0!} = e^{-5/3} = 0.1889.$$

Note that the solution to this expression exactly equals the solution to the expression when we approached the question from the exponential point of view.

Finally, we can use `dpois(0, 5/3)` to find the Poisson probability that there are 0 calls during a 5-minute interval when the mean number is 5/3:

```
dpois(0, 5/3)

## [1] 0.1888756
```

 OPTIONAL MATERIAL: A DERIVATION OF THE CUMULATIVE EXPONENTIAL PROBABILITY FUNCTION

Since we have seen that probabilities are found by calculating the area under the curve of the probability density function, let us demonstrate the connection between the exponential probability density function and the cumulative probability function:

$$f(x) = \frac{1}{\mu} e^{-x/\mu}$$

and

$$p(x \le x_0) = \int_0^{x_0} f(x)\,\mathrm{d}x = \int_0^{x_0} \frac{1}{\mu} e^{-x/\mu}\,\mathrm{d}x.$$

Now let

$$v = -\frac{x}{\mu}$$

$$\frac{dv}{dx} = -\frac{1}{\mu}$$

$$dv = -\frac{1}{\mu} dx$$

$$dx = -\mu dv.$$

Changing variables and moving the constants across the integral sign gives us

$$p(x \le x_0) = \int_0^{x_0} \frac{1}{\mu} e^{-x/\mu}\,\mathrm{d}x = \frac{1}{\mu} \int_0^{x_0} (-\mu) \mathrm{e}^{v}\,\mathrm{d}v = (-1) \int_0^{x_0} \mathrm{e}^{v}\,\mathrm{d}v = (-1) e^{v} \big|_0^{x_0}$$

and

$$(-1) e^{v} \big|_0^{x_0} = (-1) e^{-x/\mu} \Big|_0^{x_0} = (-1)\left\{e^{-x_0/\mu} - e^{-0/\mu}\right\} = (-1)\left\{e^{-x_0/\mu} - 1\right\} = 1 - e^{-x_0/\mu}.$$

Thus

$$p(x \le x_0) = \int_0^{x_0} f(x)\,\mathrm{d}x = \int_0^{x_0} \frac{1}{\mu} e^{-x/\mu}\,\mathrm{d}x = 1 - e^{-x_0/\mu}.$$

SUMMARY

This chapter, the final one dealing with probability before moving onto formal statistical methods, extends the discussion of probability distributions from the discrete to the continuous. In particular, three continuous probability distributions are introduced and developed: the continuous uniform, the normal, and the exponential. Throughout the chapter, careful attention is paid to the procedures of (a) computing the probabilities that a random variable can assume a value within a given well-defined interval and (b) finding the value of the random variable that is associated with a given level of probability. In this effort, R is used extensively.

Although the general framework for finding probabilities is the same for the discrete and continuous random variable—and the kinds of questions raised and answered are for the most part similar—an important distinction is found in the specific mechanics required to produce probabilities. Recall that in the case of the discrete random variable, probabilities are found by way of the probability function $f(x)$ which provides the probability of each value the random variable x might assume. To find the probability that x falls in an interval, we simply sum the values of the probability function for each value of x in that interval. However, in the case of the continuous random variable, the probabilities are found by deriving the area under the graph of the curve of the probability density function $f(x)$. An important difference between the discrete probability function and the probability density function is that the discrete probability function can directly provide probabilities: we find the probabilities by substituting the value of the random variable x directly into $f(x)$. However, this is not the way probabilities are found for a continuous random variable. Substituting the value of the random variable x into $f(x)$ provides the height of the graph of the function at that point, not the probability. The probability must be calculated by finding the area under the curve over an interval. The probability that the continuous random variable assumes any particular value is always 0.

The continuous uniform probability distribution has limited practical usefulness. The main reason it is introduced in this chapter is that its rectangular-shaped probability distribution makes it easy to appreciate the unique characteristics of continuous probability distributions. The normal probability distribution has many practical applications, some of which are encountered in the exercises as well as in the chapter itself. Moreover, the normal distribution is used repeatedly throughout the book once we get into the chapters dealing with statistics. The exponential probability distribution can be used to model phenomena of a continuous nature such as the time between arrivals and the distance between occurrences. Finally, if the interval of time (or distance) between occurrences is distributed exponentially, then the number of occurrences in that interval must be Poisson-distributed. The two distributions are related.

definitions

Continuous Uniform Probability Distribution A continuous uniform probability distribution is one for which all intervals of equal length have the same probability. When graphed, the distribution assumes the shape of a rectangle.

Exponential Probability Distribution A continuous probability distribution that can be used to derive the time between occurrences which themselves are Poisson-distributed.

Normal Probability Distribution A normal probability distribution is a continuous symmetric distribution for which the values of the variable are distributed in the shape of the bell curve.

Probability Density Function A probability density function provides the likelihood that a continuous random variable will assume a particular range of values. When the area under the curve of the function and over the range of values is computed, it provides the probability the random variable will fall in that interval.

Standard Normal Probability Distribution The standard normal probability distribution is simply a normal probability distribution which has mean 0 and standard deviation 1. It is used extensively in solving problems involving the general normal probability distribution by the use of a simple conversion formula.

formulae

Continuous Uniform Probability Density Function

$$f(x) = \frac{1}{b-a}, \quad \text{where } a \le x \le b$$

Continuous Uniform Probability Distribution: Expected Value

$$E(x) = \frac{a+b}{2}$$

Continuous Uniform Probability Distribution: Variance

$$\text{Var}(x) = \sigma^2 = \frac{(b-a)^2}{12}$$

Exponential Probability Density Function

$$f(x) = \frac{1}{\mu}e^{-x/\mu}, \quad \text{where } x \ge 0 \text{ and } \mu > 0$$

Exponential Probability Distribution: Cumulative Probabilities

$$p(x \le x_0) = 1 - e^{-x_0/\mu}$$

Normal Probability Density Function

$$f(x) = \frac{1}{\sigma\sqrt{2\pi}}e^{-(x-\mu)^2/2\sigma^2}, \quad \text{where } -\infty < x < +\infty$$

Standard Normal Probability Density Function

$$f(z) = \frac{1}{\sqrt{2\pi}}e^{-z^2/2}, \quad \text{where } -\infty < z < +\infty$$

R functions

`pexp(x, 1/μ)` Provides the cumulative exponential probability of x for the exponential probability distribution with mean μ.

`pnorm(x, μ, σ)` Provides the cumulative normal probability of x for the normal probability distribution with mean μ and standard deviation σ.

`pnorm(z)` Provides the cumulative standard normal probability of z for the standard normal probability distribution with mean $\mu = 0$ and standard deviation $\sigma = 1$. Since no values are defined (as arguments) for μ and σ, R assumes the function `pnorm()` is the standard normal.

`punif(x, a, b)` Provides the cumulative uniform probability of x for the uniform probability distribution with *a* as a lower bound, *b* as an upper bound.

`qnorm(α, μ, σ)` Provides the value of x that cuts off an area of α in the lower tail of the normal probability distribution with mean μ and standard deviation σ.

`qnorm(α)` Provides the value of z that cuts off an area of α in the lower tail of the standard normal probability distribution.

`qunif(α, a, b)` Provides the value of x that cuts off an area of α in the lower tail of the uniform probability distribution defined between *a* and *b*.

APPENDIX: USING R TO FIND PROBABILITIES FOR CONTINUOUS PROBABILITY DISTRIBUTIONS– UNIFORM, STANDARD NORMAL, GENERAL NORMAL, AND EXPONENTIAL

R commands for uniform, standard normal, normal, and exponential probabilities are given in Tables 6.1–6.4.

Table 6.1 R commands for the uniform probabilities

To find this probability for the uniform probability distribution defined between *a* and *b*	Use this R command
$p(x < x_0)$	`punif(x0, a, b)`
$p(x \le x_0)$	`punif(x0, a, b)`
$p(x > x_0) = 1 - p(x \le x_0)$	`1-punif(x0, a, b)`
$p(x \ge x_0) = 1 - p(x \le x_0)$	`1-punif(x0, a, b)`
If we are given α, what is x_0 where $p(x \le x_0) = \alpha$?	`qunif(α, a, b)`

Table 6.2 R commands for the standard normal probabilities

To find this probability for the standard normal probability distribution	Use this R command
$p(z < z_0)$	pnorm(z_0)
$p(z \leq z_0)$	pnorm(z_0)
$p(z > z_0) = 1 - p(z \leq z_0)$	1-pnorm(z_0)
$p(z \geq z_0) = 1 - p(z \leq z_0)$	1-pnorm(z_0)
If we are given α, what is z_0 where $p(z \leq z_0) = \alpha$?	qnorm(α)

Table 6.3 R commands for the general normal probabilities

To find this probability for the general normal probability distribution	Use this R command
$p(x < x_0)$	pnorm(x_0, μ, σ)
$p(x \leq x_0)$	pnorm(x_0, μ, σ)
$p(x > x_0) = 1 - p(x \leq x_0)$	1-pnorm(x_0, μ, σ)
$p(x \geq x_0) = 1 - p(x \leq x_0)$	1-pnorm(x_0, μ, σ)
If we are given α, what is x_0 where $p(x \leq x_0) = \alpha$?	qnorm(α, μ, σ)

Table 6.4 R commands for the exponential probabilities

To find this probability for the exponential probability distribution	Use this R command
$p(x < x_0)$	pexp(x_0, $1/\mu$)
$p(x \leq x_0)$	pexp(x_0, $1/\mu$)
$p(x > x_0) = 1 - p(x \leq x_0)$	1-pexp(x_0, $1/\mu$)
$p(x \geq x_0) = 1 - p(x \leq x_0)$	1-pexp(x_0, $1/\mu$)

exercises

6.1 A recent college graduate is moving to Houston, Texas, to take a new job, and is looking to purchase a home. Since Houston comprises a relatively large metropolitan area of about 7 million people, there are a lot of homes from which to choose. When searching for properties on the real estate websites, it is possible to select the price range of housing in which

(Continued)

(Continued)

one is most interested. Suppose the potential buyer specifies a price range of \$200,000 to \$250,000, and the result of the search returns thousands of homes with prices distributed uniformly throughout that range.

(a) What would be the probability density function that best describes this distribution of housing prices?
(b) What are $E(x)$ and σ?
(c) If the buyer ultimately selects a home from this initial list of possibilities, what is the probability she will have to pay more than \$235,000? Use R to find the solution to this question.

6.2 According to British weather forecasters, the average monthly rainfall in London during the month of June is $\mu = 2.09$ inches. Assume that the monthly precipitation is a normally distributed random variable with a standard deviation of $\sigma = 0.48$ inches.

(a) What is the probability that London will have between 1.5 and 2.5 inches of precipitation next June?
(b) What is the probability that London will have an extraordinarily dry month of June with 1 inch or less of precipitation?
(c) If London authorities worry about local flooding when the monthly precipitation falls in the upper 5% of the monthly average, how much rain would London have to receive to cause local authorities to consider preparing for flood conditions?

Use R to answer these questions.

6.3 The time required by students to complete an organic chemistry examination is normally distributed with a mean of $\mu = 200$ minutes and a standard deviation of $\sigma = 20$ minutes. Use R to answer all questions.

(a) What is the probability a student will complete the examination in 180 minutes or less?
(b) What is the probability a student will take between 180 and 220 minutes to complete the examination?
(c) Since this particular class is a large lecture section of 300 students, and the final examination period lasts 240 minutes, how many students would we expect to submit the completed exam on time?

6.4 A large agricultural producer in Spain produces melons with diameters that are normally distributed with a mean of $\mu = 15$ centimeters (cm) and a standard deviation of $\sigma = 2$ cm. Use R to find the solutions to these questions.

(a) What is the probability a melon will have a diameter of at least 12 cm?
(b) What is the probability that a randomly selected melon will have a diameter of no less than 12 cm but no more than 16 cm?
(c) The producer has an arrangement with several gourmet shops by which it will receive a slightly higher price for melons with a diameter that falls in the top 10%. What is the minimum diameter a melon must have in order to qualify for the higher price?

6.5 The number of visits to the Book4Less.com discount travel website is a Poisson-distributed random variable with a mean of 10 visits per minute. Use R to answer all questions.

(a) What is the mean of the associated exponential probability distribution?
(b) Write out the exponential probability density function $f(x)$.
(c) Write out the cumulative probability function.
(d) What is the standard deviation σ of the distribution?
(e) If the internet server experiences an 18-second power failure during which time people would be denied access to the website, what is the probability that no one attempted to visit and thus no business was lost during the down-time?

https://study.sagepub.com/stinerock

Point Estimation and Sampling Distributions

contents

learning objectives

1. Understand the importance of sampling and how the results from sampling can be used to provide estimates of population characteristics such as the population mean, standard deviation, and proportion.
2. Learn about the methods commonly used to draw samples and the important role played by one of those methods, simple random sampling.
3. Understand the concept of the sampling distribution and how it provides the foundation for statistical estimation and inference.
4. Understand the central limit theorem and how it makes it possible to use sampling distributions for purposes of estimation and inference.
5. Know the characteristics of the sampling distribution of the sample mean $\bar{x}$ and the sample proportion $\bar{p}$.

Thus far, we have covered the first two sections of this book: descriptive statistics (Chapters 1–3) and probability (Chapters 4–6). The final section deals entirely with statistics. In this chapter we introduce and develop the important ideas of point estimation, sampling, and sampling distributions. In Chapter 8 we build directly on the ideas introduced here, extending point estimation to interval estimation.

Before considering the methods of estimation, however, let us briefly review where we have been, where we are, and where we are going. This book deals with three broad but sequentially related areas. In the first area, descriptive statistics, we learn to use various methods of organizing, summarizing, and presenting data for the purposes of analysis and interpretation. The main objective of these methods is to provide insights about the data, and the story they tell, that cannot be quickly or easily obtained by looking only at the data in their raw, original state. The main approaches of descriptive statistics consist of tabular, graphical, and numerical methods.

In the second section of the book, we learn that probability problems arise when we draw a sample from a larger body of items, called a population, and wish to make statements about the probability that the sample has certain characteristics. We assign probability estimates based on our knowledge of the properties of the population. Recall the situation in which we draw a single card from a deck of 52, and ask "What is the probability the card is an ace?" We know that the probability of drawing an ace is 4 / 52, and we know this because of our knowledge of the properties of the population: a deck of 52 playing cards includes 4 aces.

In the third section, we see that statistics is concerned with questions that are opposite in nature to the one characterizing the selection of a single playing card. In a probability problem, we begin with a knowledge of the characteristics of the population and then go on to raise questions about the properties of the sample that might be drawn, whereas in statistics, we start with a knowledge of the properties of the sample and then raise questions about the unknown characteristics of the population. With probability, we start with the population and end up with statements about the sample; with statistics, we start with the sample and end with statements about the population.

7.1 POPULATIONS AND SAMPLES

As a beginning, we recapitulate two important definitions—population and sample.

Definition 7.1. Population. A population consists of all the entities of interest in an investigative study. Very often, working with a population is impractical, even impossible, and working with a sample is the best alternative. The choice of working with a sample is a trade-off decision that involves sacrificing some richness and accuracy in the findings for the advantage of working with a more manageable, more readily available, more affordable set of data.

Definition 7.2. Sample. A sample is a portion or subset of the population, selected for the purpose of the study.

Pulling these definitions together, the purpose of statistics, then, is to obtain information about a population from the information contained in a sample.

Consider the problem faced by the chair of a university's statistics department who wants to develop her understanding of the preparation of students enrolling in one of two different types of introductory-level statistics courses. She knows that there has been a problem involving a mis-assignment of (1) students with weaker backgrounds to the calculus-based course and (2) stronger students to the section of what is popularly known as "statistics for poets," the non-calculus-based course offering. Accordingly, students are now required to take a placement exam before enrolling in a statistics course. This year 1250 students completed the exam, which is scored between 0 and 100 points, with 100 points being a perfect result. The chair has also requested data on each student indicating whether he or she has completed a calculus course, either in high school or at university. To begin, the chair wants a profile of all students in terms of two variables: the mean test score and the proportion of students lacking a background in calculus. There are two general approaches to developing this type of information: a census where one collects the data on all members of the population, and a sample where one collects the data on a subgroup of the population. We begin with the census before moving on to a sample.

For the entire population of all 1250 students, the population mean exam score is

$$\mu = \frac{\sum x_i}{N} = 63,$$

while the population standard deviation is

$$\sigma = \sqrt{\sigma^2} = \sqrt{\frac{\sum(x_i - \mu)^2}{N}} = 7.$$

Finally, the population proportion of students not completing a course in calculus is

$$p = 0.62.$$

These are the population characteristics of interest—$\sigma = 7$, $\mu = 63$, and $p = 0.62$—and they are referred to as the population parameters. It is worth noting that these numbers are not statistics, even though the non-statistician might refer to them as such. In fact, at any given point in time they are constant values that do not vary from one measure to the next. Since we use the terms "population parameters" and "sample statistics" throughout this chapter, we repeat their definitions here.

Definition 7.3. Population Parameters. These are the characteristics of interest in a study. Unless we are working with the entire population, however, we will rarely if ever know with certainty the value of the population parameters. Population parameters are often referred to simply as parameters.

Definition 7.4. Sample Statistics. These are the characteristics of interest derived from a sample rather than a population. While the values of the parameters are typically true but unknown—that is, they are unobservable, fixed, and represent the unvarying truth at a given moment in time—the values of the sample statistics vary from one sample to the next. Finally, sample statistics are often referred to simply as statistics.

At this point, we raise two questions which lie at the heart of statistical thinking. First, is it really necessary to use the entire population of all 1250 students to develop the desired information? If one only wants a general feel for the lay of the land—of the overall quantitative competence of the students—is it possible to obtain this information using a sample of, say, 30 students? This question becomes all the more relevant if some of the information is not so easily obtained, for example, if the academic transcript of each and every student must be examined carefully to determine who has taken a course in calculus. But if a sample provides good enough information about the population parameters of interest, then it makes sense to work with the sample instead of the population. Second, assuming a population is not being used, how should a sample be selected for the study? Are some methods of drawing samples better than others? What are the characteristics of a good sample?

7.2 THE SIMPLE RANDOM SAMPLE

Although we discuss later in this chapter several methods of selecting a sample, we will make abundant use of one of them, simple random sampling. Here is the definition.

Definition 7.5. Simple Random Sample from a Finite Population. A simple random sample (SRS) of size n drawn from a finite population of size N is one in which each sample of size n has an equal chance of selection.

As an example of an SRS, consider the following small-scale problem. A sales manager has a sales force of five sales representatives, and would like to randomly sample two sales reps (of the five) to determine if the entire five-member sales force is moving toward its sales quota. Let us express the problem in terms of the ball-and-urn framework where each of five balls represents one of the sales reps. First, paint a single letter—A, B, C, D, or E—on each ball so that there is a one-to-one correspondence between balls and sales reps. Second, place the balls in the urn, stir, and draw two balls at random. Viewed as an experiment, one can write out the sample space S consisting of all possible pairs that might be selected:

$$S = \{(A,B), (A,C), (A,D), (A,E), (B,C), (B,D), (B,E), (C,D), (C,E), (D,E)\}.$$

It is clear that there is a finite number of samples that might be drawn, even if one were to repeat this experiment again and again. In fact, there are only 10 possible samples, or sample points. Ultimately, the sample the manager selects must be one of these 10.

An SRS of size $n = 2$ can be selected by making sure that each of the 10 possible samples has an equal probability of selection. Does drawing samples using the ball-and-urn method above represent a simple random sampling procedure? Yes, it probably does. As long as the SRS requirement is satisfied that all possible samples have an equal chance of being selected, then the method can be considered simple random sampling. That is,

$$\begin{aligned} p(A,B) &= p(A,C) = p(A,D) = p(A,E) = p(B,C) = p(B,D) \\ &= p(B,E) = p(C,D) = p(C,E) = p(D,E) = 0.10. \end{aligned}$$

Applying the classical rule for assigning probabilities to equally likely outcomes (see Chapter 4), the probability of each outcome is simply 1/10 since there are 10 outcomes.

Even though this is a relatively trivial example involving small sample and population sizes, it is possible to develop a more general approach to the larger-scale problem. When a sample of size n is drawn from a finite population of size N, how many unique samples are possible? The answer involves the combination of N objects taken n at a time:

$$C_n^N = \binom{N}{n} = \frac{N!}{n!(N-n)!}.$$

Accordingly, for any single SRS of size n drawn from a finite population of size N:

$$p(\text{any SRS}) = \frac{1}{C_n^N}.$$

Example 7.1. If $N = 5$ and $n = 2$, what is the probability of each SRS?

Answer: 0.10.

$$C_n^N = \binom{N}{n} = \frac{N!}{n!(N-n)!} = \frac{5!}{2!3!} = 10$$

$$p(\text{any SRS}) = \frac{1}{C_n^N} = \frac{1}{C_2^5} = \frac{1}{10} = 0.10.$$

```
#Comment1. The number of ways n=2 can be selected from N=5.
choose(5, 2)

## [1] 10

#Comment2. The probability of each SRS of size n=2 from N=5.
1 / choose(5, 2)

## [1] 0.1
```

An SRS requires that each of the 10 samples has an equal chance of being selected.

Example 7.2. If $N = 10$ and $n = 2$, what is the probability of each SRS?

Answer: 0.02222.

$$C_2^{10} = \binom{10}{2} = \frac{10!}{2!8!} = 45$$

$$p(\text{any SRS}) = \frac{1}{C_n^N} = \frac{1}{C_2^{10}} = \frac{1}{45} = 0.02222$$

```
#Comment. The probability of each SRS of size n=2 from N=10.
1 / choose(10, 2)

## [1] 0.02222222
```

Randomness is a property of the sampling procedure—such as selecting balls from an urn—and not the particular SRS that happens to result. We can use a simple random sampling procedure and still draw a non-random-looking sample because all possible samples (even the non-representative ones) are equally likely. For example, we could use an SRS procedure to draw four playing cards from a deck of 52, and still end up with four aces. The probability of drawing four aces—a sample some might consider non-random—is equal to the probability of drawing any other hand. The procedure is random but the results look anything but random. On average, however, SRS provides the most representative sample results.

Note that the above discussion concerns drawing samples from finite populations. However, when the population involves a continuing process—such as customers entering a shopping mall, visiting a website, or contacting a customer-service call center—it cannot be characterized as finite since there is no way of specifying N in advance. Statisticians often refer to such populations as *infinite*. Since there is nothing infinite about such a population, however, the most that can be said about it is that no one knows beforehand exactly how large it might turn out to be. Accordingly, the conditions under which an SRS can be developed when the population is an ongoing process—that is, when a population is described as infinite—need to be specified.

Definition 7.6. Simple Random Sample from an Infinite Population. An SRS from an infinite population is one for which (1) each item of the sample is chosen from the population, and (2) each item of the sample is chosen independently.

Consider the problem faced by an international bank wishing to conduct a satisfaction survey among those clients calling its toll-free number about some aspect of its service. To this end, the bank often (subsequently) emails those clients, inviting them to participate in an online survey of their satisfaction with the service encounter. One way the bank could develop an SRS from this infinite population of callers is to select the next client placing a call immediately after a caller from North America. Even North American clients are not excluded, since they are as likely to follow a North American caller as anyone else. The two conditions required for developing an SRS from an infinite population appear to be met: the first because only those calling the customer-service number are included; the second because the clients are chosen independently since the calls they place are made randomly.

7.3 THE SAMPLE STATISTIC: $\bar{x}$, S, AND $\bar{p}$

Let us return to the problem of the chair wishing to understand her students' preparation for statistics courses. Recall that we first approached this issue by working with the entire population, and learned that $\mu = 63$, $\sigma = 7$, and $p = 0.62$. Suppose that instead of working with the entire population of $N = 1250$, we (1) draw an SRS of $n = 30$ students, (2) compile data on placement exam scores and calculus course completion for all 30 students, and (3) determine the sample statistics $\bar{x}$, s, and $\bar{p}$. Suppose they are

$$\bar{x} = \frac{\Sigma x_i}{n} = 60,$$

$$s = \sqrt{\frac{\Sigma(x_i - \bar{x})^2}{n-1}} = 6,$$

$$\bar{p} = \frac{20}{30} = 0.67.$$

It should not be surprising that the values of $\bar{x}$, s, and $\bar{p}$ do not exactly equal those of the population parameters. After all, the sample contains different data items than does the population, and only 30 of them at that.

Finally, note that a sample statistic is also referred to as a point estimator because it is the numerical value that estimates a population parameter. In other words, $\bar{x}$ is the point estimator of μ, s is the point estimator of σ, and $\bar{p}$ is the point estimator of p.

Now that we have considered several of the most important foundational ideas underpinning the concept of sampling, let us turn our attention to one of the most important topics in all of statistics, the sampling distribution.

7.4 THE SAMPLING DISTRIBUTION OF $\bar{x}$

Consider a hypothetical question: if we were to collect an additional 999 SRSs, each of size $n = 30$, and then calculate $\bar{x}$ and $\bar{p}$ for each SRS, would all 999 values of $\bar{x}$ (or $\bar{p}$) be the same? No, they would vary from one SRS to the next because the different samples would not contain the same 30 students. To emphasize this point, several values of $\bar{x}$ and $\bar{p}$ are reported in Table 7.1. (The values for $\bar{x}$ and $\bar{p}$ from Section 7.3 above are entered in the first row.) Figure 7.1 is a histogram of the relative frequencies of $\bar{x}$ values from 1000 simple random samples, each of size $n = 30$.

Now recall two definitions last seen in Chapter 5: *experiment* and *random variable*.

Definition 7.7. Experiment. An experiment is any process that can result in any one of multiple well-defined outcomes that cannot be predicted with certainty beforehand.

Definition 7.8. Random Variable. A function that assigns numerical values to the outcome of an experiment.

Table 7.1 Sample means and proportions for 1000 SRSs: $n = 30$

Sample number	Sample mean $\bar{x}_i$	Sample proportion $\bar{p}_i$
1	$\bar{x}_1 = 60$	$\bar{p}_1 = 0.67$
2	$\bar{x}_2 = 64$	$\bar{p}_2 = 0.63$
3	$\bar{x}_3 = 65$	$\bar{p}_3 = 0.60$
⋮	⋮	⋮
1000	$\bar{x}_{1000} = 61$	$\bar{p}_{1000} = 0.57$

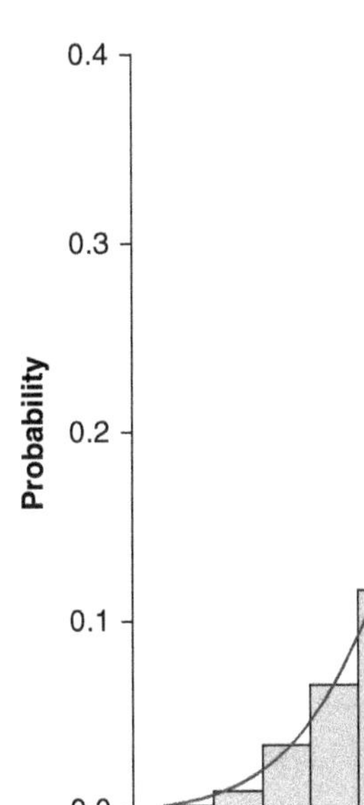

Figure 7.1 Histogram of values of $\bar{x}$ for 1000 SRSs: $n = 30$

The act of selecting an SRS of n items is an experiment in that the sampling process itself results in well-defined outcomes, in this case the SRSs. The sample statistics, $\bar{x}$ and $\bar{p}$, are both random variables because they are numerical characterizations of the outcome of the experiment of drawing SRSs. In other words, both $\bar{x}$ and $\bar{p}$ assign numerical values to each SRS that might be selected. Like other random variables, $\bar{x}$ has a distribution with an expected value, standard deviation, and a form. (The distribution of $\bar{p}$ is discussed in Section 7.5.) This leads to the next definition, the sampling distribution of $\bar{x}$.

Definition 7.9. Sampling Distribution of $\bar{x}$. The sampling distribution of $\bar{x}$ derived from samples of size n is the probability distribution of all possible values of $\bar{x}$.

Clearly, there are many more SRSs than the 1000 referred to in Table 7.1 and depicted in Figure 7.1. How many SRSs are possible if $n = 30$ from a finite population of $N = 1250$?

Example 7.3. If $N = 1250$ and $n = 30$, how many unique samples are possible?

Answer: 2.144×10^{60}.

$$C_n^N = \binom{N}{n} = \frac{N!}{n!(N-n)!} = \frac{1250!}{30!1220!} = 2.144 \times 10^{60}.$$

```
#Comment. Use function choose(1250,30) to find the number of ways
#n=30 can be selected from N=1,250.
choose(1250, 30)

## [1] 2.144385e+60
```

(Note that 2.144e+60 is simply 2.144×10^{60}.) Since there are 2.144×10^{60} possible samples, there are 2.144×10^{60} sample means $\bar{x}$, one for each sample. Therefore, the sampling distribution of $\bar{x}$ is the probability distribution of all 2.144×10^{60} sample means.

When considering the histogram in Figure 7.1, the distribution of the 1000 values of the sample mean $\bar{x}$ seems to be centered near $\mu = 63$. Moreover, the form (or shape) of the histogram appears to approach that of the normal bell curve. When estimating how close $\bar{x}$ is to μ, we make use of three important properties of the sampling distribution of $\bar{x}$:

1 What is the expected value of $\bar{x}$, or $E(\bar{x})$?
2 What is the standard deviation of $\bar{x}$, or $\sigma_{\bar{x}}$?
3 What is the form (or shape) of the sampling distribution of $\bar{x}$?

We are now in a position to answer these questions both in a general way and in terms of the specific problem faced by the chair of the statistics department.

1 The expected value of $\bar{x}$, the mean of all possible sample means $\bar{x}$, is defined as $E(\bar{x}) = \mu$, the population mean. Since in this case we have the luxury of knowing what the population mean is, we can say that

$$E(\bar{x}) = \mu = 63.$$

In other words, if we draw all 2.144×10^{60} possible samples and calculate the sample mean for each, we have 2.144×10^{60} values of $\bar{x}$. If we then calculate the mean of all 2.144×10^{60} values of $\bar{x}$, we would recover the original population mean, $\mu = 63$.

2 The standard deviation of $\bar{x}$ depends on the size of the sample n relative to the size of the population N. Accordingly, there are two possible formulations for this expression, also known as the *standard error of the mean*.

(a) If $n / N \leq 0.05$, then the standard error of the mean is equal to the ratio of the population standard deviation σ to the square root of the sample size n:

$$\sigma_{\bar{x}} = \frac{\sigma}{\sqrt{n}}.$$

This is the formulation generally used when the size of the sample n is 5% or less than the size of the population N.

(b) If $n/N > 0.05$, then the standard error of the mean is

$$\sigma_{\bar{x}} = \sqrt{\frac{N-n}{N-1}}\left(\frac{\sigma}{\sqrt{n}}\right).$$

That is, if the size of the sample exceeds 5% of the size of the population, we introduce a term called the *finite population correction factor*.

Since, in this example, $n / N = 30 / 1250 = 0.0240 \leq 0.05$, we use form (a):

$$\sigma_{\bar{x}} = \frac{\sigma}{\sqrt{n}} = \frac{7}{\sqrt{30}} = 1.2780.$$

In other words, if we draw all 2.144×10^{60} possible samples and calculate the sample mean for each, we will have 2.144×10^{60} values of $\bar{x}$. If we then calculate the standard deviation of all 2.144×10^{60} values of $\bar{x}$, we will have the standard deviation of the sampling distribution of $\bar{x}$, $\sigma_{\bar{x}} = 1.2780$, the standard error of the mean.

Expression (b) always provides the correct value for $\sigma_{\bar{x}}$. Expression (a) is introduced only because under certain circumstances—when $n / N \leq 0.05$—it provides a value that is *close enough* while being more convenient to use. In fact, applying expression (b) to our data, we have $\sigma_{\bar{x}} = 1.2483$, a value only about 2% different from that derived using expression (a).

Finally, it is worth considering the behavior of $\sigma_{\bar{x}}$ as the sample size varies. It stands to reason that because larger samples contain more information, the dispersion of $\bar{x}$ should decrease; whereas smaller samples contain less information, with the result that the dispersion of $\bar{x}$ should increase. Putting this idea a bit more formally,

$$\lim_{n \to N} \sqrt{\frac{N-n}{N-1}}\left(\frac{\sigma}{\sqrt{n}}\right) = 0,$$

since the finite population correction factor vanishes when $n \to N$:

$$\sqrt{\frac{N-n}{N-1}} \to 0.$$

In other words, when n approaches N, $\sigma_{\bar{x}}$ approaches zero. Imagine drawing samples which comprise the entire population, over and over, and calculating the mean for each. What would be the variability of the values of $\bar{x}$ in such a case? It would be 0 since the values of $\bar{x}$ would be constant, and there would be no variability at all.

At the other extreme, when the sample size becomes small (so that $n = 1$) then

$$\lim_{n \to 1} \sqrt{\frac{N-n}{N-1}} \left(\frac{\sigma}{\sqrt{n}} \right) = \sigma,$$

since the finite population correction factor becomes 1:

$$\sqrt{\frac{N-n}{N-1}} \to 1.$$

Put another way, when the sample size shrinks to $n = 1$, we recover the original data. The mean of any sample with $n = 1$ is simply the single value in that sample.

We now consider the third issue listed above, the shape of the sampling distribution of $\bar{x}$. Recall that our objective is to describe the three important properties of the sampling distribution of $\bar{x}$: the expected value $E(\bar{x})$, the standard deviation $\sigma_{\bar{x}}$, and the shape of the distribution. We do this because understanding these qualities enables us to make probability statements about how close $\bar{x}$ is to μ. We have specified the first two characteristics; we now turn to the final one, the shape.

3 The question of the shape of the sampling distribution of $\bar{x}$ can be considered under two different cases, one where the shape of the *population distribution* is known to be normal, the other where its shape is unknown.

(a) When the shape of the population distribution is known to be normal, the sampling distribution of $\bar{x}$ is also normal, no matter what the sample size *n*.

(b) When the shape of the population distribution is unknown, we rely on one of the most important concepts in statistics, the central limit theorem, which states that whenever we draw an SRS of size *n* from a population with mean μ and standard deviation σ, the sampling distribution of $\bar{x}$ approaches the shape of the normal bell curve with mean μ and standard deviation $\sigma_{\bar{x}}$ as the sample size $n \to 30$.

To summarize the three important properties of the sampling distribution for our current problem: (1) the expected value of $\bar{x}$ is $E(\bar{x}) = 63$; (2) the standard deviation of $\bar{x}$ is $\sigma_{\bar{x}} = 1.2780$; and (3) the shape approaches the normal bell curve since $n = 30$.

The sampling distribution is sometimes referred to as a theoretical distribution because it is not something with which we work directly in a practical way. Rather, we can view it as the population distribution of all values of $\bar{x}$ based on all possible samples of size $n = 30$ drawn from a population of $N = 1250$. Since there are 2.144×10^{60} possible samples (and values of $\bar{x}$), the sampling distribution of $\bar{x}$ looks as it does in Figure 7.2. Also, since $n = 30$, the central limit theorem confirms that $\bar{x}$ is distributed normally.

At this point, one might ask why we go to all the trouble of defining the properties of the sampling distribution of $\bar{x}$. The reason is that it is now possible to answer the question of how close the sample statistic $\bar{x}$ might be to the population parameter μ. That is, how large is the sampling error $|\bar{x} - \mu|$ likely to be? While the last formulation may seem rather abstract and not

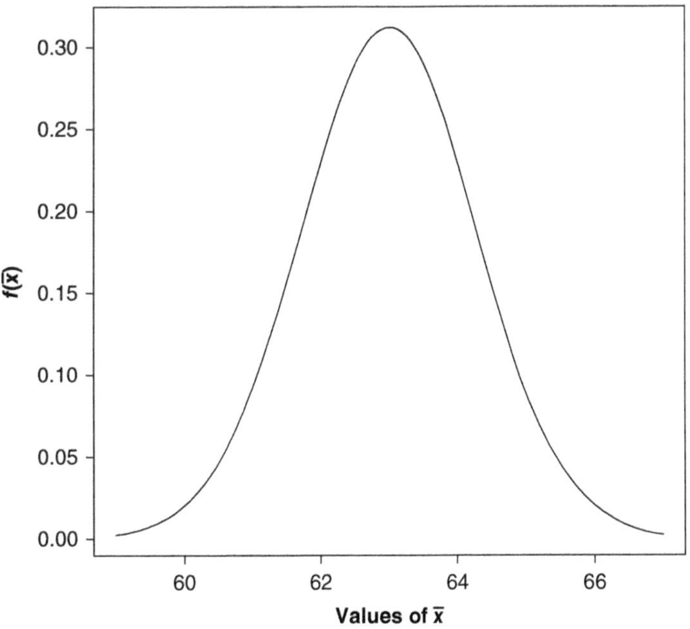

Figure 7.2 The sampling distribution of $\bar{x}$: n = 30

very useful in a practical sense, there are various ways to pose this question in a more concrete manner. Here is one approach.

Example 7.4. Given an SRS of size $n = 30$, what is the probability that $\bar{x}$ will be within ±1 of μ = 63? That is, what is $p(62 \leq \bar{x} \leq 64)$?

Answer: 0.5661. This is because

$$p(62 \leq \bar{x} \leq 64) = p(-0.78 \leq z \leq +0.78) = 0.5661.$$

We can confirm the result using R:

#Comment. Subtract pnorm(62,63,7/sqrt(30)) from pnorm(64,63,7/sqrt(30)).

```
pnorm(64, 63, 7 / sqrt(30)) - pnorm(62, 63, 7 / sqrt(30))
```

```
## [1] 0.5660562
```

That is, if we draw an SRS of $n = 30$ from a population with mean $\mu = 63$ and standard deviation $\sigma = 7$, the value of $\bar{x}$ falls in the interval from 62 to 64 with a probability of almost 0.57. Clearly, the value of $\bar{x}$ can be almost anything. The concern here is to get some idea of how close $\bar{x}$ is likely to be to μ. Let us build on this idea by raising the same question while increasing the width of the interval from 2 to 4.

Example 7.5. Given an SRS of size $n = 30$, what is the probability that $\bar{x}$ will be within ±2 of $\mu = 63$? That is, what is $p(61 \leq \bar{x} \leq 65)$?

Answer: 0.8824. Now

$$p(61 \le \bar{x} \le 65) = p(-1.56 \le z \le +1.56) = 0.8824.$$

```
#Comment. Subtract pnorm(61,63,7/sqrt(30)) from pnorm(65,63,7/sqrt(30)).
pnorm(65, 63, 7 / sqrt(30)) - pnorm(61, 63, 7 / sqrt(30))

## [1] 0.8823987
```

Note that by increasing the width of the interval around $\mu = 63$ from 2 to 4, we have also increased the probability that the sample mean $\bar{x}$ will fall in that much wider interval from 0.5661 to 0.8824. This should not be surprising. After all, we know that the sample mean $\bar{x}$ varies over a range of values. By expanding the interval into which that sample mean might fall, we also increase the likelihood that it will end up in that interval. By expanding the interval width from 4 to 6, the probability should be even higher.

Example 7.6. Given an SRS of size $n = 30$, what is the probability that $\bar{x}$ will be within ±3 of $\mu = 63$? That is, what is $p(60 \le \bar{x} \le 66)$?

Answer: 0.9811. In this case

$$p(60 \le \bar{x} \le 66) = p(-2.35 \le z \le +2.35) = 0.9811$$

```
#Comment. Subtract pnorm(60,63,7/sqrt(30)) from pnorm(66,63,7/sqrt(30)).
pnorm(66, 63, 7 / sqrt(30)) - pnorm(60, 63, 7 / sqrt(30))

## [1] 0.9810942
```

Thus, it is almost certain that $\bar{x}$ will fall into an interval when it is so wide. Table 7.2 summarizes the relationship between the interval width and probability for this example.

Table 7.2 Trade-off between the interval width and probability

Interval width	Probability
2	0.5661
4	0.8824
6	0.9811

Note that higher probabilities are necessarily accompanied by wider—that is, less precise—intervals, a trade-off relation that always exists unless we are able to increase the sample size. In reworking Example 7.4 with a larger sample size of $n = 60$, we see that it is possible to achieve higher probabilities even as we narrow the interval width.

Example 7.7. Given an SRS of size $n = 60$, what is the probability that $\bar{x}$ will be within ±1 of $\mu = 63$? That is, what is $p(62 \le \bar{x} \le 64)$?

In order to answer this question, we need to recalculate the standard error of the mean $\sigma_{\bar{x}}$, which now has a different value because of the larger sample size. We also need to check that the new sample size is less than or equal to 5% of the population size: $n / N = 60 / 1250 = 0.0480 \leq 0.05$. Therefore, the new value for $\sigma_{\bar{x}}$ is

$$\sigma_{\bar{x}} = \frac{\sigma}{\sqrt{n}} = \frac{7}{\sqrt{60}} = 0.9037.$$

Thus the probability is now 0.7315:

$$p(62 \leq \bar{x} \leq 64) = p(-1.11 \leq z \leq +1.11) = 0.7315.$$

#Comment. Subtract pnorm(62,63,7/sqrt(60)) from pnorm(64,63,7/sqrt(60)).

```
pnorm(64, 63, 7 / sqrt(60)) - pnorm(62, 63, 7 / sqrt(60))
```

```
## [1] 0.7315187
```

This result also should not be surprising since by increasing the sample size from $n = 30$ to $n = 60$, more information is included in the sample. This manifests in a smaller value of $\sigma_{\bar{x}}$ which in turn provides more accurate estimates: when $n = 30$, the probability that $\bar{x}$ is within ± 1 of μ is 0.5661, whereas when $n = 60$, the probability that $\bar{x}$ is within ± 1 of μ is 0.7315. As we will see in the context of $\bar{p}$, the same relationship between sample size and accuracy of estimate extends to sample statistics other than the sample mean $\bar{x}$.

Before continuing, we discuss some fundamental ideas concerning variation:

1 In statistical analysis, there are two important sources of variation: natural variation and sampling-outcome variation. Natural variation is the variation from one student to another in placement exam scores; sampling-outcome variation is the variation across sampling results. (Table 7.1 reports sampling-outcome variation of $\bar{x}$ for different samples we might select: $\bar{x}_1 = 60$, $\bar{x}_2 = 64$, $\bar{x}_3 = 65$, and so on.)
2 Natural variation is measured by the standard deviation σ.
3 Sampling-outcome variation is captured by the standard error of the mean $\sigma_{\bar{x}}$.
4 In practice, no one would repeatedly draw samples for the purpose of compiling a list of $\bar{x}$ values, as we have in Table 7.1; instead they would select a single sample, calculate its $\bar{x}$, and draw conclusions about how close that $\bar{x}$ might be to μ. (Although this is exactly what we did in Examples 7.4-7.7, we introduce a more practical method of doing this in Chapter 8.) The conclusions we draw about how close $\bar{x}$ might be to μ are based on the properties of the sampling distribution of $\bar{x}$.
5 The central limit theorem states that as the sample size n approaches 30, the variation in sampling outcomes follows the normal distribution even when the underlying natural variation does not.

7.5 THE SAMPLING DISTRIBUTION OF $\bar{p}$

Definition 7.10. Sampling Distribution of $\bar{p}$. The sampling distribution of $\bar{p}$ derived from samples of size n is the probability distribution of all possible values of $\bar{p}$.

Recall that the population proportion p in this example concerns the proportion of students lacking a coursework background in calculus, and that the question relates to how close $\bar{p}$ is likely to be to p. How large is the sampling error $|\bar{p} - p|$? To answer this question, we make use of three important properties of the sampling distribution of $\bar{p}$:

1 What is the expected value of $\bar{p}$, or $E(\bar{p})$?
2 What is the standard deviation of $\bar{p}$, or $\sigma_{\bar{p}}$?
3 What is the shape of the sampling distribution of $\bar{p}$?

We answer these questions both in a general way and in terms of the specific problem we have been considering in this chapter.

1 The expected value of $\bar{p}$, the mean of all sample proportions $\bar{p}$, is defined as $E(\bar{p}) = p$, the population proportion. Since we have the luxury of knowing $p = 0.62$, then

$$E(\bar{p}) = p = 0.62.$$

In other words, if we draw all 2.144×10^{60} samples and calculate the sample proportion for each, we would have 2.144×10^{60} values of $\bar{p}$. If we then calculate the mean of all 2.144×10^{60} values of $\bar{p}$, we recover the population proportion, $p = 0.62$.

2 The standard deviation of $\bar{p}$ depends on the size of the sample n relative to the size of the population N. Accordingly, there are two possible formulations for this expression, also known as the *standard error of the proportion*:

(a) If $n / N \leq 0.05$, then the standard error of the proportion is equal to

$$\sigma_{\bar{p}} = \sqrt{\frac{p(1-p)}{n}}.$$

This is the formulation typically used when the size of the sample n is 5% or less than the size of the population N.

(b) If $n / N > 0.05$, then the standard error of the proportion is

$$\sigma_{\bar{p}} = \sqrt{\frac{N-n}{N-1}}\sqrt{\frac{p(1-p)}{n}}.$$

That is, if the size of the sample exceeds 5% of the size of the population, we introduce the term for the finite population correction factor.

For this example, since $n / N = 30 / 1250 = 0.0240 \leq 0.05$, we use form (a):

$$\sigma_{\bar{p}} = \sqrt{\frac{p(1-p)}{n}} = \sqrt{\frac{0.62 \times 0.38}{30}} = 0.0886.$$

The explanation should by now be familiar. If we draw all 2.144×10^{60} samples and calculate the sample proportion for each, we have 2.144×10^{60} values of $\bar{p}$. If we then calculate the standard deviation of all 2.144×10^{60} values of $\bar{p}$, we have the standard deviation of the sampling distribution of $\bar{p}$, $\sigma_{\bar{p}} = 0.0886$, or the standard error of the proportion.

3 The shape of the sampling distribution of $\bar{p}$ approaches the normal bell curve when two conditions are met:

(a) $np \geq 5$;
(b) $n(1-p) \geq 5$.

Since $np = 30 \times 0.62 = 18.60 \geq 5$ and $n(1-p) = 30 \times 0.38 = 11.40 \geq 5$, the shape of the sampling distribution can be approximated by the normal bell curve.

Thus, the three important properties of the sampling distribution are: (1) the expected value of $\bar{p}$ is $E(\bar{p}) = 0.62$; (2) the standard deviation of $\bar{p}$ is $\sigma_{\bar{p}} = 0.0886$; and (3) the shape approaches the normal bell curve since both $np = 18.60 \geq 5$ and $n(1-p) = 11.40 \geq 5$.

Before we continue, let us revisit the sample proportions described in the hypothetical example at the beginning of Section 7.4. In that instance, we said that we had collected 1000 SRSs and calculated the value of $\bar{p}$ (and $\bar{x}$) for each. We then reported four values of $\bar{p}$ in the right-hand column of Table 7.1. The purpose of that exercise was to demonstrate how sample proportions $\bar{p}$ vary from one sample to the next.

Figure 7.3 is a frequency histogram of all 1000 sample proportions $\bar{p}$ that provides a more illustrative representation of that variability of $\bar{p}$. What is notable about the Figure 7.3 histogram is that despite being based on only 1000 SRSs, the characteristics of the sampling distribution of $\bar{p}$—which of course are based on all 2.144×10^{60} values of $\bar{p}$—are beginning to emerge: the mean of the histogram is approximately 0.62; the standard deviation is (roughly) 0.0886; and the shape of the histogram approaches that of a normal bell curve. The smooth bell curve that is imposed on the histogram allows us to compare the distribution of 1000 values of $\bar{p}$ with what that distribution might look like if we plotted all 2.144×10^{60} values of $\bar{p}$.

It is now possible to answer the question of how close the sample statistic $\bar{p}$ might be to the population parameter p; that is, how large the sampling error $|\bar{p} - p|$ is likely to be. Recall that the reason we select a sample from a population is to draw conclusions about some characteristic of that population. Consider the following practical approach to this important question.

Example 7.8. Given an SRS of size $n = 30$, what is the probability that $\bar{p}$ will be within ±0.10 of $p = 0.62$? That is, what is $p(0.52 \leq \bar{p} \leq 0.72)$?

Answer: 0.7409.

$$p(0.52 \leq \bar{p} \leq 0.72) = p(-1.13 \leq z \leq +1.13) = 0.7409.$$

```
#Comment. Subtract pnorm(0.52,0.62,sqrt(0.62*0.38/30)) from
#pnorm(0.72,0.62,sqrt(0.62*0.38/30))
pnorm(0.72, 0.62, sqrt(0.62 * 0.38 / 30)) -
  pnorm(0.52, 0.62, sqrt(0.62 * 0.38 / 30))

## [1] 0.7408598
```

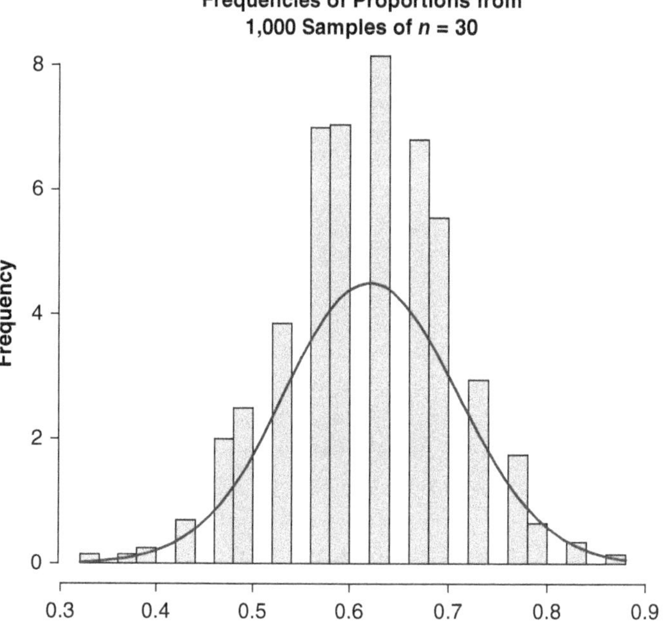

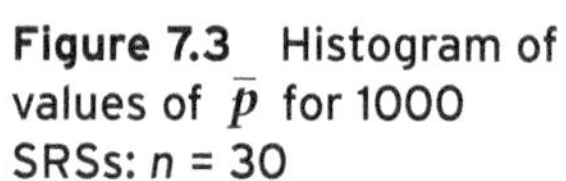

Figure 7.3 Histogram of values of $\bar{p}$ for 1000 SRSs: n = 30

Example 7.9. Given an SRS of size $n = 30$, what is the probability that $\bar{p}$ will be within ± 0.15 of $p = 0.62$? That is, what is $p(0.47 \le \bar{p} \le 0.77)$?

Answer: 0.9095.

$$p(0.47 \le \bar{p} \le 0.77) = p(-1.69 \le z \le +1.69) = 0.9095.$$

```
#Comment. Subtract pnorm(0.47,0.62,sqrt(0.62*0.38/30)) from
#pnorm(0.77,0.62,sqrt(0.62*0.38/30))
pnorm(0.77, 0.62, sqrt(0.62 * 0.38 / 30)) -
  pnorm(0.47, 0.62, sqrt(0.62 * 0.38 / 30))

## [1] 0.9094757
```

Revisiting Example 7.8, what happens when the sample size is doubled from $n = 30$ to $n = 60$?

Example 7.10. Given an SRS of size $n = 60$, what is the probability that $\bar{p}$ will be within ± 0.10 of $p = 0.62$? That is, what is $p(0.52 \le \bar{p} \le 0.72)$?

In order to answer this question, we need to recalculate the standard error of the proportion $\sigma_{\bar{p}}$ which now has a different value because of the larger sample size. We also need to check that the new sample size is less than or equal to 5% of the population size: $n / N = 60 / 1250 = 0.0480 \le 0.05$. Therefore, the new value for $\sigma_{\bar{p}}$ is

$$\sigma_{\bar{p}} = \sqrt{\frac{p(1-p)}{n}} = \sqrt{\frac{0.62 \times 0.38}{60}} = 0.0627.$$

The probability is therefore now 0.8895:

$$p(0.52 \le \bar{p} \le 0.72) = p(-1.60 \le z \le +1.60) = 0.8895.$$

```
#Comment. Subtract pnorm(0.52,0.62,sqrt(0.62*0.38/30)) from
#pnorm(0.72,0.62,sqrt(0.62*0.38/30))
pnorm(0.72, 0.62, sqrt(0.62 * 0.38 / 60)) -
  pnorm(0.52, 0.62, sqrt(0.62 * 0.38 / 60))

## [1] 0.8894744
```

This result should not be surprising since by increasing the sample size from $n = 30$ to $n = 60$, more information is included in the sample. When $n = 30$, the probability that $\bar{p}$ is within ±0.10 of p is 0.7409, whereas when $n = 60$, the probability that $\bar{p}$ is within ±0.10 of p is 0.8895. With larger sample sizes, the probability increases that $\bar{p}$ lies within a given distance from p.

In this chapter we have an advantage over the normal situation in real-world data analysis: we have advance knowledge of the population parameters—$\mu = 63$, $\sigma = 7$, and $p = 0.62$—values we seldom have in any situation requiring statistical analysis. Since the parameters are usually unknown, we select a sample from the population for the purpose of obtaining statistical information about those parameters. That we actually have knowledge of those parameters before drawing a sample is an artificial circumstance.

In Chapter 8 we introduce a method that makes it possible to obtain probability-based statistical estimates of the population parameter based entirely on the information contained in a sample. This approach, referred to as the method of confidence interval estimation, builds on what we have done in this chapter.

7.6 SOME OTHER COMMONLY USED SAMPLING METHODS

The process of simple random sampling is the gold standard against which other sampling methods are compared. There are several reasons for this, not least of which is that many statisical methods assume that the data have been collected using a random sampling approach. However, for reasons of cost and simplicity, analysts often use other methods. In this section, we discuss several of those alternative approaches to sampling.

Definition 7.11. Systematic Sampling. Systematic sampling is a convenient-to-use probabilistic method of obtaining a sample by (1) defining a value for i where $i = N / n$; (2) randomly choosing one of the first i elements of the list; and (3) selecting every ith element throughout the list. For example, suppose a sample of n = 1000 is to be selected from a population consisting of a directory of all known N = 100,000 alumni of a large university. The first step requires defining a value for i, referred to as the sampling interval, by dividing N by n, and rounding to the nearest integer: i = 100,000 / 1000 = 100. The second step involves randomly selecting a number from the interval 1 to 100. Suppose that number is 47. The third step requires compiling the sample by including items 47, 147, 247, 347, 447, 547, ... through the entire population.

Use of systematic sampling requires a clear understanding of the purpose of the research question. If a list is alphabetically ordered by the individuals' last names (as may be the case with the alumni directory), then systematic sampling may very well result in a representative sample. However, if the data items are arranged in a cyclical pattern, systematic sampling can produce samples that may be random but do not serve the purpose behind the research question. For example, if the purpose is to gain insight into the sales of a seasonal product (such as woolen sweaters or swimwear) across all periods of the calendar year, we would not want to approach this question using a sample of monthly sales data composed only of December (or even July) sales. The cyclical pattern of the data cannot be captured when the sample itself includes little of that variability. One possible solution might be to redefine the sampling interval itself from 12 months to 3 months so that unit sales are measured on January, April, July, and October of each year. In this way, the data include measurements during winter, spring, summer, and fall periods.

Definition 7.12. Stratified Random Sampling. Stratified random sampling is a probabilistic method of selecting samples which uses a two-stage procedure that (1) decomposes the population into mutually exclusive, collectively exhaustive subgroups, or strata, and (2) uses a random sampling method to draw items from each stratum. The second step is probabilistic in nature and is typically conducted by using a simple random sampling method or, in some cases, systematic sampling.

The different subgroups are defined by stratification variables which might be any characteristic of interest as long as the resulting within-strata elements are as homogeneous as possible while the between-strata elements are as heterogeneous as possible. For example, if the main stratification variable is household income, this approach might assign households to strata based on the quartile (first, second, third, or fourth) into which its income falls. The resulting sample would then be constructed, adding households to the four strata, until the desired sample size is attained.

It is not necessary that the strata all have the same number of elements, but the general practice is to bring the stratum membership levels as close as possible to one another when there is no cost to doing so. Even so, real-world data constraints—such as time pressure, financial expense, and the availability of trained personnel who actually carry out the data-collection effort—sometimes limit our ability to achieve sample size equivalency across all strata.

Statisticians often use more than one stratification variable, but the cost and complexity of doing so rise rapidly as the number of variables and strata increases. It is one thing to assign households based on income. It is quite another to also include the head of household's age, gender, and racial category. For example, if we also form strata around five racial categories (Asian, African, Latino, White, and Other), two gender categories, and four age categories for the head of household (18–29, 30–45, 46–65, and 66 and older), we have increased the number of strata from 4 to 160—that is, $4 \times 5 \times 2 \times 4 = 160$. As rich as the resulting sample might seem in theory, in practice this type of sampling plan would pose enormous difficulties—especially in terms of the time and expense involved—in the execution stage.

Definition 7.13. Cluster Sampling. Cluster sampling is a probabilistic method of drawing samples which employs a three-stage procedure that (1) decomposes the population into mutually exclusive, collectively exhaustive groups, or clusters, (2) uses a random sampling method to select a sample of clusters, and (3) includes either all elements or a random sample of elements in the final sample. When all the elements in each selected cluster are included in the sample, we call this one-stage cluster sampling, but when only a subsample is drawn (probabilistically) from each selected cluster, we refer to this as two-stage cluster sampling. Cluster sampling, or some variation of it, is often used by political polling organizations as they attempt to estimate, for example, voters' views on issues like the recent UK Brexit campaign.

Cluster sampling and stratified random sampling are sometimes confused with one another. When using stratified random sampling, we randomly select elements from all strata. None is excluded from sampling. However, when employing cluster sampling, we first randomly select a sample of clusters, and then draw elements from those selected clusters. We select no elements from those clusters which we did not choose in the earlier stage.

It is considered a good quality if the resulting clusters represent the population well. Put another way, the resulting within-cluster elements should be as heterogeneous as the larger population from which they are formed, implying that the between-cluster elements are as homogeneous as possible. Seen from this perspective, if a cluster provides a valid representation of the general population from which it is being drawn, then one cluster should be sufficient. But since this is rarely true in practice, we usually find it necessary to randomly select multiple multiple clusters.

Definition 7.14. Convenience Sampling. Convenience sampling (also known as accidental sampling) is a non-probabilistic method of obtaining a sample by which items are chosen simply by virtue of their being convenient for the analyst to identify and select. It is the easiest, most inexpensive, and least time-consuming of all sampling methods. However, since convenience samples are not selected probabilistically, they are not representative of any well-defined population. Accordingly, any results drawn from studies involving convenience samples must be viewed with skepticism.

The reason why we mention convenience sampling at all is because it is so widely used and commonly misunderstood. Examples of instances where convenience sampling is often used include, but are certainly not limited to, mall-intercept interviews, tear-out survey questionnaires from magazines, people-on-the-street interviews, customer-satisfaction surveys, and television/radio call-in polls. Convenience samples are sometimes referred to as accidental samples because the items included in the sample are selected by accident rather than by design.

Definition 7.15. Snowball Sampling. Snowball sampling is a non-probabilistic method of creating a sample which is useful in those research settings where the objective is to learn about some issue that is relatively unusual in the larger world. Snowballing is typically conducted in stages. In the first stage, subjects are contacted, interviewed, and asked to refer other individuals as possible interviewees. When these subjects are subsequently contacted and interviewed, they are also requested to refer still other individuals. This process is often extended until no new names are uncovered. When this process is continued until no additional subjects emerge, the sampling approach is referred to as exhaustive snowballing.

The author used this method when conducting research into the decision-making behavior of individuals responsible for the purchase of an expensive, high-risk product on behalf of their organization. In this instance, our research team wished to identify those decision-makers in a large New York City hospital who would be making a multi-million-dollar purchase of CT scan machines.

After speaking with the hospital purchasing agent, we learned that we should also speak with the financial vice-president who had the final decision-making authority. During the interview with the vice-president, we were advised to also speak with the hospital construction engineer with whom the vice-president was working to ensure that the CT scan machines would actually fit into their designated space. When we spoke with the engineer, he informed us that we should also interview the radiologists who would be using the new technology once the machines were installed.

This process continued through numerous stages until we uncovered no new names. Thus, by snowballing, we were able to compile an exhaustive list, or sample, of all the members comprising the decision-making unit. Although the vice-president would ultimately make the final decision, she relied heavily on the advice and expertise of other role-players. In the end, the only practical way of obtaining this kind of information was to employ exhaustive snowball sampling.

There are numerous other sampling methods not introduced here, some of which combine one or more of the above approaches. Ultimately, there is no perfect way to obtain the best possible sample; there are only methods which provide, on average, samples that are appropriate for the specific research purpose. Those readers who are interested are encouraged to consult other sources on sampling and survey research.

SUMMARY

Our introduction to statistical estimation makes abundant use of some new concepts and ideas: the simple random sample, point estimation, sampling distributions, sampling error, and the central limit theorem. We remind the reader that $\bar{x}$ provides only a point estimate of the population mean μ, just as $\bar{p}$ does for the population proportion p. As with other sample statistics, the values that $\bar{x}$ and $\bar{p}$ might assume are literally spread over an entire range. Even though all possible $\bar{x}$ values are centered around μ, we know that $\bar{x}$ is almost certain to be different from μ. In the same way, even though all possible values of $\bar{p}$ are centered around p, $\bar{p}$ is most likely different from p. The magnitude of this difference is referred to as the sampling error and is defined as $|\bar{x} - \mu|$; in the case of the sample proportion p, the sampling error is defined as $|\bar{p} - p|$.

We also know that both $\bar{x}$ and $\bar{p}$ are themselves random variables which have probability distributions, referred to as sampling distributions. In the case where $\bar{x}$ is obtained from a large sample (where large generally means $n \geq 30$), the central limit theorem tell us that the shape of the sampling distribution of $\bar{x}$ can be approximated by the normal probability distribution (see Figure 7.1); moreover, the expected value of $\bar{x}$ is $E(\bar{x}) = \mu$ and the standard deviation of $\bar{x}$, $\sigma_{\bar{x}}$ or standard error of the mean, is derived using the ratio of the population standard deviation σ to the square root of the sample size n. If the size of the sample exceeds 5% of the size of the population, we introduce the finite population correction factor. The characteristics of the sampling distribution of $\bar{p}$ are developed in a similar way and are detailed in Section 7.5.

This chapter and the next introduce a class of procedures referred to as statistical estimation; Chapter 9 extends these methods to an approach known as statistical inference. While the terms are sometimes used interchangeably, they represent different ways to find things out.

Generally speaking, the motivation behind the use of the methods of statistical estimation usually involves the attempt to determine how large or small something might be; the purpose of statistical inference entails our drawing conclusions about the likelihood of a formal statement being true. While this characterization may seem abstract, it forms the very heart of statistical methods and thinking.

definitions

Cluster Sampling Cluster sampling is a probabilistic method of drawing samples which employs a three-stage procedure that (1) decomposes the population into mutually exclusive, collectively exhaustive groups, or clusters, (2) uses a random sampling method to select a sample of clusters, and (3) includes either all elements or a random sample of elements in the final sample.

Convenience Sampling Convenience sampling is a non-probabilistic method of obtaining a sample by which items are chosen by virtue of their being convenient.

Finite Population Correction Factor A term which is included in the calculation of both the standard error of the mean $\sigma_{\bar{x}}$ and the standard error of the proportion $\sigma_{\bar{p}}$ when the size of the sample exceeds 5% of the size of the finite population.

Population A population consists of all the entities of interest in a research study.

Population Parameter A characteristic or quality of the population in terms of the variable of interest. Also referred to simply as *parameter*.

Sample The portion of the population selected for the purposes of the study.

Sample Statistic A characteristic or quality of the sample in terms of the variable of interest. Also referred to simply as *statistic*.

Sampling Distribution of $\bar{p}$ The sampling distribution of $\bar{p}$ derived from samples of size n is the probability distribution of all possible values of $\bar{p}$.

Sampling Distribution of $\bar{x}$ The sampling distribution of $\bar{x}$ derived from samples of size n is the probability distribution of all possible values of $\bar{x}$.

Sampling with Replacement A sampling approach in which the items selected for the sample are replaced in the population from which they are drawn, making possible the resampling of elements already included in the sample.

Sampling without Replacement A sampling approach in which the elements selected for the sample are removed from the population from which they are drawn, ensuring that elements cannot be sampled more than once.

Simple Random Sample from a Finite Population A simple random sample of size n drawn from a finite population of size N is one in which each sample of size n has an equal chance of selection.

Simple Random Sample from an Infinite Population A simple random sample from an infinite population is one for which (1) each item of the sample is a member of the population, and (2) each item of the sample is chosen independently.

Snowball Sampling Snowball sampling is a non-probabilistic method of creating a sample which is particularly useful in those research questions where the objective is to learn about some issue that is relatively unusual in the larger world.

Standard Error of the Mean The standard deviation of the sample means $\bar{x}$, usually denoted as $\sigma_{\bar{x}}$.

Standard Error of the Proportion The standard deviation of the sample proportions $\bar{p}$, usually denoted as $\sigma_{\bar{p}}$.

Stratified Random Sampling Stratified random sampling is a probabilistic method of selecting samples which uses a two-stage procedure that (1) decomposes the population into mutually exclusive, collectively exhaustive groups, or strata, and (2) uses a random sampling method to draw items from each.

Systematic Sampling Systematic sampling is a convenient-to-use, straightforward probabilistic method of obtaining a sample by (1) randomly choosing one of the first *i* elements of the list, and (2) selecting every *i*th element throughout the list.

formulae

Expected Value of $\bar{p}$

$$E(\bar{p}) = p$$

Expected Value of $\bar{x}$

$$E(\bar{x}) = \mu$$

Finite Population Correction Factor

$$\sqrt{\frac{N-n}{N-1}}$$

Sampling Error for p and $\bar{p}$

$$|\bar{p} - p|$$

Sampling Error for μ and $\bar{x}$

$$|\bar{x} - \mu|$$

Standard Error of the Proportion: Small-Sample Case

$$\sigma_{\bar{p}} = \sqrt{\frac{p(1-p)}{n}}, \quad \text{when } \frac{n}{N} \le 0.05$$

Standard Error of the Proportion: Large-Sample Case

$$\sigma_{\bar{p}} = \sqrt{\frac{N-n}{N-1}}\sqrt{\frac{p(1-p)}{n}}, \quad \text{when } \frac{n}{N} > 0.05$$

Standard Error of the Mean: Small-Sample Case

$$\sigma_{\bar{x}} = \frac{\sigma}{\sqrt{n}}, \quad \text{when } \frac{n}{N} \le 0.05$$

Standard Error of the Mean: Large-Sample Case

$$\sigma_{\bar{x}} = \sqrt{\frac{N-n}{N-1}}\frac{\sigma}{\sqrt{n}}, \quad \text{when } \frac{n}{N} > 0.05$$

R functions

`abs()` Returns the absolute value of the expression within the parentheses.

`data[sample(nrow(data),n), ]` Selects a random sample of size *n* from a data object named `data`.

data sets

1 `exit`
2 `temps`
3 `tv_hours`

APPENDIX: USING R TO SELECT A RANDOM SAMPLE FROM A DATA SET

It is possible to select a random sample of observations from a larger data set. The function to use is `data[sample(nrow(data),n),]` where `data` is the name of the data set (note that it appears twice), and n is the size of the random sample.

1 Draw a random sample of $n = 5$. Apply function `data[sample(nrow(data), n)]`. Use data set `tv_hours` from the website (https://study.sagepub.com/stinerock).

```
#Comment1. Use function tv_hours[sample(nrow(tv_hours),5),]
#to select a random sample of n=5 from tv_hours and name it C7_1.
C7_1 <- tv_hours[sample(nrow(tv_hours), 5), ]

#Comment2. Examine the contents of C7_1.
C7_1

## [1] 11.73 13.68 14.61 3.29 9.61
```

2 Draw a random sample of $n = 10$. Apply function `data[sample(nrow(data), n)]`. Use data set `tv_hours` from the website.

```
#Comment1. Use function tv_hours[sample(nrow(tv_hours),10),]
#to select a random sample of n=10 from tv_hours and name it C7_2.
C7_2 <- tv_hours[sample(nrow(tv_hours), 10), ]

#Comment2. Examine the contents of C7_2.
C7_2

## [1] 16.09 6.31 11.73 11.19 6.38 12.22 12.63 8.49 15.27 14.95
```

The sample size of the random sample is now $n = 10$. Note that n is adjusted by changing the argument value n in `data[sample(nrow(data), n), ]`.

3 Draw a random sample of $n = 7$. Apply function `data[sample(nrow(data), n)]`. Use data set `temps` from the website.

```
#Comment1. Use function temps[sample(nrow(temps),7),]
#to select a random sample of n=7 from temps and name it C7_3.
C7_3 <- temps[sample(nrow(temps), 7), ]

#Comment2. Examine the contents of C7_3.
C7_3

##          City  Daytemp  Nighttemp
## 3       Dublin        6          1
## 7       Munich        4         -2
## 10   Stockholm        2         -4
## 6       Moscow        2          1
## 8       Naples       14         11
## 5   Luxembourg        3         -2
## 1       Athens       21         12
```

The sample contains seven randomly selected observations consisting of the three variables.

exercises

7.1 Use the function `data[sample(nrow(data), n)]` to draw a random sample of $n = 9$ observations from data set `tv_hours` (from the website).

(a) Display the first three rows of data.
(b) Using this sample, what is the point estimate of the population mean μ?
(c) What is the point estimate of the population standard deviation σ?

7.2 During the 2012 US Presidential election, 1500 voters were interviewed upon exiting from a Manhattan polling station where they had just cast their votes. The data are recorded as 1 for a Barack Obama vote and 0 for a Mitt Romney vote. Draw a random sample of $n = 25$. Apply function `data[sample(nrow(data), n), ]` and use the data set `exit` from the website.

(a) Display all 25 observations.
(b) Using this sample, find the point estimate of the population proportion.

7.3 The mean level of debt carried by students graduating from US universities has now reached $27,000 (*Forbes*, January 29, 2013). Use this value as the population mean μ and assume that the population standard deviation is $\sigma = \$4500$. If an SRS of size $n = 121$ is selected, answer the following questions. Use R to answer the questions.

(a) What is the probability that $\bar{x}$ will fall within ±$500 of μ? That is, what is $p(26{,}500 \leq \bar{x} \leq 27{,}500)$?
(b) What is the probability that $\bar{x}$ will fall within ±$250 of μ? That is, what is $p(26{,}750 \leq \bar{x} \leq 27{,}250)$?

(Continued)

(Continued)

7.4 The percentage of people who are left-handed is not known with certainty but it is thought to be about 12%. Assume the population proportion of left-handed people is $p = 0.12$.

(a) If a sample of $n = 400$ people is chosen randomly, what is the probability that the proportion of left-handers will be within ± 0.02 of p? Put another way, what is $p(0.10 \leq \bar{p} \leq 0.14)$?

(b) If a sample of $n = 800$ people is chosen randomly, what is the probability that the proportion of left-handers will be within ± 0.02 of p? Put another way, what is $p(0.10 \leq \bar{p} \leq 0.14)$?

7.5 A quality control inspector is always on the lookout for substandard parts and components provided to her manufacturing company by outside suppliers. Because most shipments contain some defective items, each must be subjected to inspection. Naturally, some shipments contain more defectives than others, and it is the job of the inspector to identify the most defective-laden shipments so that they can be returned to the supplier. Suppose the inspector selects a sample of $n = 100$ items from a given shipment for testing. Unbeknownst to the inspector, this particular shipment includes 9% defective components. If the policy is to return any shipment with at least 5% defectives, what is the probability that this bad shipment will be accepted as good anyway?

https://study.sagepub.com/stinerock

Confidence Interval Estimation

contents

learning objectives

1. Know how to construct and interpret an interval estimate of a population mean μ and a population proportion p.
2. Understand and be able to derive the margin of error.
3. Learn about the t-distribution and its use in constructing an interval estimate for a population mean.
4. Be able to determine the size of sample necessary to estimate a population mean and population proportion with a specified level of precision.

In Chapter 7 our discussion of statistical estimation introduces several new concepts, including the simple random sample (SRS), sampling distributions, and the central limit theorem. In this chapter we build on those concepts by introducing a powerful method known as confidence interval estimation; we also provide an approach for determining the sample size required for a desired level of statistical precision. (What exactly this means will become clear in this chapter.) Our concern here, as it was in Chapter 7, is to estimate how precise a given sample statistic, such as $\bar{x}$ or $\bar{p}$, might be in terms of its respective population parameter. As we learn in this chapter, confidence interval estimation is a statistical procedure that provides a probabilistic statement about how close $\bar{x}$ is likely be to μ, and $\bar{p}$ is likely to be to p. First, however, we introduce a few new terms.

Definition 8.1. Precision. Precision is a probabilistic measure of the distance between a sample statistic and the population parameter it is intended to estimate. Its magnitude is usually a function of the population distribution and the sample size n.

Definition 8.2. Confidence Interval. This is a range of values which is likely to contain the population parameter being estimated. In this chapter it is an empircally based estimate of the population mean μ or the population proportion p.

In Chapter 7 we benefited from knowing the value of the population parameters, μ, σ, and p. For the remainder of this book, however, all we have to operate with are samples and their statistics, a situation characterizing most real-world data analysis situations. Interval estimation is one of the most important methods that statisticians have developed for the purpose of puzzling out how close a statistic is likely to be to its parameter.

In general, an interval estimate takes this form: point estimate ± margin of error. For the population mean μ, the interval estimate is $\bar{x}$ ± margin of error; for the population proportion p, it is $\bar{p}$ ± margin of error.

Definition 8.3. Margin of Error. A value which is added to and subtracted from a point estimate for the purpose of finding an interval estimate of a population parameter.

The term "margin of error" is a commonly used but widely misunderstood expression that has a very specific meaning in the present context. In the case of the interval estimate of μ, the value of the margin of error depends on the sample size n and on whether we use the population standard deviation σ or the sample standard deviation s. We return later in the chapter to the case of the interval estimate of the population proportion p.

8.1 INTERVAL ESTIMATE OF μ WHEN σ IS KNOWN

We first provide a definition of a precision statement that expresses the relationship between precision, or the sampling error, and confidence.

Definition 8.4. Precision Statement. A precision statement expresses the relationship between confidence and precision. For an estimate of μ, we say that there is a $1-\alpha$ probability that $\bar{x}$ will result in a sampling error $|\bar{x}-\mu|$ of $z_{\alpha/2}\sigma_{\bar{x}}$ or less.

While this expression is abstract, even austere, it is an accurate and concise statement of the important trade-off relationship between confidence and precision. The specific form for the interval estimate of μ when the population standard deviation σ is known is

$$\bar{x} \pm z_{\alpha/2}\frac{\sigma}{\sqrt{n}},$$

where $\bar{x}$ is the sample mean, n is the sample size, σ is the population standard deviation, $1-\alpha$ is the confidence coefficient, and $z_{\alpha/2}$ is the value of the standard normal variable z with an area of $\alpha/2$ to its right.

Definition 8.5. Confidence Level. An interval estimate has associated with it a percentage confidence level: 90% of the time, a 90% interval estimate is expected to contain the population parameter; 95% of the time, a 95% interval estimate can be expected to contain the population parameter; and 99% of the time, a 99% interval estimate is expected to contain the population parameter.

Definition 8.6. Confidence Coefficient. The confidence coefficient is the confidence level expressed as a probability. That is, if the confidence level is 90%, the confidence coefficient is $1-\alpha=0.90$; if the confidence level is 95%, the confidence coefficient is $1-\alpha=0.95$; and if the confidence level is 99%, the confidence coefficient is $1-\alpha=0.99$.

To apply these terms to a real-world situation, we return to the Section 7.1 example in which the chair of a university's statistics department seeks a better grasp of her students' preparation for statistics classes. In this example, we are told that the population parameters are $\mu = 63$ and $\sigma = 7$ across all $N = 1250$ students who sat for the placement examination. In Section 7.3 the chair selects an SRS of size $n = 30$ from this population and calculates the sample statistic $\bar{x}$. This was done not because anyone would draw a sample from a population with known parameters (because there would be no point) but only for the purpose of demonstrating the three important properties of the sampling distribution of $\bar{x}$: $E(\bar{x}) = \mu = 63$; $\sigma_{\bar{x}} = \sigma/\sqrt{n} = 1.2780$; and the shape of the sampling distribution is normal because $n = 30$ (see Figure 7.2).

We are now in a position to revisit the above definitions in terms of the present example. To begin with, we provide numeric values to four of the five elements of the above expression for an interval estimate of μ when σ is known:

1 $\bar{x}$ is undetermined until we select an SRS
2 $n = 30$
3 $\sigma = 7$

4 $1-\alpha = 0.95$ is the confidence coefficient

5 $z_{\alpha/2} = 1.96$ is the value of z that cuts off an area of 0.025 to its right. If $1-\alpha = 0.95$, then $\alpha = 0.05$ and $\alpha / 2 = 0.025$. Therefore, we know that $z_{\alpha/2} = z_{0.025} = 1.96$.

Now that we have specified all but one of the elements of the confidence interval estimate, we can substitute them into the expression above:

$$\bar{x} \pm z_{\alpha/2} \frac{\sigma}{\sqrt{n}}$$

$$\bar{x} \pm 1.96 \frac{7}{\sqrt{30}}$$

$$\bar{x} \pm 2.50 \quad \text{or} \quad [\bar{x} - 2.50,\ \bar{x} + 2.50].$$

The final two expressions provide the 95% confidence interval estimate of the population mean μ; one form is the same as the other. We know from Definition 8.5 (above) that 95% of the time—that is, 95% of the SRSs we might collect—the 95% confidence interval can be expected to contain μ, while the remaining 5% of the time the interval probably does not. The margin of error is 2.50; the point estimate $\bar{x}$ of course varies from one sample to the next. Substituting the relevant values into our precision statement, we say that there is a $1-\alpha = 0.95$ probability that $\bar{x}$ will result in a sampling error $|\bar{x} - \mu|$ of $z_{\alpha/2}\sigma_{\bar{x}} = 2.50$ or less.

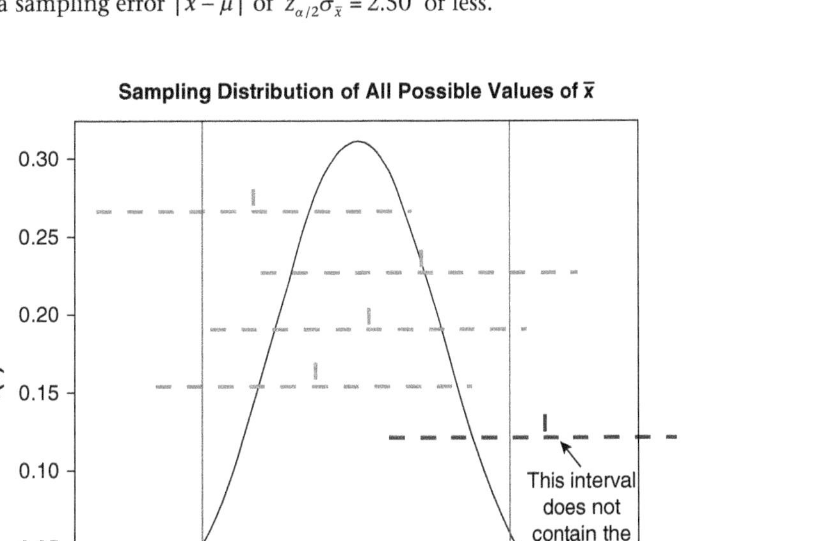

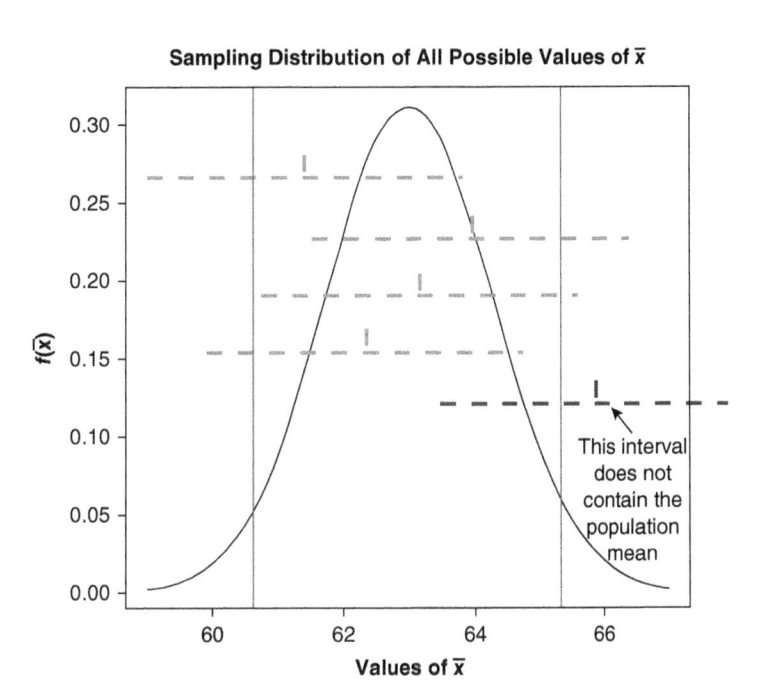

Figure 8.1 Five confidence intervals: four contain the population mean, one does not

Figure 8.1 illustrates this process for five different samples. Each confidence interval is represented by a dashed horizontal line with a small vertical notch centered at the location of the sample mean. The distance from each notch to the end of its respective line is 2.50, the size of the margin of error; thus, the width of the confidence interval is 5. Note that four samples, represented by the first four dashed lines, provide intervals that contain μ; the other sample, as shown by the bottom line, does not. Note also that when a notch (i.e., the sample mean) falls within the two vertical lines, the left-hand one at 60.50, the right-hand one at 65.50, the corresponding interval contains μ; if the notch falls outside of this range, the interval does not contain μ.

The best way to learn how to find confidence interval estimates is to begin by applying the above expression to some practical problems.

Example 8.1. In Chapter 4 we considered the case of the Bon Voyage travel agency. Suppose that every month Bon Voyage emails surveys to an SRS of 100 of the previous month's clients with the purpose of determining how well the agency is serving its customers. Each person completing the questionnaire is asked to rate her overall satisfaction with Bon Voyage on a 0–100 scale—with 0 being the worst, 100 the best—and the mean score $\bar{x}$ of all 100 completed surveys is then used as a measure of that month's customer service quality. Since for many months, the population standard deviation has hovered around $\sigma = 25$, Bon Voyage assumes that the value of σ is 25 for the current study as well. For the most recent month, the sample mean satisfaction score has come in at $\bar{x} = 75$.

Finally, the confidence level, $1-\alpha$, must be specified by the analyst. If the desired confidence level is 95%, we set the confidence coefficient equal to 0.95 and solve for the value of $\alpha/2$, the subscript on $z_{\alpha/2}$:

$$\begin{aligned} 1-\alpha &= 0.95 \\ \alpha &= 0.05 \\ \alpha/2 &= 0.025 \\ z_{\alpha/2} &= z_{0.025} = 1.96. \end{aligned}$$

```
#Comment. Use qnorm(0.975) to find the value of z which divides
#the area under the curve into 2 pieces with 0.975 to the left and
#0.025 to the right.
qnorm(.975)

## [1] 1.959964
```

We now have all the elements required to create the interval estimate: $n = 100$, $\sigma = 25$, $\bar{x} = 75$, and $z_{0.025} = 1.96$. Since these are the ingredients, we assemble them all in the way prescribed by the recipe:

$$\bar{x} \pm z_{\alpha/2} \frac{\sigma}{\sqrt{n}}$$

$$75 \pm 1.96 \frac{25}{\sqrt{100}}$$

$$75 \pm 4.90 \quad \text{or} \quad [70.10,\ 79.90].$$

The 95% confidence interval estimate of μ is expressed in the last line; both parts are identical. Some prefer the first form since the margin of error, 4.90, is reported unambiguously; others opt for the second form because they feel it is more quickly and easily interpretable. If the exercise of drawing a sample and calculating the interval is repeated, over and over again, then 95% of the resulting intervals will contain the true value of μ, but 5% will not. The interval $[70.10, 79.90]$ may be one of the intervals that contains μ or it may not. What we can say, however, is that we are 95% confident that any 95% confidence interval does indeed contain μ. We just cannot be 100% certain that this particular interval does.

With these values, the precision statement (above) assumes a more practical meaning:

1. The formal precision statement: there is a $1-\alpha$ probability that $\bar{x}$ will result in a sampling error $|\bar{x}-\mu|$ of $z_{\alpha/2}\sigma_{\bar{x}}$ or less.
2. The specific statement: there is a 0.95 probability that $\bar{x}$ will result in a sampling error of 4.90 or less.

This is a good point to consider the slightly artificial circumstance of σ being ***known***. Remember that the purpose of interval estimation of μ is precisely that: to estimate the value of μ. But if σ is assumed to be known, then the value of μ must be known as well. Recall that

$$\sigma = \sqrt{\sigma^2} = \sqrt{\frac{\Sigma(x_i-\mu)^2}{N}}.$$

The value of μ must be supplied first for σ to be known. But if μ is known, there is no need for an interval estimate of it. In the next section, the assumption that σ is known is discarded, and a slightly different way to create interval estimates is introduced.

Example 8.2. Referring to Example 8.1, give the 99% interval estimate of μ.

$$\begin{aligned} 1-\alpha &= 0.99 \\ \alpha &= 0.01 \\ \alpha/2 &= 0.005, \\ z_{\alpha/2} &= z_{0.005} = 2.576. \end{aligned}$$

```
#Comment. Use qnorm(0.995) to find value of z which divides area
#under curve into 2 pieces with 0.995 to the left, 0.005 to the right.
qnorm(.995)

## [1] 2.575829
```

Pulling together what we know (n = 100, $\sigma = 25$, $\bar{x} = 75$, and $z_{0.005} = 2.576$), we now have all the required elements for constructing the 99% confidence interval estimate:

$$\bar{x} \pm z_{\alpha/2}\frac{\sigma}{\sqrt{n}}$$

$$75 \pm 2.576\frac{25}{\sqrt{100}}$$

$$75 \pm 6.44 \quad \text{or} \quad [68.56,\ 81.44].$$

That the 99% interval estimate of μ has widened—the margin of error has increased from 4.90 to 6.44—should come as no surprise. If we want to be 99% confident that our interval actually contains μ, it stands to reason that we need to widen it. If we repeat the exercise of drawing a sample and calculating the interval, over and over again, 99% of the resulting intervals will contain μ, but roughly 1% will not. In other words, we are 99% confident that any 99% confidence interval, including this one, contains μ. Finally, in light of the above result, the new precision statement is: there is a 0.99 probability that $\bar{x}$ will result in a sampling error of 6.44 or less.

Example 8.3. Referring to Example 8.1, provide the 90% interval estimate of μ.

$$\begin{aligned} 1-\alpha &= 0.90 \\ \alpha &= 0.10 \\ \alpha/2 &= 0.05 \\ z_{\alpha/2} &= z_{0.05} = 1.645. \end{aligned}$$

#Comment. Use qnorm(0.95) to find value of z which divides area
#under curve into 2 pieces with 0.95 to the left, 0.05 to the right.

```
qnorm(.95)
```

```
## [1] 1.644854
```

Using $n = 100$, $\sigma = 25$, $\bar{x} = 75$, and $z_{0.05} = 1.645$ to construct the interval estimate:

$$\bar{x} \pm z_{\alpha/2}\frac{\sigma}{\sqrt{n}}$$

$$75 \pm 1.645\frac{25}{\sqrt{100}}$$

$$75 \pm 4.11 \quad \text{or} \quad [70.89,\ 79.11].$$

While we have a narrower, more precise interval, we are less confident that it actually contains μ. What we do know is that if we repeat the exercise of drawing a sample and calculating the interval, we can expect that on average only 90% of the resulting intervals will actually contain the value of μ, while 10% will not. Does the interval [70.89, 79.11] contain μ? Although this is unknowable, we can say that we are 90% confident that it does.

For each of the three interval estimates, the connection between the margin of error, or precision, and percent confidence now emerges. This relationship is summarized in Table 8.1.

Table 8.1 Intervals, margins of error, and percent confidence

Interval	Margin of error	Percent confidence
[70.89, 79.11]	4.11	90%
[70.10, 79.90]	4.90	95%
[68.56, 81.44]	6.44	99%

As percent confidence increases (because the width of the interval expands to include a wider range of values), we have a lower level of precision (as reflected in the larger margin of error). Higher precision is purchased at the price of lower confidence; higher confidence results in lower precision. The only way out of the trade-off relationship between precision and confidence is to increase the sample size n. As we see later in this chapter, by adjusting the sample size we can increase precision and confidence simultaneously.

8.2 INTERVAL ESTIMATE OF μ WHEN σ IS UNKNOWN

Recall that because the true value of σ is seldom known, the above form of the interval estimate is rarely used in most real-world data analysis problems. What do we do then? We make a simple two-part adjustment: we use the sample standard deviation s in place of σ, and employ the t-distribution in the place of the standard normal; that is, we change $\bar{x} \pm z_{\alpha/2}\sigma/\sqrt{n}$ to

$$\bar{x} \pm t_{\alpha/2,n-1}\frac{s}{\sqrt{n}}.$$

Definition 8.7. *t*-distribution. The t-distribution is a family of probability distributions that resemble the standard normal probability distribution. Each t-distribution is defined by the value of its parameter, the degrees of freedom, df (see Figure 8.2).

Definition 8.8. Degrees of Freedom. The degrees of freedom, df, constitute the parameter of the particular t-distribution that is used (in this case) to find the margin of error for an interval estimate of μ. Note that $df = n - 1$, where n is the sample size.

Let us make a few points about the t-distribution and the margin of error:

1 By using the sample standard deviation s rather than σ, we use the same sample data to estimate σ as we do to estimate μ.

2 $t_{\alpha/2,n-1}$ is the value of t that cuts off an area of $\alpha/2$ in the upper tail of the t-distribution with $n-1$ degrees of freedom. The subscript on t is a single indicator consisting of two pieces of information, $\alpha/2$ and $n-1$.

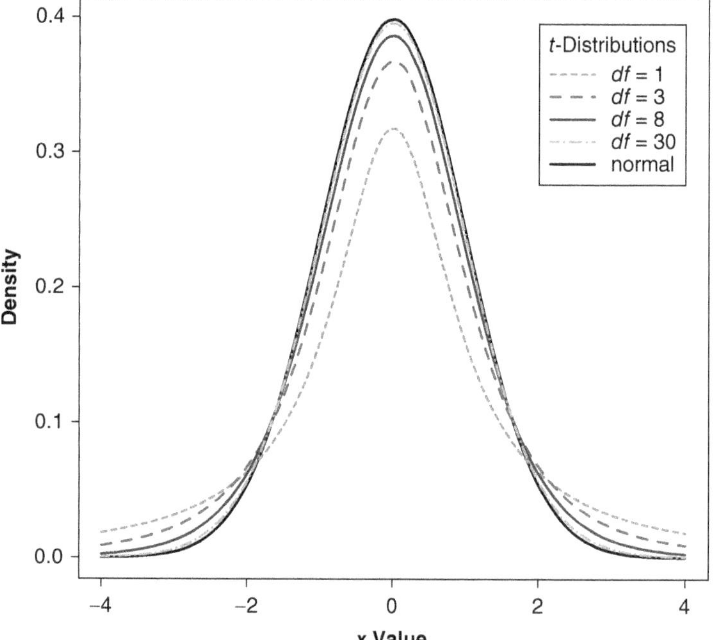

Figure 8.2 The standard normal plus four different *t*-distributions

3 When using the *t*-distribution to construct interval estimates of μ, select the one having $n - 1$ degrees of freedom where n is the size of the sample. For example, to construct an interval estimate of μ and when $n = 31$, choose the *t*-distribution with $n - 1 = 31 - 1 = 30$ degrees of freedom.

4 Note that as n becomes large, and df also becomes large, the associated *t*-distribution looks more and more like the standard normal distribution. As n (and *df*) become small, the associated *t*-distribution still resembles the standard normal distribution, but is flatter and less peaked near the mean. Both tails are thicker (see Figure 8.2).

5 The mean of every *t*-distribution is zero.

6 To derive a 95% confidence interval estimate of μ using a sample of *n* = 21, the relevant value of *t* is specified by incorporating this information into the subscript with the two pieces of information, $n - 1 = 20$ and $\alpha / 2 = 0.025$, as follows: $t_{\alpha/2,n-1} = t_{0.025,20}$.

7 If using R to find the value of $t_{0.025,20}$, use the function `qt(0.975, 20)`.

#Comment. Use qt(0.975, 20) to find value of t that divides area
#under curve of t-distribution (df = 20) with 0.975 to the left and

```
#0.025 to the right.
qt(.975, 20)
```

```
## [1] 2.085963
```

The following exercises provide practice using R to find values of t and their probabilities.

Example 8.4. If $n = 28$, what is $p(t > 1.314)$?

Answer: $0.09995 \approx 0.10$.

```
#Comment. 1 minus probability t is less than 1.314 when df=28-1=27.
1 - pt(1.314, 27)
```

```
## [1] 0.09995069
```

Example 8.5. If $n = 71$, what is $p(t > 1.994)$?

Answer: $0.02502 \approx 0.025$.

```
#Comment. 1 minus probability t is less than 1.994 when df=71–1=70.
1 - pt(1.994, 70)
```

```
## [1] 0.02502444
```

Example 8.6. If $n = 23$, what is $p(t < 0)$?

Answer: 0.5000.

```
#Comment. Use pt(0,22) to find probability t is less than 0 when df = 22.
pt(0, 22)
```

```
## [1] 0.5
```

Example 8.7. If $n = 38$, what is $p(t < 2.431)$?

Answer: 0.99.

```
#Comment. Use pt(2.431,37) to find probability t is less than 2.431
#when df=37.
pt(2.431, 37)
```

```
## [1] 0.9899894
```

Example 8.8. If $n = 15$, what is $p(-1.345 \leq t \leq 2.145)$?

Answer: 0.8750.

```
#Comment. Subtract pt(–1. 345,14) from pt(2.145,14) when df=14.
pt(2.145, 14) - pt(-1.345, 14)
```

```
## [1] 0.8750051
```

Example 8.9. What is the value of $t_{\alpha/2,n-1}$ when $1-\alpha = 0.95$ and $n = 20$?

Answer: $t_{\alpha/2,n-1} = t_{0.025,19} = 2.093$.

```
#Comment. Use qt(0.975,19) to find value of t that divides area
#under curve of t-distribution (de=19) with 0.975 to the left and
#0.025 to the right.
qt(.975, 19)

## [1] 2.093024
```

Example 8.10. What is the value of $t_{\alpha/2,n-1}$ when $1-\alpha = 0.99$ and $n = 33$?

Answer: $t_{\alpha/2,n-1} = t_{0.005,32} = 2.738$.

```
#Comment. Use qt(0.995,32) to find value of t that divides area
#under curve of t-distribution (df=32) with 0.995 to the left and
#0.005 to the right.
qt(.995, 32)

## [1] 2.738481
```

Example 8.11. What is the value of $t_{\alpha/2,n-1}$ when $1-\alpha = 0.90$ and $n = 18$?

Answer: $t_{\alpha/2,n-1} = t_{0.05,17} = 1.74$.

```
#Comment. Use qt(0.95,17) to find value of t that divides area
#under curve of t-distribution (df=17) with 0.95 to the left.
qt(.95, 17)

## [1] 1.739607
```

Examples 8.12–8.14 require interval estimates of μ using s and the t-distribution. Example 8.12 uses `tv_hours` from the website. Recall that `tv_hours` has $n = 100$.

Example 8.12. Using `tv_hours`, find a 95% confidence interval estimate of μ.

Approach 1. Assemble all elements of the interval estimate using an easy-to-follow, four-step template: (a)–(d) below. Use R to find the values for parts (a)–(c).

Recall that the form for the interval estimate is: $\bar{x} \pm t_{\alpha/2,n-1}\frac{s}{\sqrt{n}}$.

(a) What is the relevant t value, $t_{\alpha/2,n-1}$?
Answer: $t_{0.025,99} = 1.984$.

```
#Comment. Use qt(0.975,99)
qt(.975, 99)

## [1] 1.984217
```

(b) What is the sample mean, $\bar{x}$?
Answer: $\bar{x} = 11.64$.

```
#Comment. Use mean() to find mean of tv_hours.
mean(tv_hours$hours)

## [1] 11.6397
```

(c) What is the standard error of the mean, $s_{\bar{x}}$?

Answer: $s_{\bar{x}} = \frac{s}{\sqrt{n}} = \frac{3.977}{\sqrt{100}} = 0.3977.$

```
#Comment. Use sd() to find standard deviation of tv_hours and
#divide by square root of the sample size.
sd(tv_hours$hours) / sqrt(100)

## [1] 0.3975926
```

(d) What is the interval estimate of μ?

Answer: $11.64 \pm 1.984 \times 0.3977$, or 11.64 ± 0.7890; i.e., 11.64 ± 0.7890, or $[10.85, 12.43]$.

Thus, the 95% confidence interval estimate is 11.64 ± 0.7890. That is, we can be 95% confident that μ falls in the interval from 10.85 to 12.43.

Approach 2. Use the function `t.test()` to derive the 95% interval estimate of μ. Along with the data set and variable name, the confidence level is specified at 0.95.

```
#Comment. Use function t.test() to find 95% interval estimate.
t.test(tv_hours$hours, conf = 0.95)

##
## One Sample t-test
##
## data: tv_hours$hours
## t = 29.275, df = 99, p-value < 2.2e-16
## alternative hypothesis: true mean is not equal to 0
## 95 percent confidence interval:
##   10.85079 12.42861
## sample estimates:
## mean of x
##   11.6397
```

The 95% interval estimate of μ is reported on the fifth and sixth lines of the output above. The other information provided can be ignored for now; it is not used until Chapter 10.

Example 8.13. For the `LakeHuron` data set, find a 99% interval estimate μ. (Recall from Chapters 1–3 that the `LakeHuron` data set is part of the R system, and is made up of 98 annual measurements of the level of Lake Huron, from 1875 to 1972.) Use both Approach 1 and 2 from Example 8.12.

Approach 1. Use the four-step template that is applied in Approach 1 of Example 8.12.

(a) What is the relevant *t* value, $t_{\alpha/2,n-1}$?

Answer: $t_{0.005,97} = 2.627$.

```
#Comment. Use qt(0.995,97).
qt(0.995, 97)

## [1] 2.627468
```

(b) What is the sample mean, $\overline{x}$?
Answer: $\overline{x} = 579$.

```
#Comment. Use mean() to find mean of LakeHuron.
mean(LakeHuron)

## [1] 579.0041
```

(c) What is the standard error of the mean, $s_{\overline{x}}$?
Answer: $s_{\overline{x}} = s / \sqrt{n} = 1.318 / \sqrt{98} = 0.1332$.

```
#Comment. Standard error of mean is found with sd()/sqrt().
sd(LakeHuron) / sqrt(98)

## [1] 0.1331683
```

(d) What is the interval estimate of μ?
Answer: $579 \pm 2.627 \times 0.1332$ or 579 ± 0.3499, which we can also write as [578.65, 579.35].
We can be 99% confident that μ is no less than 578.65 but no greater than 579.35.

Approach 2. Use the function `t.test(LakeHuron, conf = 0.99)` to find the 99% interval estimate of μ. The confidence level is specified at 0.99. Note that both Approaches 1 and 2 report the same confidence interval values.

```
#Comment. Use function t.test(LakeHuron, conf = 0.99) to
#report the 99% interval estimate.
t.test(LakeHuron, conf = 0.99)

##
## One Sample t-test
##
## data: LakeHuron
## t = 4347.9, df = 97, p-value < 2.2e-16
## alternative hypothesis: true mean is not equal to 0
## 99 percent confidence interval:
##    578.6542 579.3540
## sample estimates:
## mean of x
##    579.0041
```

The function `t.test()` produces the same interval estimate as does the template.
Example 8.14 uses `housing` from the `introstats` package; the variable name is `rent`.

Example 8.14. Using `housing`, find a 90% confidence interval estimate of μ.

Approach 1. Use the four-step template that is applied in Approach 1 of Example 8.12.

(a) What is the relevant t value, $t_{\alpha/2,n-1}$?
Answer: $t_{0.05,69} = 1.667$.

#Comment. Use qt(.95,69)

```
qt(.95, 69)
## [1] 1.667239
```

(b) What is the sample mean, $\bar{x}$?
Answer: $\bar{x} = 3915$.

#Comment. Use mean().

```
mean(housing$rent)
## [1] 3914.571
```

(c) What is the standard error of the mean, $s_{\bar{x}}$?
Answer: $s_{\bar{x}} = s / \sqrt{n} = 451.3 / \sqrt{70} = 53.94$.

#Comment. Standard error of mean is found with sd()/sqrt().

```
sd(housing$rent) / sqrt(70)
## [1] 53.93902
```

(d) What is the interval estimate of μ?
Answer: $3915 \pm 1.667 \times 53.94 = 3915 \pm 89.92$, or $[3825, 4005]$.
We are 90% confident that μ is no less than 3825 but no greater than 4005.

Approach 2. Use function `t.test()` to find the 90% interval estimate of μ.

#Comment. Use t.test() to report the 90% interval estimate.

```
t.test(housing$rent, conf = 0.90)

##
## One Sample t-test
##
## data:  housing$rent
## t = 72.574, df = 69, p-value < 2.2e-16
## alternative hypothesis: true mean is not equal to 0
## 90 percent confidence interval:
##   3824.642 4004.501
## sample estimates:
## mean of x
##   3914.571
```

The function `t.test()` produces the same interval estimate as does the template.

8.3 SAMPLE SIZE DETERMINATION IN THE CASE OF μ

Even though in the preceding examples we have been free to set any level of confidence $(1 - \alpha)$ we desire, we have had no control over the margin of error or level of precision. But by adjusting the sample size n it is possible to control both level of confidence and degree of precision simultaneously. Recall that the interval estimate of μ takes this form: $\bar{x} \pm$ margin of error. In the case where σ is known, this form becomes

$$\bar{x} \pm z_{\alpha/2} \frac{\sigma}{\sqrt{n}},$$

where the margin of error (ME) is

$$ME = z_{\alpha/2} \frac{\sigma}{\sqrt{n}}.$$

If the desired precision is designated as the *planned* margin of error (PME) then

$$PME = z_{\alpha/2} \frac{\sigma}{\sqrt{n}}.$$

Solving for the sample size n that results in a specified level of confidence and precision,

$$\sqrt{n} = \frac{(z_{\alpha/2})\sigma}{PME}$$

and

$$n = \frac{(z_{\alpha/2})^2 \sigma^2}{(PME)^2}.$$

When σ is unknown, as it usually is, this expression can be used only if some other value is substituted in its place. For example, if a similar study has been done in the past, the standard deviation from that study can be used. But if not, a pilot study might be conducted and the standard deviation found using that sample. Suppose we are conducting a study into the average monthly mortgage payment based on a cross-section of +1000 homeowners, but do not know the value of n required to provide the desired levels of confidence and precision. We might collect information on a preliminary sample of, say, 40 households and then calculate the value of s from this sample. Once we have an estimate of σ, the sample size determination expression above can be used.

Referring to Example 8.1, recall that a 95% interval estimate of μ based on $n = 100$ is found to be 75 ± 4.90 or [70.10, 79.90].

Example 8.15. Suppose the Bon Voyage manager complains that a margin of error of 4.90 is too large and that she would prefer it to be only 2.50. What must n be? Note that in this case, the value of σ is provided by the *assumed* standard deviation of $\sigma = 25$. Then

$$n = \frac{(z_{\alpha/2})^2 \sigma^2}{PME^2} = \frac{1.96^2 \times 25^2}{2.5^2} = 384.16 \approx 385.$$

We can check that $n = 385$ provides both $1 - \alpha = 0.95$ and a PME of 2.5:

$$75 \pm 1.96 \times \frac{25}{\sqrt{385}} \text{ or } 75 \pm 2.5.$$

As we see, $n = 385$ results in a 95% interval estimate with a margin of error of 2.5. We note that this ability to set both the precision and confidence level simultaneously comes at the cost of increasing n from 100 to 385, something which may not be practical or even possible to do. In many situations, information is neither free nor easy to come by. At the very least, this method provides an idea of how much information might be required.

Example 8.16. The manager states that while she is pleased that the margin of error is now 2.5, she would also prefer to be 99% confident that the resulting interval actually contains μ. Is the margin of error still 2.5 at 99% confidence with a sample size $n = 385$?

With $1 - \alpha = 0.99$, we have $z_{0.005} = 2.576$ so the confidence interval is now

$$75 \pm 2.576 \times \frac{25}{\sqrt{385}} = 75 \pm 3.28.$$

As we see, while the confidence level is now set at 99%, the margin of error has floated upward from 2.5 to 3.28. In fact, it will return to 2.5 at the 99% level of confidence only if n is increased to something greater than 385.

Example 8.17. What should the sample size be if the manager requests a confidence level of 99% and a margin of error of 2.5?

$$n = \frac{(z_{\alpha/2})^2 \sigma^2}{PME^2} = \frac{2.576^2 \times 25^2}{2.5^2} = 663.06 \approx 664.$$

We can check that $n = 664$ provides both $1 - \alpha = 0.99$ and a PME of 2.5:

$$75 \pm 2.576 \frac{25}{\sqrt{664}} = 75 \pm 2.5.$$

Thus, with $n = 664$, we can be 99% confident that μ lies in the interval 75 ± 2.5.

8.4 INTERVAL ESTIMATE OF *p*

Recall that an interval estimate takes the general form of point estimate ± the margin of error, so for p the interval estimate assumes the form $\bar{p}$ ± margin of error. When $np \geq 5$ and $n(1-p) \geq 5$, the full expression for the interval estimate of p is

$$\bar{p} \pm z_{\alpha/2}\sigma_{\bar{p}} \quad \text{or} \quad \bar{p} \pm z_{\alpha/2}\sqrt{\frac{p(1-p)}{n}}.$$

Since p is unknown (we want an interval estimate of p precisely because its value is unknown), we must use something else in place of p. When we substitute the sample proportion $\bar{p}$ for p, the interval estimate form becomes

$$\bar{p} \pm z_{\alpha/2}\sqrt{\frac{\bar{p}(1-\bar{p})}{n}}.$$

Here $\bar{p}$ is the sample proportion, n is the sample size, $1 - \alpha$ is the confidence coefficient, and $z_{\alpha/2}$ is the value of z with an area of $\alpha/2$ to its right.

Example 8.18. Find a 95% interval estimate of p using the data set `exit` from the website. This data set consists of $n = 1500$ voters exiting a New York polling station after casting their ballots in the 2012 US Presidential election; for this sample, 930 of the 1500 respondents voted for Obama. The data are coded 0 for a Romney vote, 1 for an Obama vote.

Approach 1. Assemble all the elements of the interval estimate using a four-step template similar to that used for Example 8.12.

(a) What is the relevant z value, $z_{\alpha/2}$?
Answer: $z_{0.025} = 1.96$.

(b) What is the sample proportion, $\bar{p}$?
Answer: The sample proportion is

$$\bar{p} = \frac{930}{1500} = 0.62.$$

(c) What is the standard error of the proportion, $\sigma_{\bar{p}}$?
Answer: The standard error is

$$\sigma_{\bar{p}} = \sqrt{\frac{\bar{p}(1-\bar{p})}{n}} = \sqrt{\frac{0.62 \times 0.38}{1500}} = 0.0125.$$

(d) What is the interval estimate of p?
Answer: $0.62 \pm 1.96 \times 0.0125$ or $[0.5954, 0.6446]$.
We are 95% confident that p is no less than 0.5954 but no more than 0.6446.

Approach 2. Use R as a calculator to find the 95% confidence interval estimate for p.

```
#Comment1. Find variable name in exit.
names(exit) #exit has one variable: "Obama".

## [1] "Obama"

#Comment2. Find the sample proportion pbar.
n <- length(exit$obama); n #n=1500 is sample size in exit

## [1] 1500

k <- sum(exit$obama); k #k=930 is number of 1's in exit

## [1] 930

pbar <- k / n; pbar #pbar=0.62 is the sample proportion

## [1] 0.62

#Comment3. Find the standard error of the proportion SEP.
SEP <- sqrt(pbar * (1 - pbar) / n); SEP #SEP=0.01253.

## [1] 0.01253262
```

#Comment4. Find margin of error MOE for 95% interval estimate.

```
MOE <- qnorm(0.975) * SEP; MOE

## [1] 0.02456349
```

#Comment5. Find 95% interval estimate of population proportion.

```
pbar + c(-MOE, MOE)

## [1] 0.5954365 0.6445635
```

Approach 3. Use the `t.test()` function to find the interval estimate.

```
t.test(exit$obama, conf.level = 0.95)

##
## One Sample t-test
##
## data:  exit$obama
## t = 49.454, df = 1499, p-value < 2.2e-16
## alternative hypothesis: true mean is not equal to 0
## 95 percent confidence interval:
##   0.5954085 0.6445915
## sample estimates:
## mean of x
##      0.62
```

As we see, the results of all approaches are the same: the 95% interval estimate of p is [0.5954, 0.6446].

8.5 SAMPLE SIZE DETERMINATION IN THE CASE OF *p*

While we are free to set confidence at whatever level we desire, we do not control the magnitude of the margin of error. Here is an expression for adjusting the sample size for purposes of controlling both the level of confidence and precision when finding an interval estimate of p. If desired precision is designated as *planned* margin of error (*PME*) then

$$PME = z_{\alpha/2}\sqrt{\frac{\bar{p}(1-\bar{p})}{n}}.$$

Solving for the value of n that results in a specified level of confidence and precision,

$$PME^2 = (z_{\alpha/2})^2 \frac{\bar{p}(1-\bar{p})}{n}$$

so

$$n = \frac{(z_{\alpha/2})^2 \bar{p}(1-\bar{p})}{PME^2}.$$

In using this sample size determination expression, however, $\bar{p}$ is unknown until the sample has been collected, and so some other value must be used in its place. If we designate the substituted value as $\dot{p}$, the sample size determination expression becomes

$$n = \frac{(z_{\alpha/2})^2 \dot{p}(1-\dot{p})}{PME^2}.$$

There are several approaches to setting a value for $\dot{p}$. If a study similar to the current one has been done in the past, we could use $\bar{p}$ from the earlier study. But if there has been no previous study, and the current one is the first of its kind, we may run a pilot study and use the $\bar{p}$ from that pilot sample. Finally, the safest approach is to assign $\dot{p} = 0.50$. The reason why $\dot{p} = 0.50$ is the most conservative choice for the new value of p is illustrated in Table 8.2.

Table 8.2 Different values for $\dot{p}$ and the product $\dot{p}(1-\dot{p})$

$\dot{p}$	$(1-\dot{p})$	$\dot{p}(1-\dot{p})$
0.65	0.35	0.2275
0.62	**0.38**	**0.2356**
0.60	0.40	0.2400
0.50	**0.50**	**0.2500**
0.40	0.60	0.2400
0.38	0.62	0.2356
0.35	0.65	0.2275

That the product of $\dot{p}(1-\dot{p})$ is maximized when $\dot{p} = 0.50$ is the reason why setting $\dot{p} = 0.50$ is the safest approach to determining n. In fact, it provides the largest sample size of all because anything that maximizes the product of $\dot{p}(1-\dot{p})$, by definition, also maximizes the required sample size n.

Example 8.19. Referring to Example 8.18, the margin of error is $1.96 \times 0.0125 = 0.0245$. What n is needed to reduce the margin of error from 0.0245 to 0.02 at 95% confidence?

Answer: Using $\dot{p} = 0.62$ from the previous example yields

$$n = \frac{(z_{\alpha/2})^2 \dot{p}(1-\dot{p})}{PME^2} = \frac{1.96^2 \times 0.62 \times 0.38}{0.02^2} = 2262.70 \approx 2263.$$

We can check that $n = 2263$ brings about both a 95% confidence level and a margin of error of 0.02:

$$0.62 \pm 1.96\sqrt{\frac{0.62 \times 0.38}{2263}} = 0.62 \pm 0.0200.$$

Example 8.20. If $\dot{p} = 0.50$ is used rather than $\dot{p} = 0.62$, what is the new value of n?

Answer: Using $\dot{p} = 0.50$ from the previous example yields

$$n = \frac{(z_{\alpha/2})^2 \dot{p}(1-\dot{p})}{PME^2} = \frac{1.96^2 \times 0.50 \times 0.50}{0.02^2} = 2401.$$

Using the most conservative value for $\dot{p}$ has increased n from 2263 to 2401.

Finally, the reader is reminded that the inverse relationship between precision and sample size n is the same whether finding interval estimates of μ or p: for a given level of confidence, to improve the precision (or margin of error) by a factor of 2, n must ordinarily be quadrupled. This is an important consideration to bear in mind when making decisions about what might be a desirable, and practicably attainable, margin of error.

SUMMARY

This chapter introduces and develops the statistical method known as interval estimation. The motivation for interval estimation is the same as that for point estimation, the principal topic of Chapter 7, which is to estimate some characteristic or property of a larger population when the only information we have comes from a sample. The advantage of interval estimation over point estimation, however, is that an interval estimate is accompanied by a statement of precision that reports the point estimate in the context of how precise that estimate is likely to be. An important part of this statement is the margin of error.

In both Chapters 7 and 8 our central concern has been how precise a sample statistic is in its estimate of a population parameter. In Chapter 7 we were able to consider this question only in view of the unrealistic assumption that, even before sampling, we know the value of the population parameter. In the real world, this is of course a pointless thing to do since if we are already in possession of the actual value of a parameter there is no reason to do any sampling for the purpose of estimation. Since we already know the value of the parameter, why would we want to estimate it? In this chapter, however, we relax the assumption that we know the value of the parameter, and learn to use a method more adapted to the real world of messy data analysis where the parameter value is unknown.

To this end, in the current chapter, we use interval estimation as a statistical procedure to provide a statement about the quality, or the precision, of the point estimates $\bar{x}$ and $\bar{p}$. (We extend the method of interval estimation to other parameters in later chapters.) In general, the interval estimate takes the following form: point estimate $\pm$ margin of error. The expression for the margin of error depends on the population parameter in which we are interested, the sample size n, and (in the case of $\bar{x}$) whether we use the population standard deviation σ (because we assume that it is known) or the sample standard deviation s. If we assume that σ is known, it is an open question why we might want to estimate μ in the first place, since knowing σ implies that we know μ, which is the point of the estimation procedure. If we do not assume σ is known, then we must use the sample data to estimate both σ and μ. In this case, we use the t-distribution instead of the standard normal probability distribution in the calculation of the margin of error.

The calculations of the confidence interval estimate of the population proportion p vary slightly because of the distributions used. In this chapter, we use both the standard normal as well as the t-distribution, depending on which of the R functions are invoked: `t.test()` relies on the t-distribution, whereas `prop.test()` depends on the normal distribution. (We make extensive use of `prop.test()` in Chapter 10.) Both are approximations of a phenomenon which is essentially discrete rather than continuous. These choices do not pose a practical problem, however, since the interval estimates are all very close to one another.

This chapter concludes the introduction to the class of methods known as statistical estimation. Although we return to estimation in later chapters, we move on to the topic of statisical inference in Chapter 9. What distinguishes statistical inference from statistical estimation? Statistical estimation—point or interval estimation—involves working out how large or how small something might be; statistical inference entails testing formal hypotheses for the purpose of drawing conclusions or inferences. Which class of methods we use depends on what we wish to know and on the motivation of our study. In Chapter 9 we introduce an important method of statistical inference, hypothesis testing.

definitions

Confidence Coefficient The confidence coefficient is the confidence level expressed as a probability. That is, if the confidence level is 90%, the confidence coefficient is $1 - \alpha = 0.90$; if the confidence level is 95%, the confidence coefficient is $1 - \alpha = 0.95$; if the confidence level is 99%, the confidence coefficient is $1 - \alpha = 0.99$.

Confidence Interval This is a range of values which is likely to contain the population parameter being estimated. In this chapter it is an empircally based estimate of the population mean μ or population proportion p.

Confidence Level An interval estimate has associated with it a percent confidence level. For example, 90% of the time, a 90% interval estimate contains the population parameter; 95% of the time, a 95% interval estimate contains the population parameter; and 99% of the time, a 99% interval estimate contains the population parameter. The confidence levels are expressed as percentages.

Degrees of Freedom The parameter of the particular t-distribution which is used in finding the margin of error for an interval estimate of the population mean μ.

Margin of Error A quantitative value which is added to, and subtracted from, a point estimate for the purpose of finding a confidence interval estimate of a population parameter.

Precision A probabilistic measure of the distance between a sample statistic and the population parameter it is intended to estimate. Its magnitude is usually a function of the population distribution and the sample size n.

Precision Statement In the context of a confidence interval estimate, a precision statement expresses the trade-off relationship between confidence and precision.

Sampling Error of the Mean A measure of the positive distance between the sample mean and the population mean: $|\bar{x} - \mu|$.

(Continued)

(Continued)

Sampling Error of the Proportion A measure of the positive distance between the sample proportion and the population proportion: $|\bar{p} - p|$.

t-distribution The *t*-distribution represents a family of probability distributions which resemble the symmetric bell curve. A particular *t*-distribution is defined by the degrees-of-freedom parameter, $n - 1$, where n is the relevant sample size.

formulae

Confidence Interval Estimate of a Population Mean ↔: σ Known

$$\bar{x} \pm z_{\alpha/2} \frac{\sigma}{\sqrt{n}}$$

Confidence Interval Estimate of a Population Mean μ: σ Unknown

$$\bar{x} \pm t_{\alpha/2, n-1} \frac{s}{\sqrt{n}}$$

Confidence Interval Estimate of a Population Proportion *p*

$$\bar{p} \pm z_{\alpha/2} \sqrt{\frac{\bar{p}(1-\bar{p})}{n}}$$

Sample Size Determination for Interval Estimate of Mean μ

$$n = \frac{(z_{\alpha/2})^2 \sigma^2}{PME^2}$$

Sample Size Determination for Interval Estimate of Proportion *p*

$$n = \frac{(z_{\alpha/2})^2 \dot{p}(1-\dot{p})}{PME^2}$$

R functions

`t.test(name, conf = 0.90)` Provides the interval estimate of a parameter at the 90% level of confidence using a data set called `name`.

`t.test(name, conf = 0.95)` Provides the interval estimate of a parameter at the 95% level of confidence using a data set called `name`.

`t.test(name, conf = 0.99)` Provides the interval estimate of a parameter at the 99% level of confidence using a data set called `name`.

data sets

Note that some of the data sets listed below are used in the exercises, found on the book's website (https://study.sagepub.com/stinerock), but not in this chapter. The practice of using data sets either in the website exercises or in the chapters is followed elsewhere in this book.

1	`benefits`	6	`housing`
2	`cafe_ratings`	7	`insurance`
3	`cs`	8	`LakeHuron`
4	`dining`	9	`membership`
5	`exit`	10	`tv_hours`

exercises

8.1 According to a survey, the average British household is expected to spend £868 on holiday-related expenses during the Christmas period 2013. This amount covers not only gifts, but also food, beverages, and decorations. Assume the study was based on $n = 94$ randomly sampled households throughout Great Britain. Assume that the sample standard deviation was £162.

(a) What is the 60% confidence interval estimate of the population mean amount-to-be spent μ during the 2013 Christmas holiday period?

(b) What is the 80% confidence interval estimate of the population mean amount-to-be spent μ during the same period?

(c) What is the 90% confidence interval estimate of the population mean amount-to-be spent μ during the same period?

8.2 The manager of an insurance office wishes to gain a better understanding of the dollar value of the newly purchased automobiles his firm has insured over the previous 12 months. To this end, he randomly selects 70 insurance applications from the previous year which specified the total cost of each vehicle insured, including market value, taxes, and licensing fees. Use R and the data set `insurance` from the website to answer the following questions.

(a) Find the 90% confidence interval estimate of the mean dollar value of newly purchased automobiles μ.

(b) Find the 95% confidence interval estimate of the mean dollar value of newly purchased automobiles μ.

(c) Find the 99% confidence interval estimate of the mean dollar value of newly purchased automobiles μ.

8.3 The commute-to-work time for the residents of the world's large cities has been investigated extensively. A pilot study involving an SRS (simple random sample) of residents of Toronto is used to provide an estimate of 10 minutes for the population standard deviation σ. Answer the following questions.

(a) If we want to estimate the population mean commute-to-work time μ for the residents of Toronto with a margin of error of 2 minutes, what sample size n should you recommend? Assume 90% confidence.

(Continued)

(Continued)

(b) If we want to estimate the population mean commute-to-work time μ for the residents of Toronto with a margin of error of 1 minute, what sample size n should you recommend? Assume 90% confidence.

8.4 In a study of consumer confidence among middle-class Indian families, 450 were interviewed in the metropolitan area of Mumbai. When asked about having to cut back on discretionary purchases of big-ticket items, 212 of 450 responded that their families had done so over the previous 6 months.

(a) What is the 90% confidence interval estimate of the population proportion p of this type of household cutting back on discretionary spending?
(b) What sample size would you recommend to achieve a margin of error of 0.03?
(c) How large a sample size would be required to achieve a 99% confidence interval estimate of p with a margin of error of 0.03?
(d) How large a sample size would be required to achieve a 99% confidence interval estimate of p with a margin of error of 0.025?

8.5 A human resources manager at a small university in the US has been considering a change to the structure of employee benefits (in terms of healthcare coverage and pension savings). To get an idea of how receptive the faculty, administrators, and staff members might be to the proposed changes, she has decided to conduct a survey in which $n = 188$ respondents could register their support or opposition. Use R and the data set `benefits` from the website to answer the following questions.

(a) Find the 90% confidence interval estimate of p.
(b) Find the 95% confidence interval estimate of p.
(c) Find the 99% confidence interval estimate of p.

https://study.sagepub.com/stinerock

Hypothesis Tests: Introduction, Basic Concepts, and an Example

content

learning objectives

1. Learn how to formulate and test a hypothesis about an unknown construct.
2. Understand the types of errors that can occur when we conduct a hypothesis test.
3. Be able to calculate the probability of committing an error during a test.
4. Be able to use the sample results to draw inferences.

In Chapters 7 and 8 we considered both point estimation and interval estimation. In this chapter we move from estimation to a widely used inferential framework—the hypothesis test—and we do so in the context of a practical real-world problem faced by businesses in the food and beverage industry: identifying those individuals who are qualified by virtue of their sensitive palates to work as tasters.

For example, the identification of tasters is a problem faced by new micro-breweries of high-quality designer beer. These were common forms of new business start-ups a few years ago in the US when more people began to travel to countries where the tradition of beer-brewing had achieved a high form, most notably the UK, Ireland, Europe, Latin America, Asia, and Australia. At the time, the reaction of many young Americans to the variety and quality of the beers they encountered was to come home and start their own breweries.

The challenges they faced were daunting. Apart from having to raise start-up capital, there was also the problem of running the business on a day-to-day basis. Quality control emerged as an important aspect of their management philosophy, especially because their competitive space was populated by so many other brewers. In fact, the first micro-breweries lacked the usual ingredients for business success: they had no brand-name recognition, they could not afford advertising, they had no distribution, and of course they had high prices. All they had going for them was a tasty, high-quality product.

Since it was essential to the success of the new breweries that their product be not only tasty but consistently so, several different efforts were undertaken each day to monitor both the quality of the beer being brewed and the amount of naturally occurring variability in that quality. First, the brewers sent samples to commercial laboratories specializing in qualitative and quantitative chemical analysis to make sure that all (and only) the intended ingredients were included in their beer, and included in the correct ratios to one another. Second, the brewers employed human tasters to sample each batch of beer, monitoring the flavor to make sure that the taste was not only good but invariably good.

Now as then, the first part of this quality-control effort—having a laboratory break down each sample of beer into its constituent elements—was the easy part. The methods of chemical analysis are well known and well established in the industry. The real challenge facing the brewer is the second part: identifying a person who is qualified to serve as the brewery taster by virtue of his or her sensitive palate. Unfortunately, most of us simply do not have very sensitive palates and cannot consistently discern one beer from another. Naturally, the brewer wishes to avoid hiring a person with no taste-discrimination ability as taster: if the brewing process gets out of control, the taster might not even notice, and the brewery would end up selling beer of compromised quality—exactly the type of failure the new business can least afford.

How might the brewer identify a person having highly sensitive, taste-discrimination ability? One way involves requiring job applicants to participate in a triangle taste test. The design of the triangle taste test is very simple. During the job interview, an applicant is presented with three cups of beer, two of which contain the same beer, and is asked to identify the cup containing the odd sample. Apart from a subtle difference in flavor, the beer samples are as alike as possible: the three identical cups are filled to exactly the same height with beer of the same color and temperature. When the applicant feels certain she has identified the odd sample, she must announce her choice.

The applicant is presented with a series of identical triangle taste tests, or trials, in which the placement of the odd sample is randomized. While a single trial may not expose someone having no taste-discrimination ability, a series of trials is much more likely to do so. That is, in a single trial, the applicant lacking ability may identify the odd sample by luck alone, but on (say) 15 trials, her lack of ability is bound to become more obvious.

There are four elements that form the following conceptual framework:

1 If we let p be the probability that the job applicant correctly identifies the odd sample in a single trial of the triangle taste test, then one of the following conditions must be true: if the applicant has no taste-discrimination ability, then $p = 1/3$; if the applicant has *some* ability, then $p > 1/3$. (Note that $p = 1/3$ because even a no-ability person has a one-in-three chance of selecting the odd sample just by luck.) For each applicant, one of the two conditions must be true; there is no third possibility. While each applicant is associated with a value of p, there is heterogeneity of p values across individuals. In other words, p can be thought of as a true but unknown characteristic or parameter which varies across individuals: those with highly sensitive palates will have a value of $p > 1/3$, whereas others, the majority, who lack taste-discrimination ability will have a value of $p = 1/3$.

We next express the problem in the context of a formal hypothesis-testing framework. The first step in constructing a hypothesis test is to define the two conditions specified above in terms of two hypotheses, the null hypothesis and the alternative hypothesis.

Definition 9.1. Null Hypothesis. The condition stated in the null hypothesis H_0 is tentatively assumed to be true unless and until compelling evidence casts strong doubt on it. In that case, we say that we reject H_0.

Definition 9.2. Alternative Hypothesis. The condition stated in the alternative hypothesis H_a is concluded to be true whenever the null hypothesis is rejected.

In the case of the triangle taste test, the null hypothesis is H_0: $p = 1/3$, while the alternative hypothesis is H_a: $p > 1/3$.

In general, H_0 represents the condition that nothing interesting is going on: nothing is different from what might be expected. It embodies a conservative, skeptical point of view. In the present case, H_0: $p = 1/3$ expresses the view that the applicant has no taste-discrimination ability. Recall that H_0 is tentatively assumed true until we see strong evidence that it is not. What might that strong evidence be? Data. Data that in this case would be a high number of successful identifications over a number of trials. When that happens, we say that we reject H_0 and accept H_a, where

H_a expresses the view that the applicant does indeed have some taste-discrimination ability. But what number of successful identifications would lead us to reject H_0? To answer this question, we move on to the second element of our framework.

2 Let *x* be the random variable indicating the number of successful identifications out of *n* trials. That is, when the applicant completes the series of *n* triangle taste tests, she will achieve some number *x* of identifications, where *x* is a discrete random variable which may assume any value from 0 (no identifications) to *n* (a perfect score). Of the discrete probability distributions, the binomial best describes the behavior of *x*. In this and other hypothesis tests, *x* is often referred to as the *test statistic*.

Definition 9.3. Test Statistic. The empirical result of the hypothesis test that is used to either reject or not reject the null hypothesis H_0.

We note that *x* has a binomial probability distribution because it satisfies the five properties of the binomial experiment (see Section 5.4):

(a) The overall experiment consists of a series of *n* identical trials. The *n* triangle taste tests are all identical to one another.
(b) On each trial, there are two possible outcomes, one designated success *S* (identify), the other designated failure *F* (fail to identify).
(c) On each trial, the probability of success is $p(S) = p$ and the probability of failure is $p(F) = 1 - p$. Each person's taste-discrimination ability is stable and stationary; an applicant's *p* value neither degrades nor improves over the trials.
(d) The trials are independent.
(e) The question to be answered is this: what is the probability of *x* successful identifications in *n* triangle taste-test trials?

Before introducing the third element of the framework, recall that the binomial probability function $f(x)$ takes the form

$$f(x) = p(x \mid n, p) = \binom{n}{x} p^x (1-p)^{n-x}, \quad \text{where } x = 0, 1, 2, \ldots, n,$$

and where $f(x) = p(x \mid n, p)$ is the probability of *x* successes in *n* trials and where *p* is the probability of success and $1 - p$ the probability of failure.

3 The third element of the framework is the *rejection region (RR)*, and it forms an important part of the hypothesis test.

Definition 9.4. Rejection Region. A rejection region *RR* specifies the range of values the test statistic *x* might assume that would lead to rejection of H_0.

In the case of the triangle taste test, defining the rejection region requires that we decide *before the test* which values of *x*—that is, how many correct identifications—should lead to rejection of H_0. Clearly, when the test statistic *x* is large because the applicant has made many correct identifications, H_0 should be rejected because the empirical evidence casts doubt on H_0. Assuming the triangle taste test consists of $n = 15$ trials, let us consider two possible rejection regions, RR_7 and RR_9, where

$$RR_7 = \{7, 8, 9, 10, 11, 12, 13, 14, 15\} \text{ and } RR_9 = \{9, 10, 11, 12, 13, 14, 15\}.$$

For RR_7, if an applicant correctly identifies the odd sample at least 7 out of 15 times, we reject $H_0 : p = 1/3$ and accept $H_a : p > 1/3$. But if there are 6 or fewer correct identifications, we do not reject H_0, and no longer consider the person for employment as a taster. The same reasoning applies when using RR_9: if an applicant correctly identifies the odd sample at least 9 out of 15 times, we reject $H_0 : p = 1/3$ and accept $H_a : p > 1/3$. However, if there are 8 or fewer correct identifications, we do not reject H_0, and thus do not consider the person for the taster's position.

There is nothing special about these two particular rejection regions; they only represent different standards that might be applied. Indeed, we could just as well select RR_8 or RR_{10}, bearing in mind the question of which the best rejection region is for the purpose at hand. But what do we mean by the best rejection region? To answer this question, we turn to the fourth and final element of the framework, the two types of error that may occur as a result of a hypothesis test.

4 Applying a hypothesis test may lead to the wrong conclusion. No matter how large our sample, and no matter how sophisticated the testing methodology may be, it is still possible to commit an error. The desire to reduce the amount of uncertainty we face is one of the reasons why hypothesis testing is so widely used. Even so, the methodology is not perfect, and there are two types of error that are possible with any hypothesis test, the *Type I error* and *Type II error*.

Definition 9.5. Type I Error. A Type I error occurs when we reject the null hypothesis H_0 when it is true.

Definition 9.6. Type II Error. A Type II error occurs when we do not reject the null hypothesis H_0 when it is false.

In the case of the brewery, we commit a Type I error if we conclude that an applicant has ability when in fact she has none; we reject $H_0 : p = 1/3$ when we should not. This can happen when a taste-insensitive person makes a large number of successful identifications just by luck, and the practical outcome of such an error is that we hire someone who cannot distinguish one beer from another. Clearly, to the extent possible, we want to control the likelihood of committing this sort of error.

On the other hand, we commit a Type II error when we conclude that an applicant does not have ability when in fact she does; that is, we fail to reject H_0 when we should. This can happen when a taste-sensitive person has a bad day—perhaps because she has an allergy or head cold—and underperforms as a result. The outcome of this type of error is that we fail to identify and hire a good candidate for the taster's position, and must keep interviewing applicants until another talented person applies.

The way we assess the strength of a hypothesis test is by computing the probabilities of committing these two types of errors. Traditionally, the probability of committing a Type I error is designated by the Greek letter alpha (α); the probability of committing a Type II error is denoted by another Greek letter, beta (β).

Definition 9.7. Alpha. The Greek letter α is used in hypothesis testing to denote the probability of a Type I error.

Definition 9.8. Level of Significance. α is also known as the level of significance.

Definition 9.9. Beta. The Greek letter β is used in hypothesis testing to denote the probability of a Type II error.

To summarize these relationships:

$$p(\text{Type I error}) = p(\text{we reject } H_0 \mid H_0 \text{ is true}) = \alpha,$$

$$p(\text{Type II error}) = p(\text{we fail to reject } H_0 \mid H_0 \text{ is false}) = \beta.$$

Example 9.1. What is α for RR_7?

To find the value of α for rejection region $RR_7 = \{7, \ldots, 15\}$, we sum the binomial probabilities for each value of x from 7 through 15 (Table 9.1 reports these individual probabilities). We obtain

$$\begin{aligned}\alpha &= p(x \geq 7 \mid n = 15, p = \tfrac{1}{3}) = \sum_{x=7}^{15} \binom{15}{x} \left(\frac{1}{3}\right)^x \left(\frac{2}{3}\right)^{15-x} \\ &= p(x=7) + p(x=8) + \ldots + p(x=15) \\ &= 0.1148 + 0.0574 + 0.0223 + 0.0067 + 0.0015 + 0.0003 + 0.0000 + 0.0000 + 0.0000 \\ &= 0.2030.\end{aligned}$$

Table 9.1 Binomial probabilities for $x = 7, \ldots, 15$, for $n = 15$ and $p = 1/3$

$p(x = 7 \mid n = 15, p = 1/3) = 0.1148$
$p(x = 8 \mid n = 15, p = 1/3) = 0.0574$
$p(x = 9 \mid n = 15, p = 1/3) = 0.0223$
$p(x = 10 \mid n = 15, p = 1/3) = 0.0067$
$p(x = 11 \mid n = 15, p = 1/3) = 0.0015$
$p(x = 12 \mid n = 15, p = 1/3) = 0.0003$
$p(x = 13 \mid n = 15, p = 1/3) = 0.0000$
$p(x = 14 \mid n = 15, p = 1/3) = 0.0000$
$p(x = 15 \mid n = 15, p = 1/3) = 0.0000$

The following observations are in order:

(a) When $\alpha = 0.2030$, the probability that a taste-insensitive applicant might pass the test defined by rejection region RR_7–and fool us into thinking she has the taste-discrimination ability the brewery seeks–is 0.2030. That is, in using RR_7, there is a roughly 20% chance that the wrong person might be hired.

(b) In setting RR_7 as the rejection region, the level of significance is 0.2030.

(c) We can look at this statistical method as a means by which to *quantify* the level of risk to which we are exposed when we use this particular rejection region.

(d) Note that the probability that a taste-insensitive person makes 7 correct identifications (0.1148) exceeds the probability she makes 8 correct identifications (0.0574); the probability she makes 8 correct identifications exceeds the probability she makes 9 correct identifications (0.0223); and so on. This conforms with our intuition about how the probabilities should be distributed over the different values that x might assume for the test-insensitive person: higher numbers of correct identifications are less likely when the person has no ability.

(e) A Type I error occurs only when H_0 is true; it cannot occur when H_a is true.

(f) A Type I error occurs whenever a true H_0 is rejected; it cannot occur when a true H_0 is not rejected.

(g) When we say that we tentatively assume $H_0 = 1/3$ is true, we have acted on that assumption by setting $p = 1/3$ for each of the binomial computations.

Example 9.2. What is α for RR_9?

To find the value of α for rejection region $RR_9 = \{9, \ldots, 15\}$, we sum the binomial probabilities for each value of x from 9 through 15 (see Table 9.1). We obtain

$$\begin{aligned}\alpha &= p(x \geq 9 \mid n = 15, p = \tfrac{1}{3}) = \sum_{x=9}^{15} \binom{15}{x} \left(\frac{1}{3}\right)^x \left(\frac{2}{3}\right)^{15-x} \\ &= p(x=9) + p(x=10) + \ldots + p(x=15) \\ &= 0.0223 + 0.0067 + 0.0015 + 0.0003 + 0.0000 + 0.0000 + 0.0000 \\ &= 0.0308.\end{aligned}$$

We can use the `pbinom()` function to derive the probabilities for both rejection regions.

```
#Comment1. 1 minus probability that x assumes value between 0 and 6.
1 - pbinom(6, 15, 1/3)

## [1] 0.2030389

#Comment2. 1 minus probability that x assumes value between 0 and 8.
1 - pbinom(8, 15, 1/3)

## [1] 0.03082792
```

By removing $x = 7$ and $x = 8$ from the rejection region, α has fallen from 20% to 3%, and we reduce the likelihood that a taste-insensitive applicant might be misclassified as qualified for the taster position. RR_9 provides a margin of safety that RR_7 cannot. Obviously, the brewer will prefer RR_9 but the job applicant would rather face RR_7. The bar has been raised; the standard is now higher. But in moving from RR_7 to RR_9 to lower α, we automatically increase the probability of committing a Type II error β. We now consider this trade-off aspect of hypothesis testing.

If H_a is true—and H_0 is false—then β depends on which alternative value of p we are dealing with. Clearly, if $H_0 = 1/3$ is false, then p can take any value in the range $1/3 < p \leq 1$. As a hypothetical case, assume that one particular taste-sensitive applicant is able to distinguish successfully between different beers 70% of the time. This is actually rather good. Remember that even those individuals who have ability are heterogeneous in this skill: some discriminate successfully 40% of the time, some 50% of the time, and so on. But the taste-insensitive person successfully identifies the odd sample only one-third of the time, and even then only by luck.

The brewery might consider itself fortunate to attract, identify, and hire a job candidate who is able to discriminate successfully 70% of the time.

In view of our two rejection regions, RR_7 and RR_9, what is the probability that the brewer will fail to identify this taste-sensitive applicant? That is, what is the probability of committing a Type II error?

Example 9.3. What is β for RR_9?

To find the value of β for rejection region RR_9, we sum the binomial probabilities for each value of x from 0 through 8. Let $\beta_{p=0.70}$ be the probability of a Type II error when the candidate can identify the odd sample 70% of the time. Table 9.2 gives the binomial probabilities needed for the Type II error probability calculation. For $RR_9 = \{9, \ldots, 15\}$, we obtain

$$\begin{aligned}\beta_{p=0.70} &= p(x \le 8 \mid n = 15, p = 0.70) = \sum_{x=0}^{8} \binom{15}{x} 0.70^x 0.30^{15-x} \\ &= p(x=0) + p(x=1) + \ldots + p(x=8) \\ &= 0.0000 + 0.0000 + 0.0000 + 0.0000 + 0.0006 + 0.0030 + 0.0116 + 0.0348 + 0.0811 \\ &= 0.1311.\end{aligned}$$

Table 9.2 Binomial probabilities for $x = 0, \ldots, 8$, for $n=15$ and $p=0.70$

$p(x=0 \mid n=15, p=0.70) = 0.0000$
$p(x=1 \mid n=15, p=0.70) = 0.0000$
$p(x=2 \mid n=15, p=0.70) = 0.0000$
$p(x=3 \mid n=15, p=0.70) = 0.0000$
$p(x=4 \mid n=15, p=0.70) = 0.0006$
$p(x=5 \mid n=15, p=0.70) = 0.0030$
$p(x=6 \mid n=15, p=0.70) = 0.0116$
$p(x=7 \mid n=15, p=0.70) = 0.0348$
$p(x=8 \mid n=15, p=0.70) = 0.0811$

Thus, using rejection region RR_9, there is a 0.1311 probability that we will collect sample evidence leading us to accept H_0 even though the job applicant can correctly identify the odd sample 70% of the time. This can happen whenever a taste-sensitive person has a bad day, perhaps because of a head cold or allergy, and does not score 9 or more.

Example 9.4. What is β for RR_7?

Applying the reasoning used above in Example 9.3 where $RR_7 = \{7, \ldots, 15\}$, we obtain

$$\begin{aligned}\beta_{p=0.70} &= p(x \le 6 \mid n = 15, p = 0.70) = \sum_{x=0}^{6} \binom{15}{x} 0.70^x 0.30^{15-x} \\ &= p(x=0) + p(x=1) + \ldots + p(x=6) \\ &= 0.0000 + 0.0000 + 0.0000 + 0.0000 + 0.0006 + 0.0030 + 0.0116 \\ &= 0.0152.\end{aligned}$$

Naturally, it is easier using the `pbinom()` function to find the probabilities.

```
#Comment1. Beta for rejection region {9, 10, 11, 12, 13, 14, 15}
pbinom(8, 15, 0.70)

## [1] 0.1311426

#Comment2. Beta for rejection region {7, 8, 9, 10, 11, 12, 13, 14, 15}
pbinom(6, 15, 0.70)

## [1] 0.01524253
```

Table 9.3 α and β for RR_7 and RR_9

	α	β
RR_7	0.2030	0.0152
RR_9	0.0308	0.1311

Which rejection region is best? Table 9.3 provides a summary of the trade-off relationship between α and β in terms of RR_7 and RR_9. The values in the α column indicate that the probability of Type I error is lower when RR_9 is the rejection region. Since hiring a taste-insensitive person as taster could have serious consequences for the brewery, it might prefer RR_9 to RR_7. But the values in the β column show that in selecting RR_9 for the rejection region, the probability of Type II error is higher. This happens when a taste-sensitive applicant is misclassified as insensitive. Since the Type I error is more serious than a Type II error, the brewery should go with RR_9: while it can withstand the mistake of misclassifying a taste-sensitive applicant as unskilled (it just keeps interviewing additional applicants until the next taste-sensitive person applies), the very existence of the brewery as a successful business is threatened by hiring the wrong person as taster.

Finally, we review and extend on several important points developed in this chapter:

1 Table 9.4 summarizes the relationship between our conclusions and the world as it is.

Table 9.4 Our conclusions in the face of the true situation

Our conclusion	If H_0 is true	If H_a is true
Accept H_0	No error, probability $1 - \alpha$	Type II error, probability β
Reject H_0	Type I error, probability α	No error, probability $1 - \beta$

2 Tests of hypotheses are often referred to as significance tests. If we reject H_0 when we have set the level of α at 0.05, we say that we have rejected H_0 at the 0.05 level of significance. This means that the sample results are significantly different from those we would expect if H_0 were true. Remember that hypothesis tests are conducted under the tentative assumption that H_0 is

true, and only when we see strong evidence to the contrary—that is, only when the test statistic falls in rejection region—are we willing to accept the view of the world represented by H_a. When we reject H_0 at the 0.05 level of significance, we are saying that the sample results would have only a 0.05 or less chance of occurring if H_0 were true.

3 The hypothesis tests in Chapter 10 take one of the three following forms regardless of whether they are about μ or p: the two-tail test, the lower-tail test, and the upper-tail test. The equality sign is always placed in the null hypothesis statement.

(a) In two-tail tests the rejection region *RR* lies in both the lower and upper tails of the sampling distribution. If we hypothesize a value of μ_0 for μ then a two-tail test about μ would be

$$H_0 : \mu = \mu_0,$$

$$H_a : \mu \neq \mu_0.$$

If we hypothesize a value of p_0 for p then a two-tail test about p would be

$$H_0 : p = p_0,$$

$$H_a : p \neq p_0.$$

(b) One-tail tests in which the rejection region *RR* lies in the lower tail of the sampling distribution are known as lower-tail tests. If we hypothesize a value of μ_0 for μ then a lower-tail test about μ would be

$$H_0 : \mu \geq \mu_0,$$

$$H_a : \mu < \mu_0.$$

If we hypothesize a value of p_0 for p then a lower-tail test about p would be

$$H_0 : p \geq p_0,$$

$$H_a : p < p_0.$$

(c) One-tail tests in which the rejection region *RR* lies in the upper tail of the sampling distribution are known as upper-tail tests. If we hypothesize a value of μ_0 for μ then an upper-tail test about μ would be

$$H_0 : \mu \leq \mu_0,$$

$$H_a : \mu > \mu_0.$$

If we hypothesize a value of p_0 for p then an upper-tail test about p would be

$$H_0 : p \leq p_0,$$

$$H_a : p > p_0.$$

Definition 9.10. Two-Tail Test. A two-tail test is a hypothesis test where the rejection region lies in both the lower and upper tails of the sampling distribution.

Definition 9.11. One-Tail Test. A one-tail test is a hypothesis test where the rejection region lies in either the lower tail or the upper tail of the sampling distribution.

Definition 9.12. Lower-Tail Test. A lower-tail test is a one-tail hypothesis test where the rejection region lies in the lower tail of the sampling distribution.

Definition 9.13. Upper-Tail Test. An upper-tail test is a one-tail hypothesis test where the rejection region lies in the upper tail of the sampling distribution.

4 Because a Type I error is normally considered more serious than a Type II error, it is often helpful (when deciding which hypothesis is the null and which is the alternative) to consider the hypothesis statement we *least want to be wrong about*. For example, in the present case, we would rather fail to identify a taste-sensitive applicant (a Type II error) than hire a taste-insensitive person as taster (a Type I error). We usually seek evidence supporting the alternative hypothesis because a true alternative hypothesis often implies that we should take some sort of action. Failing to reject H_0 simply means that we keep interviewing people for the position of taste tester; we need not do anything else. But rejecting the H_0, and accepting H_a, means that we should consider the action of hiring that particular applicant.

5 Hypothesis-testing terminology may seem inelegant when we say *we do not reject* H_0 rather than *we accept* H_0. This awkward prose is used because we seldom have sufficiently strong evidence to claim that H_0 is true–and thus risk committing a Type II error. Consider that in the criminal justice systems in many nations, a defendant is presumed innocent until proven guilty. Translating this idea into the hypothesis-testing framework, the null hypothesis H_0 is that the defendant is innocent while the alternative H_a is that the defendant is guilty.

As in other hypothesis-testing settings, the Type I error of convicting an innocent person is usually viewed as a more serious mistake. The Type II error of acquitting a guilty person, while never desirable, is considered a less egregious error. The guidelines that specify how the trial should be conducted are roughly comparable to a rejection region of a hypothesis test because any rule that reduces the probability of convicting an innocent person (e.g., a rule that the defendant cannot be required to testify) also reduces the probability of convicting a guilty person. Raising the standard of evidence makes it less likely that any defendant (guilty as well as innocent) is convicted. Importantly, at the conclusion of the trial, the jury must render one of two decisions: either "We find the defendant guilty" or "We find the defendant not guilty." Juries do not say "We find the defendant innocent," just as statisticians normally do not say "We accept H_0." That a defendant is found not guilty does not mean that the jury finds him innocent. The jury might feel that the defendant is indeed guilty–it just *seems* that the defendant probably did rob the bank–but the prosecution simply failed to prove its case.

Definition 9.14. *p*-Value. The *p*-value, also known as the *observed* level of significance, is the probability of drawing a sample result that is at least as unlikely as what is observed, given that H_0 is true. When the *p*-value is less than or equal to α, H_0 is rejected; when the *p*-value is greater than α, H_0 is not rejected. Put slightly differently, the *observed level of significance* is compared with the *level of significance* α.

For example, if $\alpha = 0.05$, then a *p*-value less than or equal to 0.05 would cast strong doubt on H_0, and we would reject it. If the *p*-value is greater than 0.05, we would not reject H_0. While the practice of setting the value of α at 0.05 is very common, hypothesis tests specifying other values for α, particularly 0.01 and 0.10, are not unusual. When assigning the level of significance, most analysts set a lower value for α when the consequences of making a Type I error are more serious. When the cost of committing a Type I error are not so high, a higher value of α is often specified.

Example 9.5. What is the p-value for a job applicant who achieves $x = 9$ correct identifications in $n = 15$ trials? Should the brewery consider hiring this candidate? To answer this question, we need only compare the p-value to $\alpha = 0.05$. But what is the p-value for this person? If H_0 is true, and $p = 1/3$, the p-value is the probability that a taste-insensitive person makes 9 or more correct identifications, a value found by summing the binomial probabilities of $x = 9, \ldots, 15$ in $n = 15$ trials. Using the probabilities reported in Table 9.1, the p-value is

$$\begin{aligned} &p(x = 9) + p(x = 10) + \ldots + p(x = 15) \\ &\quad = 0.0223 + 0.0067 + 0.0015 + 0.0003 + 0.0000 + 0.0000 + 0.0000 \\ &\quad = 0.0308. \end{aligned}$$

Since $\alpha = 0.05$ and p-value=0.0308, we reject H_0 and conclude that the job candidate has sufficient taste-discrimination ability to be considered for the position of taster. One way of interpreting the meaning of a p-value of 0.0308 is this: assuming H_0 is true (and the applicant has no taste-discrimination ability with respect to beer), we would expect the applicant to achieve 9 or more successful identifications only 3 out of 100 times. Clearly, because this evidence does not support H_0, we reject it.

Using R, we can find the p-value with 1 – `pbinom(8, 15, 1/3)`.

In Chapter 10, we apply the hypothesis-testing methodology to a number of different problems and make abundant use of the p-value criterion for hypothesis tests.

SUMMARY

This chapter introduces the basic concepts of the statistical-inferential methodology known as hypothesis testing. In Chapters 7 and 8 we saw how sample data can be used for point and interval estimation for the purpose of determining how large or small something might be. In this chapter we learn that statistical inference involves using sample data to test formal hypotheses for the purpose of drawing conclusions or inferences. In the chapter example, we test two competing formal statements, one called the null hypothesis H_0, the other the alternative hypothesis H_a, concerning the taste sensitivity of job applicants.

In general, the H_0 is usually a default statement; it assumes nothing is going on, nothing is different from what is expected, nothing is new. The H_a states the opposite view that something is going on, something is new, something is different from what has been the case in other times and places. We tentatively assume that H_0 is true unless and until we see strong evidence (the sample data) that it is not. In that case, we say we reject H_0 and accept H_a.

Whenever we conduct a hypothesis test, it is possible to commit two different types of error. If we reject a true H_0, we commit a Type I error; if we do not reject a false H_0, we make a Type II error. Because the Type I error is normally considered the more serious of the two, we try to control the probability of committing this type of error. In fact, the probability of committing a Type I error is considered of such importance that we refer to it as the *level of significance* and designate it with the Greek letter α. The probability of committing a Type II error, β, though not unimportant, is not what we usually worry so much about.

In all hypothesis tests in this book, the sample data are transformed into a test statistic which is then evaluated in the context of a rejection region. The rejection region is simply those values that the test statistic might assume that would lead to rejection of H_0. If the test statistic falls in the rejection region, we reject H_0; if the test statistic does not, then we do not. In our example, the test statistic is defined as the number of correct identifications in some number of identical taste-test trials. In Chapter 10 the test statistic assumes other values that are transformed into random variables z or t with either a normal or t-distribution. Alternatively, the test statistic itself can be converted to a p-value which is then compared with α for the purpose of evaluating the two competing hypotheses. This makes possible a slightly different formulation of the rejection rule: if the p-value is less than or equal to α, we reject H_0; if the p-value is greater than α, we do not reject H_0. The p-value is simply the probability of obtaining a sample result that is at least as unlikely as what we would have observed under the assumption that H_0 is true. Like other probabilities, it is defined as existing between 0 and 1.

definitions

Alpha α is the probability of a Type I error. That is, p(Type I error) = p(we reject $H_0 \mid H_0$ is true) = α; α is also known as the *level of significance*.

Alternative Hypothesis The condition stated in the alternative hypothesis H_a is concluded to be true whenever the null hypothesis is rejected.

Beta β is the probability of a Type II error. In other words, p(Type II error) = p(we fail to reject $H_0 \mid H_0$ is false) = β.

Level of Significance The probability of committing a Type I error; that is, the probability of rejecting the null hypothesis when it is true.

Lower-Tail Test A lower-tail test is a one-tail hypothesis test where the rejection region lies only in the lower tail of the sampling distribution.

Null Hypothesis The condition stated in the null hypothesis is tentatively assumed true unless and until strong evidence casts strong doubt on it. In this case, we say that we reject H_0.

One-Tail Test A one-tail test is a hypothesis test where the rejection region lies either in the upper tail or lower tail (but not both) of the sampling distribution.

***p*-Value** The p-value is the probability of obtaining a sample result that is at least as unlikely as what we would have observed under the assumption that H_0 is true. The p-value is also known as the *observed level of significance*.

Rejection Region A rejection region specifies the range of values the test statistic might assume that would lead to rejection of the null hypothesis.

Test Statistic The empirical result of the hypothesis test that is used to either reject or not reject the null hypothesis H_0.

Two-Tail Test A two-tail test is a hypothesis test where the rejection region lies in both the lower and upper tails of the sampling distribution.

Type I Error A Type I error occurs when H_0 is rejected even though it is true.

Type II Error A Type II error occurs when H_0 is not rejected even though it is false.

Upper-Tail Test An upper-tail test is a one-tail hypothesis test where the rejection region lies only in the upper tail of the sampling distribution.

formulae

Binomial Probability Function

$$f(x) = p(x \mid n, p) = \binom{n}{x} p^x (1-p)^{n-x},$$
$$\text{where } x = 0, 1, 2, \ldots, n$$

Probability of Type I Error α for RR_7 When $p = 1/3$

$$\alpha = p\left(x \geq 7 \mid n = 15, p = \frac{1}{3}\right)$$
$$= \sum_{x=7}^{15} \binom{15}{x} \left(\frac{1}{3}\right)^x \left(\frac{2}{3}\right)^{15-x}$$

Probability of Type I Error α for RR_9 When $p = 1/3$

$$\alpha = p\left(x \geq 9 \mid n = 15, p = \frac{1}{3}\right)$$
$$= \sum_{x=9}^{15} \binom{15}{x} \left(\frac{1}{3}\right)^x \left(\frac{2}{3}\right)^{15-x}$$

Probability of Type II Error β for RR_7 When $p = 0.70$

$$\beta_{p=0.70} = p(x \leq 6 \mid n = 15, p = 0.70)$$
$$= \sum_{x=0}^{6} \binom{15}{x} (0.70)^x (0.30)^{15-x}$$

Probability of Type II Error β for RR_9 When $p = 0.70$

$$\beta_{p=0.70} = p(x \leq 8 \mid n = 15, p = 0.70)$$
$$= \sum_{x=0}^{8} \binom{15}{x} (0.70)^x (0.30)^{15-x}$$

R functions

`1-pbinom(6, 15, 1/3)` Provides the binomial probability of $x = 7$ or more successes in $n = 15$ trials with the probability of success on each trial equal to $p = 1/3$.

`1-pbinom(8, 15, 1/3)` Provides the binomial probability of $x = 9$ or more successes in $n = 15$ trials with the probability of success on each trial equal to $p = 1/3$.

`pbinom(6, 15, 0.70)` Provides the binomial probability of $x = 6$ or fewer successes in $n = 15$ trials with the probability of success on each trial equal to $p = 0.70$.

`pbinom(8, 15, 0.70)` Provides the binomial probability of $x = 8$ or fewer successes in $n = 15$ trials with the probability of success on each trial equal to $p = 0.70$.

exercises

The following exercises test your understanding of hypothesis testing in the context of the triangle-taste test described in Chapter 9. In this case, the test consists of 14 identical trials on which the subject attempts to identify the odd sample on each trial. Assume that there are 2 possible rejection regions: (1) RR_8 = {8, 9, 10, 11, 12, 13, 14} and RR_{10} = {10, 11, 12, 13, 14}.

9.1 With a rejection region of $RR_8 = \{8, 9, 10, 11, 12, 13, 14\}$, what is the probability of a Type I error? Recall that since a Type I error occurs when the subject has no taste-discrimination ability, $p = 1/3$.

9.2 With a rejection region of $RR_8 = \{8, 9, 10, 11, 12, 13, 14\}$, what is the probability of a Type II error, if the subject has a probability of $p = 0.80$ of identifying the odd sample?

9.3 With a rejection region of $RR_{10} = \{10, 11, 12, 13, 14\}$, what is the probability of a Type I error?

9.4 With a rejection region of $RR_{10} = \{10, 11, 12, 13, 14\}$, what is the probability of a Type II error, if the subject has a probability of $p = 0.80$ of identifying the odd sample?

9.5 Please answer the following questions about this triangle-test taste.

(a) Which of the rejection regions should we prefer? RR_8 or RR_{10}? Why?

(b) In general, a hypothesis test can result in 2 different types of errors. Describe those 2 errors in this case where we are attempting to identify someone with a high degree of taste-discrimination ability. Which is more serious?

(c) We saw in Chapter 9 that α and β are usually in a trade-off relationship. That is, if we select one of two possible rejection regions–such as either RR_8 or RR_{10}–we can reduce α only if we are willing to have a higher β. Can you think of anything we might do to reduce both α and β simultaneously? What would that be?

https://study.sagepub.com/stinerock

Hypothesis Tests about Means and Proportions: Applications

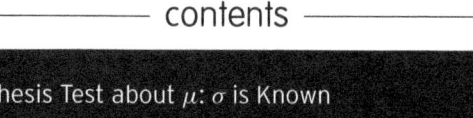

contents

learning objectives

1. Learn how to formulate hypothesis tests about population means and proportions.
2. Be able to determine α and β in the context of various hypothesis-testing problems.
3. Know how to compute and interpret *p*-values.
4. Be able to adjust the sample size for the purpose of controlling β.

Now that we have seen an application of hypothesis testing in connection with the triangle taste test of Chapter 9, we introduce a hypothesis-testing framework which consists of six easy-to-follow steps that are unambiguously stated and flexible in that they can be used for every type of hypothesis-testing situation we encounter in the chapters ahead:

1. Determine the null hypothesis H_0 in statistical terms.
2. Determine the alternative hypothesis H_a in statistical terms.
3. Set the level of significance α and decide on the sample size n.
4. Use α to specify the rejection region *RR*.
5. Collect the data and calculate the test statistic.
6. Use the value of the test statistic and the rejection region *RR* to decide whether to reject H_0. If the test statistic falls in the rejection region, reject H_0; if the test statistic falls outside the rejection region, do not reject H_0.

We apply this six-step hypothesis-testing framework to all examples in this chapter.

10.1 THE LOWER-TAIL HYPOTHESIS TEST ABOUT μ: σ IS KNOWN

We first introduce hypothesis tests concerning the population mean μ under the condition of a known value of σ. Although we conduct both one-tailed and two-tailed tests in this chapter, we begin with a lower-tail test.

Example 10.1. Agrico produces and sells ready-to-eat breakfast cereals. Because management know that consumer groups and government agencies monitor the claims by package-goods companies, their quality control group draws daily samples to make sure their packages are not being inadvertently underfilled. The company's problem is that while the advertised weight is 375 grams, the volume actually placed in each package is rarely 375 grams. Sometimes it is more, sometimes it is less. Those monitoring the packaging practices are aware of the random nature of the filling process and are content if the company simply fills its packages to a *mean* of 375 grams. If during one of the daily tests, quality control personnel find that $\bar{x}$ is less than 375, such a finding would seem to cast doubt on Agrico's claim that it is filling its packages to a mean weight of 375 grams.

Suppose that the most recent sample of size $n = 30$ has a mean of $\bar{x} = 365$ grams. In previous tests when the process was known to be in adjustment, $\sigma = 22.5$ grams. We now apply the six-step framework to test the hypothesis that the mean volume of cereal placed in each package is at least 375 grams. Use a level of significance of $\alpha = 0.05$.

1 Determine the null hypothesis H_0 in statistical terms.

$$H_0: \mu \geq 375$$

2 Determine the alternative hypothesis H_a in statistical terms.

$$H_a: \mu < 375$$

In the case of a lower-tail test, when H_0 is true, we are in effect centering the sampling distribution of $\bar{x}$ at the lowest value in the range of numbers implied in H_0. Accordingly, we reframe the null hypothesis in terms of the equality, $\mu = 375$:

$$H_0: \mu = 375.$$

Since we are not interested if Agrico is overfilling its packages, we ignore the possibility that it is. Amending H_0 at the outset is usually carried out in the case of one-tail tests. The H_a statement remains unchanged but H_0 is now framed as an equality. The assumption behind the H_0 statement is that Agrico is filling its packages to the advertised volume. That is, we are giving the company the benefit of the doubt. This is a common practice when conducting tests of this nature because no one wants to falsely accuse a company of underfilling its packages.

3 Set the level of significance α and decide on the sample size n.

$$n = 30 \text{ and } \alpha = 0.05$$

Recall that the central limit theorem states that when $n \geq 30$, the sampling distribution of $\bar{x}$ approaches that of the normal probability distribution. Because we usually prefer that the sampling distribution is normal (so that we can find probabilities easily) it is a good practice to make sure that, whenever possible, $n \geq 30$.

The three characteristics of the sampling distribution of $\bar{x}$ are: (1) the standard error of the mean is $\sigma_{\bar{x}} = \sigma / \sqrt{n} = 22.5 / \sqrt{30} = 4.11$; (2) the sampling distribution of $\bar{x}$ is approximately normal since $n = 30$; and (3) $E(\bar{x}) = \mu_0 = 375$ (we tentatively assume H_0 is true). This is the practical reason why we express H_0 as an equality, $\mu = 375$, and not as an inequality $\mu \geq 375$. Thus, assuming H_0 is true, the sampling distribution has these three characteristics: (1) $\bar{x}$ is normally distributed with (2) $E(\bar{x}) = 375$ and (3) $\sigma_{\bar{x}} = 4.11$.

Recall that a Type I error happens when the sample provides a value of $\bar{x}$ that leads to the conclusion that Agrico is underfilling its 375-gram packages when in reality it is not underfilling. Since we have set $\alpha = 0.05$, a Type I error can happen only if the sample is one that would be drawn very infrequently: only 5 or fewer times out of 100. We could set another value for α (0.01 or 0.10, for example) but in this test we use the level that many statisticians consider the gold standard, $\alpha = 0.05$.

4 Use α to specify the rejection region RR.

$$RR: z \leq -1.645$$

That is, reject H_0 if $z \leq -z_{\alpha} = -z_{0.05} = -1.645$, where $z = (\bar{x} - \mu_0)/\sigma_{\bar{x}}$.

```
qnorm(0.05)
## [1] -1.644854
```

The value of z that cuts off an area of 0.05 in the lower tail is $z = -1.645$. Therefore, if the sample mean $\bar{x}$ transforms into a value of z that is less than or equal to -1.645, we reject H_0 and accept H_a; if z is greater than -1.645, we do not reject H_0. By plugging in $\mu_0 = 375$ and $\sigma_{\bar{x}} = 4.11$, $\bar{x}$ transforms to z. That is, $z = (\bar{x} - 375) / 4.11$.

5 Collect the data and calculate the test statistic.
If a sample of $n = 30$ packages provides a mean weight of $\bar{x} = 365$ grams, then

$$z = \frac{\bar{x} - \mu_0}{\sigma_{\bar{x}}} = \frac{\bar{x} - 375}{4.11} = \frac{365 - 375}{4.11} = -2.43$$

and $\bar{x} = 365$ corresponds to $z = -2.43$.

6 Use the value of the test statistic and the rejection region RR to decide whether to reject H_0. If the test statistic falls in the rejection region, reject H_0; if the test statistic falls outside the rejection region, do not reject H_0.
Recall that the rejection region is $RR: z \leq -1.645$. Since $z = -2.43 < -1.645$, we reject $H_0: \mu = 375$ and accept $H_a: \mu < 375$.

In other words, there is evidence that the process has gotten out of control and is underfilling the packages. We expand on this discussion in two different but related ways:

1 Recall the definition of the p-value: assuming H_0 is true, the p-value is the probability of obtaining a sample that is at least as unlikely as what is observed. If $p \leq \alpha$, reject H_0; otherwise, do not reject H_0. We first calculate the p-value for the Agrico case, and then use it as the test statistic in the hypothesis test.

   (a) Since the sample mean $\bar{x} = 365$ transforms to $z = -2.43$, and because the rejection region is in the lower tail of the standard normal probability distribution, the p-value is the probability of z being less than -2.43. Thus the p-value is

   $$p(\bar{x} \leq 365) = p(z \leq -2.43) = 0.0075.$$

   ```
   pnorm(-2.43)
   ## [1] 0.007549411
   ```

   (b) Recall the rejection rule that is used in conjunction with the p-value: reject H_0 if $p\text{-value} \leq \alpha$. Since p-value=0.0075 and α =0.05, H_0 should be rejected.

   How do we interpret a p-value of 0.0075? We say that if H_0 is true, and Agrico really is not underfilling its packages, we would expect to select a sample providing a mean of 365 grams (or less) no more than 75 out of 10,000 times. Since that is a highly unlikely occurrence, it seems far more likely that H_0 is false and μ really is less than 375 grams after all. Recall that the p-value is often called the observed level of significance, and it is the value we compare with α, the level of significance.

2 It is also possible to define RR in terms of $\bar{x}$. Since RR is expressed in terms of z, we can easily recover the value of $\bar{x}$ that would trigger rejection of H_0 by setting two expressions for z equal to one another and solving for the corresponding value of $\bar{x}$.

(a) Recall that z is defined as $z = (\bar{x} - \mu_0) / \sigma_{\bar{x}}$.
(b) The rejection region RR expressed in terms of z is $z \leq -1.645$.

Substituting expression (a) into expression (b): $(\bar{x} - \mu_0) / \sigma_{\bar{x}} \leq -1.645$.
If $\mu_0 = 375$ and $\sigma_{\bar{x}} = 4.11$, then $\bar{x} \leq \mu_0 - 1.645\sigma_{\bar{x}} = 375 - 1.645 \times 4.11 = 368.24$.

What does this mean? Agrico is looking for evidence that its packaging process is underfilling. We know that even when the process is in adjustment, $\bar{x}$ is distributed across a range of values, sometimes above 375, sometimes below 375. To conclude that there is evidence of underfilling, $\bar{x}$ has to be less than 375. The question is *how much less than* 375 is sufficient to draw a conclusion of underfilling? We now have an answer: 6.76 below 375, or 368.24 grams. If $\bar{x} = 370$, a shortfall of this magnitude is not considered large enough to reject H_0; but if $\bar{x}$ comes in at 368.24 (or less), then we reject H_0. If H_0 is true, how often would $\bar{x}$ be 368.24 or less? Only 5% (or less) of the time. Since this occurrence is so rare, it casts doubt on the likelihood that H_0 is true. It is simply more plausible that H_a is true, and Agrico really is underfilling its packages. Note that there is still a 0.05 chance that $\bar{x}$ will fall in *RR* even when Agrico is not underfilling. When this happens, and we are applying the criterion set down by the rejection rule, we commit a Type I error.

All three test statistics—whether we use z, the p-value, or $\bar{x}$—provide the same conclusion because they are interrelated: the p-value is derived from z and z in turn is based on $\bar{x}$. In fact, we could easily use either the p-value or $\bar{x}$, instead of z, in steps 4, 5, and 6, and end up with the same conclusion. Even so, the p-value is widely used today because it has advantages. For one thing, the same rejection criteria (reject H_0 if p-value $\leq \alpha$) is used in many types of hypothesis tests; for another, p-values are provided as output by almost all statistical programs, including R. Although in the Agrico example we could easily use either the p-value or $\bar{x}$ instead of z in Steps 4, 5, and 6, we continue the use of z in the next example—a two-tail test—before adopting the now-ubiquitous p-value.

10.2 THE TWO-TAIL HYPOTHESIS TEST ABOUT μ: σ IS KNOWN

In this section, we use the six-step hypothesis-testing framework to perform a two-tail test about μ when σ is assumed known.

Example 10.2. A manufacturer of machine tools purchases inputs from outside suppliers. One particular component, a metal cylindrical-shaped piece, must meet very precise standards in that it must be exactly 7.25 centimeters in length. Pieces that are too short leave a gap when fitted into the housing, and do not function as designed; pieces that are too long cannot be fitted into the tight space at all. Because precision is important, the quality control manager monitors each shipment carefully. A two-tail test is appropriate in this case since there is trouble in both tails of the distribution. If the manager concludes that the components in a shipment are either too long or too short, the entire shipment is returned to the supplier as defective. Use the six-step framework to test the H_0 that a given shipment consists of components that meet the strict standard. Set the test at the 0.01 level of significance; the sample size is $n = 60$. Suppose that the most recent sample mean is $\bar{x} = 7.318$, and assume the population standard deviation is known to be $\sigma = 0.18$.

1 Determine the null hypothesis H_0 in statistical terms.

$$H_0: \mu = 7.25$$

2 Determine the alternative hypothesis H_a in statistical terms.

$$H_a: \mu \neq 7.25$$

3 Set the level of significance α and decide on the sample size n.

$$n = 60 \text{ and } \alpha = 0.01$$

At this point, we can describe the relevant sampling distribution: assuming H_0 is true, $\bar{x}$ is normally distributed with a mean of $E(\bar{x}) = \mu_0 = 7.25$ and a standard deviation of $\sigma_{\bar{x}} = \sigma / \sqrt{n}$ $= 0.18 / \sqrt{60} = 0.0232.$

4 Use α to specify the rejection region RR.

$$RR: z \geq 2.576 \text{ and } z \leq -2.576$$

That is, reject H_0 if $z \geq z_{\alpha/2} = z_{0.005} = 2.576$, or $z \leq -z_{\alpha/2} = -z_{0.005} = -2.576$.

```
qnorm(0.005)
## [1] -2.575829
qnorm(0.995)
## [1] 2.575829
```

The value of z that cuts off an area of 0.005 in the upper tail is $z = 2.576$; likewise, the value of z that cuts off an area of 0.005 in the lower tail is $z = -2.576$. Therefore, if $\bar{x}$ transforms into a value of z that is greater than 2.576, or less than -2.576, reject H_0 and accept H_a; if z falls in the region from -2.576 to 2.576, do not reject H_0.

5 Collect the data and calculate the test statistic.
If a sample of $n = 60$ items provides a mean length of $\bar{x} = 7.318$ centimeters, then

$$z = \frac{\bar{x} - \mu_0}{\sigma_{\bar{x}}} = \frac{\bar{x} - 7.25}{0.0232} = \frac{7.318 - 7.25}{0.0232} = 2.93$$

and $\bar{x} = 7.318$ corresponds to $z = 2.93$.

6 Use the value of the test statistic and the rejection region RR to decide whether to reject H_0. If the test statistic falls in the rejection region, reject; if the test statistic falls outside the rejection region, do not reject H_0.
Recall that the rejection region is $RR: z \geq 2.576$ and $z \leq -2.576$. Since $z = 2.93 > 2.576$, we reject $H_0: \mu = 7.25$ and accept $H_a: \mu \neq 7.25$.

The quality control manager has found evidence that the current shipment of components does not meet specifications, and they should return the shipment to the supplier.

Example 10.3. (1) What is the p-value? (2) Compare the p-value with α.

1 Because RR is in both the upper and lower tails of the standard normal probability distribution, the p-value is the probability that z is greater than 2.93 *plus* the probability that z is less than −2.93. Thus, the p-value is

$$p(z \geq 2.93) + p(z \leq -2.93) = 0.0017 + 0.0017 = 0.0034.$$

```
pnorm(2.93, lower.tail = FALSE) + pnorm(-2.93)
## [1] 0.00338962
```

2 Since p-value $= 0.0034$ and $\alpha = 0.01$, we know that p-value $< \alpha$ and so we reject H_0. In two-tail tests, the p-value is the probability that z falls in both tails of the RR.

Example 10.4. Define the rejection region RR in terms of $\bar{x}$.

1 Recall that z is defined as $z = (\bar{x} - \mu_0) / \sigma_{\bar{x}}$.
2 The rejection region expressed in terms of z is $RR: z \geq 2.576$ and $z \leq -2.576$.
3 We substitute $\mu_0 = 7.25$ and $\sigma_{\bar{x}} = 0.0232$ and solve for $\bar{x}$. For the upper tail,

$$\frac{\bar{x} - \mu_0}{\sigma_{\bar{x}}} \geq 2.576$$

so

$$\bar{x} \geq 7.25 + 2.576 \times 0.0232 = 7.3098.$$

For the lower tail,

$$\frac{\bar{x} - \mu_0}{\sigma_{\bar{x}}} \leq -2.576$$

so

$$\bar{x} \leq 7.25 - 2.576 \times 0.0232 = 7.1902.$$

Thus, the rejection region defined in terms of $\bar{x}$ is $RR: \bar{x} \geq 7.3098$ and $\bar{x} \leq 7.1902$.

10.3 THE UPPER-TAIL HYPOTHESIS TEST ABOUT μ: σ IS UNKNOWN

We now extend the use of the six-step framework to situations where σ is unknown. This condition characterizes most hypothesis-testing problems since it is difficult to obtain estimates of σ prior to sampling. In such cases, the sample is used to provide estimates of both μ and σ. The steps of the procedure for the σ-unknown case are similar to those we use above for the σ-known examples, but with two differences: first, s is used in place of σ; and second, the test statistic is no longer z but t (with $n - 1$ degrees of freedom, where n is the sample size). Using t rather than z makes sense since t has slightly more variability because $s_{\bar{x}} = s / \sqrt{n}$ varies from one sample to the next in a way that $\sigma_{\bar{x}} = \sigma / \sqrt{n}$ does not.

Example 10.5. In the US, many programs have been set up whereby senior citizens qualify for various types of assistance. One such program makes it possible for elderly people to obtain economic assistance for in-home care as long as they can demonstrate that they have savings of \$65,000 or less. The program administrator worries, however, that many of those recently joining this program might not be qualified because their savings exceed \$65,000. The oversight has been haphazard in the last few years, and as newer (and relatively wealthier) seniors enroll for assisance, the mean savings amount may be floating upward above \$65,000. Accordingly, she has directed her staff to collect financial data on 40 recently enrolled beneficiaries with the purpose of confirming or refuting this suspicion. When the data are collected, it is found that $\bar{x} = \$66{,}642$ and $s = \$8318$. Do the data lend support to the adminstrator's concern that unqualified recipients are taking advantage of a program for which they are ineligible? Using the six-step framework, test at the 0.01 level of significance.

1 Determine the null hypothesis H_0 in statistical terms.

$$H_0: \mu \leq 65{,}000$$

2 Determine the alternative hypothesis H_a in statistical terms.

$$H_a: \mu > 65{,}000$$

H_0 is expressed so that its rejection leads to the conclusion that recent recipients of assistance have a mean level of savings exceeding \$65,000, and that there should be tighter monitoring of people enrolling in the program. Note that $H_a: \mu > 65{,}000$ is expressed in terms of what we are seeking evidence of.

3 Set the level of significance α and decide on the sample size n.

$n = 40$ and $\alpha = 0.01$

Assuming a true H_0, once $\bar{x}$ is transformed, it has a t-distribution with $df = 39$, a mean of $E(\bar{x}) = \mu_0 = 65{,}000$, and a standard deviation of $s_{\bar{x}} = s / \sqrt{n} = 8318 / \sqrt{40} = 1315$.

4 Use α to specify the rejection region RR.

$$RR: t > 2.426$$

That is, reject H_0 if $t > t_{\alpha,n-1} = t_{0.01,39} = 2.426$, where $t = (\bar{x} - \mu_0) / s_{\bar{x}}$.

```
qt(0.99, 39)
## [1] 2.425841
```

The value of t that cuts off an area of 0.01 in the upper tail is $t = 2.426$. Therefore, if the sample mean $\bar{x}$ transforms into a value of t that is greater than or equal to 2.426, we reject H_0 and accept H_a; if t is less than 2.426, we do not reject H_0.

5 Collect the data and calculate the test statistic.
If a sample of $n = 40$ provides a mean of $\bar{x} = \$66{,}642$, then

$$t = \frac{\bar{x} - \mu_0}{s_{\bar{x}}} = \frac{\bar{x} - 65{,}000}{1315} = \frac{66{,}642 - 65{,}000}{1315} = 1.25$$

and $\bar{x} = 66{,}642$ corresponds to $t = 1.25$.

6 Use the value of the test statistic and the rejection region RR to decide whether to reject H_0. If the test statistic falls in the rejection region, reject H_0; if the test statistic falls outside the rejection region, do not reject H_0.
Recall that the rejection region is RR: $t > 2.426$. Since $t = 1.25 < 2.426$, we do not reject $H_0: \mu = 65{,}000$. The evidence is not sufficiently strong to reject H_0.

Example 10.6. (1) What is the p-value? (2) Compare the p-value with α.

1 Since $\bar{x} = 66{,}642$ transforms to $t = 1.25$, and because RR lies in the upper tail of the t-distribution ($df = 39$), the p-value is the probability that $t > 1.25$. Thus, the p-value is

$$p(t \geq 1.25,\ df = 39) = 0.1094.$$

```
1 - pt(1.25, 39)
## [1] 0.1093743
```

2 Since p-value $= 0.1094$ and $\alpha = 0.01$, we should not reject H_0. The evidence is not sufficiently strong to conclude that the mean level of elderly savings exceeds $65,000.

Example 10.7. Define the rejection region RR in terms of $\bar{x}$.

1 Recall that t is defined as $t = (\bar{x} - \mu_0) / s_{\bar{x}}$.
2 The rejection region expressed in terms of t is: $RR: t \geq 2.426$.
3 Substituting $\mu_0 = 65{,}000$ and $s_{\bar{x}} = 1315$ and solving for $\bar{x}$:

$$\bar{x} \geq 65{,}000 + 2.426 \times 1315$$

$$RR: \bar{x} \geq 68{,}190.$$

While it is possible in theory to define the rejection region in terms of $\bar{x}$ when σ is unknown, we would not do so in practice since the value of s (the point estimator of σ) would not be known until the sample is collected. The most convenient method of conducting a hypothesis test relies on the use of R.

Example 10.8. Use the `t.test()` function to conduct the hypothesis test. The data set is `elderly`, the variable name is `savings`. If the `t.test()` function looks familiar, it should. We last saw it in Chapter 8 while constructing confidence interval estimates.

```
#Comment. Use function t.test(); variable name is savings.
t.test(elderly$savings, conf.level = 0.99, mu = 65000, alternative = 'g')
##
## One Sample t-test
##
## data: elderly$savings
## t = 1.2486, df = 39, p-value = 0.1096
## alternative hypothesis: true mean is greater than 65000
## 99 percent confidence interval:
## 63451.71 Inf
## sample estimates:
## mean of x
## 66642.15
```

The four arguments of `t.test()` are:

1 The object and variable names are `elderly$savings`.
2 The significance level is set at 0.01 by `conf.level = 0.99`.
3 The null hypothesis is expressed as `mu = 65000`.
4 An upper-tail test is specified by `alternative = 'g'`; a lower-tail test is defined by `alternative = 'l'`. If the argument is omitted, a two-tail test is indicated.

When `t.test()` is executed, three pieces of information relevant to the test are reported: the value of the test statistic (t = 1.249); the degrees of freedom (df = 39); and the observed level of significance (p-value = 0.1096). That the formal rejection region RR is not provided poses no problem since we need only compare the p-value of 0.1096 with the level of significance $\alpha = 0.01$ to know that we do not reject H_0.

10.4 THE TWO-TAIL HYPOTHESIS TEST ABOUT μ: σ IS UNKNOWN

Example 10.9. A South African vineyard has purchased a new bottling machine. New equipment of this type typically requires a period of daily recalibrations to ensure the bottles are being filled to an average of 750 ml of product. While the manager wishes to avoid underfilling the bottles, exposing the vineyard to charges of defrauding its customers, she also wants to avoid overfilling, thus giving away free product. To this end, 25 bottles are selected and tested daily. For the most recent sample, $\bar{x} = 760.68$ ml and $s = 46.2085$ ml. At $\alpha = 0.05$, test to determine if an average of 750 ml is being placed in each bottle.

1 Determine the null hypothesis H_0 in statistical terms.

$$H_0 : \mu = 750$$

2 Determine the alternative hypothesis H_a in statistical terms.

$$H_a : \mu \neq 750$$

Rejection of H_0 leads to the conclusion that the filling process is out of adjustment. Accordingly, we are looking for evidence that either $\mu > 750$ or $\mu < 750$ is true.

3 Set the level of significance α and decide on the sample size n.

$n = 25$ and $\alpha = 0.05$

Assuming H_0 is true, once $\bar{x}$ is transformed, it has a t-distribution with $df = 24$, a mean of $E(\bar{x}) = \mu_0 = 750$, and a standard deviation of $s_{\bar{x}} = s / \sqrt{n} = 46.2085 / \sqrt{25} = 9.2417$.

4 Use α to specify the rejection region RR.

RR: $t \geq 2.064$ and $t \leq -2.064$

Or, reject H_0 if $t \geq t_{\alpha/2,n-1} = t_{0.025,24} = 2.064$, or $t \leq t_{\alpha/2,n-1} = -t_{0.025,24} = -2.064$, where $t = (\bar{x} - \mu_0) / s_{\bar{x}}$.

```
qt(0.025, 24)
## [1] -2.063899
qt(0.975, 24)
## [1] 2.063899
```

The value of t that cuts off an area of 0.025 in the upper tail is $t = 2.064$; the value of t that cuts off an area of 0.025 in the lower tail is $t = -2.064$. Therefore, if $\bar{x}$ transforms into a value of t that is greater than 2.064 or less than −2.064, reject H_0 and accept H_a; if t falls in the region from −2.064 to 2.064, do not reject H_0.

5 Collect the data and calculate the test statistic.

Since the most recent sample statistics are $\bar{x} = 760.68$ and $s_{\bar{x}} = 9.2417$, we have

$$t = \frac{\bar{x} - \mu_0}{s_{\bar{x}}} = \frac{\bar{x} - 750}{9.2417} = \frac{760.68 - 750}{9.2417} = 1.156.$$

Thus, $\bar{x} = 760.68$ corresponds to $t = 1.156$.

6 Use the value of the test statistic and the rejection region RR to decide whether to reject H_0. If the test statistic falls in the rejection region, reject H_0; if the test statistic falls outside the rejection region, do not reject H_0.

Recall that the rejection region is $RR : t \geq 2.064$ and $t \leq -2.064$. Since $t = 1.156$ does not fall in the rejection region, we do not reject $H_0 : \mu = 750$. The evidence is not sufficently strong to conclude that the filling process is out of adjustment.

Example 10.10. (1) What is the p-value? (2) Compare the p-value with α.

1 Because RR lies in both the upper and lower tails of the t-distribution, the p-value is the probability that t is greater than 1.156 *plus* the probability that t is less than −1.156. Thus, the p-value is

$$p(t \geq 1.156) + p(t \leq -1.156) = 0.1296 + 0.1296 = 0.259.$$

```
pt(1.156, 24, lower.tail = FALSE) + pt(-1.156, 24)
```

```
## [1] 0.2590597
```

2 Since p-value = 0.259 and $\alpha = 0.05$, p-value > α and we do not reject H_0.

Example 10.11. Use the `t.test()` function to conduct the hypothesis test. The data set is `wine`, the variable name is `ml`, the significance is defined by `conf.level = 0.95`, and the null hypothesis is specified by `mu = 750`. Recall that for the two-tail test, the argument alternative is omitted.

```
#Comment. Use function t.test(); variable name is ml.
t.test(wine$ml, conf.level = 0.95, mu = 750)
```

```
##
## One Sample t-test
##
## data: wine$ml
## t = 1.1556, df = 24, p-value = 0.2592
## alternative hypothesis: true mean is not equal to 750
## 95 percent confidence interval:
##  741.6061 779.7539
## sample estimates:
## mean of x
##    760.68
```

Note that the third line reports a p-value of 0.2592. We need only compare this p-value with the level of significance $\alpha = 0.05$ to know that we do not reject H_0.

10.5 HYPOTHESIS TESTS ABOUT *p*

The six-step framework can also be used for tests about p. The departure from what we have used above lies in the use of the sample proportion $\bar{p}$, the standard error of the proportion $\sigma_{\bar{p}}$, the sampling distribution of $\bar{p}$, and z (rather than t) as the test statistic.

Example 10.12. A survey of European Union nations has found that 70% of drivers admit to having used their cellphones while driving. In light of this, several EU countries have introduced measures to combat the phenomenon now referred to as "distracted driving." After an extensive public relations campaign in one country intended to dissuade drivers from engaging in such distracted driving, a survey has found that 1190 drivers in a sample of 1776 report using their cellphones to speak or text while driving. Conduct a lower-tail test at the $\alpha = 0.05$ level of significance to determine if the public relations effort has been successful.

1 Determine the null hypothesis H_0 in statistical terms.

$H_0: p \geq 0.70$

2 Determine the alternative hypothesis H_a in statistical terms.

$H_a: p < 0.70$

3 Set the level of significance α and decide on the sample size n.

$n = 1776$ and $\alpha = 0.05$

Assuming H_0 is true, $\bar{p}$ has a normal distribution with a mean of $E(\bar{p}) = p_0 = 0.70$ and a standard deviation of

$$\sigma_{\bar{p}} = \sqrt{\frac{p_0(1-p_0)}{n}} = \sqrt{\frac{0.70 \times 0.30}{1776}} = 0.0109.$$

Note that in conducting hypothesis tests about the population proportion p, p_0 (and not $\bar{p}$) is used in the expression for the standard error of the proportion $\sigma_{\bar{p}}$.

4 Use α to specify the rejection region RR.

$$RR : z < -1.645$$

That is, reject H_0 if $z < -z_\alpha = -z_{0.05} = -1.645$, where $z = (\bar{p} - p_0) / \sigma_{\bar{p}}$.

```
qnorm(0.05)
## [1] -1.644854
```

The value of z that cuts off an area of 0.05 in the lower tail is $z = -1.645$. Therefore, if the sample proportion $\bar{p}$ transforms into a value of z that is less than -1.645, we reject H_0 and accept H_a; if z is greater than -1.645, we do not reject H_0.

5 Collect the data and calculate the test statistic.
Since 1190 of 1776 drivers admitted to using their cellphones while driving, $\bar{p} = 1190/1776 = 0.67$. Translating $\bar{p} = 0.67$ into its associated value of z,

$$z = \frac{\bar{p} - p_0}{\sigma_{\bar{p}}} = \frac{0.67 - 0.70}{0.0109} = -2.76.$$

Thus, $\bar{p} = 0.67$ corresponds to $z = -2.76$.

6 Use the value of the test statistic and the rejection region RR to decide whether to reject H_0. If the test statistic falls in the rejection region, reject H_0; if the test statistic falls outside the rejection region, do not reject H_0.
Recall that the rejection region is $RR : z < -1.645$. Since $z = -2.76 < -1.645$, we reject $H_0 : p = 0.70$, and accept $H_a : p < 0.70$. The evidence supports the conclusion that the PR campaign may be working.

Example 10.13. (1) What is the p-value? (2) Compare the p-value with α.

1 Since the sample proportion $\bar{p} = 0.67$ translates to $z = -2.76$, and because the rejection region is in the lower tail of the standard normal probability distribution, the p-value is the probability that z is less than -2.76. Thus, the p-value is

$$p\text{-value } (z \le -2.76) = 0.0029.$$

```
pnorm(-2.76)
## [1] 0.002890068
```

2 Since p-value $= 0.0029$ and $\alpha = 0.05$, we know that p-value $< \alpha$, and so we reject H_0.

Example 10.14. Use the `prop.test()` function to conduct the test. Note that the first two arguments include the frequency information that must be known in advance.

```
#Comment. Use prop.test() to test hypothesis.
prop.test(1190, 1776, conf.level = 0.95, p = 0.70, alternative = 'l',
          correct = FALSE)

##
## 1-sample proportions test without continuity correction
##
## data: 1190 out of 1776, null probability 0.7
## X-squared = 7.5886, df = 1, p-value = 0.002937
## alternative hypothesis: true p is less than 0.7
## 95 percent confidence interval:
## 0.0000000 0.6881263
## sample estimates:
##        p
## 0.670045
```

The six arguments of the function `prop.test()` are:

1 The frequency that 1 (using cellphone) occurs in the sample.
2 The number of observations in the sample, in this case $n = 1776$.
3 The significance level is set at 0.05 by `conf.level = 0.95`.
4 The null hypothesis is expressed as `p = 0.70`.
5 A lower-tail test is specified by defining `alternative = 'l'`.
6 `correct = FALSE` disables the insertion of a continuity correction factor, something which is not required here.

To find the frequencies of a data set, we simply apply the `table()` function. (This function is used in Section 2.2 and produces tabular representations of categorical data.) For the current example, the data set `distract` is found on the website and includes the variable `cellphone`.

```
#Comment. Use function table() to recover frequencies of 1 and 0.
table(distract$cellphone)

##
##    0    1
## 586 1190
```

These frequencies (1776 observations, consisting of 1190 ones and 586 zeros) are then used as the first two arguments in the function `prop.test(1190, 1776, conf.level = 0.95, ...)`.

Since the third line of the output reports a p-value of 0.002937, we need only compare it with $\alpha = 0.05$ to know that we reject H_0. Also included in the output are statements of H_0 ("null probability 0.7") and H_a ("alternative hypothesis: true p is less than 0.7").

It is interesting to consider why we do not use `t.test()` instead, as we did above when performing hypothesis tests on μ when σ is unknown, preferring instead the new form `prop.test()`. While `t.test()` would give us approximately the same results, they are not exactly the same for the reason that `t.test()` uses a *t*-distribution while `prop.test()` uses the standard normal probability distribution.

Finally, we conduct a two-tail test on the population proportion p.

Example 10.15. In a recent survey, 1161 registered US voters were asked "If the election between Barack Obama and Mitt Romney were to be held today, would you vote for Obama?" Of the 1161 respondents, 557 reported that they would vote for Obama if the election were to be held again. Since Obama won 51.1% of the popular vote, the question is whether he gained or lost support after the 2012 election. Thus, the null hypothesis is $p = 0.511$ and a two-tail test is required. Use $\alpha = 0.01$ as level of significance.

1 Determine the null hypothesis H_0 in statistical terms.

$H_0: p = 0.511$

2 Determine the alternative hypothesis H_a in statistical terms.

$H_a: p \neq 0.511$

3 Set the level of significance α and decide on the sample size n.

$n = 1161$ and $\alpha = 0.01$

Assuming H_0 is true, $\bar{p}$ has a normal distribution with mean $E(\bar{p}) = p_0 = 0.511$ and standard deviation

$$\sigma_{\bar{p}} = \sqrt{\frac{p_0(1-p_0)}{n}} = \sqrt{\frac{0.511 \times 0.489}{1161}} = 0.0147.$$

Remember that in conducting hypothesis tests about the population proportion p, p_0 (and not $\bar{p}$) is used in the expression for the standard error of the proportion $\sigma_{\bar{p}}$.

4 Use α to specify the rejection region *RR*.

RR: $z \geq 2.576$ and $z \leq -2.576$. That is, reject H_0 if $z \geq z_{\alpha/2} = z_{0.005} = 2.576$ or $z \leq -z_{\alpha/2} = -z_{0.005} = -2.576$.

```
qnorm(0.005)
## [1] -2.575829
```

```
qnorm(0.995)
## [1] 2.575829
```

The value of z that cuts off an area of 0.005 in the upper tail is $z = 2.576$; the value of z that cuts off an area of 0.005 in the lower tail is $z = -2.576$. Therefore, if $\bar{p}$ transforms into a value of z that is greater than 2.576, or less than -2.576, we reject H_0 and accept H_a; if z falls in the region from -2.576 to 2.576, we do not reject H_0.

5 Collect the data and calculate the test statistic.
Since 557 of 1161 voters responded that they would vote for President Obama, $\bar{p} = 557/1161 = 0.4798$. Translating $\bar{p} = 0.4798$ into its associated value of z,

$$z = \frac{\bar{p} - p_0}{\sigma_{\bar{p}}} = \frac{\bar{p} - 0.511}{0.0147} = \frac{0.4798 - 0.511}{0.0147} = -2.13.$$

Thus, $\bar{p} = 0.4798$ corresponds to $z = -2.13$.

6 Use the value of the test statistic and the rejection region RR to decide whether to reject H_0. If the test statistic falls in the rejection region, reject H_0; if the test statistic falls outside the rejection region, do not reject H_0.
Recall that the rejection region is $RR: z \geq 2.576$ and $z \leq -2.576$. Since $z = -2.13$ does not fall in the rejection region, we do not reject $H_0: p = 0.511$. The evidence is not sufficiently strong for us to reject H_0.

Example 10.16. (1) What is the p-value? (2) Compare the p-value with α.

1 Since the sample proportion $\bar{p} = 0.4798$ translates to $z = -2.13$, and because the rejection region is in both the upper and lower tails of the standard normal probability distribution, the p-value is the probability that z is greater than 2.13 *plus* the probability that z is less than −2.13. Thus, the p-value is

$$p(z \geq 2.13) + p(z \leq -2.13) = 0.0166 + 0.0166 = 0.0332.$$

```
pnorm(-2.13) + pnorm(2.13, lower.tail = FALSE)
## [1] 0.03317161
```

2 Since p-value = 0.0332 and α = 0.01, we do not reject H_0. The evidence is not sufficiently strong to conclude that President Obama's support among the voters has changed since the election of 2012.

Example 10.17. Use the R function `prop.test()`.

```
#Comment. Use the function prop.test() to conduct the hypothesis test.
prop.test(557, 1161, conf.level = 0.99, p = 0.511, correct = FALSE)

##
##  1-sample proportions test without continuity correction
##
## data: 557 out of 1161, null probability 0.511
## X-squared = 4.5348, df = 1, p-value = 0.03321
## alternative hypothesis: true p is not equal to 0.511
## 99 percent confidence interval:
##  0.4422139 0.5175338
## sample estimates:
##         p
## 0.4797588
```

The five arguments of the `prop.test()` function are:

1 The frequency that 1 occurs in the sample.
2 The number of observations in the sample, n=1161.
3 The significance level is set at 0.01 by `conf.level = 0.99`.
4 The null hypothesis is expressed as `p = 0.511`.
5 `correct = FALSE` disables the insertion of the continuity correction factor.

Since the output reports a p-value of 0.03321, we need only compare it with $\alpha = 0.01$ to know that we do not reject H_0. Also included are H_0 ("null probability 0.511") as well as H_a ("alternative hypothesis: true p is not equal to 0.511").

10.6 CALCULATING THE PROBABILITY OF A TYPE II ERROR: β

We now return to a discussion of β, the probability of a Type II error, a topic that was introduced in Chapter 9. We have not revisited the concept of the Type II error since then; nor have we extended our discussion of β in this chapter to any of the previous examples. The reason is that for many hypothesis tests, controlling α is more important than worrying about Type II errors. We set the probability of a Type I error whenever we specify the level of α, an action that makes it possible to say whenever we reject H_0 that we also *accept* H_a. It is because we normally do not specify the size of β that we cannot say *we accept* H_0, preferring instead the more conservative statement that *we do not reject* H_0. Tests for which we specify α but not β are referred to as *significance tests*.

Of course, it is not the case with every testing application that we are concerned only with α; sometimes we are interested in β as well. Indeed, it is possible, even necessary, in some testing situations to control β as well as α. Whenever this is done, it is appropriate to use the term *accept* H_0 even though until now our practice has been to use the expression *do not reject* H_0. As an example, consider the following quality-control problem.

Example 10.18. A manufacturer of toner cartridges for laser and inkjet printers regularly tests its own advertising claim that one of its products prints at least 550 pages before streaking or fading. Each day, the quality manager selects and tests a sample of 36 cartridges to determine $\bar{x}$, the mean number of clearly printed pages per cartridge. Based on the sample result, she must decide whether to shut down the manufacturing process for adjustment or let the process continue on in its current state.

In this case, the manager is forced to make a decision both when $H_0: \mu = 550$ is rejected (in which case she must shut down the manufacturing process for adjustment) and when H_0 is not rejected (in which case she allows the manufacturing process to continue). A Type I error occurs when she concludes that the cartridges are providing fewer clearly printed pages than advertised and decides to shut down the process even though it actually is generating at least 550 pages.

A Type II error happens when she concludes the cartridges are printing at least 550 pages when they are in fact defective and cannot perform to the required standard. In this instance, controlling both α and β is important. Note that $\bar{x}$ is used to estimate μ, the mean number of pages provided by the population of all cartridges manufactured during a given day. During previous tests when the process was known to be in control, $\sigma = 18$ pages. Let us write out the first four steps of the six-step hypothesis-testing framework and setting $\alpha = 0.05$.

1 Determine the null hypothesis H_0 in statistical terms.

$H_0: \mu \geq 550$

2 Determine the alternative hypothesis H_a in statistical terms.

$H_a: \mu < 550$

3 Set the level of significance α and decide on the sample size n.

$n = 36$ and $\alpha = 0.05$

4 Use α to define RR in terms of $\bar{x}$.

$RR: \bar{x} \leq 545.07$

(a) Reject H_0 if $z \leq z_\alpha = -z_{0.05} = -1.645$, where $z = (\bar{x} - \mu_0) / \sigma_{\bar{x}}$.

```
qnorm(0.05)
## [1] -1.644854
```

(b) Since $z \leq -1.645$ and because

$$\sigma_{\bar{x}} = \frac{\sigma}{\sqrt{n}} = \frac{18}{\sqrt{36}} = 3,$$

we can substitute the right-hand side of the expression for z, in (a) above, and solve for $\bar{x}$:

$$z \leq -1.645$$

$$\frac{\bar{x} - \mu_0}{\sigma_{\bar{x}}} \leq -1.645$$

$$\bar{x} \leq \mu_0 - 1.645\sigma_{\bar{x}}$$

$$\bar{x} \leq 550 - 1.645 \times 3 = 545.07.$$

If we prefer, we can find $\bar{x}$ directly:

```
qnorm(.05, 550, 18 / sqrt(36))
## [1] 545.0654
```

Once the RR has been expressed in terms of $\bar{x}$, we know that the manager will shut down the manufacturing process for adjustment if $\bar{x} \leq 545.07$ because H_0 has been rejected; and that she will leave the manufacturing process running whenever $\bar{x} > 545.07$ since H_0 has not been rejected. If H_0 is not rejected, however, the manager cannot conclude that H_0 is true. Nonetheless, she acts as if it were true when she allows the manufacturing process to continue without adjustment. When faced with this type of problem, the ability to calculate and control β becomes more important.

In this era of "big data" when samples seemingly of infinite size are suddenly and freely available in nearly all contexts, many students feel that sample size calculations are not so important. After all, if we can collect and analyze enormous samples without extra effort, time, or expense, why not use all the data we can and not worry about determining the optimal sample size? The reason why sample size determination is still important is that there are many instances—this example is one of them—when there simply are no "big data" available. When testing printer cartridges for the mean number of clearly printed pages is the problem at hand, it should be obvious that this is a time-consuming, laborious, and expensive process. We really do not want to analyze samples that are any larger than they need to be for the purpose at hand.

In this context, we commit a Type II error whenever the cartridge-printing capacity falls short of the 550-page standard, yet we do not reject H_0 and allow the process to continue anyway. In order to calculate β, we must choose a value of μ which is *less than* 550. Suppose the process has gotten out of adjustment, and the cartridges are providing an average of only $\mu = 540$ pages. What is the probability that $\bar{x} > 545.07$ when $\mu = 540$? Assuming $\mu = 540$ and $\sigma_{\bar{x}} = 3$, the probability that $\bar{x} > 545.07$ is

$$\beta = p(\bar{x} > 545.07 \mid \mu = 540, \sigma_{\bar{x}} = 3) = 0.0455.$$

```
pnorm(545.07, 540, 18 / sqrt(36), lower.tail = FALSE)
## [1] 0.04551398
```

Thus, it is possible that the manager would select a sample providing $\bar{x} > 545.07$ even though $\mu = 540$. In fact, we would expect this to happen about 4.55% of the time.

Table 10.1 Probability of Type II error β for different values of μ

Value of μ	$\beta = p(\text{Type II error}) = p(\bar{x} > 545.07)$	**Power = $1 - \beta$**
540	$\beta = p(\bar{x} > 545.07 \mid \mu = 540, \sigma_{\bar{x}} = 3) = 0.0455$	0.9545
542	$\beta = p(\bar{x} > 545.07 \mid \mu = 542, \sigma_{\bar{x}} = 3) = 0.1531$	0.8469
544	$\beta = p(\bar{x} > 545.07 \mid \mu = 544, \sigma_{\bar{x}} = 3) = 0.3607$	0.6393
545.07	$\beta = p(\bar{x} > 545.07 \mid \mu = 545.07, \sigma_{\bar{x}} = 3) = 0.5000$	0.5000
546	$\beta = p(\bar{x} > 545.07 \mid \mu = 546, \sigma_{\bar{x}} = 3) = 0.6217$	0.3783
548	$\beta = p(\bar{x} > 545.07 \mid \mu = 548, \sigma_{\bar{x}} = 3) = 0.8356$	0.1644
549.99	$\beta = p(\bar{x} > 549.99 \mid \mu = 540, \sigma_{\bar{x}} = 3) = 0.9495$	0.0505

We can find the values of β (in the center column of Table 10.1) by repeatedly applying `pnorm()` to the different values of μ:

```
pnorm(545.07, 540, 18 / sqrt(36), lower.tail = FALSE)
## [1] 0.04551398

pnorm(545.07, 542, 18 / sqrt(36), lower.tail = FALSE)
## [1] 0.1530751

pnorm(545.07, 544, 18 / sqrt(36), lower.tail = FALSE)
## [1] 0.3606707

pnorm(545.07, 545.07, 18 / sqrt(36), lower.tail = FALSE)
## [1] 0.5

pnorm(545.07, 546, 18 / sqrt(36), lower.tail = FALSE)
## [1] 0.6217195

pnorm(545.07, 548, 18 / sqrt(36), lower.tail = FALSE)
## [1] 0.8356329

pnorm(545.07, 549.99, 18 / sqrt(36), lower.tail = FALSE)
## [1] 0.9494974
```

The probabilities of committing a Type II error for seven different values of μ, including $\mu = 540$, are reported in Table 10.1. We note that the closer μ is to the hypothesized value of 550, the more likely we are to commit a Type II error. We also point out that the reason why we calculate β for values of μ up to but not including 550 is that there can be no Type II error when $\mu = 550$ or above: a Type II error occurs only when $\mu < 550$. Finally, we point out that the right-hand column in Table 10.1 reports the *power of the test*, which is defined as the probability of rejecting H_0 when it is false, and is calculated as $1 - \beta$.

10.7 ADJUSTING THE SAMPLE SIZE TO CONTROL THE SIZE OF β

Now that we understand how to calculate the probability of a Type II error, let us turn our attention to how we might actually control its size. Although when we specify the level of α in the third step of our hypothesis-testing framework, we control the probability of committing a Type I error, we have thus far done nothing to control the probability of making a Type II error. We may do so, however, by using the following expression to determine the sample size n required to select the desired levels of β and α for a one-tail test:

$$n = \frac{(z_\alpha + z_\beta)^2 \sigma^2}{(\mu_0 - \mu_a)^2},$$

where z_α is the value of z providing an area of α in the tail of the standard normal distribution, z_β is the value of z providing an area of β in the tail of the standard normal distribution, σ is the population standard deviation, μ_0 is the value of the population mean in H_0, and μ_a is the value of the population mean selected for the Type II error. (If a two-tailed hypothesis test is required, we substitute $z_{\alpha/2}$ for z_α above.)

Example 10.19. Let us return to the example in which the quality manager for a manufacturer of toner cartridges wants to control the size of both α and β. She has set α at 0.05 but now must specify a level of β as well. Suppose she decides that if the mean number of clearly printed pages is 6 pages under the required standard (i.e., the mean is actually 544 rather than 550), she would like to have an 80% chance of identifying it. That is, she would be willing to expose herself to a 20% chance of missing this fact. (In Table 10.1, we see that β for $\mu = 544$ is 0.3607, or about 36%.) This sets the desired probability of a Type II error at $\beta = 0.20$. In view of this information, what is the required sample size?

Since $\alpha = 0.05$, $z_\alpha = z_{0.05} = 1.645$; and since $\beta = 0.20$, $z_\beta = z_{0.20} = 0.84$.

```
qnorm(0.95)
## [1] 1.644854
qnorm(0.80)
## [1] 0.8416212
```

Furthermore, the population standard deviation is $\sigma = 18$; the value of the population mean in H_0 is $\mu_0 = 550$; and the value of the population mean selected for the Type II error is $\mu_a = 544$. Plugging these values into the above expression for sample size yields

$$n = \frac{(z_\alpha + z_\beta)^2\sigma^2}{(\mu_0 - \mu_a)^2} = \frac{(1.645 + 0.84)^2 18^2}{(550 - 544)^2} = 55.58 \approx 56.$$

Thus, the sample size associated with $\beta = 0.20$ and $\alpha = 0.05$ is $n = 56$.

Example 10.20. Let us check that $n = 56$ does indeed control the probability of a Type II error at the level of $\beta = 0.20$. That is, is $\beta = 0.20$ when $\mu_a = 544$ and $n = 56$? To answer this question, we write out the first four steps of our hypothesis-testing framework while remembering to incorporate the new, larger sample size.

1 Determine the null hypothesis H_0 in statistical terms.

 $H_0: \mu \geq 550$

2 Determine the alternative hypothesis H_a in statistical terms.

 $H_a: \mu < 550$

3 Set the level of significance α and decide on the sample size n.

 $n = 56$ and $\alpha = 0.05$

4 Use α to specify RR in terms of $\bar{x}$.

 $RR: \bar{x} \leq 546.04$

 (a) Reject H_0 if $z < -z_\alpha = -z_{0.05} = -1.645$, where $z = (\bar{x} - \mu_0) / \sigma_{\bar{x}}$.

```
qnorm(0.05)
## [1] -1.644854
```

(b) Because the sample size is now $n = 56$, we must recalculate $\sigma_{\bar{x}}$:

$$\sigma_{\bar{x}} = \frac{\sigma}{\sqrt{n}} = \frac{18}{\sqrt{56}} = 2.41.$$

(c) Now we substitute the right-hand side of the expression for z and solve for $\bar{x}$:

$$z \leq -1.645$$

$$\frac{\bar{x} - \mu_0}{\sigma_{\bar{x}}} \leq -1.645$$

$$\bar{x} \leq \mu_0 - 1.645\sigma_{\bar{x}}$$

$$\bar{x} \leq 550 - 1.645 \times 2.41 = 546.04.$$

(d) We can also use `qnorm()` to solve for this new value more directly. We just need to make sure to increase the sample size from $n = 36$ to $n = 56$:

```
qnorm(0.05, 550, 18 / sqrt(56))
## [1] 546.0435
```

Because $RR: \bar{x} \leq 546.04$, $\beta = p(\bar{x} > 546.04) = 0.1999 \approx 0.2000$. Thus, by increasing n from 36 to 56, β is 0.2000 and α is 0.05.

Once the rejection rule has been reexpressed in terms of $\bar{x}$ in view of the larger sample size, we know that the manager will shut down the manufacturing process for adjustment if $\bar{x} \leq 546.04$ because H_0 has been rejected; and she will leave the manufacturing process running whenever $\bar{x} > 546.04$ since H_0 has been accepted. Note that this is the first time we have employed the term *accept* the H_0. In fact, the manager can use the terms reject and accept H_0 because the probabilities of both Type I and Type II errors are now controlled.

Finally, it is worth noting that in this example we would round the value to a whole number since the problem concerns the number of printed pages. In this case, the rejection region is amended to $RR: \bar{x} \leq 546$. If $\bar{x} \leq 546$, we reject $H_0: \mu \geq 550$; otherwise we accept $H_0: \mu \geq 550$.

SUMMARY

In this chapter we apply the hypothesis-testing framework to problems involving tests of two different population parameters, μ and p. In all instances, we perform both two-tail and one-tail tests. Since this chapter applies the concepts and methods set out in Chapter 9, no additional definitions or terms are introduced here.

In the case of a test of μ, we encounter two examples where we assume σ is known, in which case the standard normal variable z is used. We also work through two examples where σ is unknown. In this instance, the sample data are used to calculate s as an estimate of σ; additionally we use the appropriate t-distribution with $n - 1$ degrees of freedom. Finally, we also conduct both two-tail and one-tail tests of the population proportion p, and in the process once again make use of the standard normal variable z.

Calculating β, the probability of a Type II error, in the case of hypothesis tests on μ requires finding the probabilities of values of μ for which the null hypothesis is false. It is important to remember that a Type II error can occur only when H_0 is false. The power of the test is the probability of rejecting H_0 when it is false; it is defined as simply $1 - \beta$. In many applications, we are more interested in controlling α than β; when this is the case, the hypothesis tests are called significance tests. Whether or not we need to be concerned with β depends entirely on the seriousness of committing a Type II error. Sometimes it matters, sometimes it does not. The judgment of the analyst is usually required to resolve whether the calculation of β is something that should be done or something that can be safely ignored.

As we saw in the taste-testing example in Chapter 9, selecting a lower value for α generally results in a higher value of β; and by allowing a higher value of α, it is possible to achieve a lower value for β. In other words, α and β are normally in a trade-off relationship with one another. Even so, we saw in Section 10.7 that it is possible to adjust the sample size n for the purpose of controlling the size of α and β simultaneously. You should note, though, that whether this is a necessary step depends on the context of the problem. Bear in mind that the sample size calculation provides the smallest value of n that will result in specified (lower) values of α and β. In those instances when data are essentially free—increasingly common during the age of "big data"—it is difficult to see what the point of sample size determination might be: since increasing the amount of data available for a study decreases both α and β, we may want to use data sets of enormous size. If adding additional data is free, why not? However, in those instances where adding additional observations is costly or time-consuming, the importance of sample size determination becomes more apparent. For example, if a tire manufacturer wants to test the useful life of a new line of automobile tires for the purpose of an advertising claim—"Our tires are guaranteed to last at least 40,000 miles"—then measuring the useful life of a tire involves testing and wearing out each one, obviously a costly and time-consuming exercise. Once again, whether to do sample size determination is a decision that depends on the judgment and experience of the analyst.

definitions

Alpha α is the probability of a Type I error. That is, p(Type I error) = p(we reject $H_0 \mid H_0$ is true) = α; α is also known as the *level of significance*.

Alternative Hypothesis The condition stated in the alternative hypothesis H_a is concluded to be true whenever the null hypothesis is rejected.

Beta β is the probability of a Type II error. In other words, p(Type II error) = p(we fail to reject $H_0 \mid H_0$ is false) = β.

Level of Significance The probability of committing a Type I error; that is, the probability of rejecting the null hypothesis when it is true.

(Continued)

(Continued)

Lower-Tail Test A lower-tail test is a one-tail hypothesis test where the rejection region lies only in the lower tail of the sampling distribution.

Null Hypothesis The condition stated in the null hypothesis is tentatively assumed true unless and until strong evidence casts significant doubt on it. In this case, we say that we reject H_0.

One-Tail Test A one-tail test is a hypothesis test where the rejection region lies either in the upper tail or lower tail (but not both) of the sampling distribution.

***p*-Value** The *p*-value is the probability of obtaining a sample result that is at least as unlikely as what we would have observed under the assumption that H_0 is true. The *p*-value is also known as the *observed level of significance*.

Rejection Region A rejection region specifies the range of values the test statistic *x* might assume that would lead to rejection of the null hypothesis.

Test Statistic The empirical result of the hypothesis test that is used to either reject or not reject the null hypothesis H_0.

Two-Tail Test A two-tail test is a hypothesis test where the rejection region lies in both the lower and upper tails of the sampling distribution.

Type I Error A Type I error occurs when H_0 is rejected even though it is true.

Type II Error A Type II error occurs when H_0 is not rejected even though it is false.

Upper-Tail Test An upper-tail test is a one-tail hypothesis test where the rejection region lies only in the upper tail of the sampling distribution.

formulae

Sample Size Determination to Set β for One-Tail Hypothesis Test of μ

$$n = \frac{(z_\alpha + z_\beta)^2 \sigma^2}{(\mu_0 - \mu_a)^2}$$

Sample Size Determination to Set β for Two-Tail Hypothesis Test of μ

$$n = \frac{(z_{\alpha/2} + z_\beta)^2 \sigma^2}{(\mu_0 - \mu_a)^2}$$

Test Statistic for Hypothesis Test about μ: σ is Known

$$z = \frac{\bar{x} - \mu_0}{\sigma_{\bar{x}}}$$

Test Statistic for Hypothesis Test about μ: σ is Unknown

$$t = \frac{\bar{x} - \mu_0}{s_{\bar{x}}}$$

Test Statistic for Hypothesis Test about p

$$z = \frac{\bar{p} - p_0}{\sigma_{\bar{p}}} \text{ where } \sigma_{\bar{p}} = \sqrt{\frac{p_0(1 - p_0)}{n}}$$

R functions

```
prop.test(r, n, conf.level=0.95,
p=p0,alternative='l',correct=FALSE)
```

Performs a lower-tail hypothesis test on the population proportion at the 0.05 level of significance.

`prop.test(r, n, conf.level = 0.90, p =` p_0`, alternative = 'g', correct = FALSE)` Performs an upper-tail hypothesis test on the population proportion at the 0.10 level of significance.

`prop.test(r, n, conf.level = 0.99, p =` p_0`, correct = FALSE)` Performs a two-tail hypothesis test on the population proportion at the 0.01 level of significance.

`t.test(name, conf.level = .90,` $\mu = \mu_0$`, alternative = 'l')` Performs a lower-tail test on the population mean at the 0.10 level of significance using a data set called `name`.

`t.test(name, conf.level = .99, mu =` μ_0`, alternative = 'g')` Performs an upper-tail test on the population mean at the 0.01 level of significance using a data set called `name`.

`t.test(name, conf.level = .95, mu =` μ_0`)` Performs a two-tail test on the population mean at the 0.05 level of significance using a data set called `name`.

data sets

1 `distract`
2 `elderly`
3 `wine`

exercises

10.1 Referring to the Agrico example (Section 10.1), suppose the quality-control manager decides that while Agrico does not want to underfill its packages, neither does it wish to overfill. Clearly, giving away product in overfilled packages costs Agrico money, and provides little or no goodwill among customers who are unaware they are reaping a windfall in free bran flakes. Suppose that the sample size is adjusted upward to $n = 100$ and α is reset to 0.10. Using the six-step hypothesis-testing framework, test $H_0: \mu \leq 375$ against $H_a: \mu > 375$. Recall that $\sigma = 22.5$. Suppose the sample of $n = 100$ provides a mean weight of 377.50 grams. What is the *p*-value?

10.2 Family physicians in Tampa, Florida reportedly earn an average annual salary of $141,300. Suppose we conduct a survey on a sample of $n = 64$ family physicians from New Orleans, Louisiana to test whether their mean annual salary is different from the reported mean in Tampa, and find that the sample mean is $138,000. Assume σ = $18,000. At the level of $\alpha = 0.01$, use the six-step framework to test $H_0: \mu = 141{,}300$ against $H_a: \mu \neq 141{,}300$. What is the *p*-value?

10.3 The student newspaper at a large business school claims that 55% of graduating students have an offer of employment even before they graduate. The Office of Student Affairs decided to investigate this claim to see whether it is true. When they carried out the survey, they found that 321 of 535 graduating students reported having a job offer. At a level of $\alpha = 0.10$, use the six-step framework to test $H_0: p = 0.55$ against $H_a: p \neq 0.55$. What is the *p*-value?

(Continued)

(Continued)

10.4 While campaigning for higher political office during a recent election, a certain candidate claimed that "At least 75% of voters want the country to end all foreign aid to all countries." When a polling organization conducted a survey to investigate this claim, they found that 242 out of a sample of $n = 346$ expressed agreement with the statement. At a level of $\alpha = 0.02$, use the six-step framework to test $H_0: p \geq 0.75$ against $H_a: p < 0.75$. What is the *p*-value?

10.5 An Italian farmer who grows and packs agricultural produce for the export market claims that his packages contain an average of 750 grams of tomatoes. To ensure that the company consistently meets this standard, the manager conducts a study to test $H_0: \mu \geq 750$ against $H_a: \mu < 750$. Based on previous studies, $\sigma = 25$. What sample size should the manager use if he wants a 0.90 probability of identifying when the mean weight falls short of 750 grams by 10 grams? Let $\alpha = 0.01$.

https://study.sagepub.com/stinerock

11 Comparisons of Means and Proportions

contents

learning objectives

1. Know the properties of the sampling distribution of $\bar{x}_1 - \bar{x}_2$.
2. Be able to conduct hypothesis tests about, and obtain interval estimates of, the difference between two means μ_1 and μ_2 when the samples are independent.
3. Learn how to conduct hypothesis tests of, and obtain estimates of, the difference between two means μ_1 and μ_2 when the samples are paired.
4. Know the properties of the sampling distribution of $\bar{p}_1 - \bar{p}_2$.
5. Be able to conduct hypothesis tests about, and construct interval estimates of, the difference between two proportions p_1 and p_2 when the samples are independent.

Thus far, we have considered the three forms of hypothesis test involving a single population mean μ and a single population proportion p: the lower-tail, the upper-tail, and the two-tail tests. In this chapter we extend this inferential framework to tests about the difference between two population means, μ_1 and μ_2, as well as to the difference between two population proportions, p_1 and p_2. We also learn how to construct confidence interval estimates of the difference between the means and proportions of two populations.

This chapter marks a departure from what we have discussed thus far in the book in that, until this point, we have considered inferences about only one population at a time. We now extend this discussion by describing the confidence interval estimation procedure when we have two random samples, one from each of two populations, and then introducing the forms of hypothesis tests to be used in this situation. We begin by describing the properties of the sampling distributions of $\bar{x}_1 - \bar{x}_2$ and, later, $\bar{p}_1 - \bar{p}_2$: the expected value, the standard error, and the *shape* of the sampling distribution.

11.1 THE DIFFERENCE BETWEEN μ_1 AND μ_2: INDEPENDENT SAMPLES

The different forms of the confidence interval estimate and of the null and alternative hypotheses follow a pattern similar to those introduced in Chapters 8 and 9. In this instance, however, instead of estimating a single mean μ or proportion p, we now estimate the *difference between* population means, $\mu_1 - \mu_2$. Later in the chapter we also estimate the difference between population proportions, $p_1 - p_2$.

When we estimate the difference between μ_1 and μ_2, we select one random sample of size n_1 from a population with mean μ_1 and standard deviation σ_1, and an (independent) random sample of size n_2 from another population with mean μ_2 and standard deviation σ_2. Since σ_1 and σ_2 are unknown, we use s_1 and s_2 as estimates.

The Confidence Interval Estimate of $\mu_1 - \mu_2$

The parameter of interest is the difference between these two values, $\mu_1 - \mu_2$, and is estimated by the statistic $\bar{x}_1 - \bar{x}_2$, where $\bar{x}_1$ and $\bar{x}_2$ are obtained from independent random samples of size

n_1 and n_2. Like other sample statistics, $\bar{x}_1 - \bar{x}_2$ has a sampling distribution: the expected value of the sampling distribution is $E(\bar{x}_1 - \bar{x}_2) = \mu_1 - \mu_2$, while the standard error is $s_{\bar{x}_1 - \bar{x}_2} = \sqrt{s_1^2 / n_1 + s_2^2 / n_2}$. Since we use s_1 and s_2 in place of σ_1 and σ_2, we use the t-distribution with $n_1 + n_2 - 2$ degrees of freedom, not the standard normal z. The shape of the sampling distribution of $\bar{x}_1 - \bar{x}_2$ approaches the t-distribution when either both $n_1 \geq 30$ and $n_2 \geq 30$ or (if not) the population distributions from which the samples are drawn are approximately normal. Recalling that the interval estimate takes the form: point estimate ± margin of error; we use

$$(\bar{x}_1 - \bar{x}_2) \pm t_{\alpha/2, n_1+n_2-2}\sqrt{\frac{s_1^2}{n_1} + \frac{s_2^2}{n_2}},$$

where the margin of error is the product of the t value and the standard error.

Example 11.1. Portugal has a number of popular tourist destinations during the summer months, including the Algarve, in the far south, and Cascais, just west of Lisbon. Until the 1990s, Cascais enjoyed great success as one of the tourist destinations of choice, but as the Algarve became more accessible—with the construction of superhighways and the introduction of numerous flights from all over Europe—it soon surpassed all other areas of Portugal as the preferred holiday venue. A UK-based travel agent would like to know if the mean monthly rent of holiday properties differs between the two locations. One of the ways of resolving the uncertainty surrounding this issue is to construct a confidence interval estimate of the difference between the two population means.

In this case, we define population 1 as all holiday rental properties located in the Algarve, and population 2 as all comparable holiday rental properties situated in Cascais. Defined in this manner, μ_1 is the mean of population 1 (i.e., the mean rent of all holiday properties in the Algarve) and μ_2 is the mean of population 2 (i.e., the mean rent of all similar rentals in Cascais). The parameter of interest is the difference between these two values, $\mu_1 - \mu_2$, and is estimated by the statistic $\bar{x}_1 - \bar{x}_2$, where $\bar{x}_1$ and $\bar{x}_2$ are obtained from independent random samples of size n_1 (from the Algarve) and n_2 (from Cascais).

The travel agent has visited the websites of several Portuguese estate agents and compiled information about the monthly rents for holiday properties for both locations. A summary of the findings is reported in Table 11.1.

Table 11.1 Monthly rents (€) for holiday rentals in the Algarve and Cascais

	Algarve	**Cascais**
Sample size	$n_1 = 34$	$n_1 = 27$
Sample mean	$\bar{x}_1 = €2031$	$\bar{x}_2 = €1860$
Sample standard deviation	$s_1 = €278$	$s_1 = €325$

To estimate the difference between the mean monthly rent for comparable holiday apartments in the Algarve and Cascais, we construct the 95% confidence interval estimate of the difference in the same way we did in Chapter 8:

$$
\begin{aligned}
&(\bar{x}_1 - \bar{x}_2) \pm t_{\alpha/2, n_1+n_2-2}\sqrt{\frac{s_1^2}{n_1} + \frac{s_2^2}{n_2}} \\
&= (2031 - 1860) \pm t_{0.025,59}\sqrt{\frac{278^2}{34} + \frac{325^2}{27}} \\
&= 171 \pm 2.00 \times 79 \\
&= 171 \pm 158 \text{ or } [13, 329].
\end{aligned}
$$

We can use R to find the required value of $t_{0.025,59}$:

```
qt(0.025, 59, lower.tail = FALSE)
## [1] 2.000995
```

Thus, the point estimate of the difference between the mean rents for holiday apartments in the Algarve and Cascais is €171. The 95% interval estimate of the difference between μ_1 and μ_2 can be found by adding and subtracting the margin of error €158: 171–158 = €13 and 171 + 158 = €329.

A Two-Sample Hypothesis Test about $\mu_1 - \mu_2$

We first describe the general forms of the null and alternative hypotheses in the context a test of the difference $\mu_1 - \mu_2$ for both two-tail and one-tail tests.

Definition 11.1. Two-Tail Test. A two-tail test of the difference between two population means, μ_1 and μ_2, is one in which the rejection region falls in both the lower and upper tails of the sampling distribution of $\bar{x}_1 - \bar{x}_2$.

In the forms below, δ_0 is the hypothesized difference between μ_1 and μ_2. When $\delta_0 = 0$, H_0 says that there is no difference between the means of the two populations whereas H_a says that there is a difference, either positive or negative:

$$
\begin{aligned}
&H_0 : \mu_1 - \mu_2 = \delta_0, \\
&H_a : \mu_1 - \mu_2 \neq \delta_0.
\end{aligned}
$$

Definition 11.2. One-Tail Test. A one-tail test of the difference between two population means, μ_1 and μ_2, is a test where the rejection region falls either in the upper tail or lower tail (but not both) of the sampling distribution of $\bar{x}_1 - \bar{x}_2$. Lower-tail and upper-tail tests are always one-tail tests.

Definition 11.3. Lower-Tail Test. A lower-tail test of the difference between two population means, μ_1 and μ_2, is one in which the rejection region falls in the lower tail of the sampling distribution of $\bar{x}_1 - \bar{x}_2$. H_0 expresses the view that $\mu_1 \geq \mu_2$, while H_a states that $\mu_1 < \mu_2$. The forms of H_0 and H_a are:

$$
\begin{aligned}
&H_0 : \mu_1 - \mu_2 \geq \delta_0, \\
&H_a : \mu_1 - \mu_2 < \delta_0.
\end{aligned}
$$

Definition 11.4. Upper-Tail Test. An upper-tail test of the difference between two population means, μ_1 and μ_2, is one in which the rejection region falls in the upper tail of the sampling distribution of $\bar{x}_1 - \bar{x}_2$. H_0 expresses the view that $\mu_1 \le \mu_2$, while H_a states that $\mu_1 > \mu_2$. The forms of H_0 and H_a are:

$$H_0 : \mu_1 - \mu_2 \le \delta_0,$$

$$H_a : \mu_1 - \mu_2 > \delta_0.$$

To demonstrate how to conduct a test about the difference between μ_1 and μ_2, we apply the six-step framework (used in Chapter 10) to Example 11.1. The structure and reasoning are exactly the same.

Example 11.2. Use the six-step framework to test the H_0 that the mean monthly rent is the same in Cascais as it is in the Algarve. Set the level of significance at $\alpha = 0.05$. Note that this is a two-tail test where $\delta_0 = 0$.

1 Determine the null hypothesis in statistical terms.

$$H_0 : \mu_1 - \mu_2 = 0$$

2 Determine the alternative hypothesis in statistical terms.

$$H_a : \mu_1 - \mu_2 \ne 0$$

3 Set the level of significance α and decide on the sample sizes n_1 and n_2.

$\alpha = 0.05$, $n_1 = 34$, $n_2 = 27$

4 Use α to specify the rejection region *RR*.
The rejection region is

$$RR : t \ge 2 \text{ and } t \le -2,$$

where

$$t = \frac{(\bar{x}_1 - \bar{x}_2) - \delta_0}{\sqrt{s_1^2/n_1 + s_2^2/n_2}}.$$

That is to say, reject H_0 if $t \ge t_{\alpha/2, n_1+n_2-2} = t_{0.025,59} = 2$ and $t \le -t_{\alpha/2, n_1+n_2-2} = -t_{0.025,59} = -2$, where once again:

```
qt(0.025, 59, lower.tail = FALSE)
## [1] 2.000995
```

The value of t that cuts off an area of 0.025 in the upper tail is $t = 2$; the value of t that cuts off an area of 0.025 in the lower tail is $t = -2$. Therefore, if $\bar{x}_1 - \bar{x}_2$ transforms into a value of t that is greater than 2, or less than –2, reject H_0 and accept H_a; if t falls in the region from –2 to 2, do not reject H_0.

5 Collect the data and calculate the test statistic.
For the Algarve, the sample of $n_1 = 34$ provides $\bar{x}_1 = 2031$ and $s_1 = 278$; for Cascais, the sample of $n_2 = 27$ results in $\bar{x}_2 = 1860$ and $s_2 = 325$. Then

$$t = \frac{(\bar{x}_1 - \bar{x}_2) - \delta_0}{\sqrt{s_1^2 / n_1 + s_2^2 / n_2}} = \frac{(2031 - 1860) - 0}{\sqrt{278^2 / 34 + 325^2 / 27}} = \frac{171}{78.65} = 2.17.$$

6 Use the test statistic and RR to decide whether to reject H_0.
Recall that the rejection region is $RR: t \geq 2$ and $t \leq -2$.

Since $t = 2.17 > 2.0$, we reject $H_0: \mu_1 - \mu_2 = 0$ and accept $H_a: \mu_1 - \mu_2 \neq 0$.

Thus we infer that the mean monthly rents of holiday apartments in the Algarve and Cascais are not equal to one another. Moreover, since the value of t is positive, it appears that the rents in the Algarve are actually higher, thus confirming the confidence interval estimate of $\mu_1 - \mu_2$ that we derived in Example 11.1.

Example 11.3. (1) What is the p-value? (2) Compare the p-value with α.

1 Because RR lies in both the upper and lower tails of the t-distribution, the p-value is the probability that t is greater than 2.17 plus the probability that t is less than –2.17. This is

$$p(t \geq 2.17) + p(t \leq -2.17) = 0.0170 + 0.0170 = 0.0340.$$

```
pt(2.17, 59, lower.tail = FALSE) + pt(-2.17, 59)
## [1] 0.03404507
```

2 Since $p = 0.0340$ and $\alpha = 0.05$, the p-value is less than α, so we reject H_0.

Example 11.4. Use the `t.test()` function to conduct the hypothesis test. The data set is named `holidays` and can be found on the book's website; the variable names are `algarve` and `cascais`.

```
head(holidays, 3) #a quick inspection of the new data set: holidays.

##    algarve cascais
## 1  1800    1745
## 2  1980    2210
## 3  1775    2145

t.test(holidays$algarve, holidays$cascais, conf.level = 0.95)

##
## Welch Two Sample t-test
##
## data: holidays$algarve and holidays$cascais
```

```
## t = 2.1751, df = 51.413, p-value = 0.03425
## alternative hypothesis: true difference in means is not equal to 0
## 95 percent confidence interval:
##    13.20271 328.87354
## sample estimates:
## mean of x mean of y
##  2030.853 1859.815
```

Here is an explanation of the results:

1. The value of the test statistic, $t = 2.1751$, is very close to what we worked out using the six-step framework. See Example 11.2, step 5.
2. The degrees of freedom reported by R, 51.413, is clearly different from the value we used in Examples 11.1 and 11.2. An explanation for this peculiarity is provided below.
3. Related to the preceding point, the test is now named the `Welch Two Sample t-test`.
4. The *p*-value, 0.03425, is about the same as we found in Example 11.3.
5. As with the Chapter 10 examples, the alternative hypothesis is spelled out clearly. In this case, it is that the true difference in means is not equal to 0.
6. The 95% confidence interval estimate of the difference between μ_1 and μ_2 is [13, 329], and confirms what we found in Example 11.1.
7. The sample means are reported on the last line and confirm the values we used in Example 11.1.

There are three assumptions underlying the above statistical approaches to the two-sample problem: (1) both populations are normal; (2) the variances of the populations are equal; that is, $\sigma_1^2 = \sigma_2^2$; and (3) the random samples are selected separately and independently. In many sampling situations, however, it is neither practical nor even feasible to ensure that these conditions are met. In that case, do these methods yield reliable estimates? Are these methods *robust* in the face of violations of the requirements behind their use?

When we cannot be sure that the population variances are equal, the above approach usually works well. Note that most of the findings from the R analysis conform with the results found using the six-step hypothesis-testing framework.

However, in those situations where we have reason to believe that the population variances are equal, we modify the test slightly. (This can happen, for example, when we conduct an experiment in which subjects are randomly assigned to different treatments for the purpose of estimating and comparing the effect of each treatment.) The R function we use is the same as above except that we include an additional argument, `var.equal = TRUE`.

```
t.test(holidays$algarve, holidays$cascais, conf.level = 0.95,
       var.equal = TRUE)

##
## Two Sample t-test
##
## data: holidays$algarve and holidays$cascais
```

```
## t = 2.2142, df = 59, p-value = 0.03069
## alternative hypothesis: true difference in means is not equal to 0
## 95 percent confidence interval:
##    16.46938 325.60688
## sample estimates:
## mean of x mean of y
##  2030.853 1859.815
```

Note the difference in the results produced by inclusion of this argument:

1 The test is now named "two-sample *t*-test," not "Welch two-sample *t*-test."
2 The value of the test statistic has increased to $t = 2.2142$, while the *p*-value has fallen to 0.03069. These are not major changes, but they suggest that in assuming equal population variances, we have more precision in our estimates than is justified.
3 The value reported for degrees of freedom now conforms with what we used in the six-step framework (see Examples 11.1 and 11.2).
4 The 95% confidence interval estimate has narrowed to [16, 326] from [13, 329].

When there is no reason to assume the population variances are equal, the Welch test—also known as Welch's unequal variances *t*-test—is the preferred procedure for testing the difference between μ_1 and μ_2. Both procedures typically produce similar results, except in those situations where both the variances and the sample sizes vary greatly from one another. Finally, note that the Welch test in R is the default, while conducting the test under the assumption that the variances are equal requires the inclusion of the argument `var.equal =TRUE` in the `t.test()` function. Strictly speaking, when we wish to err on the conservative side, it is safer to use the Welch test because it does not assume that the population variances are equal.

11.2 THE DIFFERENCE BETWEEN μ_1 AND μ_2: PAIRED SAMPLES

We now build on the material in Section 11.1 by extending the methods of interval estimation and hypothesis testing to the case of paired samples. To understand the distinction between independent and paired samples, however, let us first briefly reconsider the three assumptions underlying the above statistical approaches to the two independent-sample problem: (1) both populations are normal; (2) the variances of the populations are equal; and (3) the random samples are selected separately and independently. In some cases, however, we need to estimate the difference between μ_1 and μ_2 when the two samples are not independent but are *paired*. When we say that the samples are paired, we mean that there are two measurements on the same observation—such as the same city, the same person, the same activity, and so on. To clarify this distinction further, consider the following example.

Example 11.5. Many high schools attempt to prepare their university-bound students for the Scholastic Aptitude Test (SAT) with Saturday test-preparation classes in which students take timed practice examinations in the hope of boosting self-confidence, improving accuracy, and reducing the time taken to complete the test modules. Most students find sitting for the SAT a stressful experience, since a strong result is considered an important element of a successful application for admission to the more selective universities. The idea behind the test-preparation classes is that practice makes perfect and so some students take the practice exams every single Saturday morning of the academic year, which normally commences the first week of September. The basic SAT itself typically consists of two components, one testing verbal ability, the other testing competence in mathematics.

At one school, the superintendent is considering adopting the latest cutting-edge test-preparation software to assist students as they get ready for their SATs. However, before she purchases it for her school she wants to know if the new software really makes a difference in how the students perform on the mathematics section of the SAT. The new software provides immediate feedback on a student's correct versus incorrect answers as well as helpful suggestions on incorrect answers. The current test-preparation software, in use for 10 years, provides only the correct answers at the end of the session and is in no way interactive. Before making a final decision, the superintendent's specific question is this: are students who drill using the new test-preparation software able to complete a 30-question mathematics practice exam in less time than when they prepare using the older software?

To answer this question, the superintendent asks her assistant to obtain an estimate of the difference between (a) the mean time μ_1 students take to complete a 30-question practice exam after preparing with the current software and (b) the mean time μ_2 students require to finish a nearly identical 30-question practice exam after preparing with the new software. How might this be done?

Consider the following contrasting data-collection designs for estimating the difference between the means, $\mu_1 - \mu_2$, one using independent samples, the other using paired samples.

1 **Independent samples.** We used this design in Section 11.1 when we worked through the Portuguese holiday rental example. Applied in this case, however, we would select one random sample of n_1 students who would prepare for the practice exam using the old software, and a second (different) random sample of n_2 students who would prepare for the same practice exam using the new software. The estimate of the difference between the means $\mu_1 - \mu_2$ is found the same way it was in Section 11.1.

2 **Paired samples.** A single random sample of students is chosen, and each student rehearses for the practice exam, first with one software and then (one week later) with the other. In other words, each student is now measured twice, where each measurement consists of the time (in minutes) taken to complete the 30-question practice exam. The order is randomized as to which test-preparation software is used, from one student to the next, with half the students using the old software first and the new software second, and the other half of students using the new software first and the old software second. The same exam (apart from slightly different numerical values) is used on both measurements.

In this instance, suppose a sample of $n = 20$ students is selected randomly from the population of all students who are preparing for the SAT. Of this sample, 10 are assigned randomly to the group that uses the old software first, the new software second; the remaining 10 use the new software first, then the old software. The first measurements are taken on the first Saturday of the new school year, September 1, 2012; the second measurements on the second Saturday, September 8. After all 20 students have taken both exams, the data consist of 20 measurements on t_1 and t_2, where we define t_1 as the time required to complete the exam following the use of the old software; and t_2 as the time required to finish the exam following the use of the new software. Thus, the sample statistic $D = t_1 - t_2$ is used to estimate the population mean difference $\mu_1 - \mu_2$. Figure 11.1 depicts the paired-sample data-collection design.

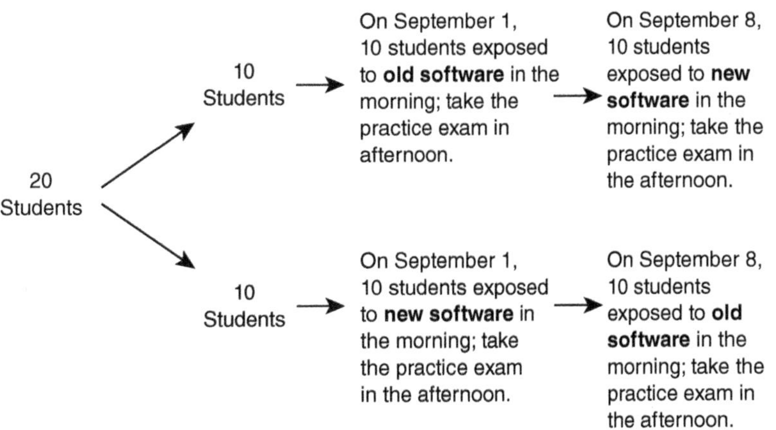

Figure 11.1 The paired-sample data-collection design

Because we cannot be sure whether the new method helps or hurts students in terms of the time they take to complete the practice exam, the null hypothesis is $H_0 : \mu_1 - \mu_2 = 0$ and the alternative is $H_a : \mu_1 - \mu_2 \neq 0$. However, since we can express the difference in means as $D = t_1 - t_2$, it is convenient to restate the hypotheses as $H_0 : \mu_D = 0$ and $H_a : \mu_D \neq 0$, where μ_D is population mean of D. We also use the one-sample hypothesis-testing approach described in Section 10.4. If H_0 is rejected, then we conclude that the mean times differ, and the superintendent should prefer the test-preparation software associated with the shortest mean time. Table 11.2 reports the findings, including D in the right-hand column.

Table 11.2 Time (in minutes) taken by 20 students to complete two practice exams

Student	t_1 in minutes	t_2 in minutes	$D = t_1 - t_2$
1	60	58	2
2	52	48	4
3	41	43	-2
4	58	54	4
5	62	59	3

6	58	53	5
7	54	50	4
8	64	61	3
9	67	64	3
10	64	63	1
11	72	69	3
12	53	51	2
13	51	49	2
14	58	56	2
15	57	58	–1
16	36	39	–3
17	45	41	4
18	53	48	5
19	55	51	4
20	57	55	2

We now use the six-step hypothesis-testing framework to test the null hypothesis that the mean time taken to complete the practice exam is the same whether students use the new or old software. The level of significance is $\alpha = 0.05$. Note that the standard deviation of D (needed in step 3 below) is $s = 2.183$.

1 Determine the null hypothesis in statistical terms.

$H_0 : \mu_D = 0$

2 Determine the alternative hypothesis in statistical terms.

$H_a : \mu_D \neq 0$

3 Set the level of significance α and decide on the sample size n.

$n = 20$ and $\alpha = 0.05$

Assuming H_0 is true, $\overline{D}$ has a t-distribution with $df = n - 1 = 19$, a mean of $E(\overline{D})$ $\mu_D = 0$, and a standard deviation of

$$s_{\overline{D}} = \frac{s}{\sqrt{n}} = \frac{2.183}{\sqrt{20}} = 0.488134.$$

4 Use α to specify the rejection region *RR*.
The rejection region is

$$RR: t \geq 2.093 \text{ and } t \leq -2.093,$$

where

$$t = \frac{\overline{D} - \mu_D}{s_{\overline{D}}},$$

that is, reject H_0 if $t \leq -t_{\alpha/2,n-1} = -t_{0.025,19} = -2.093$ or $t \geq t_{\alpha/2,n-1} = t_{0.025,19} = 2.093$.

```
qt(0.025, 19)
## [1] -2.093024

qt(0.025, 19, lower.tail = FALSE)
## [1] 2.093024
```

The value of t that cuts off an area of 0.025 in the upper tail is $t = -2.093$; the value of t that cuts off an area of 0.025 in the lower tail is $t = -2.093$. If $\overline{D}$ transforms into a value of t that is greater than 2.093, or less than −2.093, reject H_0 and accept H_a; if t falls in the region from −2.093 to 2.093, do not reject H_0.

5 Collect the data and calculate the test statistic.
Since the sample statistics are $\overline{D} = 2.35$ (the mean of the right-hand column values of Table 11.2) and $s_{\overline{D}} = 0.488134$ (see step 3 above), we have

$$t = \frac{\overline{D} - \mu_D}{s_{\overline{D}}} = \frac{\overline{D} - 0}{0.488134} = \frac{2.35 - 0}{0.488134} = \frac{2.35}{0.488134} = 4.814.$$

6 Use the value of the test statistic and rejection region *RR* to decide whether to reject H_0.
Recall that the rejection region is $RR: t \geq 2.093$ and $t \leq -2.093$. Since $t = 4.814 > 2.093$, we reject H_0. When students prepare using the new software, the time they need to complete the practice exam is less than it is when they prepare using the old software.

Example 11.6. (1) What is the p-value? (2) Compare the p-value with α.

1 Because *RR* lies in both the upper and lower tails of the t-distribution, the p-value is the probability that t is greater than 4.814 plus the probability that t is less than −4.814. Thus, the p-value is

$$p(t \geq 4.814) + p(t \leq -4.814) = 0.0001206.$$

```
pt(4.814, 19, lower.tail = FALSE) + pt(-4.814, 19)
## [1] 0.0001206086
```

2 Since $p = 0.0001206$ and $\alpha = 0.05$, $p \leq \alpha$, and we reject H_0.

Example 11.7. Use the `t.test()` function to conduct the hypothesis test. The data set `cad` is on the website; the two variable names are `old` and `new`. The null hypothesis is $H_0: \mu_D = 0$.

(Recall that for the two-tail test involving `t.test()`, the argument `alternative =` must be omitted.) Finally, when the data consist of observations that are made up of paired samples (and not independent samples) we must include `paired = TRUE` as a fourth argument. If this argument is omitted, the analysis proceeds as if the data consist of independent samples.

```
head(cad, 3) #a quick inspection of the new data set: cad.

##      old    new
## 1    60     58
## 2    52     48
## 3    41     43

t.test(cad$old, cad$new, conf.level = 0.95, paired = TRUE)

##
## Paired t-test
##
## data: cad$old and cad$new
## t = 4.8141, df = 19, p-value = 0.0001206
## alternative hypothesis: true difference in means is not equal to 0
## 95 percent confidence interval:
##  1.328292 3.371708
## sample estimates:
## mean of the differences
##                     2.35
```

Below is an explanation of the results:

1 The test is called "paired *t*-test."
2 The value of the test statistic is $t = 4.8141$, the same as that found in step 5 above.
3 The *p*-value is 0.0001206, confirming what we found in Example 11.6.
4 The alternative hypothesis is that the "true difference in means is not equal to 0."
5 The 95% confidence interval estimate of the *difference* in means is approximately [1.33, 3.37].
6 The mean of the *differences* is 2.35.

Thus, based on this sample of 20 students, we conclude that the two exam-preparation software methods are not the same in terms of the time students take to complete a practice examination. Moreover, we can conclude that when students prepare using the new software, they finish the practice exam sooner by between 1.33 and 3.37 minutes—valuable time which allows students to review their exam before submission.

Since there are no statistical methods that test whether the data are paired, a decision about whether data are independent or paired requires that we understand how the data are collected in the first place. In this case, we know the data are in no way independent because the samples consist of two measurements on the same person. Since the measurements are not independent, we cannot use either the Welch two-sample *t*-test or the equal-variance two-sample *t*-test, as we did in Section 11.1. When the samples are paired, the paired *t*-test is the preferred (even required) test.

To specify that we want a paired test, we must remember to include the argument `paired = TRUE` in the `t.test()` function.

In the case of paired samples, many external sources of variation are controlled, resulting in more precise and efficient statistical estimates. To see why, consider the possible sources of variation that might account for test-time differences had we instead used independent samples as the data collection design. If one group of students uses only the old software, and another, independently selected group of students uses only the new software, there would be many uncontrolled sources of variation besides new versus old software that might account for the variation in test times such as the differences in student motivation, interest, and aptitude. But with paired samples, there is no variation between measurements based on any of these qualities since they are taken on the same person.

From a practical point of view, consider the results of the Welch two-sample *t*-test when applied to the same data when the pairing is not considered.

```
t.test(cad$old, cad$new, conf.level = 0.95)

##
## Welch Two Sample t-test
##
## data: cad$old and cad$new
## t = 0.90904, df = 37.713, p-value = 0.3691
## alternative hypothesis: true difference in means is not equal to 0
## 95 percent confidence interval:
##  -2.884681 7.584681
## sample estimates:
## mean of x mean of y
##     55.85     53.50
```

When using the independent-sample *t*-test, we note that the difference in times is no longer significant. Not only is the *p*-value of 0.3691 much greater than $\alpha = 0.05$; the confidence interval estimate of the difference is now much wider and even includes zero, [–2.88, 7.58]. For this reason we normally prefer using a paired-sample design whenever possible. Clearly, however, this is not always practicable (for reasons of expense, time, or effort) or even possible. For example, we would not be able to design a paired data-collection method in the case of Example 11.1 where we want an estimate of the difference between apartment rents in Cascais and the Algarve area of Portugal. In that case, an independent-sample design is the best we can do.

Example 11.8. The coach of a university's track and field team wants to estimate the mean difference in winning marathon times between men and women. Assuming that the winning times from the London Marathon form a representative sample of the population of all winning marathon times, find the 99% confidence interval estimate of the mean difference in winning times for men and women marathoners. The data set `londontimes` can be found on the website and includes the times (rounded to the closest minute) for men and women winners for the years 1990–2015; the variable names are `Women` and `Men`. Note that this can be looked at as a paired-sample design.

```
options(scipen = 999)
head(londontimes, 3) #quick inspection of the new data set: londontimes.

##      Year   Women   Men
## 1    1990   147     130
## 2    1991   146     129
## 3    1992   150     130

t.test(londontimes$Women, londontimes$Men, paired = TRUE,
       conf.level = 0.99)

##
## Paired t-test
##
## data: londontimes$Women and londontimes$Men
## t = 24.479, df = 25, p-value < 0.00000000000000022
## alternative hypothesis: true difference in means is not equal to 0
## 99 percent confidence interval:
##  14.41665 18.12181
## sample estimates:
## mean of the differences
##              16.26923
```

Based on the sample of London winners, we can be 99% confident that the mean winning marathon time for men is between 14.42 and 18.12 minutes faster than the mean winning marathon time for women.

11.3 THE DIFFERENCE BETWEEN p_1 AND p_2: INDEPENDENT SAMPLES

The mechanics of confidence interval estimation and hypothesis testing about $p_1 - p_2$ are not greatly different from those concerning $\mu_1 - \mu_2$. When we estimate the difference between p_1 and p_2, we select one random sample of size n_1 from one population and an (independent) random sample of size n_2 from another population.

The Confidence Interval Estimate of $p_1 - p_2$

The parameter of interest is estimated by the statistic $\bar{p}_1 - \bar{p}_2$, where $\bar{p}_1$ and $\bar{p}_2$ are obtained from independent random samples of size n_1 and n_2, respectively. Like other sample statistics, $\bar{p}_1 - \bar{p}_2$ has a sampling distribution: the expected value of the sampling distribution is $E(\bar{p}_1 - \bar{p}_2) = p_1 - p_2$

while the standard error is $s_{\bar{p}_1-\bar{p}_2} = \sqrt{\bar{p}_1(1-\bar{p}_1)/n_1 + \bar{p}_2(1-\bar{p}_2)/n_2}$. When contructing a confidence interval, we may use the standard normal z value as long as n_1p_1, $n_1(1-p_1)$, n_2p_2, and $n_2(1-p_2)$ all exceed 5 because, in this case, the shape of the distribution of $\bar{p}_1 - \bar{p}_2$ approaches the normal. Since the general form of an interval estimate is point estimate ± margin of error, when estimating the difference between p_1 and p_2, we can use

$$(\bar{p}_1 - \bar{p}_2) \pm z_{\alpha/2}\sqrt{\frac{\bar{p}_1(1-\bar{p}_1)}{n_1} + \frac{\bar{p}_2(1-\bar{p}_2)}{n_2}},$$

where the margin of error is the product of the z value and the standard error.

Example 11.9. After the 2012 US Presidential election in which Barack Obama was reelected for his second term in office, there was considerable discussion about the "gender gap" that existed between male and female voters in terms of their choice of candidate. In particular, women seemed to vote disproportionately for candidates who are Democrats, such as President Obama, while men voted much more often for candidates who are Republicans, such as Mitt Romney. Many polling organizations explored this issue after the election, among them some of the most respected social scientists and survey groups. Gallup conducted a poll of voting behavior among $n = 2551$ voters. The results of their findings, based on exit-poll interviews conducted outside voting stations, are reported in Table 11.3.

To estimate the difference between the proportion of women and men who voted for President Obama in the 2012 US election, we construct a 95% confidence interval estimate. Note that the proportion of the sample of women who voted for Obama was $\bar{p}_1 = 749/1337 = 0.5602$, while the proportion of the sample of men who voted for Obama was only $\bar{p}_2 = 558/1214 = 0.4596$.

Table 11.3 Exit poll of men and women voters: Obama versus Romney, 2012

	Men	Women	Totals
Obama	558	749	1307
Romney	656	588	1244
Totals	1214	1337	2551

To construct the confidence interval estimate, we use the above expression:

$$(\bar{p}_1 - \bar{p}_2) \pm z_{\alpha/2}\sqrt{\frac{\bar{p}_1(1-\bar{p}_1)}{n_1} + \frac{\bar{p}_2(1-\bar{p}_2)}{n_2}}$$

$$= (0.5602 - 0.4596) \pm 1.96\sqrt{\frac{0.5602 \times 0.4398}{1337} + \frac{0.4596 \times 0.5404}{1214}}$$

$$= 0.1006 \pm 0.0387 \text{ or } [0.0619, 0.1393].$$

```
qnorm(0.025, lower.tail = FALSE)
## [1] 1.959964
```

The point estimate of the difference between the proportions of women and men who voted for Obama in 2012 is 0.1006. The 95% interval estimate of the difference between p_1 and p_2 is found by adding and subtracting the margin of error of 0.0387: 0.1006 – 0.0387 = 0.0619, and 0.1006 + 0.0387 = 0.1393. We can say with 95% confidence that the difference in the proportion of women who voted for Obama and the proportion of men who voted for him was between 6.19% and 13.93%.

A Two-Sample Hypothesis Test about $p_1 - p_2$

Although the test of $p_1 - p_2$ has lower- and upper-tail analogs similar to those described in Definitions 11.2 and 11.3, we do not consider them here but instead illustrate the two-tail test. The hypothesis test of the difference between two population proportions, p_1 and p_2, is one for which the rejection region falls in both the lower and upper tails of the sampling distribution of $\bar{p}_1 - \bar{p}_2$. In the expressions below, and similar to those set out in Definition 11.1, δ is the hypothesized difference between p_1 and p_2. When $\delta_0 = 0$, H_0 states that there is no difference between the two population proportions, while H_a asserts that there is a difference, either positive or negative. Here they are:

$$H_0 : p_1 - p_2 = \delta_0,$$

$$H_a : p_1 - p_2 \neq \delta_0.$$

Example 11.10. Use the six-step framework to test the null hypothesis that the proportion of women and men voting for Barack Obama in the 2012 election is the same. In line with the interval estimation done in Example 11.9, we set the level of significance at $\alpha = 0.05$. Remember that in the two-tail test, $\delta_0 = 0$.

1 Determine the null hypothesis in statistical terms.

$$H_0 : p_1 - p_2 = 0$$

2 Determine the alternative hypothesis in statistical terms.

$$H_a : p_1 - p_2 \neq 0$$

3 Set the level of significance α and decide on the sample size n.

$\alpha = 0.05$, $n_1 = 1337$, $n_2 = 1214$

4 Use α to specify the rejection region RR.
The rejection region is

$$RR : z \geq 1.96 \text{ and } z \leq -1.96,$$

where

$$z = \frac{(\bar{p}_1 - \bar{p}_2) - \delta_0}{\sqrt{\bar{p}_1(1-\bar{p}_1) / n_1 + \bar{p}_2(1-\bar{p}_2) / n_2}}.$$

```
qnorm(0.025, lower.tail = FALSE)
## [1] 1.959964
```

The expression for the test statistic z collapses to a simpler form for two reasons. First, since $\delta_0 = 0$, the numerator simplifies to the difference between the sample proportions, $\bar{p}_1 - \bar{p}_2$. Second, recall that when we test a hypothesis, we tentatively assume H_0 is true. In this case, since the null expresses the assumption that $p_1 = p_2$, we can set both equal to the same value p. Thus, $p_1 = p_2 = p$, and the test statistic simplifies to

$$z = \frac{\bar{p}_1 - \bar{p}_2}{\sqrt{p(1-p)/n_1 + p(1-p)/n_2}} = \frac{\bar{p}_1 - \bar{p}_2}{\sqrt{p(1-p)(1/n_1 + 1/n_2)}}.$$

A question remains as to what we use for p, the value of the population proportion p under the assumption of the null hypothesis. If $H_0 : p_1 - p_2 = 0$ is true, then the proportion of women and men voters who supported Obama is the same. Since 749 of 1337 women (or 0.5602) and 558 of 1214 men (or 0.4596) voted for Obama, we can estimate that proportion by pooling the counts of both groups and combining into one value. A pooled estimate of p can be found in the following way:

$$p = \frac{n_1\bar{p}_1 + n_2\bar{p}_2}{n_1 + n_2} = \frac{1337 \times 0.5602 + 1214 \times 0.4596}{1337 + 1214} = 0.5123.$$

That is, the overall proportion of voters who supported Obama is 0.5123.

5 Collect the data and calculate the test statistic.
We specify each piece of the expression for z before assembling: $\bar{p}_1 = 749/1337 = 0.5602$, $\bar{p}_2 = 558/1214 = 0.4596$, $n_1 = 1337$, $n_2 = 1214$, and $p = 0.5123$. Then

$$\begin{aligned} z &= \frac{\bar{p}_1 - \bar{p}_2}{\sqrt{p(1-\bar{p})(1/n_1 + 1/n_2)}} \\ &= \frac{0.5602 - 0.4596}{\sqrt{0.5123 \times 0.4877(1/1337 + 1/1214)}} \\ &= \frac{0.1006}{\sqrt{0.5123 \times 0.4877 \times 0.0016}} = \frac{0.1006}{0.0198} = 5.0753. \end{aligned}$$

6. Use the test statistic and RR to decide whether to reject H_0.
Recall that the rejection region is $RR : z \geq 1.96$ or $z \leq -1.96$. Since $z = 5.0753 > 1.96$, and thus does fall in the rejection region, we reject $H_0 : p_1 - p_2 = 0$ and accept $H_a : p_1 - p_2 \neq 0$.
Not only do we reject H_0: we also know that since the value of z is positive, women voted for Barack Obama in 2012 in greater proportions than men.

Example 11.11. (1) What is the p-value? (2) Compare the p-value with α.

1 Because the RR lies in both the upper and lower tails of the standard normal probability distribution, the p-value is the probability that z is greater than 5.0753 plus the probability that z is less than -5.0753. Thus, the p-value is

$$p(z \geq 5.0753) + p(z \leq -5.0753) = 0.000000387.$$

```
pnorm(5.0753, lower.tail = FALSE) + pnorm(-5.0753)
## [1] 0.0000003868851
```

Recall that it is necessary that we include the argument `lower.tail = FALSE` if we want the area to the right of $z = 5.0753$. If we omit this element, the result will be the area to the left of $z = 5.0753$.

2 Since $p = 0.000000387$ and $\alpha = 0.05$, $p \leq \alpha$, and we reject H_0.

Example 11.12. Use the function `prop.test()` to test H_0 against H_a.

```
options(scipen = 999)
obama <- c(749, 558)
total <- c(1337, 1214)
prop.test(obama, total, conf.level = 0.95, correct = FALSE)

##
## 2-sample test for equality of proportions without continuity
## correction
##
## data: obama out of total
## X-squared = 25.758, df = 1, p-value = 0.000000387
## alternative hypothesis: two.sided
## 95 percent confidence interval:
##  0.06192213 0.13922160
## sample estimates:
##    prop 1    prop 2
## 0.5602094 0.4596376
```

Since the function `prop.test()` is applied in a new context, some explanation of the arguments may be helpful.

1 When the result of our statistical analysis includes very small (or large) numbers, R normally reports those values in the form of scientific notation. If we would like to disable this type of display, we can enter `options(scipen = 999)` as the first line of code. In this example, R normally reports `p-value = 3.87e-07`, but by including this element on line 1, it is reported instead as 0.000000387. The advantage of the latter form is that it allows more direct comparison to α and to the Example 11.11 answers without having to visually convert from scientific to standard notation.

2 Use the concatenate function `c()` to create the vectors `obama` and `total` for inclusion as arguments in the function `prop.test()`. In this instance, `obama` contains the number of Obama voters among both women (749) and men (558); and `total` contains both the total number of women (1337) and total number of men (1214) included in the sample.

3 The function `prop.test()` includes the following arguments: (a) `obama` (the number of women and men, respectively, who voted for Obama); (b) `total` (the number of women and men, respectively, in the sample); (c) `conf.level = 0.95` specifies the significance level at $\alpha = 0.05$; and (d) `correct = FALSE` disables the application of the Yates correction for continuity, an element whose inclusion is rarely appropriate when the sample sizes are sufficiently large.

The entry order is important for both `obama` and `total`. Note that when comparing lines 2 and 3 of the R block above, it is possible to recover the structure of Table 11.3: of 1337 women, 749 (or 56.02%) voted for Obama, whereas of 1214 men, 558 (or 45.96%) voted for Obama. Note also that when using `prop.test()` to test the difference between p_1 and p_2, the original data set is unnecessary as long as we have the counts of men and women Obama voters as well as the total count for each category. However, if we must work with the data set, the frequencies can be found using the `table()` function. Consult the methods of Chapter 2, if necessary.

Finally, we call attention to several items reported in the R block: (a) the procedure is named `2-sample test for equality of proportions without continuity correction`; (b) the p-value is 0.000000387, the same value we found in Example 11.11; (c) H_a is reported as `alternative hypothesis: two.sided`; (d) the 95% confidence interval of the difference between p_1 and p_2 is reported as [0.06192213, 0.13922160], conforming with what we found in Example 11.9; and (e) the sample estimates (i.e., the sample proportions) are 0.5602094 and 0.4596376, for women and men respectively. Note that the test statistic is reported not as $z = 5.0753$ (see step 5, Example 11.10) but as `X-squared = 25.758`. The reason for this is that the `prop.test()` function bases the p-value calculation on a chi-square statistic x^2 which itself is related to the square of the z statistic. Although we do not discuss this further here, we point out that if $z = 5.0753$, then $z^2 = 5.0753^2 = \chi^2 = 25.758$.

SUMMARY

In Chapter 11, we extend the inferential and estimation methodologies involving tests of a single parameter to those concerning the differences between two population means, μ_1 and μ_2, and two population proportions, p_1 and p_2. In this connection, we develop this discussion by describing the confidence interval estimation procedure when we have two random samples, one from each of two populations, and by introducing the forms of hypothesis tests to be used in this situation. In each instance, we introduce this material with a review of the properties of the sampling distributions of $\bar{x}_1 - \bar{x}_2$ and $\bar{p}_1 - \bar{p}_2$, respectively.

We begin with a test of the difference between population means in the case of two independent random samples. When we estimate the difference between μ_1 and μ_2, we select one random sample of size n_1 from a population with mean μ_1 and standard deviation σ_1, and a second (independent) random sample of size n_2 from another population with mean n_2 and standard deviation σ_2. Since σ_1 and σ_2 are unknown, we use s_1 and s_2 as estimates instead. To obtain the confidence interval estimate of $\mu_1 - \mu_2$, we use the form: $(\bar{x}_1 - \bar{x}_2) \pm t_{\alpha/2, n_1+n_2-2}\sqrt{\frac{s_1^2}{n_1} + \frac{s_2^2}{n_2}}$.

When testing the hypothesis that the population means are equal, $\mu_1 - \mu_2$, the null hypothesis is $H_0 : \mu_1 - \mu_2 = 0$, and the alternative hypothesis $H_a : \mu_1 - \mu_2 \neq 0$. In those situations where we believe that the population variances are equal (i.e., when $\sigma_1^2 = \sigma_2^2$) we should take advantage of this condition by including the argument `var.equal = TRUE` in the function `t.test()`. Population variances are sometimes equal when we conduct an experiment in which subjects are assigned randomly to different treatments for the purpose of estimating and comparing the effect of each treatment. In this case, the standard error is smaller, the test statistic t is larger, the p-value returns a more significant value, and the confidence interval estimate is narrower.

In those cases where the random samples are not independent but paired, the test of the difference between μ_1 and μ_2 reverts back to a simple one-sample test. Paired samples are also known as matched samples, and are found when there are two measurements on the same observation (e.g., on the same person, the same city, or the same process). The advantage of using paired rather than independent samples lies in the fact that many external sources of variation are controlled because both measurements are taken on the same element. Even so, it is not always possible to work with paired samples, and when it is not we often resort to the earlier methods of testing on independent samples.

The approaches to testing the difference between p_1 and p_2 are similar to those used above: we select one random sample of size n_1 from one population with proportion p_1, and another random sample of size n_2 from another (independent) population with proportion p_2. (Recall that in Example 11.9, the population proportions were the proportion of women p_1 and the proportion of men p_2 who voted for President Obama in the 2012 Presidential election.) To obtain the confidence interval estimate of $p_1 - p_2$, we use the form $(\bar{p}_1 - \bar{p}_2) \pm z_{\alpha/2}\sqrt{\frac{\bar{p}_1(1-\bar{p}_1)}{n_1} + \frac{\bar{p}_2(1-\bar{p}_2)}{n_2}}$.

In the instance where we wish to test for the equality of p_1 and p_2, the null hypothesis is $H_0 : p_1 - p_2 = 0$ and the alternative $H_a : p_1 - p_2 \neq 0$. Since $p_1 = p_2 = p$ is assumed under H_0, the standard error simplifies from that used in the interval estimate above to a less complicated form employing the pooled estimate of p: $\sqrt{p(1-p)(1/n_1 + 1/n_2)}$.

In the next chapter we extend this inferential framework to hypothesis tests and interval estimates in the context of simple and multiple regression. As we will see, regression is one of the most versatile and powerful of the basic tools of statistical analysis, and in many ways it is the pay-off for all we have learned up to this point.

definitions

Independent Random Samples
Independent random samples are those that are selected independently of one another. The elements that are selected for one sample do not affect, nor are affected by, the selection of elements of the other sample.

Lower-Tail Test of the Difference between Two Population Means A lower-tail test of the difference between two population means, μ_1 and μ_2, is one in which the rejection region falls in the lower tail of the sampling distribution of $\bar{x}_1 - \bar{x}_2$. H_0 expresses the view that $\mu_1 \geq \mu_2$, while H_a states that $\mu_1 < \mu_2$.

Lower-Tail Test of the Difference between Two Population Proportions A lower-tail test of the difference between two population proportions, p_1 and p_2, is one in which the rejection region falls in the lower tail of the sampling distribution of $\bar{p}_1 - \bar{p}_2$. H_0 expresses the view that $p_1 \geq p_2$, while H_a states that $p_1 < p_2$.

One-Tail Test A one-tail test of the difference between two population means, μ_1 and μ_2, is a test where the rejection region falls either in the upper tail or lower tail (but not both) of the sampling distribution of $\bar{x}_1 - \bar{x}_2$. In a similar vein, a one-tail test of the difference between two population proportions, p_1 and p_2, is a test where the rejection

(Continued)

(Continued)

region falls either in the upper tail or lower tail of the sampling distribution of $\bar{p}_1 - \bar{p}_2$. Lower-tail and upper-tail tests are always one-tail tests.

Paired Samples Paired (or matched) samples are those for which the two measurements are taken on the same or similar elements. A common form of paired samples is when the same person is measured twice, *before* and *after* some type of treatment. Another example of paired sampling may be done by grouping together elements (e.g., people, organizations, locations) into homogeneous clusters and comparing them with other clusters that are different.

Pooled Estimator of *p* Used in the hypothesis test about the difference between two population proportions, the pooled estimator is found by taking a weighted average of the two sample proportions.

Two-Tail Test A two-tail test of the difference between two population means, μ_1 and μ_2, is one in which the rejection region falls in both the lower and upper tails of the sampling distribution of $\bar{x}_1 - \bar{x}_2$. Similarly, a two-tail test of the difference between two population proportions, p_1 and p_2, is one in which the rejection region falls in both the lower and upper tails of the sampling distribution of $\bar{p}_1 - \bar{p}_2$.

Upper-Tail Test of the Difference between Two Population Means An upper-tail test of the difference between two population means, μ_1 and μ_2, is one in which the rejection region falls in the upper tail of the sampling distribution of $\bar{x}_1 - \bar{x}_2$. H_0 expresses the view that $\mu_1 \leq \mu_2$, while H_a states that $\mu_1 > \mu_2$.

Upper-Tail Test of the Difference between Two Population Proportions An upper-tail test of the difference between two population proportions, p_1 and p_2, is one in which the rejection region falls in the upper tail of the sampling distribution of $\bar{p}_1 - \bar{p}_2$. H_0 expresses the view that $p_1 \leq p_2$, while H_a states that $p_1 > p_2$.

formulae

Confidence Interval Estimate of the Difference between μ_1 and μ_2

$$(\bar{x}_1 - \bar{x}_2) \pm t_{\alpha/2, n_1+n_2-2}\sqrt{\frac{s_1^2}{n_1} + \frac{s_2^2}{n_2}}$$

Confidence Interval Estimate of the Difference between p_1 and p_2

$$(\bar{p}_1 - \bar{p}_2) \pm z_{\alpha/2}\sqrt{\frac{\bar{p}_1(1-\bar{p}_1)}{n_1} + \frac{\bar{p}_2(1-\bar{p}_2)}{n_2}}$$

Expected Value of the Sampling Distribution of $\bar{x}_1 - \bar{x}_2$

$$E(\bar{x}_1 - \bar{x}_2) = \mu_1 - \mu_2$$

Expected Value of the Sampling Distribution of $\bar{p}_1 - \bar{p}_2$

$$E(\bar{p}_1 - \bar{p}_2) = p_1 - p_2$$

Point Estimate of the Difference between Two Population Means

$$\bar{x}_1 - \bar{x}_2$$

Point Estimate of the Difference between Two Population Proportions

$$\bar{p}_1 - \bar{p}_2$$

Pooled Estimate of p **for Hypothesis Test** $H_0: p_1 - p_2 = 0$

$$p = \frac{n_1\bar{p}_1 + n_2\bar{p}_2}{n_1 + n_2}$$

Standard Error of $\bar{x}_1 - \bar{x}_2$

$$S_{\bar{x}_1 - \bar{x}_2} = \sqrt{\frac{S_1^2}{n_1} + \frac{S_2^2}{n_2}}$$

Standard Error of $\bar{p}_1 - \bar{p}_2$

$$s_{\bar{p}_1 - \bar{p}_2} = \sqrt{\frac{\bar{p}_1(1-\bar{p}_1)}{n_1} + \frac{\bar{p}_2(1-\bar{p}_2)}{n_2}}$$

Standard Error of $\bar{p}_1 - \bar{p}_2$ **under Assumption** $p_1 = p_2 = p$

$$s_{\bar{p}_1 - \bar{p}_2} = \sqrt{p(1-p)\left(\frac{1}{n_1} + \frac{1}{n_2}\right)}$$

Test Statistic for Hypothesis Test about $\mu_1 - \mu_2$**: Independent Samples**

$$t = \frac{\bar{x}_1 - \bar{x}_2}{\sqrt{s_1^2/n_1 + s_2^2/n_2}}$$

Test Statistic for Hypothesis Test about $\mu_1 - \mu_2$**: Paired Samples**

$$t = \frac{\bar{D} - \mu_D}{s_{\bar{D}}}$$

Test Statistic for Hypothesis Test about $p_1 - p_2$ **(Assuming** $p_1 = p_2 = p$**)**

$$z = \frac{\bar{p}_1 - \bar{p}_2}{\sqrt{p(1-p)(1/n_1 + 1/n_2)}}$$

R functions

`t.test(name1, name2, conf.level = 0.95)` This function, for the Welch two-sample *t*-test, performs a two-tail hypothesis test on the difference between the means of two independent populations when the population variances are not necessarily equal. It also provides a 95% confidence interval estimate of the difference, although any level of confidence can be specified by adjusting the `conf.level =` argument.

`t.test(name1, name2, conf.level = 0.95, var.equal = TRUE)` This function for the two-sample *t*-test performs a two-tail hypothesis test on the difference between the means of two independent populations when the population variances are assumed to be equal. It also provides a 95% confidence interval estimate of the difference, although any level of confidence can be specified by adjusting the `conf.level =` argument.

`t.test(name1, name2, conf.level = 0.95, paired = TRUE)` This paired *t*-test function performs a two-tail hypothesis test on the difference between the means of two paired populations. It also provides a 95% confidence interval estimate of the difference, although any level of confidence can be specified by adjusting the `conf.level =` argument.

`prop.test(counts1, totals2, conf.level = 0.95, correct = FALSE)` Known as the two-sample test for equality of proportions without continuity correction, this function performs a two-tail hypothesis test on the difference between the proportions of two

(Continued)

(Continued)

independent populations. It also provides a 95% confidence interval estimate of the difference, although any level of confidence can be specified by adjusting the `conf.level` = argument. For direction on how to define the first two arguments, `counts1` and `totals2`, see Example 11.12.

data sets

1 `cad`
2 `holidays`
3 `londontimes`
4 `temps`

exercises

11.1 A statistics instructor is concerned that after her students perform well on the first of two major examinations in the introductory-level class, their performance appears to drop off on the second. Since this pattern appears to repeat itself across many sections of the same statistics class at her university, she wants to confirm that the downward trend in performance on the two 100-point examinations is real. To this end, she collects the examination results for a random sample of $n = 12$ students from the previous academic year. The scores on Exam 1 are: 79, 92, 81, 80, 79, 80, 78, 88, 86, 88, 77, and 93. On Exam 2, they are: 80, 75, 67, 82, 76, 71, 78, 78, 80, 77, 78, and 75. Create a data frame that organizes this data into two variables and 12 observations and use R to answer questions (b) and (c).

(a) Are these data independent or paired? Why?
(b) What is the point estimate of the difference between the two population means, $\mu_1 - \mu_2$?
(c) What is the 95% confidence interval of the difference between the two population means, $\mu_1 - \mu_2$?

11.2 A recent study of the cost of living in various US cities has found regional differences in home prices. Two of the cities considered are Dallas, Texas and Minneapolis, Minnesota. The following data have been collected in the studies for those two cities: 47 homes in Dallas are for sale for an average of $151,800, with a standard deviation of $17,457; 34 comparable homes are for sale in Minneapolis for an average of $207,100, with a standard deviation of $26,510.

(a) Are these data paired or independent? Why?
(b) Find the 95% confidence interval estimate of the difference between the mean price for a home in Minneapolis and a comparable home in Dallas.

11.3 The data set `temps` can be found on the book website. The two variable names are `Daytemp` and `Nighttemp`, and report the high (`Daytemp`) and low (`Nighttemp`) temperatures in degrees Celsius for 10 European cities. The data are displayed below. Use R to answers parts (b) and (c).

```
temps
##              City     Daytemp     Nighttemp
## 1          Athens          21     12
## 2       Barcelona          12     9
## 3          Dublin           6     1
## 4          Lisbon          15     9
## 5      Luxembourg           3     -2
## 6          Moscow           2     1
## 7          Munich           4     -2
## 8          Naples          14     11
## 9           Paris           7     -1
##         Stockholm           2     -4
10
```

(a) Are these data independent or paired? Why?
(b) What is the 90% confidence interval estimate of $\mu_1 - \mu_2$?
(c) Test $H_0 : \mu_1 - \mu_2 = 0$ against $H_a : \mu_1 - \mu_2 \neq 0$ at the $\alpha = 0.10$ level of significance.

11.4 During two recent tax years, the US Internal Revenue Service (IRS) conducted an in-house investigation of the accuracy of tax filing advice given by IRS agents to individuals who call with questions about how to handle various tax issues. During the first phase, conducted in 2013, 900 calls were placed to IRS offices for tax advice, and after reviewing the accuracy of the advice provided, the investigation found that on 82 occasions the advice was incorrect. In a follow-up investigation in 2014, 800 calls were placed and on 28 occasions the advice was incorrect. Does it appear that the IRS has successfully improved the accuracy of the advice provided by its agents from one year to the next? Use R to find the 95% confidence interval estimate of $p_1 - p_2$.

11.5 In a recent consumer confidence survey of 400 adults, 54 of 200 men and 36 of 200 women expressed agreement with the statement, "I would have trouble paying an unexpected bill of $1000 without borrowing from someone or selling something." Do men and women differ on their answer to this question? Use the six-step framework to test $H_0 : p_1 - p_2 = 0$ against $H_a : p_1 - p_2 \neq 0$ at the $\alpha = 0.05$ level of significance. What is the p-value? Use R to confirm your answers.

Simple Linear Regression

contents

learning objectives

1. Understand how regression analysis can be used to obtain an equation that estimates how two variables are related.
2. Understand the improvement in precision made possible by a regression approach over point estimation and interval estimation.
3. Know how to fit an estimated regression equation to a set of sample data based upon the least-squares method.
4. Be able to determine how good a fit is provided by the estimated regression equation.
5. Understand the assumptions necessary for statistical inference and be able to test for a significant relationship.

12.1 SIMPLE LINEAR REGRESSION: THE MODEL

In Chapter 11 we extend our discussion of statistical methods from the analysis of one variable to two variables. Among the issues considered is the estimation of the difference between two population parameters, either μ_1 and μ_2 or p_1 and p_2. In all examples, the interval estimates of—and inferences about—these differences are based on random samples of sizes n_1 and n_2 selected from two populations, either independent or paired.

We now begin our discussion of a set of procedures known as regression analysis. In this chapter we introduce simple linear regression, a method which provides an equation that describes the relationship of one variable Y to another variable x. In the next chapter, we continue the coverage to multiple regression, a procedure which results in an equation that describes the relationship of one variable Y to more than one variable $x_1, x_2, \ldots, x_n$.

As a hypothetical example of simple linear regression, suppose a prospective homebuyer is interested in purchasing a condominium apartment in Winnipeg, Canada, and wishes to understand the connection between the price (in Canadian dollars) of a property and its living area (in square feet). To explore the relationship between price and area, let us analyze a sample of 14 apartments on which there are two measurements, the price Y and the area of living space x. In this situation, we have a data set consisting of $n = 14$ pairs of data, one for each property: $(x_1,y_1), (x_2,y_2), \ldots, (x_n,y_n)$. In the Winnipeg case, the data are drawn from an estate agent website in May 2016, and consist of a random sample of 14 condominium properties priced in the \$125,000 to \$325,000 range. What simple linear regression analysis does is provide an equation expressing the relationship between Y and x, or (in this case) the relationship between price and living area. If the equation describing this relationship includes an error term ε, the most basic regression model takes the form

$$y = \beta_0 + \beta_1 x + \varepsilon,$$

where y is the dependent variable, or the variable being modeled; x is the independent variable, or the variable being used to model y; β_0 is the y-intercept, or the point at which the regression line intercepts the y-axis; β_1 is the slope of the regression line (sometimes called the regression coefficient); and ε is the error term that represents the random component of the regression model.

Definition 12.1. Dependent Variable. In the context of regression analysis, the dependent variable (often denoted by Y) is what we want to predict or explain. It is also known as the *criterion variable.*

Definition 12.2. Independent Variable. While the dependent variable is what we want to predict or explain, the independent variable (often denoted by x) is what we use to make the prediction. In the case of multiple regression (Chapter 13), there are two or more independent variables.

Definition 12.3. Simple Linear Regression Model. A general expression that specifies how the dependent variable Y is related to the independent variable x plus the error term ε.

The reason why we include the error term ε is that we do not expect the regression equation to express the relationship between price and area exactly. For one thing, the equation is calibrated on only a sample of the larger population and thus omits information about all apartments in this price range; for another, the price of an apartment is influenced by many other characteristics beyond area, such as the number of bedrooms, number of bathrooms, the proximity to public transportation, and the quality of neighborhood schools. Because of this, the price of an apartment (having a given number of square feet of area) is not something that is exactly predictable. In fact, the price has a distribution of values, and like any other distribution, it has an expected value and a standard deviation. We can express this notion with a regression equation of the form

$$E(y|x) = \mu_{y|x} = \beta_0 + \beta_1 x,$$

where $E(y|x) = \mu_{y|x}$ is the expected value of y for a given value of x, or in this case the expected price for a given number of square feet of living area. Both β_0 and β_1 are population parameters: β_0 is the y-intercept of the regression line and β_1 is the slope of that line.

Definition 12.4. Simple Linear Regression Equation. A general expression that specifies how the expected value of y, or $\mu_{y|x}$, is related to the independent variable x.

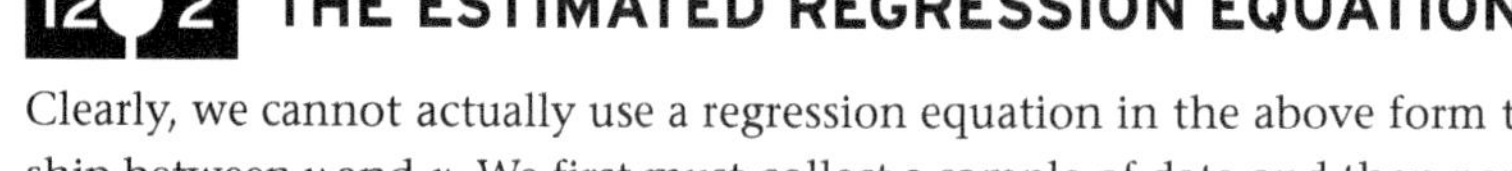

12.2 THE ESTIMATED REGRESSION EQUATION

Clearly, we cannot actually use a regression equation in the above form to describe the relationship between y and x. We first must collect a sample of data and then perform some type of statistical analysis to obtain the point estimators of both β_0 and β_1. The type of analysis we use to do this is simple linear regression. Once we replace $\mu_{y/x}$, β_0, and β_1 with $\hat{y}$, b_0, and b_1, respectively, we finally have a usable form of the estimated simple linear regression equation

$$\hat{y} = b_0 + b_1 x$$

where $\hat{y}$ is the estimator of $\mu_{y/x}$, or the mean of the dependent variable for a given level of the independent variable x; x is the independent variable; b_0 is the point estimator of the y-intercept term β_0; and b_1 is the point estimator of the population regression coefficient β_1.

Definition 12.5. Estimated Simple Linear Regression Equation. A general expression that specifies how the predicted value of the dependent variable, or $\hat{y}$, is related to the independent variable x. In this case, the estimators b_0 and b_1 (which are estimated from the sample data) replace the parameters β_0 and β_1, respectively.

The question remains as to how we might actually obtain the sample statistics b_0 and b_1 from the data described above. Our approach to this estimation problem is known as the *method of least squares* and it involves finding those values of b_0 and b_1 that minimize the difference between the actual value of the dependent variable y and the predicted value $\hat{y}$. That is, we need to know the values of b_0 and b_1 that minimize the magnitude of $y-\hat{y}$ where the estimated regression equation $\hat{y}=b_0+b_1x$ is used for prediction. It can be shown that the least-squares values of b_0 and b_1 can be found using the expressions

$$b_1=\frac{\sum(x_i-\bar{x})(y_i-\bar{y})}{\sum(x_i-\bar{x})^2}$$

and

$$b_0=\bar{y}-b_1\bar{x}.$$

Example 12.1. Table 12.1 reports and summarizes the computations required to find the point estimators of the regression equation for the Winnipeg apartment example. Note that there are

Table 12.1 Computations for the estimated regression equation: b_0 and b_1

1	2	3	4	5	6	7
Apt i	Y_i	x_i	$(y_i-\bar{y})$	$(x_i-\bar{x})$	$(x_i-\bar{x})^2$	$(y_i-\bar{y})(x_i-\bar{x})$
1	299,900	974	52,779	−93.71	8782.37	4,946,106
2	214,900	947	−32,225	−120.71	14,571.94	3,889,587
3	284,900	1065	37,779	−2.71	7.37	−102,542
4	249,900	812	2779	−255.71	65,389.80	−710,520
5	159,900	889	−87,221	−178.71	31,938.80	15,587,715
6	231,000	958	−16,121	−109.71	12,037.22	1,768,751
7	254,900	1050	7779	−17.71	313.80	−137,792
8	324,900	1403	77,779	335.29	112,416.51	26,078,044
9	199,900	834	−47,221	−233.71	54,622.37	11,036,322
10	304,900	1349	57,779	281.29	79,121.65	16,252,287
11	309,900	1668	62,779	600.29	360,342.94	37,685,080
12	269,900	1568	22,779	500.29	250,285.80	11,395,794
13	134,900	650	−112,221	−417.71	174,485.22	46,876,494
14	219,900	781	−27,221	−286.71	82,205.08	7,804,772
Totals	3,459,700	14,948	0	0	1,246,521	172,477,886

14 apartments, each of which is measured on two variables: Y is the price and x is the area. (Columns 2–3 report the price Y and the square feet of living area x; columns 4–7 provide the elements of the basic computations of b_0 and b_1.) Use Table 12.1 and the expressions for b_0 and b_1 to find the estimated regression equation.

Substituting the column 6 and 7 totals into the above expression for b_1, we have

$$b_1 = \frac{\sum(x_i - \bar{x})(y_i - \bar{y})}{\sum(x_i - \bar{x})^2} = \frac{172,477,886}{1,246,521} = 138.37,$$

and since we know $\bar{y} = 3,459,700 / 14 = 247,121.43$ and $\bar{x} = 14,948 / 14 = 1067.71$,

$$b_0 = \bar{y} - b_1\bar{x} = 247,121.43 - 138.37 \times 1067.71 = 99,384.55.$$

Plugging b_0 and b_1 into $\hat{y} = b_0 + b_1x$, the estimated regression equation is

$$\hat{y} = 99,384.55 + 138.37x$$

Figure 12.1 shows the scatter plot of the 14 data points as well as the line representing the estimated regression equation, $\hat{y} = 99,384.55 + 138.37x$.

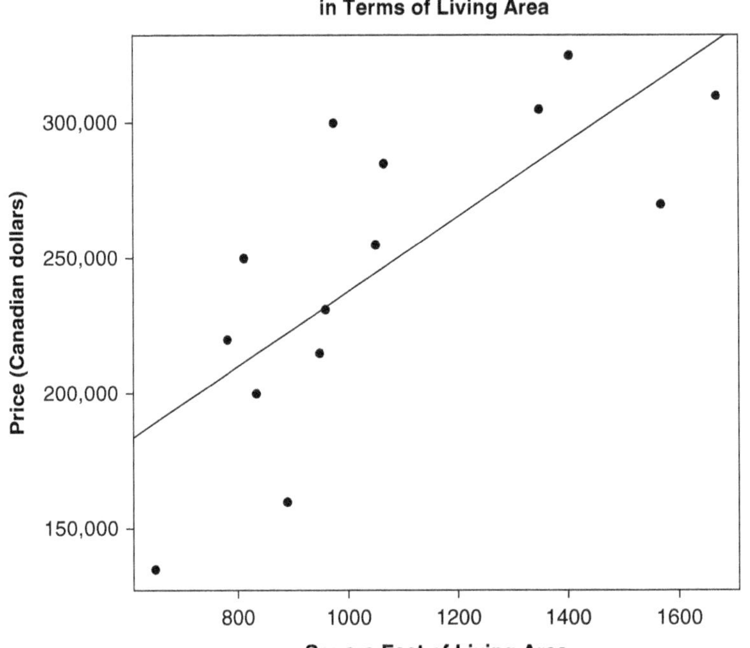

Figure 12.1 Line of the estimated regression equation for 14 apartments

Simple linear regression is often used for two different but related purposes: description and prediction. By description, we simply mean that regression can be used to confirm (or disconfirm) that two variables are linearly associated; and if they are, whether that association is positive or negative. For example, we might suspect that the price of apartments is positively associated with living area because, in general, the more square feet of space a home has, the higher the price. As the scatter plot and regression line in Figure 12.1 show, the positive association between price and living area appears to be confirmed.

In addition to description, regression can be used to predict. For example, when the prospective homebuyer wishes to predict how much she will have to pay for an apartment in Winnipeg, there are several methods she might use. In Chapter 7 we saw that the population mean can be estimated by the sample mean. Accordingly, the homebuyer might use the sample mean, $\bar{y} = \$247,121$, to predict the price she will ultimately pay for her home. But even though this is what many people who have never been exposed to statistics might use to predict home prices, we know we can do better than this.

Figure 12.2 plots the line representing the sample mean, $\bar{y} = \$247,121$, in the scatter plot from Figure 12.1 (the regression line has been removed). Observe that the mean does not do a very good job of predicting the price of a home. In fact, in only two cases does the mean *miss* the apartment price it is trying to predict by less than \$15,000; in the other instances, the prediction provided by the mean misses the mark by more than \$15,000. We see how poorly the

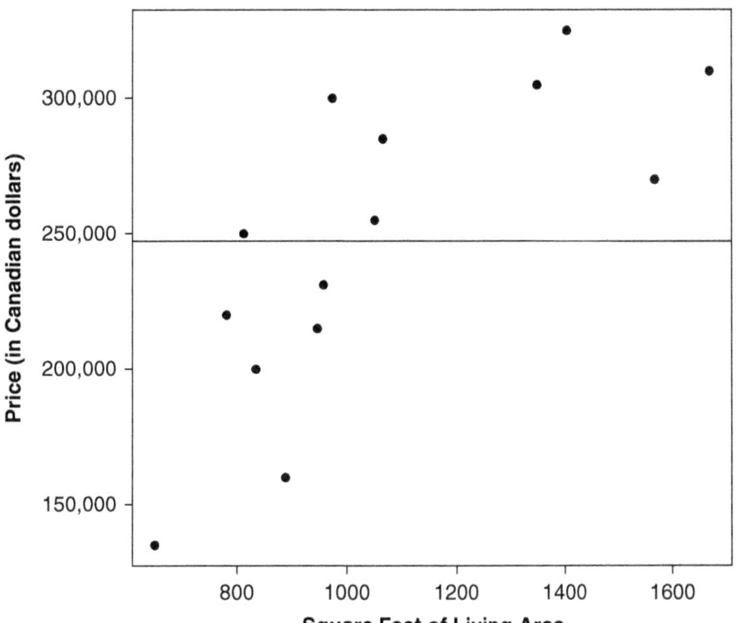

Figure 12.2 Line showing the sample mean price of 14 apartments

line representing the mean *fits* the data, especially when compared with how much better the regression line fits the data (see Figure 12.1).

We could also predict home prices more accurately than the mean by creating an interval estimate (Chapter 8) that exploits more of the information contained in the sample.

Example 12.2. Use the function `t.test()` to find the 95% confidence interval estimate of price. The data set is named `winnipeg_apt` and can be found on the website; the variable names are `price` and `sqft`.

```
t.test(winnipeg_apt$price, conf = 0.95)

##
## One Sample t-test
##
## data: winnipeg_apt$price
## t = 16.153, df = 13, p-value = 5.52e-10
## alternative hypothesis: true mean is not equal to 0
## 95 percent confidence interval:
##  214069.8 280173.0
## sample estimates:
## mean of x
##  247121.4
```

As we saw in Chapter 8, confidence interval estimates are normally preferred over point estimates like the sample mean. For one thing, when we use R to find the interval estimate, the sample mean is reported by default on the final line of the output. For another, the confidence interval estimate is provided. In this case, we can say with 95% confidence that the true population mean of price falls in the interval [$214,070, $280,173].

We are able to use simple linear regression only when we can identify some other variable that might be related in a *systematic manner* to the variable we want to predict. In the context of regression, the variable we want to predict is called the criterion or dependent variable; the variable we are using to predict is referred to as the predictor or independent variable. Once we have identified an independent variable (in this case, square feet of living area), we can make predictions about the dependent variable (the apartment price) based on our knowledge of the independent variable. And as an example of what we mean by variables that are related in a systematic manner, note that in Figure 12.1 the band of points runs from the lower left to the upper right corners of the scatter plot: more spacious amounts of living space are associated with higher prices.

Even though the terms "dependent variable" and "independent variable" imply that the independent variable *causes* the dependent variable, regression does not establish causality. Instead we say that the independent variable is *associated* with, or related to, the dependent variable. In this example, we might just as easily say that a higher price causes living area to be larger ("For what I am paying, the area better be generous!") as the other way around. Normally, regression does not deal with issues of causality but only association.

Our discussion on prediction concludes with an example.

Example 12.3. Suppose the prospective homebuyer is interested in an apartment with 1000 square feet of living area. What price might she expect to pay? Using the estimated regression equation and setting the independent variable equal to 1000, we have

$$\begin{aligned}\hat{y} &= 99{,}384.55 + 138.37x \\ &= 99{,}384.55 + 138.37 \times 1000 = 99{,}384.55 + 138{,}370 = 237{,}755.\end{aligned}$$

Thus, we predict that an apartment with 1000 square feet of living area should be priced in the neighborhood of $237,755.

In general, the regression coefficient represents the expected change in the dependent variable y when the independent variable x is changed by one unit. In this example, the regression coefficient $b_1 = 138.37$ means that we expect a 1 square-foot change in living area to be associated with a $138.37 change in price. This interpretation is valid, however, only within the range of living areas in the data, or only for those apartments having between 650 and 1668 square feet of living area. Since we have no information about homes that are either above or below that range, we cannot be sure that the regression coefficient does not have a different value outside that range.

Example 12.4. In practice, we prefer using R to conduct regression analysis. By applying the function `lm()` to the `winnipeg_apt` data set (found on the website), we are able to regress the dependent variable `price` on the independent variable `sqft`:

```
lm(price ~ sqft, data = winnipeg_apt)

##
## Call:
## lm(formula = price ~ sqft, data = winnipeg_apt)
##
## Coefficients:
## (Intercept)          sqft
##     99384.5         138.4
```

The output confirms both the coefficient and intercept term of the estimated regression equation that we have already calculated: $\hat{y} = 99{,}384.5 + 138.4x$.

When we specify the `lm()` function this way, the output is basic and straightforward. As we learn in the next section, however, we normally want to see additional analytic and diagnostic results—including, but not limited to, goodness-of-fit measures and significance tests—beyond the basic estimated regression equation. But before we consider a more complete and thorough treatment of regression analysis, we offer the following brief description of the basic elements of the `lm()` function as we use it above.

1. The function `lm()` directs R to call the regression routine. The designation `lm()` refers to "linear model."
2. The first argument, `price ~ sqft`, is referred to as the *model formula* and includes (from left to right) the dependent variable, a tilde (~), and the independent variable. We encountered the

tilde symbol earlier in this book, in Chapter 3, when using the `boxplot()` function. It can be thought of as meaning "is described by."

3 The second argument, `data = winnipeg_apt`, directs R to look in the object named `winnipeg_apt` for the variables `price` and `sqft`.

4 Finally, it is worth pointing out that this regression analysis can also be specified and executed in the following way: `lm(winnipeg_apt$price ~ winnipeg_apt$sqft)`.

```
lm(winnipeg_apt$price ~ winnipeg_apt$sqft)

##
## Call:
## lm(formula = winnipeg_apt$price ~ winnipeg_apt$sqft)
##
## Coefficients:
##       (Intercept)   winnipeg_apt$sqft
##          99384.5                138.4
```

While this eliminates the need to define a second argument, `data = winnipeg_apt`, it can be quite tedious when defining more complicated regression models (having more than one independent variable) to write out the object name for each and every variable. Because of this, we often find that the first method is the simplest and most convenient way to go.

In the next section, we extend the discussion of simple linear regression to include the concept of the goodness of fit of the regression model. Put simply, goodness of fit is measured by a statistic known as r^2, or the coefficient of determination, that provides an estimate of how well the estimated regression equation actually fits the data.

12.3 GOODNESS OF FIT: THE COEFFICIENT OF DETERMINATION, r^2

When we consider Figure 12.1, we observe that the estimated regression line does not fit the scatter plot of observations perfectly well. In fact, many observations appear to fall some distance from the line. But it is also clear that the observations seem to group more closely around the regression line (Figure 12.1) than they do around the line representing the mean (Figure 12.2). What this comparison tells us is that if we want to predict the expected price of an apartment, we can do so more accurately using the regression equation—and the information about the square feet of living area of an apartment—than using the sample mean alone, $247,121. But is there is a better way of evaluating the accuracy of the regression prediction? There is, and it is a well-known quantitative measurement called the coefficient of determination or r^2.

Definition 12.6. Coefficient of Determination, r^2. The coefficient of determination r^2 is a measure of the strength of linear association between two variables. Its value varies between 0 and 1, and it indicates the proportion of total variation in the dependent variable y that is explained by the variation in the independent variable x.

Before we discuss r^2, however, remember that one of the most important uses of simple linear regression is the prediction of a dependent variable y based on some value of x, the independent variable. But even though the estimated regression equation makes it possible to predict an expected value of y from x, we know that there is bound to be some error because other independent variables that might be used to predict y are omitted. By definition, simple linear regression involves a single independent variable.

Recall that the regression model can be expressed as $y = \beta_0 + \beta_1 x + \varepsilon$. In the discussion that follows, we refer to ε as the error term and define it as $\varepsilon = y_i - \hat{y}_i$, or the difference between the actual and predicted values of y. Why this is important should be clear: when the $y_i - \hat{y}_i$ terms are large, it is because the observations are not tightly grouped around the estimated regression line; but when the $y_i - \hat{y}_i$ values are small, the observations are grouped more closely around the line and we say that the line *fits* the data better.

An intuitive measure of the accuracy of predictions is the sum of squared errors of y_i values around the regression line. In fact, we can think of it as a measure of the *variance* of y_i around the regression line, and it is estimated from the sample data as follows:

$$s^2_{y|x} = \frac{\Sigma(y_i - \hat{y}_i)^2}{n-2}.$$

Although this expression is new, it is an easy matter to calculate its value for the Winnipeg data:

$$s^2_{y|x} = \frac{\Sigma(y_i - \hat{y}_i)^2}{n-2} = \frac{18{,}733{,}802{,}033}{12} = 1{,}561{,}150{,}169.$$

The bottom row of column 6 in Table 12.2 reports the numerator $\Sigma(y_i - \hat{y}_i)^2$ and shows how it is derived. This term is referred to as the residual sum of squares, and is denoted by $SS_{\text{res}} = \Sigma(y_i - \hat{y}_i)^2$. Note that in this case the numerator is divided by $n - 2$ since two degrees of freedom are used to calculate b_0 and b_1 for the estimated regression equation, $\hat{y} = b_0 + b_1 x$. This stands in contrast to how we calculated the sample variance around the mean (in Section 3.4) where we divided the sum of squared deviations by $n - 1$. In Figure 12.3, the vertical lines connecting the regression line to the data points provide a visual depiction of the residuals associated with each observation; the numbers situated next to the data points are the residuals, and are in fact the same values as those reported in Column 5 of Table 12.2.

Before we return to our discussion of r^2, let us briefly consider Table 12.2. Columns 1–3 of Table 12.2 are identical to columns 1–3 of Table 12.1. What is new in Table 12.2 is column 4 which reports $\hat{y}_i$, the predicted values of y_i. How are these produced? These estimates can be found by simply plugging the values of x_i, the square feet of living area (see column 3), into the estimated regression equation and working out the corresponding value of $\hat{y}_i$. Thus, for the first apartment, $\hat{y} = 99{,}384.5 + 138.4x = 99{,}384.5 + 138.4 \times 974 = \$234{,}154$; for the second apartment, $\hat{y} = 99{,}384.5 + 138.4 \times 947 = \$230{,}419$; and so on. The elements in column 5 are simply the difference between those in column 2 and those in column 4, $y_i - \hat{y}_i$; the column 6 elements are the square of those in column 5, $(y_i - \hat{y}_i)^2$, or the squared residuals.

Table 12.2 Computations for $S^2_{y|x}$ and S^2_y

1	2	3	4	5	6	7
Apt *i*	y_i	x_i	$\hat{y}_i$	$(y_i - \hat{y}_i)$	$(y_i - \hat{y}_i)^2$	$(y_i - \bar{y})^2$
1	299,900	974	234,154	65,746	4,322,480,786	2,785,577,602
2	214,900	947	230,419	–15,519	240,823,943	1,038,220,459
3	284,900	1065	246,746	38,154	1,455,738,412	1,427,220,459
4	249,900	812	211,739	38,161	1,456,269,523	7,720,459
5	159,900	889	222,393	–62,493	3,905,399,097	7,607,577,602
6	231,000	958	231,941	–941	884,625	259,900,459
7	254,900	1050	244,670	10,230	104,645,772	60,506,173
8	324,900	1403	293,514	31,386	985,077,813	6,049,506,173
9	199,900	834	214,783	–14,883	221,503,208	2,229,863,316
10	304,900	1349	286,042	18,858	355,616,260	3,338,363,316
11	309,900	1668	330,181	–20,281	411,335,968	3,941,149,031
12	269,900	1568	316,345	–46,445	2,157,107,969	518,863,316
13	134,900	650	189,323	–54,423	2,961,903,960	12,593,649,031
14	219,900	781	207,450	12,450	155,014,699	741,006,173
Totals	3,459,700	14,948	3,459,700	0	18,733,802,033	42,599,123,571

If the regression does not predict accurately, then the $y_i - \hat{y}_i$ terms in the above expression are large. When they are, $s^2_{y|x}$ is also large. But if the regression predicts with perfect accuracy—and all the observations fall exactly on the regression line—then each $y_i - \hat{y}_i$ term is 0 and (accordingly) $s^2_{y|x} = 0$. Consequently, we can think of $s^2_{y|x}$ as a measure of the variance of the y values *around the regression line* (and not around the mean). But how do we interpret the meaning of $s^2_{y|x} = 1{,}561{,}150{,}169$? Although this is a very large number, does it necessarily mean that the regression does not predict well? No. While it is a large number in *absolute* terms, it is not a large number in *relative* terms.

To complete our discussion of the coefficient of determination, we include one final element in our calculation of r^2: the variance of y_i around the mean $\bar{y}$ or s^2_y. As we are about to see, this is the standard against which the above expression $s^2_{y|x}$ must be measured if we are to get an idea of how well the regression predicts. Recall that in Section 3.4 we saw that the variance of y_i around the mean $\bar{y}$ is expressed as

$$s^2_y = \frac{\Sigma(y_i - \bar{y})^2}{n-1}.$$

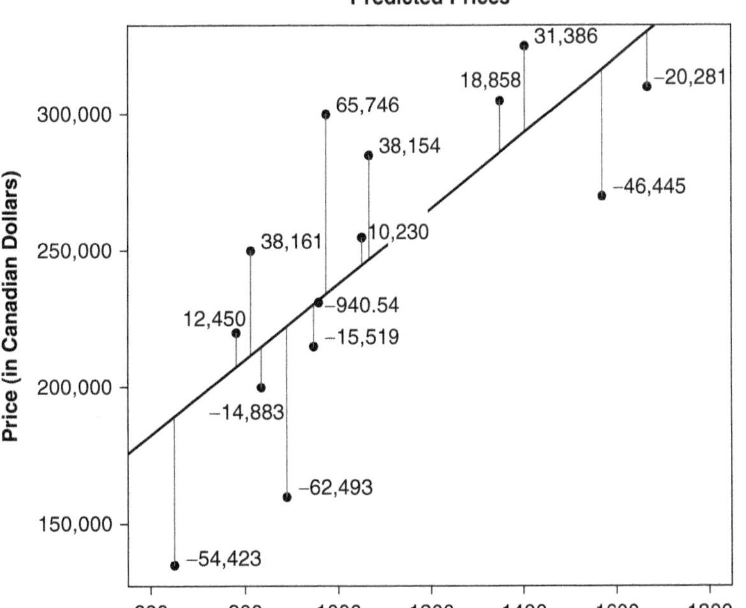

Figure 12.3 Residual values $y_i - \hat{y}_i$: actual minus predicted prices

The value of the numerator of the above expression is reported in the bottom row of column 7 of Table 12.2. When it is plugged into this expression, we find that the variance is

$$s_y^2 = \frac{\Sigma(y_i - \bar{y})^2}{n-1} = \frac{42{,}599{,}123{,}571}{13} = 3{,}276{,}855{,}659.$$

That the variance of y_i values *around the mean* exceeds the variance of y_i values *around the regression line* is evidence that we can predict the apartment prices with more accuracy using the regression than we can using the mean.

The numerator of s_y^2 is referred to as the total sum of squares, and is the measure of the total variation in the dependent variable when the point of reference is the mean. The total sum of squares is denoted by $SS_y = \Sigma(y_i - \bar{y})^2$.

Finally, these relationships lay the foundation for how we quantify the predictive accuracy of the regression or r^2. Note that the key element of the expression below is the ratio (on the right) of SS_{res} to SS_y:

$$r^2 = 1 - \frac{\Sigma(y_i - \hat{y}_i)^2}{\Sigma(y_i - \bar{y})^2} = 1 - \frac{SS_{res}}{SS_y}.$$

Example 12.5. Find the value of r^2. Substituting $\sum(y_i - \hat{y}_i)^2 = SS_{res} = 18{,}733{,}802{,}033$ and $\sum(y_i - \bar{y})^2 = SS_y = 42{,}599{,}123{,}571$ into this expression and solving, we arrive at the value of r^2. These two numbers are reported in the bottom rows of columns 6 and 7 (respectively) of Table 12.2:

$$r^2 = 1 - \frac{18{,}733{,}802{,}033}{42{,}599{,}123{,}571} = 1 - 0.4398 = 0.5602.$$

Whenever $r^2 \to 1$, it is because there is a strong linear association between the dependent variable y and the independent variable x; the observations group more or less closely around the regression line. But when $r^2 \to 0$, there is a weak (or no) linear relationship between y and x; the observations are distributed much more randomly throughout the scatter plot, and reveal no apparent pattern of a relationship between the two variables.

Example 12.6. How should we interpret the meaning of r^2? In the Winnipeg example, a coefficient of determination of $r^2 = 0.5602$ means that 56.02% of the variation in prices can be accounted for by the variation in living area. The variation in price that remains unaccounted for (43.98% of the variation) is explained by the variation in those variables that are omitted from the regression model, and it is the influence of the omitted variables that account for the ε in the formulation of the basic regression model that is introduced in Section 12.1. Recall that since $0 \le r^2 \le 1$, we know that (56.02 + 43.98)% = 100%.

Why does the above expression for r^2 provide a valid measure of the goodness of fit? Consider the following two-part answer. First, in the ratio (on the right), the denominator is the sum of squared errors when the point of reference is the mean: $\sum(y_i - \bar{y})^2$. It is the measure of the total squared error that would occur if we use the mean $\bar{y}$ to predict y_i values, and is referred to as the total error or total variation. The numerator of the ratio is the sum of squared errors when the point of reference is the predicted value of the regression equation: $\sum(y_i - \hat{y}_i)^2$. It represents that part of the total variation in the dependent variable that the regression leaves unexplained, and is often referred to as the residual error or residual variation. Following this line of reasoning, it should be clear that the ratio of $\sum(y_i - \hat{y}_i)^2$ to $\sum(y_i - \bar{y})^2$ is the proportion of total error or total variation that is left unexplained when the regression equation is used as the predictor of y.

Second, since $\sum(y_i - \hat{y}_i)^2 / \sum(y_i - \bar{y})^2$ represents the proportion of the total variation that is unexplained, 1 minus this ratio equals the proportion of the total variation that is explained when the regression equation is used as the predictor.

Finally, we extend this reasoning and these ideas to a final type of variation, the regression sum of squares, SS_{reg}. This source of variation is defined as

$$SS_{reg} = \sum(\hat{y}_i - \bar{y})^2.$$

Although we return to SS_{reg} in the next chapter, for now it is enough for us to know that the total sum of squares can be decomposed into the regression sum of squares and the residual sum of squares. These three sources of variation are related as follows:

$$\sum(y_i - \bar{y})^2 = \sum(\hat{y}_i - \bar{y})^2 + \sum(y_i - \hat{y}_i)^2$$

or, using the simpler notation,

$$SS_y = SS_{reg} + SS_{res}.$$

For our purpose in Chapter 12, we point out that one of the advantages of using this notation is that it renders the expression for r^2 into a simpler and more easily remembered form. Recalling the expression above and performing a bit of substitution and rearranging,

$$r^2 = 1 - \frac{SS_{res}}{SS_y} = \frac{SS_y}{SS_y} - \frac{SS_{res}}{SS_y}$$
$$= \frac{SS_y - SS_{res}}{SS_y} = \frac{SS_{reg}}{SS_y}.$$

Thus, we see that r^2 is simply the proportion of total variation in the dependent variable y that is accounted for or explained by the variation in the independent variable x.

Finally, it is interesting to note that for simple linear regression, the value of r^2 is equal to the square of the correlation coefficient between the dependent and independent variables. (The correlation coefficient is introduced in Section 3.6.) That is, $r = \sqrt{r^2} = \sqrt{0.5602} = 0.7485$. Note that this relationship is valid only when there is one independent variable; it is no longer true when there are two or more independent variables.

```
cor(winnipeg_apt$price, winnipeg_apt$sqft)
```

```
## [1] 0.7484854
```

12.4 THE HYPOTHESIS TEST ABOUT β_1

Thus far, whenever we have selected a sample from a population for the purpose of statistical inference, we have been concerned about the statistical significance of the result. In this regard, regression analysis is no different. To this end, we next discuss the properties of the sampling distribution of the regression coefficient b_1 and then use the six-step hypothesis-testing framework to test the significance of the regression coefficient.

There are three properties of the sampling distribution of b_1 we need to know before we can either conduct hypothesis tests about β_1 or create interval estimates of β_1: the expected value of b_1, the standard deviation, and the shape of the sampling distribution:

1 The expected value of b_1, the mean of all possible sample regression coefficients, is defined as $E(b_1) = \beta_1$, the population regression coefficient.
2 The standard deviation of b_1 is formulated as

$$\sigma_{b_1} = \frac{\sigma}{\sqrt{\sum(x_i - \bar{x})^2}},$$

where σ is the population standard deviation of the error terms $\varepsilon = y_i - \hat{y}_i$.
3 The shape of the sampling distribution of b_1 is normal.

Since the value of σ is unknown (remember that we are working with a sample, not a population), so is σ_{b_1}. Accordingly, we must estimate σ_{b_1} with s_{b_1}, where

$$s_{b_1} = \frac{s_{y|x}}{\sqrt{\Sigma(x_i - \bar{x})^2}}$$

and

$$s_{y|x} = \sqrt{\frac{\Sigma(y_i - \hat{y}_i)^2}{n-2}}.$$

Moreover, since σ_{b_1} is unknown, the transformed b_1 does not follow the normal distribution but a t-distribution with $n - 2$ degrees of freedom. (Recall that two degrees of freedom are used up in calculating the estimates of β_0 and β_1 for the estimated regression equation.) The transformed b_1 is the test statistic we use in the significance test itself:

$$t = \frac{b_1 - \beta_1}{s_{b_1}}.$$

In the Winnipeg example, the value of the standard error of b_1, or s_{b_1}, is easily calculated. From the bottom row of column 6 in Table 12.2, we have $\Sigma(y_i - \hat{y}_i)^2 = 18{,}733{,}802{,}033$, and so

$$s_{y|x} = \sqrt{\frac{18{,}733{,}802{,}033}{12}} = 39{,}511.39.$$

From the bottom row of column 6 of Table 12.1, we have $\sqrt{\Sigma(x_i - \bar{x})^2} = \sqrt{1{,}246{,}521} = 1116.48$. Substituting these two values into the expression for s_{b_1}, we have

$$s_{b_1} = \frac{s_{y|x}}{\sqrt{\Sigma(x_i - \bar{x})^2}} = \frac{39{,}511.39}{1116.48} = 35.39.$$

Thus, in this example, the sampling distribution of b_1 has an expected value of $E(b_1) = \beta_1$ and a standard deviation of $s_{b_1} = 35.39$.

The first two steps of the hypothesis test require (as usual) specification of the null and alternative hypotheses. In this case, the null hypothesis expresses the view that there is no linear association between y and x, and we state this formally as $H_0 : \beta_1 = 0$. When $\beta_1 = 0$ is true, we have $E(y) = \beta_0 + \beta_1 x = \beta_0 + (0)x = \beta_0 + 0 = \beta_0$, and there is no relationship between y and x. As in earlier chapters, we assume that $H_0 : \beta_1 = 0$ is true unless and until we see strong evidence that it is not. In that case, we say that we reject H_0 and conclude that the alternative hypothesis $H_a : \beta_1 \neq 0$ is true. The test of significance of the regression coefficient b_1 requires a two-tail test.

Example 12.7. At the $\alpha = 0.05$ level of significance, test to determine if there is a significant relationship between `price` and `sqft` for the Winnipeg example.

1 Determine the null hypothesis H_0 in statistical terms.

$H_0 : \beta_1 = 0$

2 Determine the alternative hypothesis H_a in statistical terms.

$H_a : \beta_1 \neq 0$

3 Set the level of significance α and decide on the sample size.

$n = 14$ and $\alpha = 0.05$

4 Use α to specify the rejection region RR.
The rejection region is $RR: t \ge 2.179$ and $t \le -2.179$. Or reject H_0 if $t \ge t_{\alpha/2,n-2} = t_{0.025,12} = 2.179$ or $t \le -t_{\alpha/2,n-2} = -t_{0.025,12} = -2.179$, where

$$t = \frac{b_1 - \beta_1}{s_{b_1}} = \frac{b_1 - 0}{s_{b_1}} = \frac{b_1}{s_{b_1}}.$$

```
qt(0.025, 12, lower.tail = FALSE)

## [1] 2.178813

qt(0.025, 12)

## [1] -2.178813
```

If $H_0: \beta_1 = 0$ is true, then the test statistic t collapses to the ratio of b_1 to s_{b_1}. The value of t that cuts off an area of 0.025 in the upper tail is $t = 2.179$; the value of t which cuts off an area of 0.025 in the lower tail is $t = -2.179$. Therefore, if b_1 transforms into a value of t that is greater than 2.179, or less than −2.179, reject H_0 and accept H_a; however, if t falls in the region from −2.179 to 2.179, do not reject H_0.

5 Collect the data and calculate the test statistic.
Since $b_1 = 138.37$ and $s_{b_1} = 35.39$,

$$t = \frac{b_1}{s_{b_1}} = \frac{138.37}{35.39} = 3.910.$$

Thus, $b_1 = 138.37$ corresponds to $t = 3.910$.

6 Use the test statistic and RR to decide whether to reject H_0.
Recall that the rejection region is RR: $t \ge 2.179$ and $t \le -2.179$. Since $t = 3.910 > 2.179$, we reject $H_0: \beta_1 = 0$ and accept $H_a: \beta \ne 0$.
Thus we have found evidence that the regression coefficient is significant. This result provides support for the claim that y, the price (in Canadian dollars) of a condominium apartment, is linearly associated with x, the square feet of living area.

Example 12.8. (1) What is the p-value? (2) Compare the p-value with α.

1 Because the RR lies in both the upper and lower tails of the t-distribution, the p-value is the probability that t is greater than 3.910 *plus* the probability that t is less than −3.910, that is,

$$p(t \ge 3.910) + p(t \le -3.910) = 0.00104 + 0.00104 = 0.00207.$$

```
pt(3.910, 12, lower.tail = FALSE) + pt(-3.910, 12)

## [1] 0.002072249
```

2 Since p-value = 0.00207 and $\alpha = 0.05$, p-value $< \alpha$ and we reject H_0.

Example 12.9. Use the function `lm()` to find (1) r^2 and (2) the *p*-value.

```
#Comment. Use function lm() to create a model object; name it slr.
slr <- lm(price ~ sqft, data = winnipeg_apt)
```

The `lm()` function simply repeats what we did above in Example 12.4. The only difference is that we now assign the result to an object, and we name the object `slr`. (Recall that an object can be named anything; we select the name `slr` for "simple linear regression" only because it is easy to remember for this example.) The technical term for the object we designate `slr` is *model object.* The advantage of creating a model object is that it captures and stores information and results that are produced by the regression analysis. In practical terms, this simply means that we can recover information and results by use of *extractor functions*, such as `summary()`.

```
#Comment. Use function summary() to learn r-square and p-value from slr
summary(slr)

##
## Call:
## lm(formula = price ~ sqft, data = winnipeg_apt)
##
## Residuals:
##    Min      1Q Median      3Q     Max
## -62493 -19091   4645  28254  65746
##
## Coefficients:
##             Estimate Std. Error t value Pr(>|t|)
## (Intercept) 99384.55   39233.54   2.533  0.02627 *
## sqft          138.37      35.39   3.910  0.00207 **
## --
## Signif. codes:  0 '***' 0.001 '**' 0.01 '*' 0.05 '.' 0.1 ' ' 1
##
## Residual standard error: 39510 on 12 degrees of freedom
## Multiple R-squared: 0.5602, Adjusted R-squared: 0.5236
## F-statistic: 15.29 on 1 and 12 DF, p-value: 0.002073
```

What follows is a brief discussion of the output of the `summary()` extractor function. Note that the information is organized into four sections or groupings.

1. The first entry simply repeats the details of the function call that created the model object `slr`. We note that this is not particularly useful information when the function involves a model with a single independent variable. Its usefulness becomes more apparent, however, once a regression model is significantly more complicated and includes, for example, a large number of independent variables.
2. The second section reports the residuals. These provide helpful diagnostic information which we use later when we review how to validate the assumptions behind the proper usage of regression analysis.

3 The third block is named `Coefficients` and includes a lot of information organized into four areas. Here is a summary of what is reported in the columns, from left to right.

(a) `Estimate` reports the values for the *y*-intercept term and regression coefficient. When using R to conduct regression analysis, this is where we learn that $b_0 = 99{,}384.55$ and $b_1 = 138.37$.

(b) `Std. Error` provides the standard deviations of b_0 and b_1, respectively. Note that the entry on the second line of this column confirms our finding that $s_{b_1} = 35.39$. (We worked out this value a few lines above Example 12.7.) For reasons that become more clear later, we are less concerned with either b_0 or its standard deviation, and so will not discuss these values further here.

(c) `t value` displays the test statistic, $t = b_1 / s_{b_1} = 3.910$. This value conforms with what we derived in step 5 of Example 12.7. Although we are not interested in the *t*-value for the intercept term, $t = b_0 / s_{b_0}$, its value is reported in the top row.

(d) `Pr(>|t|)` lists the *p*-values associated with both b_0 and b_1. Importantly, we learn that for b_1, the *p*-value is 0.00207, the same value we derived in part (1) of Example 12.8. The asterisks that accompany each *p*-value specify the level of significance. Because the meaning of these symbols forms an important aspect of our being able to interpret the results of any regression analysis correctly, here is a brief explanation of their meaning: three asterisks indicate a *p*-value less than 0.001 ($0.000 < p < 0.001$); two asterisks indicate a *p*-value between 0.001 and 0.01 ($0.001 \leq p < 0.01$); one asterisk indicates a *p*-value between 0.01 and 0.05 ($0.01 \leq p < 0.05$); a period indicates a *p*-value between 0.05 and 0.10 ($0.05 \leq p < 0.10$); and an empty space indicates a *p*-value greater than 0.10 ($0.10 \leq p < 1.00$).

Under normal circumstances, any statistic that is accompanied by a *p*-value with one or more asterisks is considered statistically significant; if it has a period next to it, or an empty space, then it is said to be non-significant. In the Winnipeg example, since our *p*-value is 0.00207, it has two asterisks next to it. What this means in practical terms is that the independent variable `sqft` can be used to predict the dependent variable `price` because the linear relationship is significant.
Finally, not everyone likes seeing the asterisks that are placed by default next to the *p*-values. The idea behind including these graphical indicators is that they make it easier (for some people) to identify the significant relationships at a glance; others feel that the asterisks simply introduce additional visual clutter to an already congested output space. Fortunately, it is possible to suppress the inclusion of these asterisks, if desired, by inserting the following line before executing the `summary()` function: `options(show.signif.stars = FALSE)`. Adding this line of code conceals the asterisks, and the *p*-values are reported without any graphical indicators.

4 The last section includes more information arranged in three rows. What follows is a quick review of what is reported in the rows, top to bottom.

(a) `Residual standard error` provides the standard deviation of y_i values around the regression line. This value is derived at the beginning of Section 12.4, namely $s_{y|x} = \sqrt{\Sigma(y_i - \hat{y}_i)^2 / (n-2)}$, and differs from 39,510 by only a very slight rounding error.

(b) `Multiple R-squared` reports both the coefficient of determination, $r^2 = 0.5602$, and the `Adjusted R-squared`, a measure we discuss in Chapter 13.

(c) `F-statistic` and its associated `p-value` are measures we also postpone discussing until Chapter 13.

Example 12.10. This example provides an opportunity to practise writing some very simple code using both new and old (familiar) R functions. There are three steps: (1) use the function `fitted(slr)` to create the predicted (or fitted) values of the dependent variable $\hat{y}$, and name the new object containing the predicted values `price_predicted`; (2) use the function `cbind()` to bind the new object to `winnipeg_apt`, and name the resulting object `winnipeg_apt_new`; and (3) use `head()` to review the first six lines of `winnipeg_apt_new`.

```
#Comment. Use fitted(slr) to create the predicted dependent variables;
#name the new object: price_predicted
fitted(slr) -> price_predicted

#Comment. Use cbind(winnipeg_apt,price_predicted) to bind the 2 objects
#together; name the result of the cbind() function: winnipeg_apt_new
cbind(winnipeg_apt, price_predicted) -> winnipeg_apt_new

#Comment. Use head() to review top 6 lines of winnipeg_apt_new
head(winnipeg_apt_new)

##    price sqft price_predicted
## 1 299900  974        234154.4
## 2 214900  947        230418.5
## 3 284900 1065        246745.9
## 4 249900  812        211738.9
## 5 159900  889        222393.2
## 6 231000  958        231940.5
```

What follows are explanatory comments on the three steps just executed:

1. The function `fitted()` provides the predicted values of the dependent variable for the model object `slr`. Note that the argument is not the original set of data but the model object that results from `lm()`. If we review the contents of `price_predicted`, we find the same values as those entered in column 4 of Table 12.2.
2. We first encountered the function `cbind()` in Example 2.8. Its purpose here is simply to incorporate a new variable into an existing object.
3. The function `head()` allows us to review the result of the `cbind()` function. In this case, we can confirm that the first six entries of `price_predicted` conform exactly with the first six rows of column 4 of Table 12.2.

Example 12.11. Use the function `predict()` to find the predicted prices of apartments having the following square feet of living space: 800, 900, 1000, 1100, and 1200.

```
#Comment. Use data.frame() to create new object containing 800, 900,
#1000, 1100, and 1200. Name the new object: price_new
price_new <- data.frame(sqft <- c(800, 900, 1000, 1100, 1200))
```

```
#Comment. Use function predict() to provide the predicted prices of
#apartments having 800 (and up) square feet of living space
predict(slr, price_new)

##        1        2        3        4        5
## 210078.5 223915.2 237752.0 251588.7 265425.5
```

Sometimes we want to use the regression equation to make predictions based on values of the independent variable that are not part of the original model calibration. As long as these values fall within the range of the independent variable included in the original analysis, it is valid and legitimate to use the regression model for prediction.

1 We first encountered the function `data.frame()` in the Appendix to Chapter 1. In this case, the function assigns the values 800, 900, 1000, 1100, and 1200 to the variable named `sqft`, and stores everything in the data frame named `price_new`.
2 The function `predict()` extracts from the model object `slr` the predicted values of the dependent variable for those values of the independent variable specified in step 1. In this example, the first argument of the function is the model object `slr`; the second argument is the data frame `price_new`. These types of predictions (i.e., those made on values of the independent variable not included the original sample) can be made with `predict()` but not with `fitted()`, which produces predictions only on those values used in the original sample. Note that if the `predict()` function does not specify the second argument (i.e., if the data frame `price_new` is omitted) the function defaults to executing exactly the same thing as `fitted()`.
3 The practical value of the `predict()` function lies in its ability to relieve us of having to puzzle out the predicted values manually, as we did above in Example 12.3. Note that it is confirmed that an apartment with 1000 square feet of living space (see Example 12.3) can be expected to be priced at $237,752.

12.5 ALTERNATIVE APPROACHES TO TESTING SIGNIFICANCE

Formal hypothesis testing of β_1 of the type detailed in Section 12.4 is not the only means by which the significance of a simple linear regression equation can be tested. There are two other well-known—though perhaps not so widely used—approaches: confidence interval estimates of β_1; and the *F*-test. What follows is a brief discussion of each.

Confidence interval estimate of β_1

Just as we developed interval estimates of parameters such as μ and p in Chapter 8, it is an easy matter to do so for β_1. Recall that the general form of an interval estimate is point estimate ± margin of error. In view of this, the structure of the interval estimate of β_1 is $b_1 \pm t_{\alpha/2,n-2} s_{b_1}$.

Example 12.12. Find the 95% interval estimate of β_1 for the Winnipeg example. Recall that $s_{b_1} = 35.39$. If $1-\alpha = 0.95$ and $n = 14$, then $t_{\alpha/2,n-2} = t_{0.025,12} = 2.179$.

$$\begin{aligned} b_1 &\pm t_{\alpha/2,n-2}s_{b_1} \\ &= 138.37 \pm 2.179 \times 35.39 \\ &= 138.37 \pm 77.11 \text{ or } [61.26, 215.47]. \end{aligned}$$

Thus, we can be 95% confident that β_1 falls in the interval from 61.26 to 215.47. We can confirm this result using the function `confint()`. The first argument refers to the model object `slr`; the second argument `level =` specifies the confidence level.

```
confint(slr, level = 0.95)
```

```
##                   2.5 %      97.5 %
## (Intercept) 13902.00376 184867.0930
## sqft           61.26066    215.4742
```

You are reminded that any two-tail hypothesis test can be conducted using an interval estimation procedure. Remember that whenever the hypothesized value of β_1 falls in the confidence interval, we do not reject H_0; however, if the hypothesized value of β_1 falls outside the interval, we reject H_0. Therefore, because the confidence interval $[61.26, 215.47]$ does not include 0, the value specified under null hypothesis, we reject $H_0 : \beta_1 = 0$ at the $\alpha = 0.05$ level of significance and accept $H_a : \beta_1 \neq 0$.

The *F*-test

Since this test of significance is not very useful when the regression model has only one independent variable (such as with the Winnipeg example), our discussion of it here is brief. This test is much more important in the context of models with two or more independent variables, and so we delay a more detailed discussion of it until Chapter 13. The reason why we mention this method at all in this chapter is that, under certain conditions, the *F*- and *t*-tests provide identical results because the hypothesis test behind each is the same, $H_0 : \beta_1 = 0$. For now, it is enough for us to know that the value of *F* equals the square of the value of *t*. Since the R block in Example 12.9 reports the values of both *t* and *F*, we can see that $t^2 = 3.910^2 = 15.29 = F$. In the case of simple linear regression, this relationship always holds true; in the case of multiple regression, it does not.

We could just as easily have tested the significance of the relationship between the two variables using the *F*-test rather than the *t*-test. But since both tests provide exactly the same results—and since we used the *t*-test first in Example 12.7—there is no reason to go through the hypothesis test a second time, using the *F*-test as well. In the next chapter, however, we are faced with the need to do both types of test.

12.6 SO FAR, WE HAVE TESTED ONLY b_1; WILL WE ALSO TEST b_0?

No, usually we are not concerned with testing the significance of the intercept term. Remember that b_0 is simply the predicted value of the dependent variable when the independent variable equals 0; that is, $\hat{y} = b_0 + b_1 x = b_0 + b_1(0) = b_0$.

In other cases, it simply makes no sense to try to predict $\hat{y}$ when $x = 0$. For example, the intercept term in the Winnipeg example provides the price of a home with $x = 0$ square feet of living area. But when we plug 0 into the regression equation, we learn that the expected price of an apartment with no living space should be in the neighborhood of \$99,384.50: $\hat{y} = 99{,}384.5 + 138.4x = 99{,}384.5 + 138.4 \times 0 = 99{,}384.5$.

Finally, there are times when the intercept term is a negative value simply because that is the equation of the line that fits the data best. For example, some time ago, the author received a project submitted by a group of students who investigated the relationship between the price of a digital camera and the number of megapixels. The regression equation that described the relationship best was (approximately) $\hat{y} = -150 + 50x$, where x is the number of megapixels and $\hat{y}$ the predicted price in euros. The coefficient $b_1 = 50$ is reasonable enough—there is an expected change in price of €50 for each change of 1 megapixel—but the meaning of the intercept term $b_0 = -150$ is less clear. What does it mean to say that a digital camera with 2 megapixels would be priced at –€50?

Three messages emerge in this section. First, because the intercept term b_0 does not always have a clear meaning, we are less interested in it than in the coefficient itself. Accordingly, we do not normally test its significance. Second, do not try to make predictions for values of x that fall outside the range of values that make up the sample. The world may look very different for values of x that fall above or below that range. Third, use common sense when interpreting the meaning of the regression model.

 12.7 ASSUMPTIONS: WHAT ARE THEY?

In this chapter, we have spent considerable time learning the fundamentals underpinning the theory and practice of regression analysis. But before we move on to Chapter 13, where we glimpse how to extend the power and flexibility of the regression model by including additional independent variables, we need to build on what we have learned thus far. In particular, before applying the regression analytic framework to any data problem, we need to refine our understanding of the basic assumptions upon which its correct usage rests. We have delayed until now any explicit consideration of these assumptions because many people find such a discussion abstract, even pointless, until we have achieved at least a nodding acquaintance with what regression analysis is as well as how it is used.

We begin with the assumptions about the model of the relationship between y and x. Recall that the residuals or error terms described in Section 12.3 are defined as $\varepsilon = y_i - \hat{y}_i$.

1 The residuals ε are independent of one another. Put another way, the value of y for any given value of x is unrelated to the value of y for any other given value of x.
2 The variance of ε is $\sigma^2_{y|x}$ and is constant for all values of x. In other words, the distribution of y values around the regression line is the same for each value of x.
3 The residuals ε are normally distributed with $E(\varepsilon) = 0$. That is, the distribution of y values around the regression line for any value of x is normal.

12.8 ASSUMPTIONS: HOW ARE THEY VALIDATED?

In the case of simple linear regression, an underlying assumption is that the relationship between y and x is *actually linear*. We might think that all we need to do to validate this assumption is to create and inspect a scatter plot of y against x. Unfortunately, a simple scatter plot and p-value (of the associated regression equation) can mislead us into thinking that not only are y and x linearly related, but also that the three assumptions (in Section 12.7) are satisfied. Consider Figures 12.4 and 12.5. Even though the Figure 12.4 scatter plot (p-value = 0.0481) suggests that the assumptions are satisfied, the Figure 12.5 residual plot (of the same data) casts doubt on the assumption of constant variation of ε for all values of x; that is, the variation of y values around the regression line increases as x increases. A possible reason for this is that the functional form of the equation is not linear after all, or that additional independent variables should be included in (but were omitted from) the analysis.

Comparing Figures 12.6 and 12.7, the scatter plot (p-value = 0.0275) obscures what the residual plot does not—that y and x are related *curvilinearly* rather than linearly. In this case, the residual plot reveals that y and x move together in a manner requiring a transformation of some type. Transformations typically involve transforming a variable in a way that imposes linearity where it does not exist otherwise. For example, sometimes a variable is raised to a power; other times a variable is transformed logarithmically. Regardless of the type of transformation that might be needed to impose linearity, linear regression should not be used unless and until such a transformation is made.

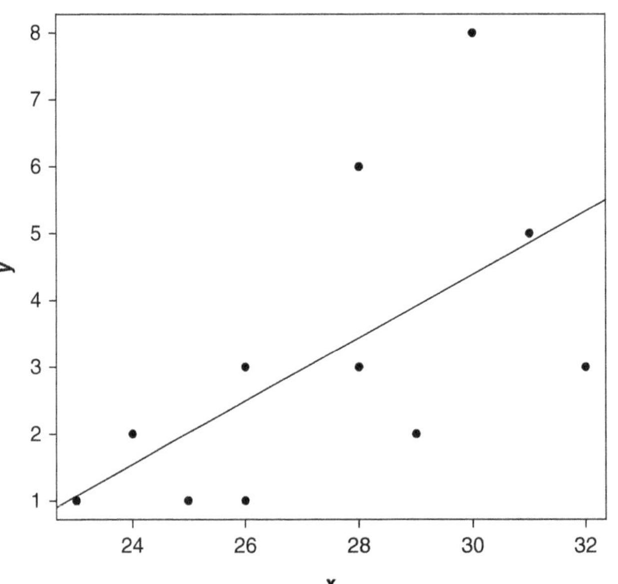

Figure 12.4 Scatter plot of y and x (p-value = 0.0481)

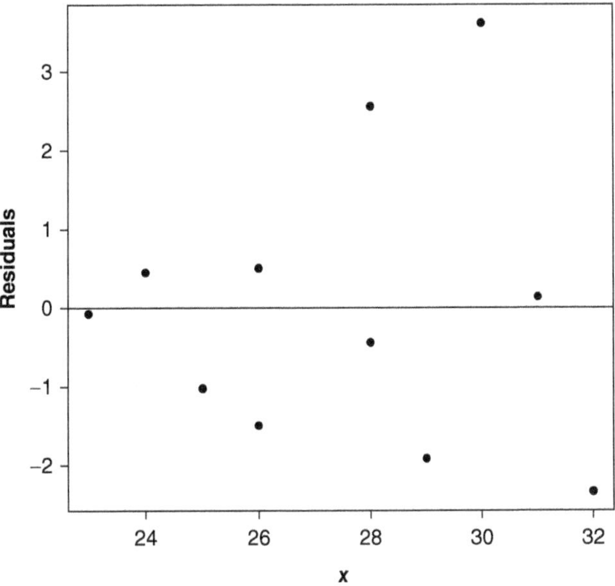

Figure 12.5 Plot of residuals $y - \hat{y}$ and x

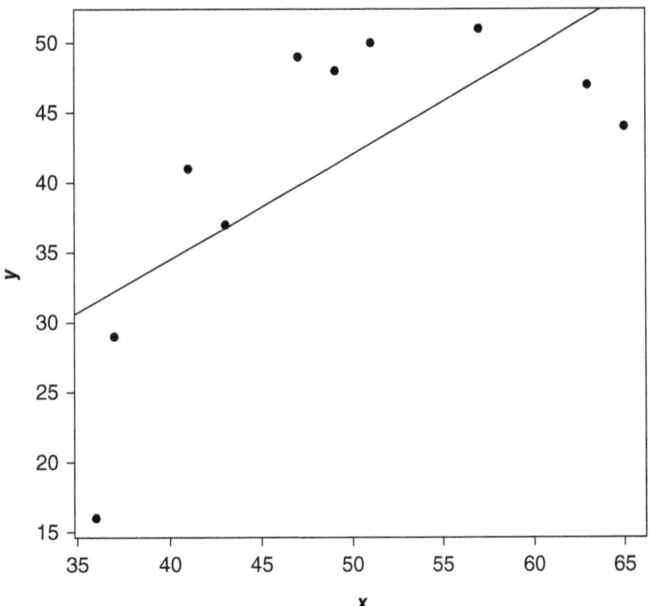

Figure 12.6 Scatter plot of y and x (p-value = 0.0275)

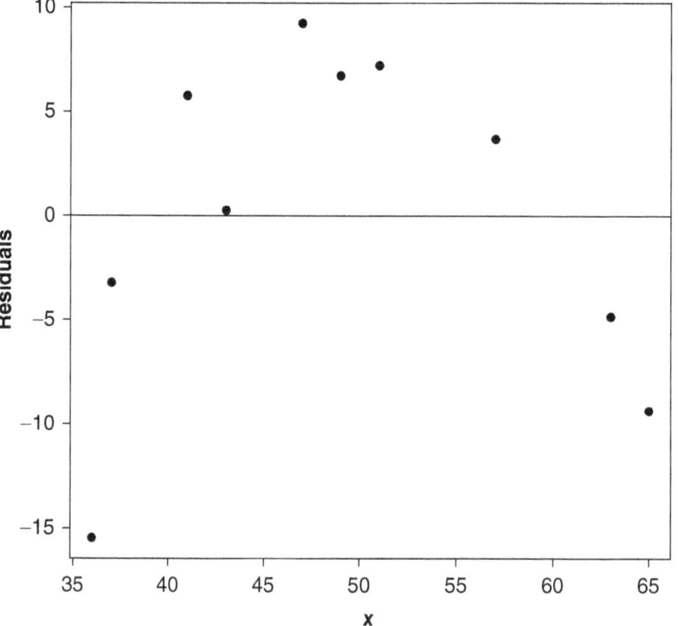

Figure 12.7 Plot of residuals $y-\hat{y}$ and x

It is important that we understand the distinction between the scatter plot and the residual plot. Before we try to fit any sample data with a linear model, we often make a scatter plot as a first step in the analysis in order to understand if there might be a linear relationship between y and x. If there is, then linear regression is often an appropriate analytic methodology. However, we cannot make the residual plot until we have estimated the regression equation itself. Since we cannot find residuals (which are the differences between the actual and predicted values, $y-\hat{y}$) without the estimated regression equation, this step typically comes later in the process. (See step 4 of the summary at the end of this chapter.) A residual plot of $y-\hat{y}$ against x often reveals patterns of nonlinearity that do not emerge in a straightforward scatter plot of y against x. We use the residual plot to validate the assumptions underlying the application of regression methodology to a given sample.

Definition 12.7. Scatter Plot. A graphical presentation of two quantitative variables. One variable is shown on the vertical axis, one on the horizontal axis. In regression analysis, the dependent variable is often (but not always) plotted on the vertical axis, and the independent variable on the horizontal axis. The general pattern of the plotted points suggests the nature of the relationship (and if it is linear or not) between the two variables.

Definition 12.8. Residual Analysis. The purpose of residual analysis, which typically involves making a residual plot, is to understand if the assumptions underlying the correct usage of the regression model are valid.

Definition 12.9. Residual Plot. In the case of simple linear regression, this is a plot of the residuals $y-\hat{y}$ against the independent variable x. In the case of multiple regression, where there are two or more independent variables, it is a plot of the residuals against the predicted dependent variable $\hat{y}$.

There are at least three important questions to raise when inspecting the residual plot. First, do the residuals $y_i-\hat{y}_i$ and x_i appear to be linearly related or are they associated in some other, perhaps curvilinear or kinked, manner? Second, does the variance of the residuals around the line representing $E(\varepsilon)=0$ appear constant for all ranges of x? Third, are there any conspicuous outliers? In Figures 12.5 and 12.7 the horizontal axis shows the independent variable x while the vertical axis displays the residual $y-\hat{y}$; each point i is plotted as $(x_i, y_i-\hat{y}_i)$. What is important is the pattern of the points of the residual plot. When all three assumptions above are satisfied and the relationship between y and x is indeed linear, the general pattern is a horizontal band of points in which the spread of points is denser nearer the line specifying $E(\varepsilon)=0$. As we have seen, there are several types of patterns that could arise in a residual plot when one (or more) of the above assumptions is not satisfied.

Creating and examining a residual plot is an important step in any simple linear regression analysis, and it should be done once the regression model has been estimated and the residuals calculated.

To create a residual plot for the Winnipeg data, we use the following `plot()` function:

```
plot(winnipeg_apt$sqft, resid(slr), pch = 19, abline(h = 0), xlab =
    'Square Feet of Living Area', ylab = 'Residuals', main = 'Winnipeg
    Homes: Residuals Against the Independent Variable')
```

A brief discussion of the arguments follows.

1. `winnipeg_apt$sqft`, square feet of living area for each observation, is plotted on the horizontal axis of the residual plot.
2. `resid(slr)` provides the residual values, $y-\hat{y}$, for the model object `slr`. The value of each residual for all 14 observations is plotted on the vertical axis of the residual plot.
3. `pch = 19` specifies the plotting character. For example, when `pch` is set to 19, the plotted point is a filled-out circle. For a full list of the available plotting options, simply enter `?pch` at the R prompt in the Console.
4. `abline(h = 0)` adds a horizontal line to the plot where the vertical axis indicates 0 (in this case, at the point where $E(\varepsilon)=0$).
5. `xlab = ''` defines the title for the horizontal axis.
6. `ylab = ''` defines the title for the vertical axis.
7. `main = ''` defines the overall title for the plot.

Even though the Winnipeg example includes only 14 sample points, the residual plot reveals nothing obvious that might cause us to question the assumptions of a linear relationship between the price of a condominium apartment and its living area. There does not appear to be a curvilinear relationship; the variance of the residual terms seems relatively constant; there are no obvious

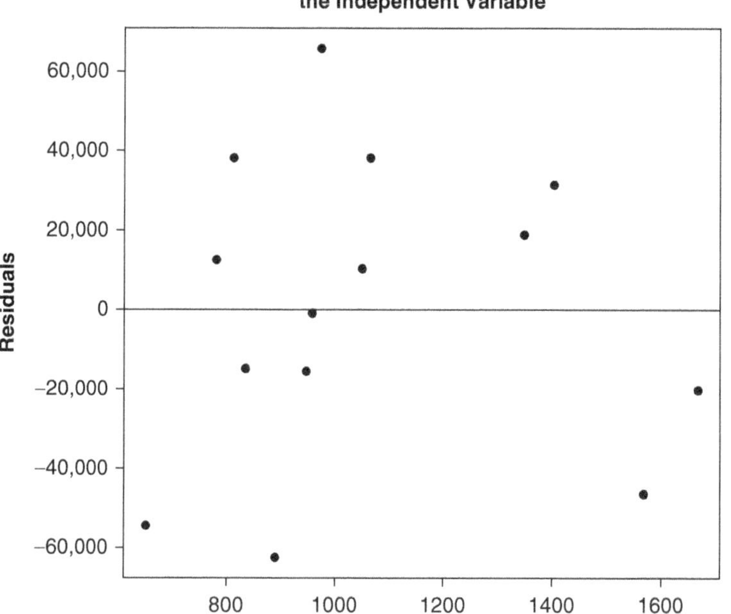

Figure 12.8 Residual plot against *x*

outlier values. For these reasons, we would say that because we have validated the assumptions about the linear model for the relationship between the dependent and independent variables, linear regression is an appropriate analytic methodology for this sample.

12.9 OPTIONAL MATERIAL: DERIVATION OF THE EXPRESSIONS FOR THE LEAST SQUARE ESTIMATES OF β_0 AND β_1

In Section 12.2 we give the expressions for the values of b_0 and b_1 that provide the equation of the best-fitting line, this being the one which minimizes the vertical distance between each observation and the line of the regression itself. But while we have already applied the expressions to find those values of b_0 and b_1, we have provided no justification for why these expressions work. The approach to this estimation problem is known as the *method of least squares* or *ordinary least squares*, and it involves finding those values of b_0 and b_1 that minimize the difference between the actual value of the dependent variable y and the predicted value $\hat{y}$. More specifically, we need to know the values of b_0 and b_1 that minimize the magnitude of $y-\hat{y}$ where the estimated regression equation $\hat{y}=b_0+b_1x$ is used for prediction. That is, using the least-squares criterion, we must minimize $\Sigma(y_i - \hat{y}_i)^2$ where the estimated regression equation $\hat{y} = b_0 + b_1 x$ is used for prediction. In other words,

$$\text{minimize } \Sigma(y_i - \hat{y}_i)^2.$$

When we substitute $b_0 + b_1 x_i$ for $\hat{y}_i$, the above expression becomes

$$\text{minimize } \Sigma(y_i - b_0 - b_1 x_i)^2.$$

In order to minimize this expression, we find the partial derivatives with respect to b_0 and b_1, one at a time, set the result equal to 0, and rearrange the terms until we arrive at an expression that is a bit easier to work with. First, we differentiate with respect to b_0:

$$\frac{\partial \Sigma(y_i - b_0 - b_1 x_i)^2}{\partial b_0} = -2\Sigma(y_i - b_0 - b_1 x_i) = 0.$$

Divide both sides of the equation by 2 and add each of the three terms separately:

$$-\Sigma y_i + \Sigma b_0 + \Sigma b_1 x_i = 0.$$

Reexpress Σb_0 as nb_0, add Σy_i to both sides of the equation, and move b_1 across the summation sign:

$$nb_0 + b_1 \Sigma x_i = \Sigma y_i.$$

From both sides of the equation, subtract $b_1 \Sigma x_i$ and divide by n to solve for b_0:

$$b_0 = \frac{\Sigma y_i}{n} - b_1 \frac{\Sigma x_1}{n}.$$

Now differentiate the expression with respect to b_1:

$$\frac{\partial \Sigma(y_i - b_0 - b_1 x_i)^2}{\partial b_1} = -2\Sigma(x_i(y_i - b_0 - b_1 x_i)) = 0.$$

Once again, divide by 2 and perform similar rearrangements of terms:

$$b_0 \Sigma x_i + b_1 \Sigma x_i^2 = \Sigma x_i y_i.$$

Now substitute the equation for b_0 into this expression and solve for b_1:

$$\left(\frac{\Sigma y_i}{n} - b_1 \frac{\Sigma x_1}{n}\right)\Sigma x_i + b_1 \Sigma x_i^2 = \Sigma x_i y_i.$$

Now if we simplify, rearrange, and solve for b_1, we have

$$b_1 = \frac{\Sigma(x_i - \bar{x})(y_i - \bar{y})}{\Sigma(x_i - \bar{x})^2},$$

and when we substitute $\bar{y} = \Sigma y_i / n$ and $\bar{x} = \Sigma x_i / n$, we arrive at the final solution for b_0:

$$\begin{aligned} b_0 &= \frac{\Sigma y_i}{n} - b_1 \frac{\Sigma x_1}{n} \\ &= \bar{y} - b_1 \bar{x}. \end{aligned}$$

SUMMARY

Today, regression has emerged as a very widely used statistical methodology. There are at least four reasons why this is so: first, in the case of simple linear regression, there are only two estimators, b_0 and b_1, and the form of the equation is simple and straightforward, $\hat{y} = b_0 + b_1 x$; second, it has an easy-to-understand measure of goodness of fit, the coefficient of determination r^2; third, for a given set of data, residual plots can help validate the model assumptions; and fourth, regression can be used for either description or prediction.

But even though (or perhaps because) regression is so popular with many people from diverse fields of application, the methodology is also commonly misunderstood and misused. One reason for this is that, like so many statistical methods, the correct application of regression involves nearly as much art as science. In view of this, here are the steps that might be taken whenever applying a simple linear regression analysis to a data set.

1 **Describe the research question in clear and unambiguous terms.** For the Winnipeg example, we might say that we want to understand the relationship (if any) between the price of a condominium apartment and its living area.

2 **Define the variables and describe the sample being used in the analysis.** In our example, price is reported in Canadian dollars, and the variable name is `price`; living area is measured in square feet, and the variable name is `sqft`. Sample data were collected in May 2016 on 14 homes being advertised by Winnipeg real estate agents.

3 **Verify tentatively that the two variables are linearly related.** This involves constructing and inspecting a scatter plot. Figure 12.1 confirms that there may be a rough linear relationship; here is the full `plot()` function that is used to create it.

```
plot(winnipeg_apt$sqft, winnipeg_apt$price, pch = 19, xlab = 'Square
Feet of Living Area', ylab = 'Price (in Canadian dollars)')
```

If the scatter plot reveals a pattern of points that suggests that the relationship might be linear, we proceed to step 4.

4 **Make and inspect a residual plot.** Since we know that a scatter plot does not always reveal the relationship between the two variables, we need to take a closer look. Remember that the first step to creating a residual plot is to run the regression itself and then store the result in a model object. In this case, we specify `price` as the dependent variable and `sqft` as the independent variable.

```
slr <- lm(price ~ sqft, data = winnipeg_apt)
```

Now enter the model object name `slr` as the argument to the `resid()` function and execute the following line of code. This produces Figure 12.8.

```
plot(winnipeg_apt$sqft, resid(slr), pch = 19, abline(h = 0), xlab =
'Square Feet of Living Area', ylab = 'Residuals', main =
'Winnipeg Homes: Residuals Against the Independent Variable')
```

If the residual plot uncovers no serious violations of the assumptions described in Sections 12.7 and 12.8 (e.g., a non-constant variance, a curvilinear relationship between the two variables, or the presence of outliers), proceed to step 5. Recall that the problem of outliers is discussed in Section 3.5.

5 **Use the summary() function to unpack the important information from the model object.** In particular, find the coefficients, b_0 and b_1, the estimated regression equation, the r^2, and the *p*-value of the regression coefficient.

```
summary(slr)
```

The results below are reproduced from those in Section 12.4. Refer to the discussion of the Example 12.9 results for more detail, if necessary.

```
##
## Call:
## lm(formula = price ~ sqft, data = winnipeg_apt)
##
## Residuals:
## Min      1Q Median      3Q     Max
## -62493 -19091      4645   28254      65746
##
## Coefficients:
##             Estimate Std. Error t value Pr(>|t|)
## (Intercept)        99384.55    39233.54     2.533   0.02627 *
## sqft        138.37        35.39    3.910  0.00207 **
## --
## Signif. codes: 0 '***' 0.001 '**' 0.01 '*' 0.05 '.' 0.1 ' ' 1
##
## Residual standard error: 39510 on 12 degrees of freedom
## Multiple R-squared: 0.5602, Adjusted R-squared: 0.5236
## F-statistic: 15.29 on 1 and 12 DF, p-value: 0.002073
```

(a) The intercept term is $b_0 = 99{,}384.55$.
(b) The coefficient on the independent variable *x* is $b_1 = 138.37$.
(c) The estimated regression equation is $\hat{y} = 99{,}384.55 + 138.37x$.
(d) The coefficient of determination is $r^2 = 0.5602$.
(e) The observed level of significance is the *p*-value, 0.002073.

6 So what's new? Description, prediction, and conclusions.

(a) **Description.** Both the scatter plot and the residual plot suggest a positive and linear association between the price and living area for condominium apartments in Winnipeg. While this is not a surprising finding, it provides empirical evidence that the relationship holds up much as we might expect. The residual plot reveals no obvious outliers, and the assumption of constant variation of the residuals over the range of the independent variable seems reasonable. While a sample size of 14 is small, the $r^2 = 0.5602$ indicates that roughly 56% of the variation in price can be accounted for by the variation in living area. Finally, an observed level of significance of p-value = 0.002073 allows us to conclude that the non-zero relationship between the two variables is significant.

(b) **Prediction.** As we saw in Example 12.11, we can use the following functions to make predictions based on values of the independent variable that are not part of the original sample: `c()` nested within `data.frame()` which itself is nested within `predict()`. For visual reasons, we break the code into two lines.

```
price_new <- data.frame(sqft <- c(800, 900, 1000, 1100, 1200))
predict(slr, price_new)

##        1        2        3        4        5
## 210078.5 223915.2 237752.0 251588.7 265425.5
```

If we want to make predictions based on the values in the original sample, we can use either `predict()`, making sure we omit the second argument `price_new`, or `fitted()`. The result is the same.

(c) **Conclusions.** The estimated regression equation $\hat{y} = 99{,}384.55 + 138.37x$ allows us to conclude that a change of 1 square foot of living area is associated with a change of \$138.37 in price. (We know this because the regression coefficient is $b_1 = 138.37$.) In this case, the meaning of the intercept term, $b_0 = 99{,}384.55$, is less clear because it represents the predicted value of an apartment with no living space at all. Is this a realistic price for a home that does not exist? Even so, it is important to retain the intercept term in the equation because it must be included when we want to make predictions. But because the sample size is only 14 and because it does not include apartments having less than 650 square feet, nor those with more than 1668 square feet, the regression equation really does not describe the world outside that range.

In the next chapter, we extend the power of regression analysis by specifying models with multiple independent variables. Much of what we have learned in this chapter applies in the next. The multiple regression model tests for linear relationships between a dependent variable y and $n = 2$ or more independent variables, $x_1, x_2, \ldots, x_n$. Several of the diagnostic procedures (including the r^2 and p-values) are the same; moreover, even the regression output is comparable. What is different in the case of multiple independent variables is the problem of identifying which variables should be retained in the regression model, and which should be omitted. To this and other related issues we give attention in Chapter 13.

definitions

Coefficient of Determination The coefficient of determination r^2 is a measure of the strength of linear association between two variables. Its value varies between 0 and 1, and it indicates the proportion of total variation in the dependent variable Y that is explained by the variation in the independent variable x.

Dependent Variable In the context of regression analysis, the dependent variable (often denoted by Y) is what we want to predict or explain. It is also known as the *criterion variable.*

Estimated Simple Linear Regression Equation A general expression that specifies how the predicted value of the dependent variable, or $\hat{y}$, is related to the independent variable x. In this case, the estimators b_0 and b_1 (which are estimated from the sample data) replace the parameters β_0 and β_1, respectively.

Independent Variable While the dependent variable is what we want to predict or explain, the independent variable (often denoted by x) is what we use to make the prediction. In the case of multiple regression, there are two or more independent variables.

Residual Analysis The purpose of residual analysis, which typically involves making a residual plot, is to understand if the assumptions underlying the correct usage of the regression model are valid.

Residual Plot In the case of simple linear regression, this is a plot of the residuals $y - \hat{y}$ against the independent variable x. In the case of multiple regression, where there are two or more independent variables, it is a plot of the residuals against the predicted dependent variable $\hat{y}$.

Scatter Plot A graphical presentation of two quantitative variables. One variable is shown on the vertical axis, one on the horizontal axis. In regression analysis, the dependent variable is often (but not always) plotted on the vertical axis, and the independent variable on the horizontal axis. The general pattern of the plotted points suggests the nature of the relationship (linear or not) between the two variables.

Simple Linear Regression Equation A general expression that specifies how the expected value of Y, or $\mu_{Y|x}$, is related to the independent variable x.

Simple Linear Regression Model The general expression that specifies how the dependent variable Y is related to the independent variable x plus the error term ε.

formulae

Simple Linear Regression Model

$$y = \beta_0 + \beta_1 x + \varepsilon$$

Simple Linear Regression Equation

$$E(y \mid x) = \mu_{y|x} = \beta_0 + \beta_1 x$$

Estimated Simple Linear Regression Equation

$$\hat{y} = b_0 + b_1 x$$

Expression for Regression Coefficient of Estimated Regression Equation

$$b_1 = \frac{\sum(x_i - \bar{x})(y_i - \bar{y})}{\sum(x_i - \bar{x})^2}$$

Expression for Intercept Term of Estimated Regression Equation

$$b_0 = \bar{y} - b_1\bar{x}$$

Variance of Y_i around Regression Line

$$s^2_{y|x} = \frac{\Sigma(y_i - \hat{y}_i)^2}{n-2}$$

Variance of Y_i around Sample Mean $\bar{y}$

$$s^2_y = \frac{\Sigma(y_i - \bar{y})^2}{n-1}$$

Coefficient of Determination

$$r^2 = 1 - \frac{\Sigma(y_i - \hat{y}_i)^2}{\Sigma(y_i - \bar{y})^2}$$

Residual Sum of Squares

$$SS_{res} = \Sigma(y_i - \hat{y}_i)^2$$

Total Sum of Squares

$$SS_y = \Sigma(y_i - \bar{y})^2$$

Regression Sum of Squares

$$SS_{reg} = \Sigma(\hat{y}_i - \bar{y})^2$$

Relationship of the Three Sources of Variation

$$SS_y = SS_{reg} + SS_{res}$$

Standard Deviation of b_1

$$\sigma_{b_1} = \frac{\sigma}{\sqrt{\Sigma(x_i - \bar{x})^2}}$$

Estimate of the Standard Deviation of b_1

$$s_{b_1} = \frac{s}{\sqrt{\Sigma(x_i - \bar{x})^2}}$$

Standard Deviation of Y_i around Regression Line

$$s_{y|x} = \sqrt{\frac{\Sigma(y_i - \hat{y}_i)^2}{n-2}}$$

Test Statistic for Test of Significance

$$t = \frac{b_1}{s_{b_1}}$$

R functions

`abline()` Introduces a line into a plot. In this chapter, we use this function to include both the line of the estimated regression equation and a line representing the mean.

`confint()` An extractor function that provides confidence interval estimates of the parameters of a fitted regression model.

`fitted()` An extractor function that provides the predicted (or fitted) values of the dependent variable for the model object. Only those values included in the original sample are fitted to the model.

`lm(y ~ x, data =)` Provides the intercept term b_0 and the regression coefficient b_1 for an estimated simple linear regression equation of the form $\hat{y} = b_0 + b_1x$.

`predict()` An extractor function that predicts values of the independent variable *not* included in the original sample. If the new independent variable values are omitted as an argument, `predict()` provides the same predictions as `fitted()`.

`resid()` An extractor function that reports residuals; that is, the difference between the actual and predicted values, $y-\hat{y}$, for all values from the original sample.

`summary()` An extractor function that extracts (from the model object) the parameters, goodness-of-fit measures, and *p*-values.

data sets

1 mtcars
2 polling
3 winnipeg_apt

---

exercises

12.1 This exercise provides further opportunity to find a set of data from an online source (such as www.infoplease.com), create a data frame from scratch (see the Chapter 1 Appendix, if necessary), and analyze it using some of the methods associated with simple linear regression. Look up and record the high and low intraday temperatures (in either degrees Celsius or Fahrenheit) for the following 14 cities from around the world: Auckland, Beijing, Cairo, Lagos, London, Mexico City, Mumbai, Paris, Rio de Janeiro, Sydney, Tokyo, Toronto, Vancouver, and Zurich. This information is easily found after a brief search.

(a) Use `c()` to create three objects one for each city name, one for the high temperatures, and one for the low temperature. Data are recorded for December 19, 2016.
(b) Use `data.frame()` to create a data frame consisting of each city name and high and low temperatures. This results in an object with 14 observations on two variables. Display the results to check your work.
(c) Make a scatter plot of high against low temperatures. Create a main title, label each axis appropriately, and use `pch =` to specify how the points should appear. Does the pattern of points appear to confirm that the relationship between high and low temperatures is linear?
(d) Estimate and write out the regression equation $\hat{y} = b_0 + b_1 x$. Let the high temperature be the dependent variable, and the low temperature, the independent variable.
(e) What is the value of r^2?
(f) What is the *p*-value? Is the estimate regression equation significant? Why or why not?

12.2 A dependent variable *y* is regressed on an independent variable *x*; the sample size is $n = 32$.

(a) If $SS_{reg} = 808.89$ and $SS_{reg} = 317.16$, what is r^2?
(b) If $b_1 = -0.041215$ and $s_{b_1} = 0.004712$, what is the value of the test statistic *t*?
(c) What is the *p*-value?
(d) Is the estimated regression equation significant at the $\alpha = 0.01$ level?
(e) If $b_0 = 29.599855$, write out the regression equation $\hat{y} = b_0 + b_1 x$.

12.3 This exercise uses the `mtcars` data set that is installed in R. (Remember that to see all the installed data sets, simply enter `data()` at the R prompt in the Console; to view the `mtcars` data set itself, enter `mtcars` at the R prompt; to learn more about the data set, including the variables and observations, enter `?mtcars` at the prompt and wait for the R Help page to open.) In this case, we are interested in the relationship between an automobile's quarter-mile time and gross horsepower.

(a) Create a scatter plot of the two variables. What does the pattern of points suggest about the relationship (if any) between the variables? Are there any outliers?
(b) Letting the quarter-mile time be the dependent variable, estimate the regression equation. Write out the regression equation $\hat{y} = b_0 + b_1 x$.
(c) What is the value of r^2?
(d) What is the p-value?
(e) Is the estimated regression equation significant at the $\alpha = 0.05$ level?

12.4 Use the `mtcars` data set to answer the following questions.

(a) Find the predicted quarter-mile time for all the values of gross horsepower from the data set used in the original analysis. Report the predicted values for the last four observations.
(b) Find the predicted values of quarter-mile time for the following values of gross horsepower: 100, 125, 160, 225, and 250.
(c) Can we use the estimated regression equation to make predictions of quarter-mile time when gross horsepower is 40 or 350? Why or why not?

12.5 This exercise explores the relationship (if any) between two of the five variables comprising the data set `polling`: x_1 = age, measured in years, and x_3 = same sex, which is measured on a 1-to-7 Likert scale as a response to the statement, "I approve of the right of same-sex couples to marry." A respondent registers strong disapproval with a 1, strong approval with a 7, and relative indifference with a response in the middle of the range from 1 to 7. Note: `polling` can be found on the book's website.

(a) Make a scatter plot of x_3 against x_1. Do you see any possible violations of the assumptions underlying the correct application of simple linear regression analysis? What does the nature of the pattern tell you? Do you think regression can be used to explore the relationship between the two variables?
(b) Write out the regression equation. In this case, does it make more sense to specify x_1 or x_3 as the dependent variable? That is, should you define the model as $x_3 = b_0 + b_1 x_1$ or as $x_1 = b_0 + b_1 x_3$? Why?
(c) What is the value of r^2?
(d) What is the p-value?
(e) Is the regression equation significant at the $\alpha = 0.05$ level?
(f) Find the 95% confidence interval estimate of β_1.
(g) State in words the meaning of the confidence interval estimate of β_1.
(h) What are your conclusions about the regression analysis? Please write out your conclusions in a similar way to those written out in point 6, part (c), of the Summary section above.

Multiple Regression

contents

learning objectives

1. Understand how regression analysis can be used to obtain an equation that estimates how two or more independent variables are related to a dependent variable.
2. Know how to fit an estimated regression equation to a set of sample data based on the least-squares method.
3. Be able to determine how good a fit is provided by the estimated regression equation.
4. Understand the assumptions necessary for statistical inference and be able to test for a significant relationship.

13.1 SIMPLE LINEAR REGRESSION: A REPRISE

In Chapter 12 we introduced a method known as regression and applied it to a simple example. We learned that simple linear regression analysis provides a linear equation that describes the relationship of one variable y, the dependent variable, to another variable x, the independent variable. In this chapter we extend this discussion to multiple regression, a procedure that provides an equation that describes the relationship of a dependent variable y to more than one independent variable $x_1, x_2, \ldots, x_n$.

Consider the following application of multiple regression. Meals on Wheels (MOW), the organization that meets the support needs of the elderly and persons recovering from hospital stays, is well represented in Australia, where services are delivered to thousands of people in their homes on an almost daily basis. Throughout the country, volunteers and staff members deliver meals to home-bound persons and provide one-on-one personal well-being visits. All this requires considerable planning because, as with social service agencies elsewhere, financial support is insufficient to conduct operations without it. To this end, the Brisbane MOW supervisor would like to understand the factors associated with the time MOW vehicles spend on the road each day conducting client visits.

As a first step, the supervisor collects data on 18 randomly selected daily schedules in terms of the total time a vehicle is on the road during a day of client visits and the total distance travelled during that time. It stands to reason that the greater the distance covered during a day of scheduled client visits, the longer the time a vehicle will be on the road making those visits. The `brisbane` data set can be found on the book's website, and includes two variables of interest for our present purposes, `minutes` and `kilometers`. In what follows, we go through all six steps detailed in the Summary section of Chapter 12.

1. **Describe the research question in clear and unambiguous terms.** We want to understand the relationship (if any) between the total daily time a MOW vehicle is on the road and the total daily distance it must cover.
2. **Define the variables and describe the sample being used in the analysis.** Each of the 18 randomly selected schedules is drawn from the record of recently scheduled daily client visits by the Brisbane MOW organization and is specified in terms of the two variables. The variable `minutes` has been converted from hours for ease of analysis and subsequent interpretation; naturally, the variable `kilometers` is expressed in terms of kilometers.

3 **Verify tentatively that the two variables are linearly related.** This step normally requires that we construct and inspect a scatter plot. In this case, we can simply use the `plot()` function and the website data set `brisbane`.

```
plot(brisbane$kilometers, brisbane$minutes, pch = 19, xlab =
     'Kilometers the Vehicle Travels on the Daily Client Visits',
     ylab = 'Minutes the Vehicle is on the Road')
```

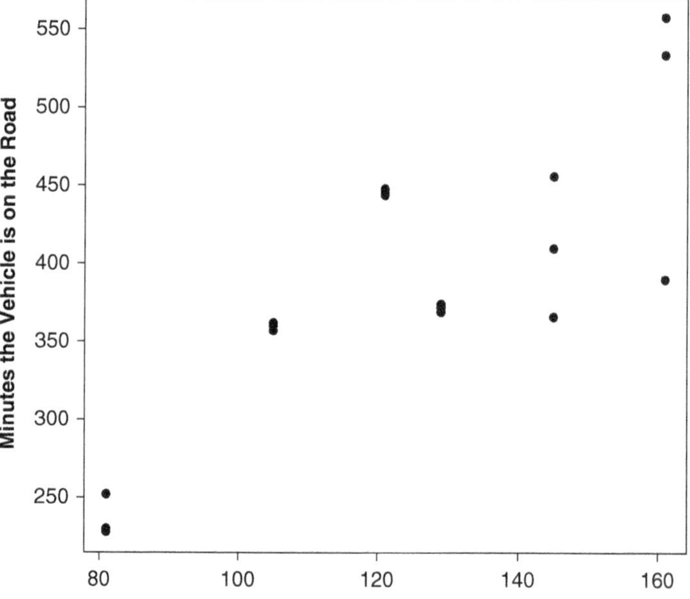

Figure 13.1 A scatter plot of daily travel time against distance for MOW vehicles

That the points in Figure 13.1 run in a band from the lower left to the upper right corners of the scatter plot suggests that the relationship is roughly linear. The only possible problem is that the variation of `minutes` does not seem constant for all values of `kilometers`. In fact, the variation of `minutes` seems to increase as `kilometers` increases. This is an issue we explore further in step 4.

4 **Make and inspect a residual plot.** Because we know that a scatter plot does not always reveal the real nature of the relationship between two variables, it is important that we create and examine a residual plot. The first step to doing this is to estimate the regression equation itself. (We cannot examine the residuals without first finding them, but to find them we must begin with the regression analysis.) The regression equation $\hat{y} = b_0 + b_1x$ can be estimated the same way as it was in Chapter 12, using the `lm()` function; the residuals are then found using the function `resid()`. The two-step approach is demonstrated in the R block below. See Comments 1 and 2.

```
#Comment1. The first step to making a residual plot is to create
#a regression model object. In this case, use function lm()
#to create a model object. Name it slr.
slr <- lm(minutes ~ kilometers, data = brisbane)

#Comment2. Create plot of residuals against kilometers; use
#resid(slr) as an argument in plot() function.
plot(brisbane$kilometers, resid(slr), pch = 19, abline(h = 0),
     xlab = 'Kilometers the Vehicle Travels on the Daily Client
     Visits', ylab = 'Residuals')
```

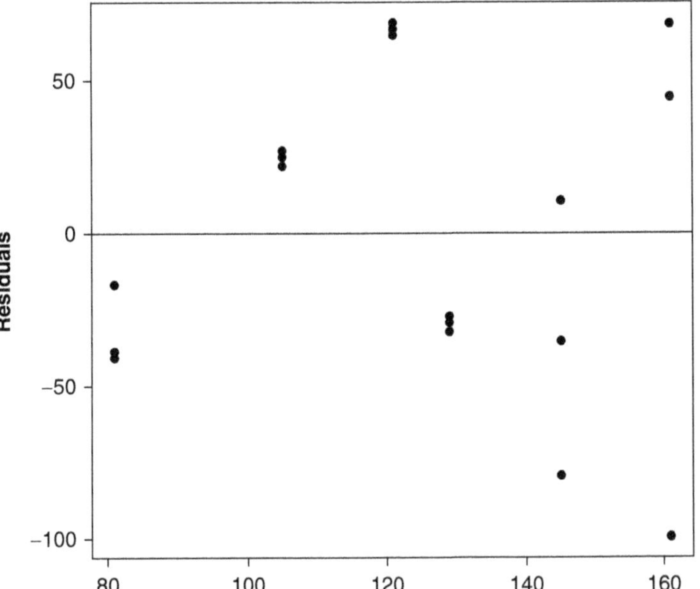

Figure 13.2 A plot of the residuals against the independent variable (kilometers)

The residual plot (Figure 13.2) casts some doubt on the assumption of constant variation of $\varepsilon = y_i - \hat{y}_i$ for all values of `kilometers`, the independent variable. Put another way, the variation of `minutes`, the dependent variable, around the regression line increases as `kilometers` increases. Although it is difficult to diagnose the reasons for this, it is very possible that the regression model should include additional independent variables.

Are we justified in using simple linear regression to model the relationship between these two variables? Yes, we probably are if we (a) bear in mind that the sample size is not very large and (b) avoid using the estimated equation to predict `minutes` using larger values of the independent variable `kilometers`. That is where the variation of dependent variable values is greatest and the fit of the regression line is least precise.

5 **Use the `summary()` function to unpack the important information from the model object.**

```
#Comment1. Invoke this option to specify that all values be reported
#in their normal format and not in scientific notation.
options(scipen = 999)

#Comment2. Use function lm() to create a model object; name it slr.
slr <- lm(minutes ~ kilometers, data = brisbane)

#Comment3. Use extractor function summary() to learn the actual
#estimated regression equation, the p-value, and the r-square
#from slr.
summary(slr)
```

```
##
## Call:
## lm(formula = minutes ~ kilometers, data = brisbane)
##
## Residuals:
##      Min      1Q  Median      3Q     Max
## -99.463 -34.525  -3.011  40.169  68.914
##
## Coefficients:
##              Estimate Std  Error t value   Pr(>|t|)
## (Intercept)    45.195     61.158   0.739      0.471
## kilometers      2.759      0.484   5.702  0.0000327 ***
## --
## Signif. codes: 0 '***' 0.001 '**' 0.01 '*' 0.05 '.' 0.1 ' ' 1
##
## Residual standard error: 53.37 on 16 degrees of freedom
## Multiple R-squared: 0.6702, Adjusted R-squared: 0.6496
## F-statistic: 32.51 on 1 and 16 DF, p-value: 0.00003274
```

(a) The intercept term is $b_0 = 45.195$.
(b) The coefficient on the independent variable (call it x) is $b_1 = 2.759$.
(c) The estimated regression equation is $\hat{y} = 45.195 + 2.759x$.
(d) The coefficient of determination is $r^2 = 0.6702$.
(e) The observed level of significance is *p-value* = 0.0000327.

Note that we now use the more convenient, general terms y and x to denote the dependent and independent variables.

6 **What do we know?** The scatter plot and the estimated regression equation indicate that there is a positive linear relationship between time on the road and distance travelled. The residual plot suggests that while there is a bit of a problem with non-constant variation of ε terms as x increases, there are no obvious outliers.

In this example, the coefficient of determination $r^2 = 0.6702$ indicates that roughly 67% of variation in time on the road can be accounted for by variation in distance travelled; the other 33% of variation is accounted for by factors not included in the analysis. The coefficient in the regression equation $\hat{y} = 45.195 + 2.759x$ tell us that a 1 kilometer change in travel distance is associated with a 2.759 minute change in time on the road. The intercept term $b_0 = 45.195$ means very little since it represents the number of minutes on the road when the vehicle drives 0 kilometers (that is, when $x = 0$). (Even so, we retain the intercept in the equation when we use it for prediction.) Finally, an observed level of significance of $p = 0.0000327$ indicates that the relationship between time and distance is highly significant.

We have taken the trouble to go through all six steps involved in regression analysis once again because it is important to encourage all students and readers at the outset to follow a sort of "best practice" approach. Even if the steps seem detailed and tedious, adhering to them can help avoid many of the most common mistakes that even experienced analysts commit occasionally. As we move on to the section introducing multiple regression, we incorporate a similar framework for conducting this type of analysis.

13.2 MULTIPLE REGRESSION: THE MODEL

Recall that the simple linear regression model takes the form $y = \beta_0 + \beta_1 x + \varepsilon$ and is estimated by the simple linear regression equation $\hat{y} = b_0 + b_1 x$. Recall also that b_0 and b_1 are the sample statistics that are used to estimate the population parameters β_0 and β_1, while y and x are the dependent and independent variables, respectively. Finally, ε is the error term that represents the random component of the regression model. In general, multiple regression can be thought of in the same terms as simple linear regression. In fact, it is an extension of simple linear regression because it allows for the introduction of additional independent variables into the model.

The analysis and interpretation of multiple regression are in large part the same as they are in the case of simple linear regression, but there are some differences. One of the differences is that we no longer refer to the regression *line* but rather to the regression *plane*, since there are always at least two independent variables. This feature—the presence of multiple independent variables—also makes it difficult (and often impossible) to render a graphical image of the regression plane on a two-dimensional page.

Definition 13.1. Multiple Regression Model. A general expression that specifies how the dependent variable y is related to the independent variables $x_1, x_2, \dots, x_k$ plus the error term ε.

The multiple regression model with k independent variables takes the form

$$y = \beta_0 + \beta_1 x_1 + \beta_2 x_2 + \dots + \beta_k x_k + \varepsilon$$

where y is the dependent or criterion variable; $x_1, x_2, \dots, x_k$ are the independent or predictor variables; β_0 is the y-intercept, or the point at which the regression plane intercepts the y-axis; $\beta_1, \beta_2, \dots, \beta_k$ are the partial regression coefficients; and ε is the error term that represents the random component of the regression model.

Note that in the case of multiple regression, the population regression coefficients $\beta_1, \beta_2, \ldots, \beta_k$ are now referred to as the *partial regression coefficients*.

Definition 13.2. Partial Regression Coefficients. Partial regression coefficients are the regression coefficients that form the multiple regression model. Unless the independent variables are perfectly uncorrelated with one another, a partial regression coefficient is not equal to the simple linear regression coefficient on the same independent variable; nor in general does the partial regression coefficient remain constant when it is accompanied by different sets of other independent variables.

13.3 MULTIPLE REGRESSION: THE MULTIPLE REGRESSION EQUATION

As with simple linear regression, the error term ε is needed because the equation does not express the relationship between y and the independent variables perfectly. In fact, there are many variables that are usually omitted from the analysis, either because we do not know about them or (even if we do) we cannot get adequate measurements on them. Because of this, in the MOW example, the dependent variable `minutes` has a distribution of values and, like other distributions, it has an expected value $E(y)$. This notion can be expressed in terms of the multiple regression equation,

$$E(y|x_1, x_2, .., x_k) = \mu_{y|x_1, x_2, .., x_k} = \beta_0 + \beta_1 x_1 + \beta_2 x_2 + \ldots + \beta_k x_k,$$

where $E(y|x_1, x_2, .., x_k) = \mu_{y|x_1, x_2, .., x_k}$ is the expected value of y for given values of $x_1, x_2, \ldots, x_k$.

Definition 13.3. Multiple Regression Equation. A general expression that specifies how the expected value of y, or $E(y|x_1, x_2, .., x_k) = \mu_{y|x_1, x_2, .., x_k}$, is related to the independent variables $x_1, x_2, \ldots, x_k$.

Indeed, in our example, the time a vehicle is on the road (for any given scheduled distance in kilometers) is not something that can be predicted with perfect accuracy, largely because other variables, known as well as unknown, also contribute to the variability in daily driving time but are omitted from the analysis.

13.4 THE ESTIMATED MULTIPLE REGRESSION EQUATION

It should be clear, however, that we cannot actually use the above multiple regression equation to describe the relationship between y and the independent variables because we seldom if ever know the values of $\beta_0, \beta_1, \beta_2, \ldots, \beta_k$. What we need to do to render this expression into a usable form is collect a sample of data and then find the estimated multiple regression equation. Once we have done this, we can replace $\mu_{y|x_1, x_2, .., x_k}$ with $\hat{y}$, the estimated value of the dependent variable y for a given level of the independent variables, and the population parameters $\beta_0, \beta_1, \beta_2, \ldots, \beta_k$ with the sample statistics $b_0, b_1, b_2, \ldots, b_k$. Once we have collected the data and run the analysis, we have the estimated multiple regression equation of the form

$$\hat{y} = b_0 + b_1 x_1 + b_2 x_2 + \ldots + b_k x_k$$

where $\hat{y}$ is the estimator of $\mu_{y|x_1, x_2, \ldots, x_k}$ or the mean of the dependent variable for a given level of the independent variables $x_1, x_2, \ldots, x_k$; b_0 is the point estimator of the y-intercept term β_0; and $b_1, b_2, \ldots, b_k$ are the point estimators of the population partial regression coefficients $\beta_1, \beta_2, \ldots, \beta_k$.

Definition 13.4. Estimated Multiple Regression Equation. A general expression that specifies how the predicted value of the dependent variable, or $\hat{y}$, is related to the independent variables $x_1, x_2, \ldots, x_k$. In this case, the estimators $b_0, b_1, b_2, \ldots, b_k$ (which are estimated from the sample data) replace the parameters $\beta_0, \beta_1, \ldots, \beta_k$, respectively.

Although in Section 12.2 we were able to solve for b_0 and b_1 using simple equations (derived in Section 12.9), we do not propose to follow this approach in the case of multiple regression. For one thing, since we have more than one independent variable for which we need to estimate a coefficient, the mathematical solution is considerably more tedious to work out. For another, because we can perform regression analysis using R, doing so any other way is unnecessary.

MULTIPLE REGRESSION: TWO INDEPENDENT VARIABLES

Returning to the example, suppose that while the manager believes that the estimated simple linear regression equation (in Section 13.1) provides a reasonable amount of explanatory and predictive power, he wants to improve on the model by identifying a second independent variable that is related to `minutes`, and incorporating it into the analysis. After consulting his drivers about what that new variable might be, the manager concludes that the number of scheduled client visits is also an important predictor of the time a vehicle must be on the road. In fact, the number of client visits that can be carried out in a scheduled workday varies, as some clients require more attention and care than others. In view of this, the manager decides to add the new variable `visits` to the `brisbane` data set. See Table 13.1 for all three variables across all 18 observations.

Note that while `kilometers` varies considerably from one schedule to the next, `visits` assumes only three values: 12, 13, or 14. Although we do not know at this point if `visits` explains very much of the variation in `minutes` that is not also explained by `kilometers`, it appears that the two independent variables, `visits` and `kilometers`, are themselves unrelated. This indicates that `visits` may tap into a source of variation in `minutes` not captured by `kilometers` and so may be a promising candidate for inclusion in the regression model. For convenience and simplicity of notation, we relabel the variables: y = `minutes`, the dependent variable; x_1 = `kilometers`, the first independent variable; and x_2 = `visits`, the second independent variable.

Compare the following schedules in Table 13.1: schedule 7 was for a day on which there were 12 visits requiring the driver to cover 161 km, but schedule 9 was for a day on which there were 12 visits requiring the driver to cover only 81 km. Clearly, `visits` and `kilometers` are measuring different aspects of the daily operating experience.

Table 13.1 Data set for Brisbane Meals on Wheels scheduling example

Schedule no.	y = minutes	x_1 = kilometers	x_2 = visits
1	558	161	14
2	448	121	13
3	228	81	13
4	369	129	12
5	534	161	14
6	446	121	13
7	390	161	12
8	410	145	13
9	252	81	12
10	357	105	14
11	372	129	12
12	362	105	14
13	444	121	13
14	374	129	12
15	360	105	14
16	230	81	13
17	456	145	13
18	366	145	12

The scatter plot in Figure 13.3 appears to support the view that `minutes` and `visits` are positively associated. However, we note that the relationship is a relatively weak one.

```
plot(brisbane$visits, brisbane$minutes, pch = 19, xlab = 'Number of
     Scheduled Daily Client Visits', ylab = 'Minutes the Vehicle is
     on the Road')
```

We also observe the peculiar pattern of some of the observations. For example, consider the six schedules when the number of client visits is 12. For five of the 12-visit schedules, `minutes` falls in the relatively narrow range from 366 to 390, but for one 12-visit schedule (see schedule 9 in Table 13.1) `minutes` is only 252 minutes. What might explain this apparent outlier? Without knowing more, we might surmise that for the first set of schedules, the 12 clients are the same from one schedule to the next or, if they are not, they at least live in the same neighborhood.

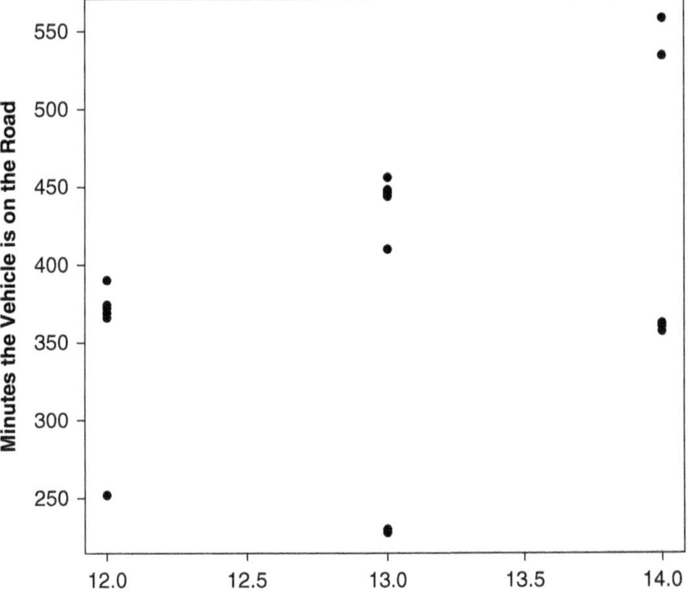

Figure 13.3 A scatter plot of daily travel time against number of client visits

The clients who are visited in schedule 9 probably live in an entirely different neighborhood in the Brisbane metropolitan area from those included in the other schedules. This pattern of observations—many observations clustered together but with outliers—also characterizes those schedules including 13 and 14 visits. Despite this strange pattern, we introduce `visits` as a second independent variable into the regression analysis because it may contribute to the explanatory and predictive power of the model.

But before we extend the regression model to include visits as an independent variable, we need to examine the extent to which it is related to the first independent variable, `kilometers`. The reason why we want to do this is that a problem known as *multicollinearity* often emerges once we move from simple linear regression, where it is not an issue, to multiple regression. Put simply, multicollinearity is a condition characterizing multiple regression models when some of the independent variables are correlated with one another. There are several ways of checking for correlation, of course, but obvious methods include calculating the correlation coefficient, and creating and examining a scatter plot.

In the first instance, the correlation coefficient is $r \approx -0.04$ and is an indication that `visits` and `kilometers` are only very weakly correlated, if they are correlated at all. We use the `cor()` function to find this measure of association:

```
cor(brisbane$kilometers, brisbane$visits)

## [1] -0.03654897
```

In the second, the lack of any discernible pattern of points in the scatter plot (Figure 13.4) confirms the weak (or non-existent) association between `visits` and `kilometers`.

```
plot(brisbane$kilometers, brisbane$visits, pch = 19, xlab = 'Kilometers
    the Vehicle Travels on the Daily Visits', ylab = 'Number of Scheduled
    Daily Client Visits')
```

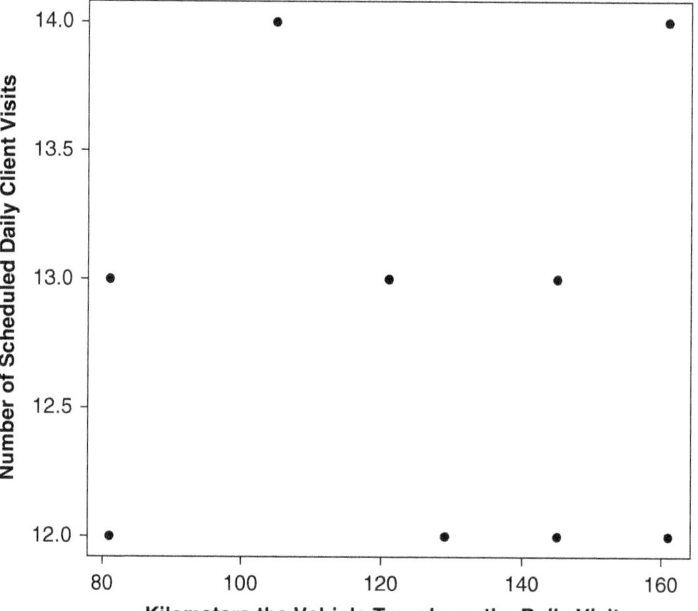

Figure 13.4 A scatter plot of number of client visits against distance traveled

It is possible to produce all scatter plots simultaneously by use of the `pairs()` function:

```
pairs(brisbane, pch = 19, lower.panel = NULL)
```

The arguments of this function require a little explanation.

1 The first argument directs the `pairs()` function to the data object `brisbane`.
2 The next argument is `pch =` which specifies the plotting character. Since we have used this argument repeatedly with other functions, we say no more about it here.
3 The final argument `lower.panel = NULL` is optional. If this argument is included and specified in this way, the resulting graphic image provides the pairwise plots in the upper diagonal (only) of the scatter plot matrix; if it is omitted, the image reproduces and reports (unnecessarily) the pairwise plots in the lower diagonal as well. We have inserted this element only because we want a less cluttered image.

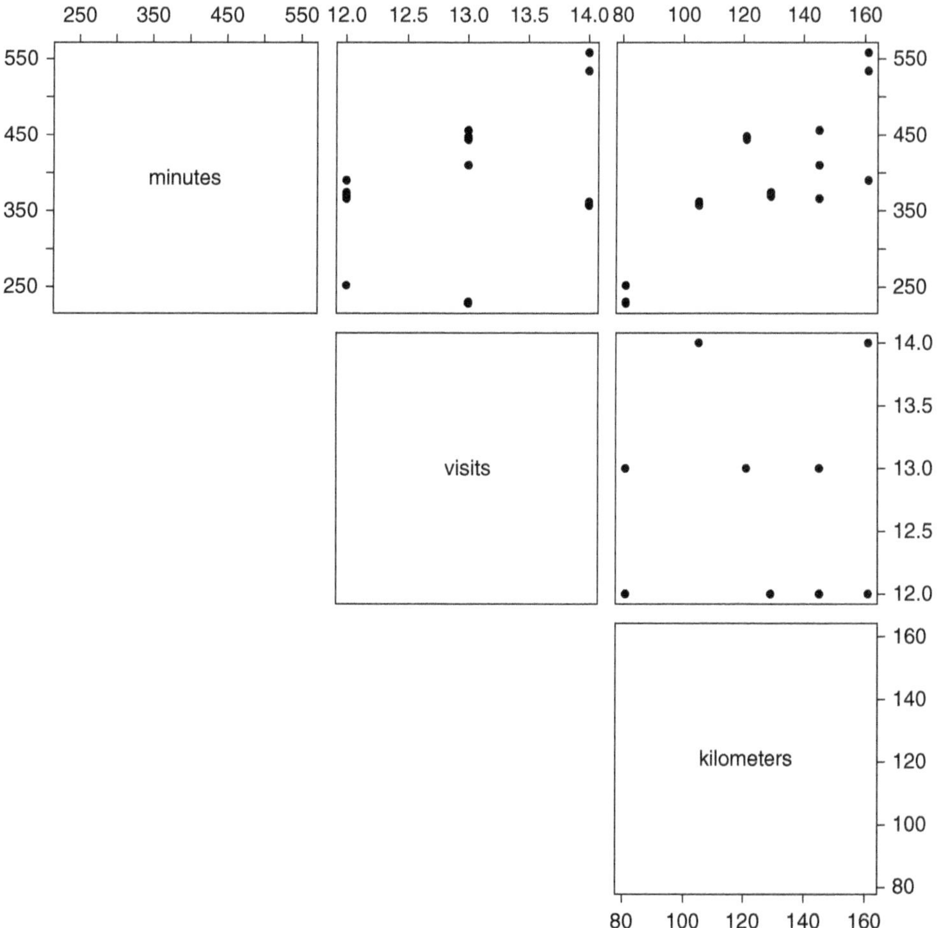

Figure 13.5 A pairwise scatter plot of all variables against one another

Figure 13.5 provides all three scatter plots simultaneously. The plot in the upper right-hand corner reproduces Figure 13.1: the variable `minutes` is plotted against `kilometers`. The plot in the center column of the top row replicates Figure 13.3: the variable `minutes` is plotted against `visits`. Finally, the plot in the second row of the right-hand column reproduces Figure 13.4: the variable `visits` is plotted against `kilometers`. The pairwise scatter plot allows us to confirm at a glance three different relationships that (in this example) we want to know about before commencing the analysis: `minutes` and `kilometers` seem to be positively related; `minutes` and `visits` appear to be positively related; and `kilometers` and `minutes` are evidently not related in any systematic way.

The `pairs()` function provides a quick and easy means by which to visualize all pairwise plots without having to go to the trouble of running individual scatter plots (as we have done in

Figures 13.1, 13.3, and 13.4). When the number of variables gets larger, however, the individual plots become smaller (because there are more of them) and more difficult to interpret since they are harder to see.

Example 13.1. Apply the `lm()` function to the `brisbane` data to find (1) the estimated multiple regression equation, $\hat{y} = b_0 + b_1x_1 + b_2x_2$, and (2) the value of r^2.

Before we conduct the regression analysis, we make a few points.

1. Use the `lm()` function (as we did for the simple linear regression in Section 13.1) but separate the independent variables `kilometers` and `visits` from one another with the + sign. Note that whenever we conduct multiple regression analysis, each independent variable must be separated from the others with the + sign, regardless of the number of variables.
2. Include `data = brisbane` as the data set to be analyzed by `lm()`.
3. Store the results in a model object and name it `mr` (for "multiple regression").
4. Use the `summary()` extractor function to reveal the relevant information that is housed in the model object `mr`.
5. Note that the output is identical in form and content (with exception of the numbers) to that obtained for simple linear regression in Section 13.1.

```
#Comment. Use lm() function; separate independent variables with + sign.
mr <- lm(minutes ~ kilometers + visits, data = brisbane)
summary(mr)

##
## Call:
## lm(formula = minutes ~ kilometers + visits, data = brisbane)
##
## Residuals:
##     Min      1Q  Median      3Q     Max
## -60.509 -34.678   2.273  19.273  66.645
##
## Coefficients:
##              Estimate Std. Error t value   Pr(>|t|)
## (Intercept) -518.7481   169.0094  -3.069    0.00779 **
## kilometers     2.8067     0.3723   7.538 0.00000178 ***
## visits        43.1148    12.4110   3.474    0.00340 **
## --
## Signif. codes: 0 '***' 0.001 '**' 0.01 '*' 0.05 '.' 0.1 ' ' 1
##
## Residual standard error: 41.03 on 15 degrees of freedom
## Multiple R-squared:  0.8172, Adjusted R-squared: 0.7928
## F-statistic: 33.53 on 2 and 15 DF,  p-value: 0.000002914
```

What follows is a discussion of the output of the `summary()` extractor function. While many of the terms and concepts are similar to what we have seen before in the case of simple linear regression, there are also several new issues to consider.

1. The estimated regression equation is $\hat{y} = -518.7481 + 2.8067x_1 + 43.1148x_2$.
2. The intercept term is b_0= -518.7481. Taken literally, it represents the `minutes` a vehicle is on the road when its schedule includes no `kilometers` and no `visits`. Since it is a negative number, we are justified in ignoring it for purposes of interpretation. Even so, it is important to retain the intercept term in the model since it must be included when we want to use the estimated equation to make predictions.
3. The partial regression coefficient on the independent variable x_1 = `kilometers` is 2.8067. Note that the relative magnitude of the coefficient on `kilometers` has changed from b_1 = 2.759, when it was reported above as part of the estimated simple linear regression equation, to b_1 = 2.8067. This change in the magnitude of the regression coefficient happens because the independent variables usually are correlated, at least to some extent. Recall that in the case of simple linear regression, x_2 = `visits` was not included in the model. Because of that, any variation in the dependent variable y = `minutes` that is shared by x_1 and x_2 is attributed to x_1 and only to x_1. But when we include both x_1 and x_2, any variation in y that is attributable to x_2 can now be reported as such.
   How should we interpret b_1, the partial regression coefficient on the independent variable x_1? It represents the estimated change in the dependent variable y when accompanied by a one-unit change in x_1 while holding x_2 constant. In the Brisbane example, because b_1 = 2.8067 we expect that a 1-km change in the independent variable x_1 should be accompanied by a 2.8067-minute change in the dependent variable y, as long as the number of client visits x_2 is held constant.
4. The partial regression coefficient on the independent variable x_2 = `visits` is 43.1148. How should we interpret b_2, the partial regression coefficient on the independent variable x_2? In a similar vein, b_2 is the estimated change in y when the independent variable x_2 changes by one unit but x_1 is held constant. In the example, because b_2 = 43.1148 we expect that a one-visit change in the independent variable x_2 should be accompanied by a 43.1148-minute change in the dependent variable y, as long as the number of kilometers x_1 is held constant.
5. The *multiple R-squared* is reported as 0.8172. This is the same r^2 (the coefficient of determination) we encountered in Section 12.3; now as then, it is an important measure of the goodness of fit of the regression model. Fortunately, the r^2 statistic is calculated and interpreted the same way, where $0 < r^2 < 1$. When the r^2 for a model approaches 1, the fit of the model to the data is good; when the r^2 approaches 0, the fit of the model to the data is poor. In the case of multiple regression analysis, the r^2 is commonly referred to as the *multiple coefficient of determination.*

Definition 13.5. Multiple Coefficient of Determination. The multiple coefficient of determination r^2 is a measure of the strength of linear association between the dependent variable y and the independent variables $x_1, x_2, \ldots, x_k$. Its value varies between 0 and 1, and it indicates the proportion of total variation in the dependent variable that is explained by the variation in the independent variables.

Recall also that in Section 12.3, we partitioned the total sum of squares SS_y into its two constituent parts, the regression sum of squares SS_{reg} and the residual sum of squares SS_{res}, where the relationship between these components can be expressed as $SS_y = SS_{reg} + SS_{res}$ or

$$\Sigma(y_i - \bar{y})^2 = \Sigma(\hat{y}_i - \bar{y})^2 + \Sigma(y_i - \hat{y}_i)^2.$$

The r^2 is expressed as

$$r^2 = \frac{SS_y - SS_{\text{res}}}{SS_y},$$

where

$$SS_y = \Sigma(y_i - \bar{y})^2 = 138{,}162.4$$

```
#Comment. To find the total sum of squares: ss_y
ss_y <- sum((brisbane$minutes - mean(brisbane$minutes)) ^ 2)
ss_y
```

```
## [1] 138162.4
```

and

$$SS_{\text{res}} = \Sigma(y_i - \hat{y})^2 = 25{,}253.43.$$

```
#Comment. To find the residual sum of squares: ss_res
ss_res <- sum((resid(mr)) ^ 2)
ss_res
```

```
## [1] 25253.43
```

Plugging the values for SS_y and SS_{res} into the expression for r^2, we find

$$r^2 = \frac{SS_y - SS_{\text{res}}}{SS_y} = \frac{138{,}162.4 - 25{,}253.43}{138{,}162.4} = 0.8172.$$

```
#Comment. Find the coefficient of determination: r_squared
r_squared <- (ss_y - ss_res) / ss_y
r_squared
```

```
## [1] 0.8172193
```

Thus, by including a second independent variable, the r^2 has increased from 0.6702 to 0.8172. We interpret this in the following way: 81.72% of the variation in the dependent variable y can be accounted for (or explained) by the variation in the two independent variables, x_1 and x_2.

It is worth contrasting the sum-of-squares values for the multiple regression with those for the simple linear regression (Section 13.1). Clearly, $SS_y = 138{,}162.4$ is the same for both models (see the SS_y column in Table 13.2) since it is simply a measure of the variability of y. Note, however, the trade-off relationship between SS_{reg} and SS_{res} for each model: SS_{res} falls and SS_{reg} rises when x_2 is introduced. (We do not show the computation of the SS values for the simple linear regression, but they can be derived the same way we found them above for the multiple regression.)

Table 13.2 Sum of squares table for the two regression models

Regression model	SS_y	SS_{reg}	SS_{res}
$\hat{y} = 45.195 + 2.759x_1$	138,162.4	92,591.75	45,570.70
$\hat{y} = -518.7481 + 2.8067x_1 + 43.1148x_2$	138,162.4	112,908.97	25,253.43

As additional independent variables are introduced into the regression model, SS_{res} becomes smaller. But because SS_y is unchanging, SS_{reg} inevitably becomes larger (recall that $SS_y = SS_{reg} + SS_{res}$). And when SS_{reg} becomes larger, so does r^2. This is true even if the independent variable makes no significant contribution to the explanatory power of the regression model. Because of this, it is possible that any model with a high value of r^2 contains independent variables that should not be included at all.

Because the r^2 always increases (and never decreases) as additional independent variables are introduced into the model, statisticians often prefer using the *adjusted* multiple coefficient of determination, or adjusted r^2, as a measure of goodness of fit. The adjusted r^2 deflates the r^2 to a somewhat lower value as additional independent variables are included. In the output (see Example 13.1), the adjusted r^2 is reported as 0.7928. Although the adjusted r^2 is provided in the output that R produces for all regressions, we did not discuss it for the simple linear regression (Section 13.1) because it is not particularly meaningful in that case; after all, the simple linear regression includes only one independent variable and the issue of additional independent variables never arises. It only becomes important for multiple regression because of the introduction of additional independent variables.

Definition 13.6. Adjusted Multiple Coefficient of Determination. The adjusted multiple coefficient of determination is a measure of the strength of linear association between the dependent variable y and the independent variables $x_1, x_2, \ldots, x_k$ that compensates for the number of independent variables.

The expression for the adjusted r^2 is

$$r^2_{\text{adj}} = r^2 - \frac{k(1-r^2)}{n-k-1},$$

where k is the number of independent variables and n is the sample size. Since, in this example, $k = 2$, $n = 18$, and $r^2 = 0.8172$, we can easily find the adjusted r^2:

$$r^2_{\text{adj}} = 0.8172 - \frac{2(1-0.8172)}{18-2-1} = 0.8172 - 0.0244 = 0.7928.$$

Since the partial regression coefficients are sample statistics (not different in essentials from the sample mean, sample standard deviation, or sample proportion), their values can be expected to change from one sample to the next. Fortunately, it is an easy matter to produce interval estimates of the regression coefficients for any multiple regression model.

Example 13.2. Find the 95% confidence interval estimates of the regression coefficients.

```
confint(mr, level = 0.95)
```

```
##                    2.5 %       97.5 %
## (Intercept) -878.983113 -158.513068
## kilometers     2.013084    3.600326
## visits        16.661275   69.568260
```

Thus, we can say that we are 95% confident that the partial regression coefficient for `kilometers` falls between 2.013084 and 3.600326; for `visits` it falls between 16.661275 and 69.568260. A couple of points of explanation follow.

1 The first argument of the `confint()` function indicates the name of the model object `mr`.
2 The second argument `level =` specifies the confidence level. This value can be set at any level of confidence that might be desired.

13.6 ASSUMPTIONS: WHAT ARE THEY? CAN WE VALIDATE THEM?

The basic assumptions about the model of the relationship between y and the independent variables $x_1, x_2, \ldots, x_k$ are similar to those underpinning the relationship between the dependent and independent variable in the instance of simple linear regression (see Section 12.7). Recall that the residuals or the error terms are defined as $\varepsilon = y_i - \hat{y}_i$.

1 The residuals $\varepsilon = y_i - \hat{y}_i$ are independent of one another. That is, the value of $y_i - \hat{y}_i$ for any given values of $x_1, x_2, \ldots, x_k$ is unrelated to the value of $y_i - \hat{y}_i$ for any other values of $x_1, x_2, \ldots, x_k$.
2 The variance of ε is $\sigma^2_{y|x_1, x_2, \ldots, x_k}$ and is constant for all values of $x_1, x_2, \ldots, x_k$. Put another way, the distribution of y values around the regression plane is the same for all values of $x_1, x_2, \ldots, x_k$.
3 The residuals ε are normally distributed with $E(\varepsilon) = 0$. In other words, the distribution of y values around the regression plane for any values of $x_1, x_2, \ldots, x_k$ is normal.

As we saw in Chapter 12, a good way to confirm whether a set of variables conforms to the assumptions underlying the correct usage of regression analysis is to create and inspect a plot of the residuals $\varepsilon = y_i - \hat{y}_i$ against the independent variable x. However, one difference between what we did in the case of simple linear regression and how we go about it for multiple regression is that we do not usually plot the residuals against the independent variable, for the reason that we now have more than one of them. (In fact, the residuals are sometimes plotted against the individual independent variables, one by one, but we do not do that here.) In view of this, we can instead plot the residuals against the predicted value of the dependent variable, $\hat{y}$. Here is the step we take to create the residual plot (see Figure 13.6). By now, all the arguments should be familiar.

```
plot(fitted(mr), resid(mr), abline(h = 0), pch = 19,
     xlab = 'Predicted Value of y', ylab = 'Residuals')
```

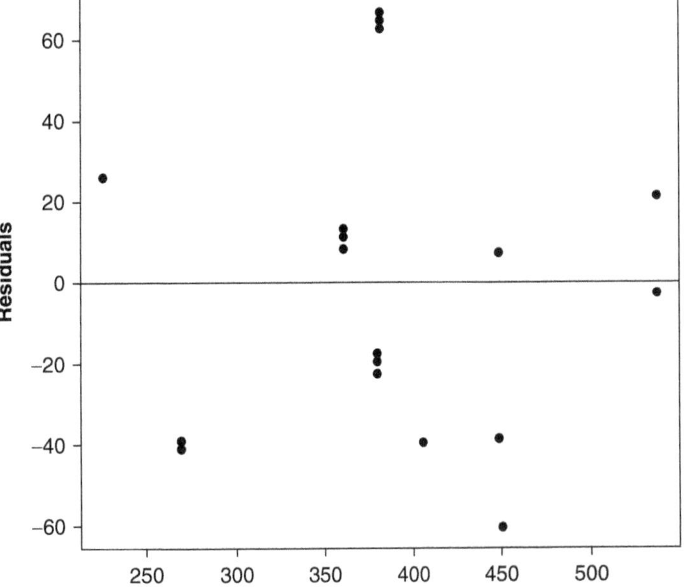

Figure 13.6 Plot of residuals $y_i - \hat{y}$ against the predicted dependent variable $\hat{y}$

A cursory inspection of the residual plot confirms that there is nothing obvious that might cause us to question whether the assumptions behind the correct application of regression analysis to the Brisbane data are satisfied. In particular, (1) there is no evidence of a nonlinear relationship (no bends, no curves, no kinks) between the residuals and the predicted dependent variable $\hat{y}$; (2) the variance of the residual terms around $\hat{y}$ seems to be relatively constant; and (3) there appear to be no conspicuous outliers. Accordingly, we might say that because we have validated the assumptions underpinning the correct application of regression analysis to the Brisbane data, regression appears to be an appropriate analytic methodology for this sample.

13.7 TESTS OF SIGNIFICANCE: THE OVERALL REGRESSION MODEL

Recall that in the case of simple linear regression, the only significance test involves testing $H_0: \beta_1 = 0$ against $H_a: \beta_1 \neq 0$. If H_0 is rejected, we conclude that a significant linear relationship exists between the dependent variable y and the independent variable x, either positive or negative. The tests of significance in the case of multiple regression are similar in rationale but different in how they are executed. In fact, for multiple regression, we must carry out two types of significance tests: one for the significance of the overall regression model itself, the other for the significance of each independent variable, taken one at a time. We begin with the first type of test, the test of the overall regression model; in the next section, we follow up with the tests of the independent variables.

Example 13.3. At the α = 0.05 level of significance, test to determine if the overall regression model is significant.

The test of the overall regression model requires that we use the *F*-statistic and the *F*-distribution. Although this is a new distribution, it is similar to other sampling distributions we have encountered thus far. In fact, there are many *F*-distributions and each is defined by two parameters, the numerator degrees of freedom (df_N) and the denominator degrees of freedom (df_D). The meaning of these terms is more easily understood within the context of the actual hypothesis test, and for the sake of continuity with how we have conducted significance tests in earlier chapters, we follow the familiar six-step hypothesis-testing framework here.

In this case, the null hypothesis is $H_0: \beta_1 = \beta_2 = \ldots = \beta_k = 0$, which expresses the view that none of the parameters is significant, that none of the independent variables is related to the dependent variable *y*. An alternative expression of this notion, and what we use below for the sake of notational simplicity, is $H_0: r^2 = 0$. In view of this, the alternative hypothesis H_a is at least one of the parameters is non-zero, or $H_a: r^2 > 0$. Put another way, when we state the null hypothesis as $H_0: r^2 = 0$, what we are doing is testing if the overall regression model offers *no benefit* in terms of explanatory or predictive power over simply modeling the dependent variable *y* using its own mean $\bar{y}$. As usual, rejection of H_0 leads us to conclude that H_a is true, and that at least one of the independent variables is significant.

1 Determine the null hypothesis H_0 in statistical terms.

$$H_0: r^2 = 0$$

2 Determine the alternative hypothesis H_a in statistical terms.

$$H_a = r^2 > 0$$

3 Set the level of significance α and decide on the sample size.

$n = 18$ and $\alpha = 0.05$

4 Use α to specify the rejection region *RR*.
The rejection region is

$$RR: F \geq F_{\alpha, df_N, df_D} = F_{\alpha,k,n-k-1} = F_{0.05,2,15} = 3.68232$$

where

$$F = \frac{SS_{\text{reg}}/k}{SS_{\text{res}}/(n-k-1)} = \frac{\Sigma(\hat{y}_i - \bar{y})^2/k}{\Sigma(y_i - \hat{y}_i)^2/(n-k-1)},$$

and where k = 2, the number of independent variables, and n – k – 1 = 18 – 2 – 1 = 15. Note that the particular *F*-distribution we need has $df_N = k = 2$ numerator degrees of freedom and $df_D = n-k-1 = 15$ denominator degrees of freedom.

Finding the value of $F_{0.05,2,15}$ is an easy matter when we use the `qf()` function. As usual, we include the argument `lower.tail = FALSE` to specify that the desired area of 0.05 is in the upper (not lower) tail. The expression below provides that value of *F* which cuts off an area of 0.05 in the upper tail of the *F*-distribution with $df_N = 2$ and $df_D = 15$.

```
qf(0.05, 2, 15, lower.tail = FALSE)
```

```
## [1] 3.68232
```

Once we complete this step, we know that if SS_{reg}, SS_{res}, k, and $n-k-1$ transform into a value of F that is greater than 3.68232, we reject H_0 and accept H_a; however, if F falls in the region less than 3.68232, we do not reject H_0 and conclude that there is not sufficiently strong evidence supporting the view that the overall regression model is significant. Worded slightly differently, if we do not reject H_0, there is insufficient evidence for us to conclude that the overall regression model predicts or explains `minutes` any better than the mean of `minutes`.

5 Collect the data and calculate the test statistic.
As we see in the above formulation, the F-statistic itself is a ratio of ratios that is easily computed if we know the values of SS_{reg}, SS_{res}, k, and $n - k - 1$. For the sake of convenience, the elements of the F-test statistic are often arranged in an analysis of variance (ANOVA) table. See Table 13.3.

Table 13.3 Analysis of variance (ANOVA) table for the Brisbane example

Source	Sum of squares	*df*	Mean square	*F*	p-value
Regression	$SS_{reg} = 112{,}908.97$	$k = 2$	56,454.485	33.5328	0.000002914
Residual	$SS_{res} = 25{,}253.43$	$n - k - 1 = 15$	1683.562		
Total	$SS_y = 138{,}162.4$	17			

We note that in the ANOVA table, SS_y is partitioned into its two sources, SS_{reg} and SS_{res}. Moving from left to right in Table 13.3, if we divide each SS term by the value of its respective degrees of freedom df, we find the mean square for both sources (both are recorded in the third column from the right). The ratio of the two mean square terms provides the F-test statistic which, in this case, is $F = 33.5328$, and is found in the second column from the right.

6 Use the test statistic and RR to decide whether to reject H_0.
Recall that the rejection region is RR: $F \geq 3.68232$. Since $F = 33.5328 > 3.68232$, we reject $H_0: r^2 = 0$ and accept $H_a: r^2 > 0$.
Thus we have found evidence that the overall regression model is significant and that (therefore) at least one of the independent variables is linearly related to the dependent variable y = `minutes`.

Example 13.4. (1) What is the p-value? (2) Compare the p-value with α.

1 Because the RR lies in the upper tail of the F-distribution, the p-value is the probability that F is greater than 33.5328:

$$p\text{-value} = p(F \geq 33.5328) = 0.000002914.$$

We can find the p-value using the `pf()` function in the usual way.

```
pf(33.5328, 2, 15, lower.tail = FALSE)
```

```
## [1] 0.000002913908
```

This conforms with the p-value found in the final line of the output above.

2 Since p-value = 0.000002914 and $\alpha = 0.05$, we have p-value $\leq \alpha$, and we reject H_0. See Example 13.1.

To get a better idea of what this particular F-distribution looks like, see Figure 13.7. In this instance, we have used R to generate 100,000 data values that are distributed according to the F-distribution with $df_N = 2$ and $df_D = 15$ and then displayed them in a histogram for visual purposes. Note that a value of $F = 33.5328$ would fall far to the right of the values of the horizontal axis; our p-value of 0.000002914 is the probability that F is larger than 33.5328.

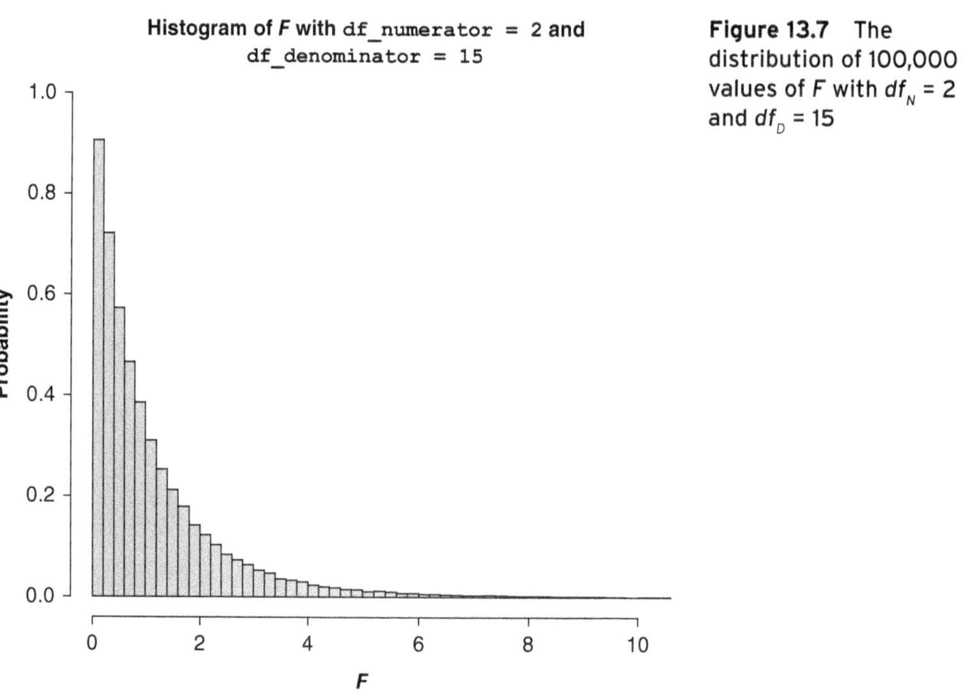

Figure 13.7 The distribution of 100,000 values of F with $df_N = 2$ and $df_D = 15$

To recreate the Figure 13.7 image, we execute two simple steps. See the R block below.

```
F215 <- rf(100000, 2, 15)

hist(F215, xlim = c(0, 10), ylim = c(0, 1), breaks = 150,
     freq = FALSE, xlab = 'F', ylab = 'Probability',
     main = 'Histogram of F with df_numerator = 2 and
     df_denominator = 15', col = 'blue')
```

What follows is an explanation of how to produce the above image.

1. Use the function `rf(100000, 2, 15)` to generate 100,000 data values that are F-distributed with $df_N = 2$ and $df_D = 15$, and store them in the object we call `F215` (named for the F-distribution with 2 and 15 degrees of freedom). Recall that we generated data values in a similar way for both the normal and uniform probability distributions in the Chapter 2 Appendix.
2. Use the `hist()` function to produce a histogram of the 100,000 data values. Here is an explanation of each of the nine arguments.
   (a) The first argument references the object name `F215`.
   (b) `xlim = c(0, 10)` specifies the range of the horizontal axis.
   (c) `ylim = c(0, 1)` defines the range of the vertical axis.
   (d) `breaks = 150` specifies the number of categories or bars for the histogram.
   (e) `freq = FALSE` indicates that the vertical axis reports probability densities rather than frequencies or counts.
   (f) `xlab = ''` defines the horizontal axis label.
   (g) `ylab = ''` defines the vertical axis label.
   (h) `main = ''` includes a main title to be placed above the image.
   (i) `col = ''` stipulates the color of the histogram bars.

Although the test of the overall regression model indicates that it is significant—and that therefore at least one of the independent variables is significant—we do not stop here. In fact, we must test each independent variable, one by one, to identify those that are significant and those that are not. We now turn our attention to this next round of hypothesis tests. Fortunately, these tests do not differ in any substantial way from the test we conducted in Chapter 12 in the case of the simple linear regression.

13.8 TESTS OF SIGNIFICANCE: THE INDEPENDENT VARIABLES

Since these tests are almost exactly the same as the one we used in Chapter 12 for simple linear regression, we turn directly to the familiar six-step hypothesis-testing framework. The only departure in the case of the multiple regression is that the test statistic has a t-distribution with $df = n - k - 1$ rather than $df = n - 2$. It is worth pointing out that the degrees-of-freedom expression, $df = n - k - 1$, is actually the same for simple linear regression as for multiple regression because when $k = 1$, $df = n - k - 1 = n - 1 - 1 = n - 2$.

Example 13.5. At the $\alpha = 0.05$ level of significance, test to determine if there is a significant relationship between y = `minutes` and x_1 = `kilometers` for the Brisbane example.

1. Determine the null hypothesis H_0 in statistical terms.

$$H_0 : \beta_1 = 0$$

The null hypothesis H_0 states that there is no linear relationship between y and x_1: that knowing x_1 in no way contributes to explaining or predicting y.

2 Determine the alternative hypothesis H_a in statistical terms.

$$H_a : \beta_1 \neq 0$$

The alternative hypothesis H_a states that there is a linear relationship between y and x_1, either positive or negative.

3 Set the level of significance α and decide on the sample size.

$$n = 18 \text{ and } \alpha = 0.05$$

4 Use α to specify the rejection region RR.
The rejection region is

$$RR : t \geq 2.131 \text{ and } t \leq -2.131.$$

Or reject H_0 if $t \geq t_{\alpha/2,n-k-1} = t_{0.025,15} = 2.131$ or $t \leq -t_{\alpha/2,n-k-1} = -t_{0.025,15} = -2.131$, where

$$t = \frac{b_1 - \beta_1}{s_{b_1}} = \frac{b_1 - 0}{s_{b_1}} = \frac{b_1}{s_{b_1}}.$$

```
qt(0.025, 15, lower.tail = FALSE)
```

```
## [1] 2.13145
```

```
qt(0.025, 15)
```

```
## [1] -2.13145
```

If $H_0 : \beta_1 = 0$ is true, then the test statistic t collapses to the ratio of b_1 to S_{b_1}. The value of t that cuts off an area of 0.025 in the upper tail is t = 2.131; the value of t that cuts off an area of 0.025 in the lower tail is t = –2.131. Therefore, if b_1 transforms into a value of t that is greater than 2.131, or less than –2.131, we reject H_0 and accept H_a; however, if t falls in the region from –2.131 to 2.131, we do not reject H_0.

5 Collect the data and calculate the test statistic.
Since $b_1 = 2.8067$ and $S_{b_1} = 0.3723$,

$$t = \frac{b_1}{s_{b_1}} = \frac{2.8067}{0.3723} = 7.538.$$

Thus, $b_1 = 2.8067$ corresponds to $t = 7.538$. To convert b_1 to t, we have taken S_{b_1} from the output (see Example 13.1) and do not work out its value (using a formula) here.

6 Use the test statistic and RR to decide whether to reject H_0.
Recall that the rejection region is $RR : t \geq 2.131$ and $t \leq -2.131$. Since $t = 7.538 > 2.131$, we reject $H_0 : \beta_1 = 0$ and accept $H_a : \beta_1 \neq 0$.

Thus, we have found evidence that the regression coefficient is significant. This result provides support for the view that y, the time (in minutes) that a Meals on Wheels driver is on the road calling on clients, is linearly associated with x_1, the number of kilometers the driver must travel.

Example 13.6. (1) What is the p-value? (2) Compare the p-value with α.

1 Because the *RR* lies in both the upper and lower tails of the *t*-distribution, the *p*-value is the probability that *t* is greater than 7.538 plus the probability that *t* is less than –7.538:

$$p\text{-}value = p(t \geq 7.538) + p(t \leq -7.538) = 0.00000089 + 0.00000089 = 0.00000178.$$

```
pt(7.538, 15, lower.tail = FALSE) + pt(-7.538, 15)

## [1] 0.000001777391
```

This conforms with the p-value for `kilometers` already reported (see Example 13.1).

2 Since *p-value* = 0.00000178 and $\alpha = 0.05$, we have $p\text{-}value \leq \alpha$, and we reject H_0.

Example 13.7. At the $\alpha = 0.05$ level of significance, test to determine if there is a significant relationship between y = `minutes` and x_2 = `visits` for the Brisbane example.

1 Determine the null hypothesis H_0 in statistical terms.

$$H_0 : \beta_2 = 0$$

The null hypothesis H_0 states that there is no linear relationship between y and x_2: that knowing x_2 in no way contributes to explaining or predicting y.

2 Determine the alternative hypothesis H_a in statistical terms.

$$H_a : \beta_2 \neq 0$$

The alternative hypothesis H_a states that there is a linear relationship between y and x_2, either positive or negative.

3 Set the level of significance α and decide on the sample size.

$$n = 18 \text{ and } \alpha = 0.05$$

4 Use α to specify the rejection region RR.
The rejection region is

$$RR : t \geq 2.131 \text{ and } t \leq -2.131.$$

Or reject H_0 if $t \geq t_{\alpha/2,n-k-1} = t_{0.025,15} = 2.131$ or $t \leq -t_{\alpha/2,n-k-1} = -t_{0.025,15} = -2.131$, where

$$t = \frac{b_2 - \beta_2}{s_{b_2}} = \frac{b_2 - 0}{s_{b_2}} = \frac{b_2}{s_{b_2}}.$$

```
qt(0.025, 15, lower.tail = FALSE)

## [1] 2.13145

qt(0.025, 15)

## [1] -2.13145
```

If $H_0 : \beta_2 = 0$ is true, then the test statistic *t* collapses to the ratio of b_2 to s_{b_2}. The value of *t* that cuts off an area of 0.025 in the upper tail is $t = 2.131$; the value of *t* that cuts off an area of 0.025 in the lower tail is $t = -2.131$. Therefore, if b_2 transforms into a value of *t* that is greater than 2.131, or less than –2.131, we reject H_0 and accept H_a; however, if *t* falls in the region from –2.131 to 2.131, we do not reject H_0.

5 Collect the data and calculate the test statistic.

Since $b_2 = 43.1148$ and $s_{b_2} = 12.4110$,

$$t = \frac{b_2}{s_{b_2}} = \frac{43.1148}{12.4110} = 3.474.$$

Thus, $b_2 = 43.1148$ corresponds to $t = 3.474$. Once again, for the purpose of converting b_2 to *t*, we have taken the value of s_{b_2} from the output, and do not derive it here.

6 Use the test statistic and RR to decide whether to reject H_0.
Recall that the rejection region is $RR: t \geq 2.131$ and $t \leq -2.131$. Since $t = 3.474 > 2.131$, we reject $H_0 : \beta_2 = 0$ accept $H_a : \beta_2 \neq 0$.
Therefore, we have found evidence that the regression coefficient is significant. This result provides support for the view that y, the time (in minutes) that a Meals on Wheels driver is on the road calling on clients, is linearly associated with x_2, the number of client visits the driver is scheduled to make.

Example 13.8. (1) What is the *p*-value? (2) Compare the *p*-value with α.

1 Because the RR lies in both the upper and lower tails of the *t*-distribution, the *p*-value is the probability that *t* is greater than 3.474 plus the probability that *t* is less than –3.474:

$$p\text{-}value = p(t \geq 3.474) + p(t \leq -3.474) = 0.0017 + 0.0017 = 0.0034.$$

```
pt(3.474, 15, lower.tail = FALSE) + pt(-3.474, 15)

## [1] 0.003400187
```

This agrees with the *p*-value for visits already reported.

2 Since *p-value* = 0.0034 and α = 0.05, we have $p\text{-}value \leq \alpha$, and we reject H_0.

Thus, we can conclude that not only is the overall regression model significant; so are both independent variables x_1 and x_2.

13.9 THERE MUST BE AN EASIER WAY THAN THIS, RIGHT?

There is a far easier way of testing for the significance of an overall multiple regression model and its independent variables, and it involves letting R do the tedious work. In fact, in the context of practical, real-world data analysis, one should not conduct regression analysis as we have above. So why have we bothered going through both types of statistical tests in such a painstakingly detailed way? The reason why we have developed the ideas as we have (using the six-step hypothesis-testing framework) is that it is important that we understand the rationale underlying the regression-analytic method.

Although we may write and execute statistical code proficiently, we must also understand the statistical methods to which that code is applied. If we do not, then we know just enough to be dangerous. But the person who understands how and why the analytic methods work has a far better chance of using it competently, even with skill.

In practice, here is how we use the statistical software to produce the results we need. Assuming we have performed the usual diagnostic tests (we return to this topic later, but for now that would include examining scatter plots, checking the residuals, etc.) and have executed the actual regression, we review the output for the relevant information. We have simplified this aspect of the analysis into the three steps that follow.

1 What is the adjusted r^2? This is found on the second-from-bottom line of the R output. If the value of the adjusted r^2 indicates that the model provides an acceptable level of goodness of fit, then proceed to step 2. If it does not, we sometimes need to collect more data or, more likely, refine our thinking about which independent variables to include (or omit) from the model.
2 Locate the *F* statistic and its *p*-value on the bottom line of the output. Is the *p*-value less than or equal to α? (For example, if we have set $\alpha = 0.05$, is *p-value* ≤ 0.05?) If the *p*-value is less than or equal to α, the overall regression model is significant. Since this tells us that at least one of the independent variables is significant, we proceed to step 3 to determine which variable(s) that might be.
3 Find the coefficients table in the output and locate the *p*-values of the independent variables in the far right-hand column (under the heading `Pr(>|t|)`). Those independent variables for which $p\text{-}value \leq \alpha$ are significant and can be retained in the model; those that are not are usually dropped from the model and the analysis is run again without them. Sometimes multiple regression models can be improved by employing any one of several variable-selection methods, including the well-known stepwise routine. One other approach to the variable-selection problem is known as the best-subsets procedure, and we discuss it in Section 13.11.

Following these three simple steps saves us from having to do everything the hard way, using (for example) the six-step hypothesis-testing framework. We are now in a position to consider how to make predictions and select our independent variables.

USING THE ESTIMATED REGRESSION EQUATION FOR PREDICTION

We saw in Example 12.10 that there are two commonly used ways of using the estimated regression equation to make predictions. One approach uses the `fitted()` function to report the predicted values of the dependent variable y that are *fitted* to the values of the independent variables existing within the original data set; the `predict()` function, on the other hand, provides the values of the dependent variable that are predicted (using the estimated equation) based on a holdout sample of values not included in the original data set. Two examples should suffice to draw the distinction between these two approaches.

Example 13.9. What are the predicted values of the dependent variable `minutes`?

```
fitted(mr)
##        1        2        3        4        5        6        7        8
## 536.7381 381.3552 269.0870 360.6940 536.7381 381.3552 450.5086 448.7161
##        9       10       11       12       13       14       15       16
## 225.9722 379.5627 360.6940 379.5627 381.3552 360.6940 379.5627 269.0870
##       17       18
## 448.7161 405.6013
```

To predict minutes for schedule 1 (Table 13.1), plug $x_1 = 161$ km and $x_2 = 14$ visits into $\hat{y} = -518.7481 + 2.8067x_1 + 43.1148x_2$ and solve. That is, $\hat{y} = -518.7481 + 2.8067 \times 161 + 43.1148 \times 14 = 536.74$ minutes. (This is the first value in the R block above.) In the same way, to predict the number of minutes for schedule 18, plug in $x_1 = 145$km and $x_2 = 12$ visits and solve: $\hat{y} = -518.7481 + 2.8067 \times 145 + 43.1148 \times 12 = 405.60$ minutes (the last value in the R block). Using the `fitted()` function with the model object name as the argument makes it easy to find the predicted values without having to work them out.

Example 13.10. Suppose we are considering two different schedules: the first is $x_1 = 155$ km and $x_2 = 12$ visits; the second is $x_1 = 110$ km and $x_2 = 14$ visits. What is the predicted value in minutes in both cases?

```
newvalues <- data.frame(kilometers = c(155, 110), visits = c(12, 14))
predict(mr, newvalues)

##        1        2
## 433.6684 393.5962
```

A word of explanation of these two steps is in order.

1 The `data.frame()` function assigns values of 155 and 110 to the variable named `kilometers` and 12 and 14 to the variable named `visits`, and stores everything in the data frame named `newvalues`.

2. The function `predict()` extracts from the model object `mr` the predicted values of the dependent variable for those values of the independent variable specified in the first step. In this example, the first argument of the function is the model object `mr`; the second argument is the data frame `newvalues` created in the first step.

To confirm that our prediction for the first schedule is correct, we simply plug $x_1 = 155$ km and $x_2 = 12$ visits into $\hat{y} = -518.7481 + 2.8067x_1 + 43.1148x_2$ and solve. That is, $\hat{y} = -518.7481 + 2.8067 \times 155 + 43.1148 \times 12 = 433.67$ minutes. And to check our prediction for the second schedule, we plug $x_1 = 110$ km and $x_2 = 14$ visits into $\hat{y} = -518.7481 + 2.8067x_1 + 43.1148x_2$ and solve: $\hat{y} = -518.7481 + 2.8067 \times 110 + 43.1148 \times 14 = 393.60$ minutes. Thus, the `predict()` function may be used to predict the dependent variable based on new values of the independent variables.

13.11 INDEPENDENT VARIABLE SELECTION: THE BEST-SUBSETS METHOD

Although the Brisbane example includes only two independent variables, much of what we have learned in this chapter is applicable to models including any number of predictor variables. The more variables we have, however, the more likely we are to experience problems when deciding which variables to include in the model and which to omit.

One of the problems we frequently encounter occurs when some of the independent variables are highly correlated with one another. This condition is known as multicollinearity, and it introduces difficulties of interpretation into the analysis results. In the Brisbane example, we can imagine a situation where multicollinearity among the independent variables would occur if, for instance, we decided to include a third independent variable, x_3, the amount of gasoline (in liters) consumed by a driver while traveling and calling on clients. Clearly, the correlation between x_1 and x_3 is bound to be high since the amount of gasoline consumed is related directly to the distance (in kilometers) one travels. If we were to add x_3 to a regression model already including x_1 and x_2, the partial regression coefficient on x_3 would be difficult to interpret. With x_1 (the distance traveled in kilometers) already in the equation, knowing x_3 adds little predictive or explanatory power beyond that provided by x_1.

Definition 13.7. Multicollinearity. A condition occurring in multiple regression where some or all of the independent variables are highly correlated.

Under most circumstances, there are at least two important qualities that we prefer in a set of independent variables. First, we usually desire that the independent variables be linearly related to the dependent variable y while being relatively uncorrelated with one another. Authorities disagree on exactly what constitutes high correlation, but we find that when intercorrelations exceed or even approach 0.50, there are bound to be issues of multicollinearity.

With this in mind, we should try to avoid including variables that are highly correlated with one another. We can identify high intercorrelations in several ways: scatter plots, correlation coefficients, *a priori* theory, and common sense (the number of liters of gasoline consumed should move pretty much in lock-step with the number of kilometers one drives).

Second, assuming the model has good predictive and explanatory power, we usually prefer that the set of independent variables be smaller rather than larger. Once the first uncorrelated variables are introduced into the model, there are fewer remaining independent variables of promise to be found. Very often, "the more variables, the merrier" is *not* an adage to live by when building a multiple regression model.

These arguments point to the need to be able to select which independent variables should be included in a model and which should be omitted. There are many statistical methods available for this purpose, including some more advanced methods (such as principal components and factor analysis) that reduce the number of variables to a minimum while retaining as much as possible of the information from the original set of variables. There are also various types of regression procedures that attempt to achieve this end, including stepwise, backward elimination, and forward elimination. These procedures suffer, however, from the limitation that because they enter variables one at a time, they may not uncover the best set of predictor variables. What follows is a discussion of a method that approaches the variable-selection challenge in an entirely different way—the best-subsets regression procedure.

We use best-subsets regression because we want to identify the best subset of independent variables, usually taken from a larger set, for inclusion in the model. (We also use it because, unlike some other statistical packages that do not include the best-subsets routine among the procedures they can perform, R does.) When we say *best*, we mean that we would like to identify the set of variables that, when analyzed, achieve some pre-specified criterion, such as maximizing the model's r^2. In the next example, the criterion we select is maximizing the adjusted r^2, though there are other possible criteria from which to choose.

Compared with the one-variable-at-a-time approach of stepwise, backward elimination, and forward elimination methods, best-subsets regression employs brute force. In fact, under certain circumstances, best-subset may run regressions on every possible combination of every possible set of independent variables. To understand this point, and to appreciate the power of the best-subset procedure, consider the challenge we face when attempting to select the best-subset of predictors from a set of eight variables: $x_1, x_2, \ldots, x_8$. The best-subsets routine identifies the model that, for example, maximizes the model's adjusted r^2 by running every possible regression analysis. How many regression models would the procedure have to execute? In the eight-variable case, there are 8 + 28 + 56 + 70 + 56 + 28 + 8 + 1 = 255 regressions to be run. And if we include the model with no independent variables, the total comes to 255 + 1 = 256 regression models.

1 There are 8 unique models with one predictor variable: $x_1, x_2, \ldots, x_8$.

$$\binom{8}{1} = 8$$

2 There are 28 unique models with two predictor variables: $x_1x_2, x_1x_3, x_1x_4, x_1x_5, \ldots, x_7x_8$.

$$\binom{8}{2} = 28$$

3 There are 56 unique models with three predictor variables: $x_1x_2x_3$, $x_1x_2x_4$, …, $x_6x_7x_8$.

$$\binom{8}{3} = 56$$

4 There are 70 unique models with four predictor variables: $x_1x_2x_3x_4$, $x_1x_2x_3x_5$, …, $x_5x_6x_7x_8$.

$$\binom{8}{4} = 70$$

5 There are 56 unique models with five predictor variables: $x_1x_2x_3x_4x_5$, $x_1x_2x_3x_4x_6$, …, $x_4x_5x_6x_7x_8$.

$$\binom{8}{5} = 56$$

6 There are 28 unique models with six predictor variables: $x_1x_2x_3x_4x_5x_6$, $x_1x_2x_3x_4x_5x_7$, …, $x_3x_4x_5x_6x_7x_8$.

$$\binom{8}{6} = 28$$

7 There are 8 unique models with seven predictor variables: $x_1x_2x_3x_4x_5x_6x_7$, $x_1x_2x_3x_4x_5x_6x_8$, …, $x_2x_3x_4x_5x_6x_7x_8$.

$$\binom{8}{7} = 8$$

8 There is 1 unique model with eight predictor variables: $x_1x_2x_3x_4x_5x_6x_7x_8$.

$$\binom{8}{8} = 1$$

In general, if we have n predictor variables, there are 2^n possible subsets (and therefore unique regression models): $2^8 = 256$. The R block below shows two ways to find the number of models that are possible with eight predictor variables.

#Comment1. Add 1 to 8 combination values to arrive at 256 unique models.

```
1 + choose(8, 1) + choose(8, 2) + choose(8, 3) + choose(8, 4) + choose(8, 5) +
    choose(8, 6)+ choose(8, 7)+choose(8, 8)
```

```
## [1] 256
```

#Comment2. As a shortcut, raise 2 to the 8th power.

```
2 ^ 8
```

```
## [1] 256
```

Clearly, no one would want to execute 250+ regressions just to find the model with the highest adjusted r^2; doing so would mean undertaking a tedious and error-prone process of combing through all the regressions in search of the highest adjusted r^2. Fortunately, the best-subsets procedure simplifies this operation considerably.

In this example, we use the data set `mtcars` which is part of the R system. (Remember that to see all the installed data sets, simply enter `data()` at the R prompt in the Console; to view `mtcars` itself, enter `mtcars` at the R prompt; to learn more about the data, such as what the variable names measure, enter `?mtcars` at the prompt and wait for the R Help page to open.) Although we worked with `mtcars` in Exercises 3 and 4 of Chapter 12, we reacquaint ourselves with it by inspecting the first three observations and variable names.

```
head(mtcars, 3)
```

```
##                mpg cyl disp  hp drat    wt  qsec vs am gear carb
## Mazda RX4     21.0   6  160 110 3.90 2.620 16.46  0  1    4    4
## Mazda RX4 Wag 21.0   6  160 110 3.90 2.875 17.02  0  1    4    4
## Datsun 710    22.8   4  108  93 3.85 2.320 18.61  1  1    4    1
```

For reasons of notational simplicity, we have changed the original variable names to y and x_1, …, x_{10}. The new data set is named `mtcarsnvn` (for `mtcars` with new variable names) and is available on the website. Here are the first three observations.

```
##               X    y x1  x2  x3   x4    x5    x6 x7 x8 x9 x10
## 1     Mazda RX4 21.0  6 160 110 3.90 2.620 16.46  0  1  4   4
## 2 Mazda RX4 Wag 21.0  6 160 110 3.90 2.875 17.02  0  1  4   4
## 3    Datsun 710 22.8  4 108  93 3.85 2.320 18.61  1  1  4   1
```

For this model, we regress the dependent variable y = `mpg` (miles per gallon) on five independent variables: x_1 = `cyl` (number of cylinders), x_2 = `disp` (cubic inches of engine displacement), x_3 = `hp` (gross horsepower), x_5 = `wt` (weight, in units of 1000 pounds), and x_6 = `qsec` (number of seconds vehicle requires to travel a distance of a quarter mile from a standing start). In selecting variables for the model, we use our judgment in deciding which variables should be included and which should not. In this, our reasoning goes something like this: fuel efficiency y should be related to number of cylinders x_1 and displacement x_2 (measures of engine size), horsepower x_3, vehicle weight x_5, and level of engine performance x_6. We omit the other variables because they do not seem related to the variable of interest, y = `mpg`.

To help us appreciate the need for a thoughtful variable-selection approach, consider the following analysis in which all the above initially screened variables are included: x_1, x_2, x_3, x_5, and x_6. The data set name is `mtcarsnvn`.

```
firstmodel <- lm(y ~ x1 + x2 + x3 + x5 + x6, data = mtcarsnvn)
summary(firstmodel)
```

```
##
## Call:
## lm(formula = y ~ x1 + x2 + x3 + x5 + x6, data = mtcarsnvn)
```

```
##
## Residuals:
##     Min      1Q  Median      3Q     Max
## -4.3117 -1.3483 -0.4352 1.2603 5.6094
##
## Coefficients:
##             Estimate Std. Error t value Pr(>|t|)
## (Intercept) 35.87361    9.91809   3.617  0.00126 **
## x1          -1.15608    0.71525  -1.616  0.11809
## x2           0.01195    0.01191   1.004  0.32484
## x3          -0.01584    0.01527  -1.037  0.30908
## x5          -4.22527    1.25239  -3.374  0.00233 **
## x6           0.25382    0.48746   0.521  0.60699
## --
## Signif. codes: 0 '***' 0.001 '**' 0.01 '*' 0.05 '.' 0.1 ' ' 1
##
## Residual standard error: 2.547 on 26 degrees of freedom
## Multiple R-squared: 0.8502, Adjusted R-squared: 0.8214
## F-statistic: 29.51 on 5 and 26 DF, p-value: 0.0000000006182
```

When inspecting the p-values associated with the independent variables, we might conclude that x_5 = wt is the only significant predictor variable. (Presumably, the variables we omitted from the analysis (x_4, x_7, x_8, x_9, x_{10}) would also be non-significant had we included them.) With all five variables included, the adjusted r^2 is $r^2_{\text{adj}} = 0.8214$. But if we rerun the analysis with x_5 as the only variable in the model, $r^2_{\text{adj}} = 0.7528$. (We leave this exercise to you.) Can we improve on this? Yes, we can if we use the best-subsets procedure.

The best-subsets procedure requires that we install two packages, leaps and car. Recall that there is a two-step procedure for each package installation. For leaps, we enter

```
install.packages("leaps")
library(leaps)
```

and for car, it is the same two steps:

```
install.packages("car")
library(car)
```

Once both packages are installed, we write and execute two lines of code.

```
bestsubsets <- regsubsets(y ~ x1 + x2 + x3 + x5 + x6,
                          data = mtcarsnvn, nbest = 1)

subsets(bestsubsets, statistic = "adjr2")
```

Here is an explanation of the first line of code.

1. The first argument of `regsubsets()` is the model object `y ~ x1 + x2 + x3 + x5 + x6`. Note that this is not different from how we specify the model for the `lm()` function.
2. The second argument is the data frame `mtcarsnvn` to be analyzed.
3. The third argument `nbest =` specifies the number of subsets to be provided for each possible subset size. That is, if `nbest = 1`, the procedure reports one set for a subset size of 1, one set for a subset size of 2, one set for a subset size of 3, and so on. If two subsets are desired, then we set `nbest = 2`, and we get two sets for a subset size of 1, two sets for a subset size of 2, two sets for a subset size of 3, and so on. In general, if we want *n* subsets, we indicate this with `nbest = n`.
4. The result of the `regsubsets()` function is stored in the model object named `bestsubsets`, although we are free to name it anything we like.

For the second line, the logic behind the arguments should by now be intuitive. It is important that the steps be executed in this order because the first step results `bestsubsets` in a model object that is used as an argument in the second step.

1. The first argument of the `subsets()` function is the model object `bestsubsets` that was created in the first line above.
2. The second argument `statistic = "adjr2"` specifies that the statistic to be scaled along the vertical axis in the plot is the adjusted r^2.

When these two steps are executed, the result is a plot (see Figure 13.8). Here is a summary of the useful information the plot reveals that we want when specfiying the set of predictor variables that results in the regression model providing the highest adjusted r^2.

1. The single best (in terms of adjusted r^2) one-variable model includes variable x_5. This comes as no surprise since x_5 emerged as the only significant predictor in the five-variable regression above. From Figure 13.8, we note that $r^2_{\text{adj}} \approx 0.74$, though this is not so useful for a simple linear regression.
2. The single best two-variable model contains x_1 and x_5.
3. The single best three-variable model includes x_1, x_3, and x_5.
4. The single best four-variable model has x_1, x_2, x_3, and x_5.
5. That the single best five-variable model includes x_1, x_2, x_3, x_5, and x_6 is a trivial case since it is also the only five-variable model. Moreover, as we know from running the five-variable regression above, four of the five predictors are non-significant. The entire point of using the best-subsets procedure is to uncover all additional significant predictor variables, if indeed any additional ones exist at all, while maximizing the adjusted r^2.

From this, it should be clear that while the subsets reported in Figure 13.8 are the ones that maximize the adjusted r^2, it does not necessarily follow that all, or even most, of the predictor variables are themselves significant. To uncover which variables are significant, we need to run regressions on all five sets of variables provided in Figure 13.8.

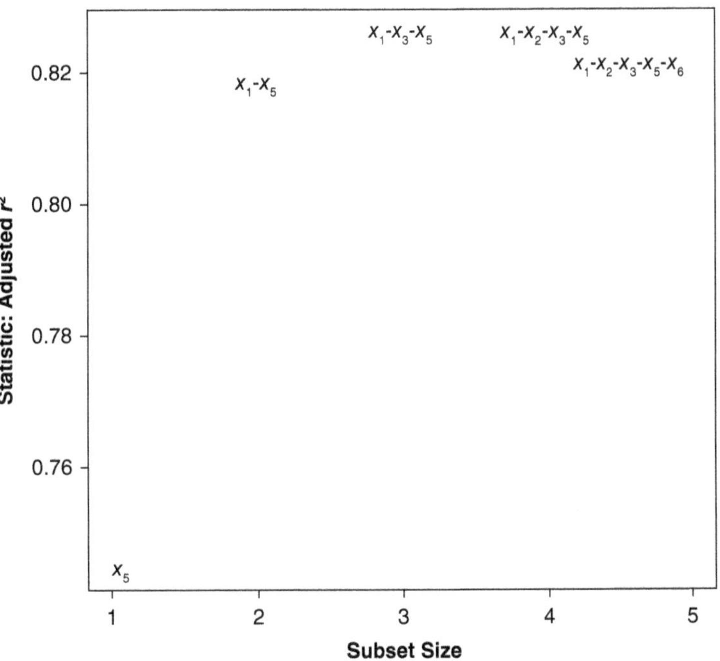

Figure 13.8 The regression models with highest adjusted r^2 values

What we want to know is this: which of these five models contains *only* those predictor variables that are significant, or those variables for which $p \leq 0.05$? (This assumes of course that $\alpha = 0.05$.) Table 13.4 organizes the information for each of the five possible models from Figure 13.8 along with (1) the adjusted r^2 and (2) the significant predictors. Both (1) and (2) are found by running regressions on all five subsets of predictor variables, though in the interest of space we do not show the results of all those analyses here.

Table 13.4 Adjusted r^2 and significant predictors for the five models identified in Figure 13.8

Regression model	Adjusted r^2	Significant predictors
$\hat{y} = b_0 + b_5x_5$	0.7446	x_5
$\hat{y} = b_0 + b_1x_1 + b_5x_5$	0.8185	x_1 and x_5
$\hat{y} = b_0 + b_1x_1 + b_3x_3 + b_5x_5$	0.8263	only x_5
$\hat{y} = b_0 + b_1x_1 + b_2x_2 + b_3x_3 + b_5x_5$	0.8262	only x_5
$\hat{y} = b_0 + b_1x_1 + b_2x_2 + b_3x_3 + b_5x_5 + b_6x_6$	0.8214	only x_5

On the basis of the information in Table 13.4, the most promising subset of predictors includes x_1 and x_5. They are both significant and the adjusted r^2 is nearly 0.82. There is no point in including non-significant independent variables in our analysis; ultimately, we would remove them anyway as we move toward identifying the best model. Looking at the results of the regression below, we note that the significance of x_1 and x_5 are 0.001064 and 0.00022, respectively—a finding that was obscured in the case of the full five-variable model. Therefore, since the model now includes (1) a high adjusted r^2, (2) a highly significant F-statistic for the overall regression model, and (3) two significant independent variables, we have improved both the predictive and explanatory power of the model.

```
secondmodel <- lm(y ~ x1 + x5, data = mtcarsnvn)
summary(secondmodel)
```

```
##
## Call:
## lm(formula = y ~ x1 + x5, data = mtcarsnvn)
##
## Residuals:
##      Min       1Q   Median      3Q     Max
## -4.2893 -1.5512 -0.4684 1.5743 6.1004
##
## Coefficients:
##              Estimate Std. Error t value              Pr(>|t|)
## (Intercept)   39.6863     1.7150  23.141 < 0.0000000000000002 ***
## x1            -1.5078     0.4147  -3.636             0.001064 **
## x5            -3.1910     0.7569  -4.216             0.000222 ***
## --
## Signif. codes: 0 '***' 0.001 '**' 0.01 '*' 0.05 '.' 0.1 ' ' 1
##
## Residual standard error: 2.568 on 29 degrees of freedom
## Multiple R-squared: 0.8302, Adjusted R-squared: 0.8185
## F-statistic: 70.91 on 2 and 29 DF, p-value: 0.000000000006809
```

SUMMARY

It is appropriate that the book ends with treatment of multiple regression analysis. For one thing, it draws on nearly every aspect of coverage dealt with thus far. For another, and because of this, it would not have been possible to develop the method and way of thinking as we have, without first acquiring a basic understanding of the foundational ideas underpinning its use. For some students and readers, this chapter no doubt heralds the end of their formal exposure to probability and statistics; for others, it marks only the beginning as they proceed to more advanced courses of study. In this, we hope that this book has provided a helpful exposure to introductory statistical methods and the R statistical programming language.

Successful application of regression to any set of data rests at least as much on the analyst's ability to see the big picture as it does on her technical skill and mathematical sophistication. There is as much art as science involved in the design and execution of any type of analysis, but with curiosity, patience, and practice, good results are achievable.

In the interest of practical application, we now describe the steps that might be taken when one wishes to apply the multiple regression methodology to real-world data. In this connection, we propose to revisit the `mtcarsnvn` data we analysed in Section 13.11.

1. **Describe the research question in clear and unambiguous terms.** For the `mtcarsnvn` example, we could say that we would like to understand the relationship (if any) between the gas mileage of a vehicle and five other variables thought initially to have some relationship to it: the number of cylinders of the engine, engine displacement, power of the engine, vehicle weight, and acceleration performance.
2. **Define the variables and describe the sample being used in the analysis.** Because the sample data were drawn from a *Motor Trend* magazine survey, and form part of the base R installation, we say the data are secondary, not primary. The data consist of 11 automobile design-and-performance measures across 32 vehicles. Thus, this data set has 11 variable measures across 32 observations comprising vehicles of various types (economy, sport, family sedan, luxury, etc.), different price points, and three regions of origin (17 European, 8 US, and 7 Japanese). The variables being analyzed have been selected by the author (based on common sense) to include the dependent variable $y =$ `mpg` as well as five predictor variables: $x_1 =$ `cyl`, $x_2 =$ `disp`, $x_3 =$ `hp`, $x_5 =$ `wt`, and $x_6 =$ `qsec`. The five excluded variables were omitted from the analysis because no connection between them and $y =$ `mpg` could be thought of.
3. **Verify tentatively that each independent variable is linearly related to the dependent variable but not strongly related to one another.** This step typically involves constructing and reviewing a scatter plot of each variable against all the others. Ideally, we look for (1) linear relationships between the dependent variable and each of the predictor variables, and (2) no discernible relationship between any one independent variable and the others. Any linear relationship (or correlation exceeding 0.50) between two predictors is evidence of possible multicollinearity.

   When we have multicollinearity in our data (most data sets have some multicollinearity, so do not worry if yours does too), we often experiment a bit, dropping one of the correlated variables identified in this way, and proceeding with the analysis without it. Typically, this iterative, trial-and-error stage of the process continues until we arrive at a final set of relatively uncorrelated variables. A quick and convenient means by which to visualize all pairwise plots without having to go to the trouble of creating individual scatter plots is to use the `pairs()` function. Because you are encouraged to carry out this step yourself, the scatter plots are not reproduced here.

   ```
   pairs(mtcarsnvn, pch = 19, lower.panel = NULL)
   ```

   For the `mtcarsnvn` example, the `pairs()` function reveals that many of the variables seem to be associated with one another, either positively or negatively, including x_1 and x_5. Despite this, we will work our way through the remaining steps of this procedure since the purpose of this section is illustrative, not investigative. Once this step has been completed, proceed to step 4.

4 **Select the best subset of independent variables from the larger set.** Assuming we would like to follow the same approach as that outlined above in Section 13.11, first make sure that both leaps and car packages have been installed. If they have not been, remember that we must execute the following two steps first.

```
install.packages("leaps")
library(leaps)

install.packages("car")
library(car)
```

When both packages are installed, execute the following two lines of code in order, the second followed by the first.

```
bestsubsets <- regsubsets(y ~ x1 + x2 + x3 + x5 + x6,
                          data = mtcarsnvn, nbest = 1)

subsets(bestsubsets, statistic = "adjr2")
```

Examine the resulting plot and decide on which predictors to include in the model. For the `mtcarsnvn` example, we identified x_1 and x_5 as the two best independent variables to include in our regression model (see Figure 13.8). Now go to step 5.

5 **Run the regression with the independent variables identified in step 4.** This involves the by-now familiar `lm()` function. We named the resulting model object `secondmodel`. (By contrast, the five-variable model was named `firstmodel`.)

```
secondmodel <- lm(y ~ x1 + x5, data = mtcarsnvn)
```

6 **Run the summary() function to unpack the important information from the model object.** Since the model object name is `secondmodel`, we use it as the argument in the `summary()` function.

```
summary(secondmodel)
```

The output for this step can been seen just above the Summary section, and so will not be reproduced here. Refer to the discussion in Section 13.11 for more detail, if necessary. Here is a summary of the relevant information from the analysis:

(a) The intercept term is $b_0 = 39.6863$.
(b) The coefficient on the independent variable x_1 is $b_1 = -1.5078$; the *p*-value is 0.001064.
(c) The coefficient on the independent variable x_5 is $b_5 = -3.1910$; the *p*-value is 0.000222.
(d) The estimated regression equation is $\hat{y} = 39.6863 - 1.5078x_1 - 3.1910x_5$.
(e) $r^2 = 0.8302$; $r^2_{adj} = 0.8185$.
(f) The significance of the overall regression model is *p* = 0.000000000006809.

As a final step to the actual analysis (but before we get to the interpretation in step 8), it is always a good idea to construct and inspect a plot of the residuals against $\hat{y}$. Since we finally have identified our *best* model, we can proceed to step 7.

7 **Make and inspect a residual plot.** Because we know that a scatter plot does not necessarily reveal the nature of the relationship between any two variables, we will want to plot the residuals against the predicted value of the dependent variable $\hat{y}$:

```
plot(fitted(secondmodel), resid(secondmodel), abline(h = 0),
     pch = 19, xlab = 'Predicted Value of y', ylab = 'Residuals')
```

An inspection of the residual plot should tell us if there is anything obvious that might raise doubts about whether the assumptions behind the correct application of the regression analysis to the `mtcarsnvn` data are satisfied. Specifically, we are interested in whether there is evidence of (1) a nonlinear relationship (such as bends, curves, or kinks) between the residuals and the values of $\hat{y}_i$; (2) a non-constant variance of the residual terms around the regression plane; or (3) any conspicuous outliers. If the residual plot reveals no serious violations of the assumptions described in Section 13.6, we have done what we can to build the best model with the data and variables we have. If the results are not all we hope for, we may want to consider incorporating new independent variables not included in the original data set.

8 **So What's New? Description, Prediction, and Conclusions.**

(a) **Description.** The scatter plot reveals a negative relationship between the dependent variable y = `mpg` and (1) the predictor variable x_1 = `cyl` and (2) the predictor variable x_5 = `wt`; it also uncovers a positive relationship between the two predictor variables x_1 and x_5. None of these associations is surprising: most of us know that gas mileage is negatively related to the number of cylinders in the engine and the weight of the vehicle. Less clear as to what accounts for it, but undeniable in light of the data, is the positive association between x_1 and x_5. Still, this relationship is not something we should ignore.
Even so, the residual plot reveals no obvious outliers although the variance of the residuals seems to increase a bit over the higher values of $\hat{y}$ (perhaps also an indicator of the correlation between x_1 and x_5). Nonetheless, the adjusted r^2 value of 0.8185 indicates that approximately 82% of the variation in gas mileage can be accounted for by variation in (1) the number of cylinders in the engine and (2) the weight of the vehicle.

(b) **Prediction.** We can use the following functions to make predictions based on values of the independent variables that are not part of the original data set: `c()` nested within `predict()`. For the sake of clarity, we separate the two steps in the following code:

```
newvalues <- data.frame(x1 = c(4, 6, 8),
                        x5 = c(5.00, 3.35, 1.75))
predict(secondmodel, newvalues)

##        1        2        3
## 17.70022 19.94974 22.03970
```

Thus, our model predicts that (1) if $x_1 = 4$ and $x_5 = 5$, then $\hat{y} = 17.70022$; (2) if $x_1 = 6$ and $x_5 = 3.35$, then $\hat{y} = 19.94974$; and (3) if $x_1 = 8$ and $x_5 = 1.75$, then $\hat{y} = 22.03970$.
If we want to make predictions based on the values in the original sample, we can use either `predict()`, making sure we omit the second argument `newvalues`, or `fitted()`, where the single argument is the model object name (in this case, `secondmodel`). The result is the same.

(c) **Conclusions.** The estimated regression equation $\hat{y} = 39.6863 - 1.5078x_1 - 3.1910x_5$ allows us to draw a few conclusions. First, the partial regression coefficient on x_1 represents the estimated change in y when accompanied by a one-unit change in x_1 while holding x_2

constant. Thus, in our example, because $b_1 = -1.5078$ we expect that a one-cylinder increase (decrease) in x_1 should be accompanied by a 1.5078-mpg decrease (increase) in y, as long as the vehicle weight x_2 is held constant. Second, the partial regression coefficient on x_2 represents the estimated change in y when accompanied by a one-unit change in x_2 while holding x_1 constant. Thus, because $b_1 = -3.1910$ we expect that a 1000-pound increase (decrease) in x_2 should be accompanied by a 3.1910-mpg decrease (increase) in y, as long as the number of engine cylinders x_1 is held constant. The value of the constant term $b_0 = 39.6863$ becomes important only when we use the estimated regression equation to make predictions.

Beyond this, because the sample size is neither large nor widely representative of all makes and types of vehicles, there are limitations to the predictive power of the model. For one thing, it is calibrated only on vehicles weighing from 1513 to 5424 pounds. If we wish to make mileage predictions based on vehicles whose weight falls below or above that range, we should proceed with caution since the model has incorporated nothing about the world outside this range.

```
min(mtcarsnvn$x5)

## [1] 1.513

max(mtcarsnvn$x5)

## [1] 5.424
```

Predictions based on the number of cylinders are less of a problem since most vehicles have either 4, 6, or 8 cylinders in the engine, and (we assume) predictions for other vehicles would include only those having 4, 6, or 8 cylinders as well. Few if any vehicles have 1, 2, or 3 cylinders or more than 8.

```
table(mtcarsnvn$x1)

##
##  4  6  8
## 11  7 14
```

definitions

Adjusted Multiple Coefficient of Determination The adjusted multiple coefficient of determination is a measure of the strength of linear association between the dependent variable y and the independent variables x_1, x_2, ..., x_k that compensates for the number of independent variables.

Estimated Multiple Regression Equation A general expression that specifies how the predicted value of the dependent variable, or $\hat{y}$, is related to the independent variables $x_1, x_2, ..., x_k$. In this case, the estimators $b_0, b_1, ..., b_k$ (which are estimated from the sample data) replace the parameters β_0, β_1, ..., β_k, respectively.

(Continued)

(Continued)

Multiple Coefficient of Determination The multiple coefficient of determination r^2 is a measure of the strength of linear association between the dependent variable y and the independent variables $x_1, x_2, \ldots, x_k$. Its value varies between 0 and 1, and it indicates the proportion of total variation in the dependent variable that is explained by the variation in the independent variables.

Multiple Regression Equation A general expression that specifies how the expected value of y, or $E(y|x_1, x_2, \ldots, x_k) = \mu_{y|x_1, x_2, \ldots, x_k}$, is related to the independent variables $x_1, x_2, \ldots, x_k$.

Multiple Regression Model A general expression that specifies how the dependent variable y is related to the independent variables $x_1, x_2, \ldots, x_k$ plus the error term ε.

Multicollinearity A condition occurring in multiple regression where some or all of the independent variables are highly correlated.

Partial Regression Coefficient Partial regression coefficients are the regression coefficients that form the multiple regression model. Unless the independent variables are perfectly uncorrelated with one another, a partial regression coefficient is not equal to the simple linear regression coefficient on the same independent variable; nor in general does the partial regression coefficient remain constant when it is accompanied by different sets of other independent variables.

formulae

Adjusted r²

$$r^2_{\text{adj}} = r^2 - \frac{k(1-r^2)}{n-k-1}$$

Multiple Regression Model

$$y = \beta_0 + \beta_1 x_1 + \beta_2 x_2 + \ldots + \beta_k x_k + \varepsilon$$

Multiple Regression Equation

$$E(y \mid x_1, x_2, \ldots, x_k) = \mu_{y|x_1, x_2, \ldots, x_k} = \beta_0 + \beta_1 x_1 + \beta_2 x_2 + \ldots + \beta_k x_k$$

Estimated Multiple Regression Equation

$$\hat{y} = b_0 + b_1 x_1 + b_2 x_2 + \ldots + b_k x_k$$

Test Statistic for the Overall Regression Model

$$F = \frac{SS_{\text{reg}}/k}{SS_{\text{res}}/(n-k-1)} = \frac{\Sigma(\hat{y}_i - \bar{y})^2/k}{\Sigma(y_i - \hat{y}_i)^2/(n-k-1)}$$

Test Statistic for the Test of the Individual Regression Coefficients

$$t = \frac{b_i}{s_{b_i}}$$

R functions

`confint(,level =)` Provides confidence interval estimates for all independent variables. The first argument is the name of the model object; the level of desired confidence is specified with the second argument `level =`.

`lm(y ~ .., data =)` Provides the intercept term b_0 and the regression coefficients $b_1, b_2, ..., b_k$ for an estimated multiple regression equation of the form $\hat{y} = b_0 + b_1x_1 + b_2x_2 + ... + b_kx_k$.

`pairs()` Produces a matrix of pairwise scatter plots of all variables simultaneously. The most important (and essential) argument to include is the name of the data object.

`regsubsets(y ~` $x_1 + x_2 + ... + x_k$`, data =, nbest =)` A regression procedure that finds and reports the best subset of predictor (independent) variables in terms of some pre-specified criterion such as the highest adjusted r^2. In R, the `regsubsets()` routine first requires the installation of the `leaps` package. See Section 13.11.

`subsets()` Plots the output from the `regsubsets()` best-subsets procedure in terms of the best subset of predictor variables (in terms of some pre-specified number of variables) as well as a summarization statistic such as the adjusted r^2. In R, `subsets()` first requires the installation of the `car` package. See Section 13.11.

data sets

1 `brisbane`
2 `mtcars`
3 `mtcarsnvn`

exercises

13.1 Consider the estimated regression equation $\hat{y} = 3536 + 1183x_1 - 1208x_2$. Suppose the model is changed to reflect the deletion of x_2 and the resulting estimated simple linear equation becomes $\hat{y} = -10{,}663 + 1386x_1$.

(a) How should we interpret the meaning of the coefficient on x_1 in the estimated simple linear regression equation $\hat{y} = -10{,}663 + 1386x_1$?
(b) How should we interpret the meaning of the coefficient on x_1 in the estimated multiple regression equation $\hat{y} = 3536 + 1183x_1 - 1208x_2$?
(c) Is there any evidence of multicollinearity? What might that evidence be?

13.2 Interpret the results below and answer the following questions. Suppose we regress the dependent variable y on four independent variables x_1, x_2, x_3, and x_4. After running the regression on $n = 16$ observations, we have the following information: $SS_{reg} = 946.181$ and $SS_{res} = 49.773$ Please answer the following questions.

(a) What is the value of r^2?
(b) What is the adjusted r^2?
(c) What is the F-statistic?
(d) What is the p-value?
(e) Is the overall regression model significant? Test at the $\alpha = 0.05$ level of significance.

(Continued)

(Continued)

13.3 Referring to Question 13.2, suppose we also have the following information about the partial regression coefficients.

Independent variables	Coefficients b_i	Standard Error s_{b_i}
x_1	$b_1 = -0.0008155$	$s_{b_1} = 0.003$
x_2	$b_2 = -2.48400$	$s_{b_2} = 0.960$
x_3	$b_3 = 0.05901$	$s_{b_3} = 0.015$
x_4	$b_4 = 0.06928$	$s_{b_4} = 0.038$

(a) Is b_1 significant at $\alpha = 0.05$? What is its *t*-value? What is its *p*-value?
(b) Is b_2 significant at $\alpha = 0.05$? What is its *t*-value? What is its *p*-value?
(c) Is b_3 significant at $\alpha = 0.05$? What is its *t*-value? What is its *p*-value?
(d) Is b_4 significant at $\alpha = 0.05$? What is its *t*-value? What is its *p*-value?

13.4 Consider the estimated multiple regression equation

$$\hat{y} = -0.59141 + 0.05800x_1 + 0.84490x_2 + 0.11419x_3 .$$

(a) Complete the missing entries in this ANOVA table.

Source	SS	df	MS	F	p-value
Regression	21.83373				
Residual					
Total	23.9	9			

(b) Complete the missing entries in this coefficients table.

Predictor	Estimates	Standard error	t	p-value
b_0	-0.59141	1.03092		
b_1		0.01082	5.362	
b_2	0.84490		3.439	
b_3		0.13877	0.823	

(c) What is the value of r^2?
(d) What is the adjusted r^2?

13.5 This exercise uses the `mtcars` data set that is installed in R.

(a) Use the `pairs()` function to create a scatter plot matrix for three variables: `mpg`, `cyl`, and `wt`. What can we say about the relationships between these variables?
(b) Regress the dependent variable `mpg` on the variables `cyl` and `wt`. Write out the estimated regression equation.
(c) Use the `fitted()` function to create the predicted dependent variables for the values of `cyl` and `wt` in the original data set. Just to check that the predictions are correct, select two observations and work out the predicted value manually.
(d) Use the `predict()` function to create the predicted dependent variable for the following pairs of values of the independent variables: for the first pair `cyl = 4` and `wt = 5`; for the second pair `cyl = 8` and `wt = 2`.

https://study.sagepub.com/stinerock

INDEX